TEL TANNINIM
EXCAVATIONS AT KROKODEILON POLIS
1996–1999

AMERICAN SCHOOLS OF ORIENTAL RESEARCH ARCHEOLOGICAL REPORTS

Joseph A. Greene, Editor

Number 10

Tel Tanninim

Excavations at Krokodeilon Polis, 1996–1999

TEL TANNINIM

EXCAVATIONS AT KROKODEILON POLIS 1996–1999

By

ROBERT R. STIEGLITZ

With Contributions By

YAʿEL D. ARNON, A. ASA EGER, DIANE EVERMAN,
ARLENE FRADKIN, OMRI LERNAU, JOHN MACSAI,
MICHAL OREN-PASKAL, RACHEL POLLAK
AND SHALOM YANKELEVITCH

AMERICAN SCHOOLS OF ORIENTAL RESEARCH • BOSTON, MA

Tel Tanninim

Excavations at Krokodeilon Polis, 1996–1999

By

Robert R. Stieglitz

The American Schools of Oriental Research © 2006

ISBN 0-89757-072-3

Library of Congress Cataloging-in-Publication Data

Stieglitz, R. Raphael.
   Tel Tanninim : excavations at Krokodeilon Polis, 1996-1999 / by
Robert R. Stieglitz ; with contributions by Ya'el D. Arnon ... [et al.].
      p. cm. -- (American schools of oriental research archeological
reports)
   Includes bibliographical references and index.
   ISBN 0-89757-072-3 (alk. paper)
   1. Tanninim Site (Israel) 2. Israel--Antiquities. 3. Excavations
(Archaeology)--Israel.   I. Arnon, Ya'el D. II. Title.
DS110.T22S75 2006
933--dc22

                                        2006022613

Printed in the United States of America on acid-free paper.

Contents

Acknowledgments

The Tanninim Archaeological Project in Israel was undertaken with the help of numerous friends who supported our researches by their contributions, made either in the field or with donations to the project. I am indebted to the financial and administrative support provided by my university, specifically, to the Office of the Dean (Faculty of Arts and Sciences, Rutgers University, Newark, NJ), and to the Office of Research and Sponsored Programs (Rutgers University, New Brunswick, NJ). Valuable assistance was provided by Kibbutz Ma'agan Mikhael (Israel), Sarah and Avie Arenson (Caesarea), and the Anglo-Israeli Friendship Society (UK). We received very beneficial advice, and material support, from Professors Elisha Linder and the late Avner Raban of the Leon Recanati Institute for Maritime Studies, University of Haifa.

I am particularly pleased to thank the dedicated staff of TAP, who excavated and supervised the volunteers, and cleaned, analyzed and registered finds, as well as performing other tasks which make for a successful expedition: A. Asa Eger (site supervisor, currently a Ph.D. candidate at the University of Chicago, discusses the stratigraphy and architecture of Areas A and A2 in Chapter II.2); Dr. Diane M. Everman (registrar and assistant site supervisor, a contract archaeologist, writes about the hydraulic installations in Areas B and B2 in Chapter II.3); Shalom Yankelevitch (site supervisor, contract archaeologist [University of Haifa], analyzes the Persian-Hellenistic ceramics in Chapter III.1). Professor John Macsai, FAIA (architect), measured and drew the site plans, sections, and reconstructions during all four seasons of excavations. TAP staff included Jessica A. Fletcher (registrar), Arnout Hyde, Jr. (photographer), Sean A. Kingsley (ceramicist), Garry F. Mohr (site supervisor), H. Katharine Sheeler (site supervisor during all four seasons), Daniel E. Stieglitz (photographer).

The initial site survey was carried out by Anna Iamim (Combined Caesarea Expeditions). Site photographs are by Dani Zorea (Kibbutz Ma'agan Mikhael) and the author. The stratigraphic sections were prepared by A. Asa Eger. Artifact drawings were made by Sappir 'Ad (Kiryat Hayim). Photographs of artifacts are by Zaraza Friedman (Haifa) and the author. Restorations of ceramics were undertaken by Naomi Pomerantz (Kfar Monash). We also benefited from the assistance of Yehudit Ayalon (Kibbutz Ma'agan Mikhael), Tsah Horowitz (IAA), architect Moshe Laner (Tirat HaCarmel), and Kemi Zehiran (Caesarea Development Corporation).

Additional specialized studies of the material culture were undertaken by Michal Oren-Paskal (The Combined Caesarea Expedition) on the Byzantine ceramics (Chapter III.2); Ya'el D. Arnon (Recanati Institute for Maritime Studies) analyzed the Later Periods pottery (Chapter III.3) and the lamps (Chapter IV.2); Rachel Pollak (Recanati Institute for Maritime Studies) studied the glass; and the fish remains (Chapter V) are discussed by Dr. Arlene Fradkin (Florida Atlantic University) and Dr. Omri Lernau (The Hebrew University).

Our expedition was very fortunate to have numerous friends who provided financial support for the Project, and we are deeply indebted to them. Major funding was provided by Isaac L. Cohen, the S. H. and Helen R. Scheuer Family Foundation, Joan and Allen Bildner, Susan and Kazem Niamir, Jessica A. Fletcher, Profs. Gloria and Irving Merker,

Maryam Niamir Fuller, Harva L. Sheeler, Katherine C. Gay, and Lisa A. Piascik. Additional donations were made by Bunie P. Veeder, Dr. Liviu Schapira, Norma Kershaw, Prof. Uri Hurwitz, Jacob Julius, Rabbi Dr. Robert Ratner, Danielle R. Rudi, Annette and Bert Bauman, Jim Terrill, Lionel Arond, Morris Diener, Benjamin Adelman, Melvin Dubin, Frances and Alan Levine, Abraham Neustadter, Shirley and Edgar Roggen, Ellen and David Cornford, Gesher Branch LZA (#975), George Mihail, Norman Roland, Murray Seeman, Joel Kirman, Abraham Walfish, and Fred Shaw.

We owe a special gratitude to the wonderful teams of volunteers—undergraduate and graduate students, professionals and a few dedicated teenagers—who worked so diligently in the excavations, pottery washing, and registration, and thereby ensured the success of the expedition. Their names are listed at the end of this volume.

List of Figures

List of Tables

Abbreviations

Annales du Congrès	*Annales du Congrès de l'Association Internationale pour L'Histoire du Verre*
BAR	British Archaeological Reports
BASOR	*Bulletin of the American Schools of Oriental Research*
BCH	*Bulletin de Correspondance Hellenique*
BIES	*Bulletin of the Israel Exploration Society (Hebrew)*
ESI	*Excavations and Surveys in Israel.* Jerusalem: IDAM
HA	*Hadashot Arkheologiyot* (Hebrew)
HUCA	*Hebrew Union College Annual*
IAA	Israel Antiquities Authority
IA-HU	Institute of Archaeology – The Hebrew University, Jerusalem
IDAM	Israel Department of Antiquities and Museums
IEJ	*Israel Exploration Journal*
IES	Israel Exploration Society
IHC	Sabino de Sandoli, *Itinera Hierosolymitana Crucesignatorum (saec. XII–XIII), Vol. II.* Jerusalem: Franciscan Printing Press, 1980
JARCE	*Journal of the American Research Center in Egypt*
JEA	*Journal of Egyptian Archaeology*
JGS	*Journal of Glass Studies*
JRA	*Journal of Roman Archaeology*
Megiddo I	R. S. Lamon and G. M. Shipton, *Megiddo I, Seasons of 1925–1934, Strata I–V.* Chicago: The Oriental Institute, 1939
Megiddo II	G. Loud, *Megiddo II, Seasons of 1935–1939.* Chicago: The Oriental Institute, 1948
MGWJ	*Monatsschrift fuer Geschichte und Wissenschaft des Judentums*
PEF	Palestine Exploration Fund
PEFQSt	*Palestine Exploration Fund Quarterly Statement*
PEQ	*Palestine Exploration Quarterly*
PPTS	Palestine Pilgrims' Text Society. London: PEF, 1895–.
QDAP	*Quarterly of the Department of Antiquities of Palestine*
RB	*Revue biblique*
TAP	Tanninim Archaeological Project
ZDPV	*Zeitschrift des deutschen Palästina Vereins*

Chapter I

The Site and Its Exploration

by Robert R. Stieglitz

The central sector of the Mediterranean coastal plain in Israel has been known as the Sharon since the second millennium B.C.E., as is known from ancient Egyptian texts and the biblical narratives. The Sharon plain is a fertile region, with diverse geographic and hydrographic features, which extends along the sea coast from Mount Carmel in the north to the Yarkon River and the coastal town of Jaffa in the south. Ancient Jaffa is now entirely within the municipality of Tel Aviv-Jaffa. The eastern border of the plain was defined by the inland hill country, consisting of the Carmel mountain range and the so-called Central Highlands of Palestine, while its western border was the shore of Mediterranean Sea.

The coastal strip of the Sharon Plain is characterized by a series of sandstone ridges which run parallel to the seashore, at various distances from the sea. The ridges are composed primarily of a relatively soft sandstone—locally named *kurkar*—which consists of a conglomerate of sand and petrified marine deposits, primarily sea shell fragments. The shell fragments had been deposited on the ancient shorelines by the continuous action of waves and winds. The existence of several such parallel *kurkar* ridges along the present coastline of the Sharon plain is ample geological testimony to the intermittent formation of several prehistoric coastlines. These shores developed during different periods in the Pleistocene era, as the level of the sea fluctuated during the cycles of the Ice Ages. The *kurkar* ridge nearest to the coast nowadays attains a maximum height of some 30 m above the mean sea level, and is situated about 1.25 km east of the present shoreline.

Tel Tanninim, "Crocodiles Mound," is the modern Hebrew name of a site known locally in Arabic as *Tell el-Melāṭ* (also *Tall al-Malāṭ*) 'Mortar Mound.' It is located in the northern region of the Sharon on the Mediterranean coast (map reference 1410 2161), at the mouth of Nahal Tanninim, "Crocodile River," a stream known in Arabic as *Nahr ez-Zerqa* (also *az-Zarqa),* "The Blue River." The river discharges into the sea 4.25 km north of Caesarea Maritima. Tel Tanninim, entirely covered by sand dunes, measures at its base approximately 180 × 125 m, an area of about 2.25 hectares, and its summit is almost 10 m above sea level (fig. 1).

The mound was much larger in ancient times, but its entire western sector has been severely damaged by marine erosion. During winter storms, the sea gradually undermines and cuts into the coastal ridge, causing small sections to collapse into the water. At least 40 percent of the original mound has been destroyed, as is apparent from the eroded outlines at the mound's seaside edge. Along the western periphery of the mound, there are substantial remains of walls and tessellated floors, some of these cut by erosion and subsequent collapse of sections into the sea. These remnants indicate the

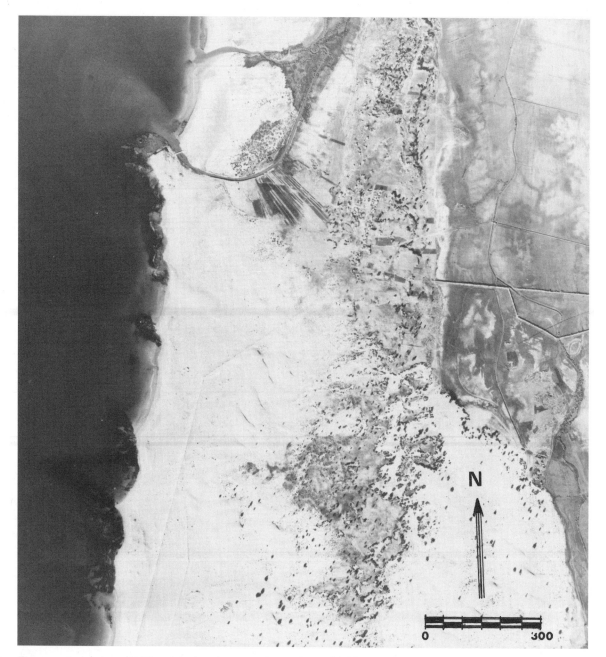

Fig. 1.   *Aerial view of Tel Tanninim (1944); note marine erosion and bridge over the river.*

existence of substantial ancient buildings in this part of the site and these structures are dated by their mosaics remnants to the Byzantine era.

The well known 1799 map of the Sharon plain—drawn by M. Jacotin in the wake of Napoleon's army retreat from Acre—had clearly depicted this (unnamed) site as a triangular promontory, jutting out into the sea in a northwestern direction. The erosion of the western sector of the site is clearly visible in the 1944 Royal Air Force aerial photograph of the area (fig. 1). Most of this eroded promontory has now become an abrasion table, about 150 m long and extending some 100 m into the shallow waters. The platform nowadays serves as a convenient platform for the local fishermen.

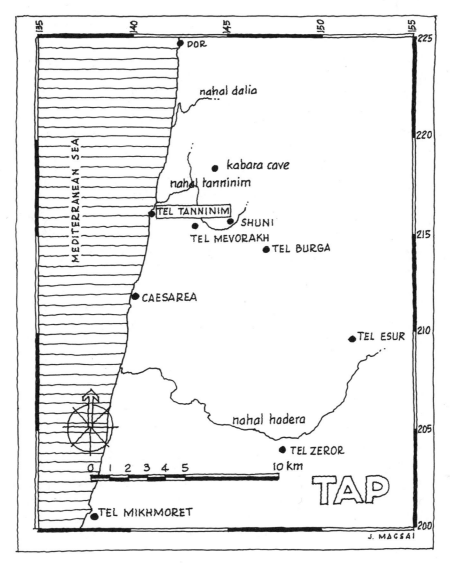

Fig. 2. *Map of the Tel Tanninim region.*

THE GEOGRAPHIC-HYDROGRAPHIC SETTING

From atop the mound, the observer is afforded an excellent view of the relatively straight coastline, with fine flat sandy beaches interrupted by an occasional sandy hill. On the horizon to the north, some 9 km distant, one can discern the silhouette of the ancient port city at Tel Dor (*Tantura*). Clearly visible on the coast to the south, about 5 km away, is the modern marina built over the sunken remains of Σεβαστός, the great artificial port constructed by King Herod to serve the city of Caesarea (fig. 2).

The most noteworthy aspect of Tel Tanninim's location was its unique hydrographic setting, which may be described as a confluence of three diverse water resources: the sea, the Crocodile River and a sizeable coastal marsh, located in the area between the coast and the sandstone ridge east of the Tel. The first settlers at Tel Tanninim were presumably attracted to this location by the favorable conditions for a fishery, as well as the presence of animals and various birds in this marshy riverine-maritime environment. The modern name of the marshy region was Ez-Zoar (Thomson 1880: 73), termed *Zōr* by Graf von Mülinen (1908: 231). During the Ottoman era, the marshland was inhabited by poor semi-nomadic farmers, some of whom tended water-buffaloes in the marshes. They lived in simple reed huts and were called *Ghawarni* "Depression-dwellers" (from *ghor* "[River] Depression"). The name was still found on maps of the British Mandate period, which label the area of the marshes as *'Arab al-Ghawarina*. Locally the swamp was known as *Al-Kabbāra*, or *El-Keb(b)āra* (also *El-Kebarah*), named after the ruins of a nearby site called Khirbet el-Kebarah (Conder and Kitchener 1882: 29), termed Khurbet Kubbar by Schumacher (1887: 79). The ruins are situated about 4 km northeast of Tel Tanninim, and the Ottoman district was also named after them. The Kabbara swamp was sustained primarily by thousands of tiny springs, many of them spouting water too salty for drinking, but which was useable in agriculture and industry. In modern times, small plots of land in this rather extensive marsh region began to be drained for farming as early as the 1880s (Schumacher 1887: 84). But most of the marsh was left intact and could still be seen in a 1918 Australian aerial photograph (Kedar 1991: 192). The entire Kabbara marshland was finally drained in a major agricultural reclamation project undertaken by the Palestine Colonization Association (PICA) during the period 1926–30.

In the fourth century C.E., the ancient marsh was totally transformed by a great Roman hydraulic engineering project. A sizeable dam, built with some very large ashlars, was constructed across the Crocodile River where the waters flowed through a gap in the *kurkar* ridge. The dam was 197 m long, 3 m wide and 5 m high, with its top situated at 9.33 m above sea level (map reference 1421 2171). In 2002, the entire length of the dam was cleared. The excavations revealed the remains of a lower aqueduct, one which led from Nahal 'Ada, a tributary of the Crocodile River, towards the intake of the Low-level Aqueduct of Caesarea. The Lower Aqueduct was built before the construction of the Crocodile River dam (Sa'id 2002).

By backing up the river flow, the Crocodile River dam created a substantial water reservoir behind it. At least one structure housing a turbine watermill was built into the dam in the second half of the fourth century (Oleson 1985; Schioler 1989).

During the Ottoman era, there were no less than six large structures constructed into the ancient dam, accommodating eleven watermills. These mills had an output of about 3,000 tons of flour *per annum* (Avizur 1990), and were in operation until 1922. The dam was wide enough to serve as a bridge over the river, hence its modern name *Jisr az-Zarqa*, "The Zerqa Bridge" (Conder and Kitchener 1882: 13).

To prevent the overflow of the reservoir waters northward, a second dam, much more massive, was constructed about 2.5 km north of the Crocodile River dam. This dam was called by the natives *Jisr al-Qanā*, "The Aqueduct Bridge" (Schumacher 1887: 80), and it stretched from Tell as-Sarris eastward to the foothills of the Carmel range. The northern dam was truly an impressive feat of engineering; 1,280 m long, 4 m wide and 3 m high, with its top situated at 9.33 m above sea level, precisely leveled with the Crocodile River dam.

The water gathered in the reservoir, between the two dams, exited from the southern tip of the Crocodile River dam, whence it was fed into the intake of the Low-level Aqueduct of Caesarea (fig. 3). When the reservoir was filled to capacity after the winter rains, its water level was at least 7.00 m above sea level (Olami and Peleg 1977). After the Low-level Aqueduct fell into disuse, the great reservoir that fed it was gradually transformed into the Kabbara swamp, as the Zerqa dam prevented the drainage of its waters through the course of the river (Thomson 1880: 73).

Since antiquity, the best known denizens of the swamp, which was situated along both banks of the Crocodile River, were indeed the crocodiles. How and when these Nilotic reptiles arrived in this region is not known, but evidently they gave their name to the river and to the ancient settlement established at the river mouth. In later times, several Crusader sources refer specifically to the crocodiles in the "river of Caesarea" (Jacques de Vitry, Godefroy Winisauf, Burchard du Mont-Sion [1283 C.E.], and Marinus Sanutus; texts quoted in Guerin 1875: 317). The Crusader-period itineraries single out these reptiles as the most noteworthy animal in the stream: *In fluminibus Cesaree sunt corcodrilli serpentes horribiles* "In the river of Caesarea there are crocodiles, horrible serpents" (*IHC* 13:46).

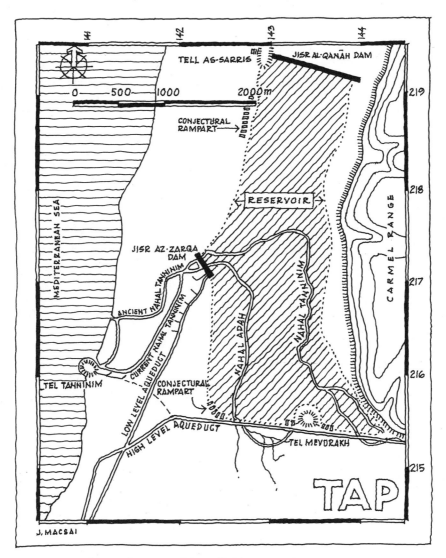

Fig. 3. *Map showing the suggested Crocodile River reservoir.*

We should note here that Nilotic crocodiles were not unique to this location in the Holy Land. Several coastal marshes, adjacent to rivers in Palestine, were associated with crocodiles, and therefore named in Arabic *Muyāt at-Timsāḥ* "Crocodile Waters" (PPTS 5: 47; Guerin 1875: 320; Abel 1914: 564). Maps of the Holy Land produced in the Ottoman period also indicated the presence of coastal swamps with crocodiles. During the nineteenth century, the crocodiles of the Zerqa River congregated at a pond within the marshland named by the locals *Birket Timsāḥ* "Crocodile Pool" (Schumacher 1887: 79). Crocodiles survived in the marsh until the beginning of the twentieth century.

The last known specimen was apparently killed shortly before World War I.

The water of the Crocodile River originates from a number of springs situated in the foothills of the modern Menashe Ridge, locally known as the *Rūḥa* (Mülinen 1908: 229), some 8 km east of the coastal plain. There, the upper course of the river consists of two branches, the Zerqa in the north and the *Wādi Timsāḥi*, "Crocodile Gully," south of it. The Timsahi gully extends eastward, well into the hill country, to the springs in the region of As-Sindiyana and Sabbarin (Kuhnen 1987: 155, map). In the Byzantine era, the upper sector of the Crocodile River was used to augment the water

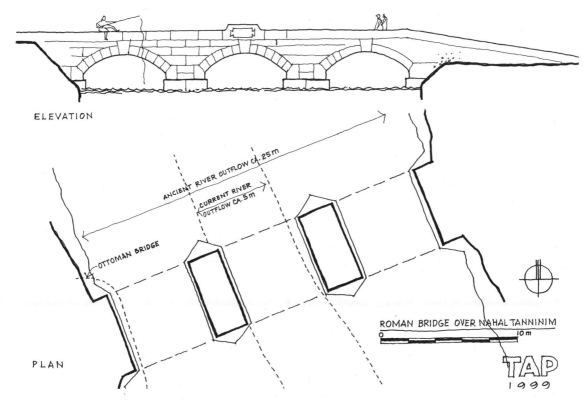

Fig. 4.   *Reconstruction of the ancient bridge over the Crocodile River.*

Fig. 5.   *Aerial view of Tel Tanninim in 1986, looking west.*

supply for Caesarea Maritima, by building a third dam, now called the Nahal Tanninim dam, near Ein 'Ami (Siegelmann 1993). The dam backed up the upper river water and fed it into an intricate system of subterranean aqueducts in the upper Nahal Tanninim region (Siegelmann 1973: 6; 1989; Siegelmann and Rawak 1995).

Winding its way westward to the sea, the flow was supplemented by additional waters from springs at Shuni (Talmudic Kefar Shumi; Khirbet ash-Shuna; map reference 1455 2157), some 6.25 km northeast of Caesarea. The river then flowed north of Tel Mevorakh through the Kabbara marsh, where its waters were augmented by the waters of Nahal 'Ada, and then continued through a gap in the *kurkar* coastal ridge, north of the village of Jisr az-Zarqa (Khirbet esh-Shomariya). From this location, about 1.75 km northeast of Tel Tanninim, its course winds to the sea, where it exits at the foot of Tel Tanninim. When the Kabbara marsh was drained, a sector of the river's lower course was altered in order to accelerate the water flow, but the location of the river mouth was not much affected since ancient times, as is proven by the remains of the ancient bridge built across very near its current mouth.

Until the twentieth century, Nahal Tanninim was a fast flowing perennial stream, one of the few along the coast of Palestine which was difficult to ford. In October 1876, Conder and Kitchener (1882: 2) observed that at the sea shore the stream has a strong current, 5 to 10 yards across, and was about 2 feet deep. Early European travelers to the Holy Land, such as Richard Pococke (1745) had already identified the Zerqa River with the *Crocodilon* river noted by Pliny *(Natural History* 5.17.75). Others sought to equate the river with the biblical stream named Shihor-libnath (Joshua 19:26). The Hebrew term *Šiḥōr*, supposedly derived from Egyptian *Š-Ḥr* "Pool of Horus", was thought by some to be another biblical name for the Nile. Thus the Egypto-biblical river name in the Book of Joshua was linked to the Egyptian Nilotic crocodiles in the Zerqa River and the nearby marshes (Thomson 1880: 74).

At the river's outflow on the coast, the travelers also noted the ruins of an ancient stone bridge, built presumably in Roman-Byzantine or Crusader times, which had three arches (fig. 4). The ruined bridge indicated that the course of the river had shifted only slightly southwards. In 1898, a new stone bridge, about 4.5 m wide, was constructed by the Ottoman authorities over the ruined ancient arches. The new bridge was built specifically for the impending tour of Kaiser Wilhelm II of Germany, who expressed the wish to tour this part of the Holy Land along the coast, from Haifa to Caesarea. The so-called *Kaiserbrücke* was intact until the late 1970s, when it was destroyed by storms and thereafter was left in ruins. A pontoon bridge, erected east of the ruined bridge (fig. 5), was also washed away by storms.

In ancient times, the nearest inland settlement to Tel Tanninim was at Tel Mevorakh (*Tall Mubarak*), called by the locals *Tell el-Fellaḥ* (Mülinen 1908: 231). The mound is located 2.5 km east of Tel Tanninim and was occupied from the end of the eleventh century B.C.E. until the Roman era, with a substantial gap in occupation from the tenth–fifth centuries B.C.E. and another break from 332–201 B.C.E. (Stern 1978: 85). The land adjacent to the lower course of the Crocodile River, between Tel Mevorakh and Tel Tanninim, was suitable for farming. Remains of a substantial Roman-Byzantine rural villa, occupied from the third to the seventh centuries, were recently unearthed ('Ad 2000). As for Tel Tanninim, the surface ceramic evidence indicated that the site had been settled, probably by Phoenician traders, during the Persian period (Stern 1973: 238).

From the first century C.E., until its final destruction in 1265, the closest urban center to Tel Tanninim was Caesarea Maritima, built by King Herod the Great. Pliny (5.14.69) noted that the Roman frontier of Palestine (*finis Palaestines*) was marked by Caesarea (*colonia Prima Flavia*). The Crocodile River north of the urban center, with the ruined settlement at its mouth, was considered to be the southern limit of Phoenicia (5.17.75). Caesarea was preceded on its site by a small harbor known in Greek sources as Στράτωνος πύργος and in Hebrew documents named *Migdal Ṡar* (Stieglitz 1996). This fortified Hellenistic site was founded in the third century B.C.E. The next port south of Caesarea was the fine natural harbor at

Tel Mikhmoret (Porath, Paley and Stieglitz 1993), known locally as *Minat Abu Zabūrā*, situated 15 km south of Tel Tanninim.

SITE IDENTIFICATIONS

The local name for the coastal mound was *Khirbet el-Melāṭ* "Mortar Ruin" (Conder and Kitchener 1882: 2; Mülinen 1908: 223). This was not an ancient name, but one evidently coined due to the ruined and heavily mortared stone structures visible atop the mound (see Arabic *milāṭ* "mortar"). Guerin (1875: 317) noted that the largest of three offshore islets, situated about 1.75 km north of the mound, was known as *Jazirat el-Melāṭ* "Mortar Island," presumably named after the nearby coastal mound. The island was also known as *Jazirat al-Ḥamām* "Pigeon Island," whence its modern Hebrew name *ʾIy ha-Yōnīm* "Pigeons Island" (map reference 1411 2179). Guerin (1875: 319) recorded the local name of the coastal mound as Kharbet Abu Tantur, a designation not found in other sources. The name Abu Tantur, however, is attested in the British Mandate period for the site of Kibbutz Sedot Yam, south of Caesarea.

Guerin identified the coastal mound with the ancient site of Κροκοδείλων πόλις "City of Crocodiles" mentioned by Strabo (16.2.27), and referred to as *Crocodilon* by Pliny (5.17.75). Both of these ancient writers had located that settlement just north of Caesarea. According to their testimony, the town was abandoned and lay in ruins, at least as early as the last quarter of the first century B.C.E.

Galling (1938) proposed to restore the name of the late Hellenistic town of Krokodeilon polis in a much earlier document, dated to the Persian period. The text he suggested to emend is a partially preserved list of Syro-Palestinian harbors by the Greek geographer Pseudo-Scylax (*Periplus* 93; ca. 350 B.C.E.). In Section 93, the *Periplus* registers most major ports and rivers of Palestine, in correct geographical order from north to south. The original text (Müller 1855) listed the following four entries south of Mount Carmel, a mountain which was qualified by the epithet "the sacred mountain of Zeus" (ὄρος ʿιερὸν Διός):

> *Arados, a city of the Sidonians*
> *[…], and river of the Tyrians*
> *Doros, a city of the Sidonians*
> *[The city of Ioppe, expo]sed there, they say,*
>   *was Androm[eda]…*

Since a harbor town named Arados is a well-known port in north Syria (the Arwad of the Bible), but is unknown along this sector of the Palestinian coast. Galling (1938: 80), followed by Avi-Yonah (1949: 129) and others, proposed to emend Arados to read *Adaros, and to identify the latter with a coastal town called by Strabo Βουκόλων (πόλις) "Herders' City" (16.2.27). This ingenuous suggestion was based on the hypothesis that the list's missing toponym had originally been a Phoenician name, such as the term * ʿAdarōt "Herds (town)," and that the name preserved by Strabo is merely its translation into Greek. Indeed, as a parallel, one could cite the biblical toponym ʿĒder "Herd" (the singular form of * ʿAdarōt), attested in Joshua 15:21.

Galling also re-arranged the original listing in this section of Pseudo-Scylax, placing the restored site name after Dor (south of it), so that the emended list now reads:

> *Adaros, a city of the Sidonians*
> *Doros, a city of the Sidonians*
> *[Krokodeilon polis], and a river of the Tyrians*
> *[The city of Ioppe, expo]sed there, they say,*
>   *was Androm[eda]…*

We find these emendations quite problematic, precisely because Section 93 of the *Periplus* is geographically accurate. As it stands, the identity of the "river of the Tyrians" depends on the identity of Arados. If we equate Arados (or *Adaros) with Athlit, then the following lacuna contained the name of a port south of Athlit, and the river in question would be the stream south of Athlit named Nahal Meʿarot (*Wādi al-Maghāra*), or possibly the stream to the south of it, namely, Nahal Maharal (*Wādi Ḥenu*). But this conjecture is not satisfactory since there are no known Persian period harbors between Athlit and Dor. This was presumably the reason why Galling sought to re-arrange the original text.

A more plausible proposal, to my mind, would be if Arados does not refer to Athlit at all, but rather to one of the several known Persian era coastal settlements situated between Mt. Carmel and Athlit. If that is the case, the missing site name in the original order in the *Periplus* of Pseudo-Scylax could well have been the ancient Phoenician name of Athlit. Perhaps it was *ʿAtlit*, a name only attested since Medieval times. The "river of the Tyrians" named in the *Periplus* would be either Nahal Meʿarot, south of Athlit, or Nahal Oren (*Wādi Falāḥ*) immediately north of Athlit. In this reconstruction, Krokodeilon polis was not listed in the *Periplus* simply because it was not an important port along this sector of the coast.

Alternatively, if we accept the re-arranged order and assume that Arados (or *ʿAdaros*) is indeed the Phoenician Athlit, then the best candidate for the missing port between Dor and Ioppe (Jaffa) would still not be the site of Krokodeilon polis, because I believe that it was much too small to be listed there. A far better candidate would be Tel Mikhmoret, ancient name unknown, some 15 km south of Tel Tanninim (fig. 3). This was a fine natural harbor quite active during the Persian era, as revealed by our brief excavations there (Porath, Paley and Stieglitz 1993). In this case, the "river of the Tyrians" associated with the missing harbor name, would be Nahal Alexander (*Nahr Iskandaruna*), which nowadays discharges into the sea some 500 m south of Tel Mikhmoret.

In summary, since the nineteenth century the mound of Tell el-Melāt at the outflow of the Zerqa river has been identified by most authors with the ancient ruined Greco-Roman settlement known as Krokodeilon polis, or Crocodilon, mentioned by Strabo and Pliny. The Greek name, transmitted to the Latin sources, indicates an occupation horizon at the settlement in the Hellenistic period, before the site was abandoned, or destroyed, probably early in the first century B.C.E. As such, this phase in the history of Tel Tanninim is similar to the later history of nearby Tel Mevorakh (Roller 1982: 47). Finally, it should be noted that the nineteenth century identifications of Tell el-Melāt with Krokodeilon polis led to its modern Hebrew name of Tel Tanninim.

Turning now to the later Roman period, there is ample archaeological and literary evidence indicating that the region of Tel Tanninim served as the northern boundary for the *territorium* of Caesarea Maritima. Two dozens Roman milestones, some of them with surviving inscriptions, were found along the old Roman coastal road leading northward from Caesarea to Dor. Three milestones were found less than 1 km south of Tel Tanninim (map reference 1410 2154), near a previously known milestone (Yankelevitch 1981). Another group of no less than nineteen milestones was found on the shore about 2 km north of the mound (map reference 1481 2185). The legible inscriptions on seven of the latter group of milestones dated them to the period 161–238 C.E. (Avi-Yonah 1959).

One of the inscriptions records the marker as being "[3] miles from Caesarea." The aerial distance measured from the center of Caesarea to this location is 6.40 km, namely, over 4 Roman miles. Evidently the proper restoration of the milestone's worn numeral should be [4]. Avi-Yonah (1959: 40) had rightly observed that the milestones confirm the assumption about the boundary between Caesarea and Dor being situated north of the Crocodile River. Throughout the Roman and Byzantine eras Tel Tanninim was certainly within the territory of Caesarea.

After the third century C.E., the settlement at Tel Tanninim was known by other names. In Late Roman and Byzantine periods it can be identified with the Talmudic toponym *Migdal Malḥāʾ* (or *Milḥāʾ*) "Saltworks Tower," a place first attested in the Palestinian Talmud (*Demai* 2:1, 22). The locality is mentioned in a legal discussion, recording three Rabbinic opinions regarding the fixing of the northern, or northeastern, territorial boundary of Caesarea. The border was essential to determine the status of agricultural produce for the fulfillment of the laws of offerings, tithing and the Sabbatical Year (Hebrew *Sheviʿit*).

In one Rabbi's view, the boundary was marked by "the waters" (*mayyāʾ*). This is an unusual designation, as it is quite general. Perhaps it was a reference to the water flowing in the Crocodile River, and to the large water reservoir formed by the two dams. One Talmudic manuscript has a variant reading "the sea" (*yammā '*), which is even more obscure, since the Mediterranean is obviously the western border. A second opinion found in this passage favored the locality named Migdal Malha as a boundary point, while the third opinion named *Me ʿ ārat Telimōn* "The Cave of Telimon."

The suggestion of Avi-Yonah (1949: 126) to identify the latter with one of the caves near Khirbet Suleimaniyat, located over 14 km northeast of Caesarea, is rather unlikely. Rabbinic opinions in another discussion (*jHallah* 2:13,14) clearly indicate that Caesarea's territorial boundary in the north and northeast was 4 miles from the city. Since the Talmudic mile was only 2,000 cubits, or about 1.15 km (the Roman mile was 1.48 km), the cave in question would have to be in the vicinity of Caesarea, much closer than 14 km away. I would thus suggest to identify the Cave of Telimon with the Kebara Cave (*Maghārat Kabbāra*; map reference 1442 2182), located some 7.4 km northeast of the center of Caesarea.

Avi-Yonah (1949: 129), following Klein (1923), further proposed to identify the site of Migdal Malha with the modern Khirbet Malhah (Melliha, or Maliha; map reference 1444 2312), situated some 20 km north of Caesarea, 3 km south of Athlit, and well north of Dor. Beyer (1936: 8 [map], 20), following a suggestion by Röhricht, had located at Khirbet Malhah the Frankish citadel called El-Mellaha, a name found in Ibn al-Furat (ca. 1375), who relates its destruction by the forces of Sultan Baybars in 1265. The fortress, situated between Caesarea and Athlit, whose Crusader name is unknown, was called in Arabic *Ḥiṣn al-Mallūha* "Al-Malluha Fort" (Lyons, Lyons and Riley-Smith 1971: 72, 206). This important citadel was also mentioned by the Egyptian historian Al-Maqrizi (ca. 1425; Beyer 1936: 20). We should note here the cogent observation of Schumacher (1887: 84) about the name of the site Khirbet Malhah, situated near Athlit:

> ... the ancient sarcophagi and holes in the rocks near it are used to a wide extent as salt basins, that is, into which sea-water is poured in order to obtain cooking salt by the evaporation of the water by the sun; this trade is practiced all along the coast, and such places generally bear

the name Mallāḥa.

As noted above, Rabbinic views concurred that the northern and northeastern territorial boundary of Caesarea was in the area of the Crocodile River and the settlement of Migdal Malha, and was thus certainly south of the territory of Dor. Indeed, there are several sources that confirm that Dor and her territory constituted the region immediately to the north of Caesarea's territory (Avi-Yonah 1949: 129). The situation of Tel Tanninim, at the outflow of the Crocodile River, and only 4.2 km from Caesarea, strongly suggest that it was the ancient settlement of Migdal Malha.

Tel Tanninim (Tell el-Melat) was later identified with a Crusader coastal estate called in contemporary sources *Turris Salinarum* "Saltworks Tower" (Cook 1900: 294). The name suggests the property was known for its salt pans, and/or salted fish production. Until 1166, the estate belonged to a certain Gervasius of Caesarea. Then Hugh the Lord of Caesarea (1154–68) transferred the estate to the Hospitallers (Röhricht 1893: 164, No. 619; Beyer 1936: 29; Tibble 1989: 150). The Crusader name *Turris Salinarum* is not new, but is an exact translation of the Byzantine Aramaic name Migdal Malha (Stieglitz 1998: 54). It is not known if the Latin name was coined in the Byzantine or in later periods.

Nearby was a Crusader site named *Pain Perdu*, associated with a Tower of St. Lazarus. *Pain Perdu* is probably not to be identified with Khirbet Kabbara (Beyer 1936: 28), but with a place closer to the coast. After the peace of 1191, the Hospitallers of Saint Lazarus, based in Jerusalem, had established their main naval base at Saint Jean d'Acre (Akko). They were also granted two sites near Caesarea: the Tower of Saint Lazarus, and the Church of Saint Lawrence. In 1253, the Order even acquired a small fleet in order to facilitate their regular communications between Europe and the Holy Land (Feigl no date: 23). It is possible that the Tower of Saint Lazarus may be the same site as *Turris Salinarum*, still, there were other Crusader settlements in the region north of Caesarea.

Pringle (1998: 152, 422, map) accepted the identification of Tel Tanninim with the Crusader estate of *Turris Salinarum* (his "Tower of the Saltings"), and also equated the site with the toponym Burj al-Malih "Saltworks Tower." The latter Arabic name is now known as a site east of Tubas in Samaria. To my knowledge, that name is not attested along the coast in Medieval sources. If Burj al-Malih referred to a coastal site, it may well be another Arabic name of the fort named *Ḥiṣn al-Mallūḥa* (El-Mellaha). The name Burj al-Malih itself is clearly a translation, either from the Byzantine Aramaic name Migdal Malha, or, less likely, from a Greek or Latin source. In any event, we believe that the Crusader citadel of El-Mellaha, or *Ḥiṣn al-Mallūḥa*, should be identified with modern Khirbet Malhah near Athlit, but not with Tel Tanninim.

ARCHAEOLOGICAL INVESTIGATIONS UNTIL 1996

In the nineteenth century, explorers and surveyors in the Holy Land reported various structural remains atop the mound at Khirbet el-Melat. Guerin (1875: 319) described the ruins of a tower and some walls, next to remains of multi-colored mosaics and other structures. Some of these colorful mosaic fragments were still visible in the 1970s (fig. 6). Mülinen noted on his map (1907–08) two towers on the mound, situated on either side of the then existing Ottoman bridge. Guerin had concluded that the ruins were the probable remains of Krokodeilon polis, and that the town was originally a much larger settlement. He also remarked that the ruined buildings had evidently served as a quarry during the construction of the Roman (High-level) aqueduct for Caesarea. Conder and Kitchener (1882: 33) noted ruins at El Helat (a misprint for El Melat), as well as ancient bridge remains, which they remarked appeared to be of Crusader times.

That the ruined structures of Tel Tanninim were used intermittently as a source for building materials, even as late as the end of the nineteenth century, is certain. Thomson noted that "Boats often call in summer to load with stones from the ruins, many of the recent buildings in Jaffa and Acre are constructed out of them" (1880: 73). We can be equally certain that when the Ottoman bridge was built across the river mouth in 1898, many stones for the bridge were derived from the ruins of the

Fig. 6. *Mosaic fragment, west of Tel Tanninim summit (courtesy of Y. Ayalon).*

structures conveniently situated directly above the construction site.

During the British Mandate period, several archaeologists of the Palestine Department of Antiquities conducted surveys of Tell el-Melat and its surrounding area, and recorded the remains visible on the mound and in its immediate vicinity. Their notes in the files of the Israel Antiquities Authority (IAA) in Jerusalem include the following observations on the structural remains at the site: A "cistern built of rubble in cement, sand blocks and tessellated pavement of red and white big tesserae on a sand hill immediately south of the [Ottoman] Jisr on the seashore" (Ory 1922); a "tower at west with aqueduct leading from it to main aqueduct" (Guy 1926); an "old building in ruins; has canal for water in its walls. Probably a bath. Water brought by built canal branching from Low-level aqueduct (from a spring)" (Makhouly 1934). The remains of the above mentioned structure called a "tower" or "bath," were later better described as "Foundations of a reservoir. Remains of aqueduct to east" (Ory 1940). Lastly, we have the following entry: "Small mound ca. 60 m inland—building remains with internal plaster and apparent water installation. Tower foundation—*kurkar* ashlars with core of

Fig. 7.   *Two salvaged marble capitals from the summit of Tel Tanninim.*

large rubble concrete. Concrete of lime, ashes, shells, and sand. Marble drains, well built, intersect wall line. Drains lined with reddish mortar. Traces of a rubble aqueduct north parallel to and south of river" (Hamilton 1943).

In the 1960s, several ornate and very well preserved marble capitals were uncovered in the sand atop the mound, illegally excavated, and removed from Tel Tanninim. The exact number of the stolen items remains unknown. Four additional capitals were later salvaged by the local IDAM staff (registration numbers 95–5034, 5035, 5045, 5057; fig. 7). The antiquities department staff also retrieved a complete monolithic marble column from the mound (IDAM 95–5037). All the finds were brought for safekeeping to the nearby field school of the Society for the Protection of Nature in Israel, located at the outskirts of Kibbutz Maʿagan Mikhael.

A brief salvage excavation was undertaken at the western perimeter of Tel Tanninim in December 1979 by Siegelmann and Yankelevitch (1981), after remains on the site sustained damage due to recent military activities. The excavators concentrated on the western edges of the mound, where they unearthed several large and well-built stone structures, including an elliptical stone tank, indicating these were remains of industrial installations for handling liquids. There were also areas of tessellated pavements, located along the western periphery of the hill. Among the finds were two rather large colored mosaics (11 × 11 m and 8.5 × 5 m). In one of them, a Greek mosaic inscription set into a *tabula ansata* read "In the days of … the commander (*hegemon*)." The ceramic and small finds indicated occupation levels from the Persian, Hellenistic, Late Roman and Late Byzantine periods. Some of remains had previously been noted in 1972 by the Israel Survey Northern team, headed by Olami (Binyaminah Sheet). In conjunction with the 1979 salvage excavation, Raban and divers of the Undersea Exploration Society of Israel conducted an underwater archaeological survey west of the tel and at the river outflow. The area revealed some underwater construction features suggesting the possibility that an ancient artificial anchorage had been built at the mouth of Nahal Tanninim.

A survey of the Tel Tanninim aqueduct conducted by Porath (1988) first led him to the conclusion that the water line had its origins in the Low-level Caesarea aqueduct, and exhibited two construction phases. The last phase appeared to date to the Byzantine era, but a more extensive examination of the aqueduct, undertaken by Porath on behalf of the IAA from November 1990 to April 1991, unearthed evidence that contradicted his earlier conclusion. Porath then established that the aqueduct line to Tel Tanninim (termed Channel E) received its water from the High-level Caesarea aqueduct (fig. 8). The earliest hydraulic plaster within various exposed sections of Channel E was typologically dated to the Late Roman period (third–fourth century C.E.), not to the Byzantine era (Porath 1993: 26).

An unusual surface find reportedly made in the western region of the site, and now in a private collection, consisted of five lead slingshots. Four of the slingshots were inscribed with Greek letters and some figures, while the fifth was only decorated

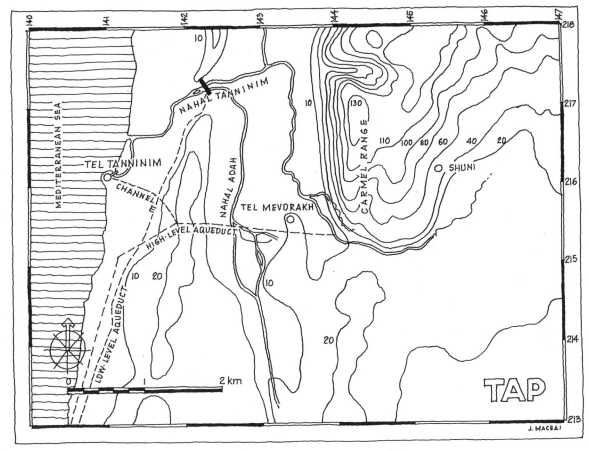

Fig. 8.   Map showing the proposed course of the Tel Tanninim aqueduct (Channel E).

with figures of a *lituus* and an anchor (Schlesinger 1984: 89). The bullets are evidence of a military presence at the site, most likely during the turbulent times of the second century B.C.E. The slingshot may well be connected with the struggles between Tryphon (142–137 B.C.E.) and Antiochus VII Sidetes (138–129 B.C.E.), centering around the city of Dor in the year 138/37 B.C.E. (Josephus, *Antiquities of the Jews* 13.203–24).

Spier (1993: 120–21) explored the shallow waters along the northwestern region of Tel Tanninim. Her search revealed the existence of three rock-cut fishponds (*piscinae*). The first, situated below the western edge of the tel, was a hewn rectangular pond measuring 4 × 2.5 m. A second rectangular pond was located in the southwest of the mound. It was smaller than the first, with dimensions of 3 × 2 m, and had its floor cut on two levels. A third and much larger fishpond, associated with a nearby

smaller cutting (measuring 1.25 × 1.2 m), was found along the south bank of Nahal Tanninim, at the river outflow. Spier estimated the dimensions of the third fishpond to be about 8 × 6.5 m.

The large pond and its associated cutting were also recorded by Horowitz (1994: 7) in his survey of the Tel Tanninim area undertaken for the Israel Department of Antiquities and Museums. He recorded the dimension of the cutting, actually a small tank (his Site #1), as being 1.5 × 1.5 m and discovered that it had a mosaic floor constructed of large white *tesserae*, with a hewn channel leading out, and two channels entering into the basin. The large pond at the river outflow (his Site #2) was determined to be 8.4 × 6.6 m, with a hewn channel leading towards the sea from its northern side. This area was subsequently excavated by the Tanninim Archaeological Project (Area D), and the fish pond was found to be associated with additional rock-cut installations, as well as a bath-house situated to its south (see Chapter II.4, below).

Among the features Horowitz described in his report on the site were the reservoir and aqueduct, known from previous surveys, and a newly discovered well, about 3 m² in area—previously noted only by Ayalon—located at the southern edge of the archaeological site, some 125 m south of Tel Tanninim and 50 m inland (his Site #8). In order to ascertain the extent of the archaeological remains south of the mound, Horowitz opened five test trenches by mechanical means (his Sections A–A to E–E) located in the southern region of the site (1994: 18, map). The numerous remains found led him to the conclusion that systematic excavations were required to determine the nature of the structural remains at the site.

During the first half of 1995, a systematic underwater survey was conducted by Galili and Sharvit (1999) on behalf of the IAA and the Israel Lands Administration. They discovered five underwater sites, whose finds consisted of pottery and stone anchors, and also noted the previously described large fish-pond at the foot of the tel, on the south bank of Nahal Tanninim. The earliest datable finds were ceramics of the fifth–fourth centuries B.C.E. The finds indicated to the surveyors that the coast north and south of Tel Tanninim served as an anchorage during various periods in antiquity.

The nautical aspects of Tel Tanninim were dramatically highlighted in the autumn of 1985, by the discovery of a small and unusually well preserved merchantman that had sunk in shallow waters and was covered by sand, off the beach at Kibbutz Maʿagan Mikhael. The wreck was situated about 1.75 km north of the tel. The shipwreck was originally dated on the basis of the ceramics found aboard to about 400 B.C.E. (Linder 1991; Linder and Rosloff 1995). Current estimates have raised the date to about 450 B.C.E. (Linder, personal communication, June 2002). It is not clear if the ship, which was a "sewn vessel" (Kahanov 1998), was attempting to reach the site at Tel Tanninim when she was wrecked.

Chapter II

Tanninim Archaeological Project Excavations, 1996–1999

1. Introduction

by Robert R. Stieglitz

In 1996, the Tanninim Archaeological Project (hereafter TAP), directed by Prof. R.R. Stieglitz on behalf of Rutgers University (Newark, NJ), initiated systematic excavations on the mound of Tel Tanninim and in its immediate vicinity. The excavations took place over the next four seasons, under IAA license nos. G-26/96, G-32/97, G-51/98, and G-15/99. A professional staff of five members and fifteen to twenty volunteers per year excavated for six weeks per season. The TAP expedition began with a surface survey and the production of a contour map of the archaeological site (IAA Site No. 1391/0). The surface survey located over two dozen features, which consisted of diverse structural remains and some pockets of material culture. In addition to pottery, the surface finds included a variety of mosaic segments, numerous marble and colorful stone pieces from paved floors and wall attachments, roof tile fragments, plaster chunks and brick components.

Exploration of the surface and its remains showed that the topography of the site may be divided into three distinct elements: (1) the mound of Tel Tanninim, situated on the shore directly above the outflow of Nahal Tanninim. The summit of the mound is at an elevation of 9.66 m above sea level, now marked by the new Israel Grid triangulation point W 2814; (2) a smaller hill located about 120 m to the southeast, with prominent wall remains of a large reservoir visible above its summit and a buried aqueduct line leading to the base of this reservoir from its source in the east; and (3) a third hillock situated some 100 m south of Tel Tanninim.

Scattered along the western periphery of the site were several short sections of well-built low walls made of *kurkar* ashlar blocks. The bedrock of the site slopes rather markedly, as may be discerned in the eroded seaward edges of the mound. The peripheral wall sections were found to have been constructed between two projecting areas of the bedrock. These were not fortification remains, but retaining walls designed to allow the construction of leveling terraces behind and above them to serve as foundations for structures (fig. 9).

We decided to begin excavations in two areas and to probe two other promising regions. The first chosen area was near the summit of Tel

Fig. 9. *Three sections of retaining walls along the periphery of the mound.*

Tanninim, where an excellent aerial photograph from 1974, and the TAP surface survey, indicated the existence of substantial structures under the sand cover. The initial excavation squares opened at the summit were designated as Area A. A second region—designated as Area B—was delineated outside the south and west walls of the protruding structure, which previous surveys had labeled a reservoir, and which was evidently the terminus of an aqueduct leading to it from the east. The hillock to the south of Tel Tanninim was designated as Area C. Just beyond the western end of the ruined Ottoman bridge, there were several wall sections of varying length, as well as hewn features in the nearby bedrock on the shore. That sector was named Area D (fig. 10).

In 1996, the TAP excavated only in two locations: Areas A and B. A third area, the hillock named Area C, was probed by a shallow east–west

trench dug mechanically across its southern part, as well as by a small test square (Area F; measuring 2 × 2 m) opened at its southwest edge. The probe in Area F had its highest point at 4.02 m above sea level. The mechanical trench, which was about 0.75 m deep, revealed remains of walls extending at least 10 meters, disarticulated segments from a white mosaic floor, and some fragments of fine colored mosaics. When the section of the trench was cleaned, a badly fragmented mosaic floor was discovered at an elevation of +6.80 m. It was clear from the test trench that there were significant structural remains buried in Area C, but the area could not be excavated owing to lack of personnel.

The test square of Area F, probed by Sean A. Kingsley, was inundated with roof tile fragments, pottery, and marble fragments, as well as disarticulated white mosaic segments, and a single lamp fragment. There were also pockets of colored stone and glass *tesserae* in black, sky blue, green and red, all found within the 15 cm of topsoil level. Below that layer was a concentration of grey veined marble, some complete *opus sectile* floor tiles, wall paneling, stepped paneling and brick fragments. The ceramics were mostly locally produced bag-shaped amphorae, dated to the late sixth to early seventh centuries, and included sherds from cooking pots, imported fine ware bowls, and two *pithoi*. The probe concluded at a depth of 65 cm.

The initial surface explorations of the entire archaeological site revealed a varied ceramic assemblage, dominated by Byzantine pottery, with significant quantities of Persian and Hellenistic wares (figs. 11–14). There were only few Late Islamic–Crusader sherds. The earliest surface sherds were datable to the fifth century B.C.E. and the latest, not counting the handful of glazed Ottoman sherds, was a Crusader bowl rim of the thirteenth century (fig. 13:7). No early Roman pottery was found on the surface. The surface evidence for a Crusader horizon was new, since previous surveys and the salvage excavation at the site in 1981 had not reported Crusader remains.

In addition to pottery, the surface yielded mosaic segments of diverse sizes and three materials. There were tiny glass and colored stone cubes from colorful mosaics, and large stone cubes and some

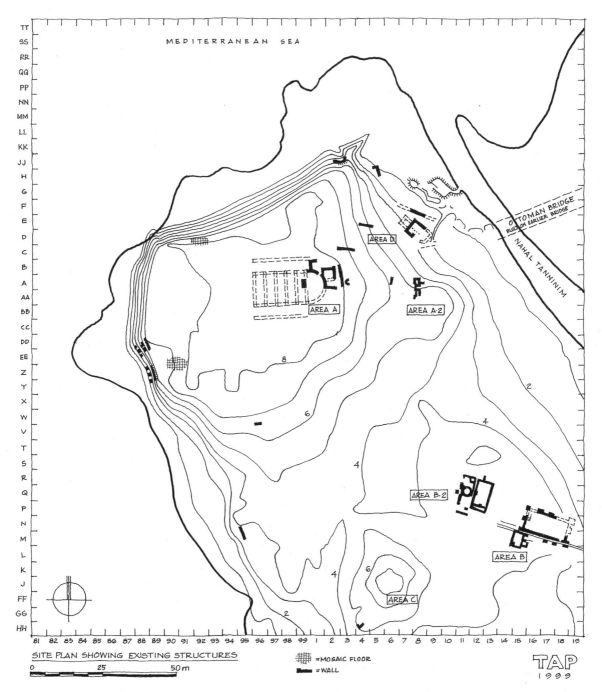

Fig. 10.   *Site plan showing existing structures.*

ceramic *tesserae* made of roof tiles, probably from industrial installations.

Other finds included marble and colored stone pieces, roof tile fragments, glass pieces, shells, and several parts of nails. These finds were predominantly from the Byzantine era. Local inhabitants related that in past years numerous coins had been found on the surface, particularly following the winter storms. The overall impression gained from the surface material culture, the relatively substantial architectural remains, and the aqueduct leading to the site, was that the settlement had once been a thriving community among the suburbs of Caesarea.

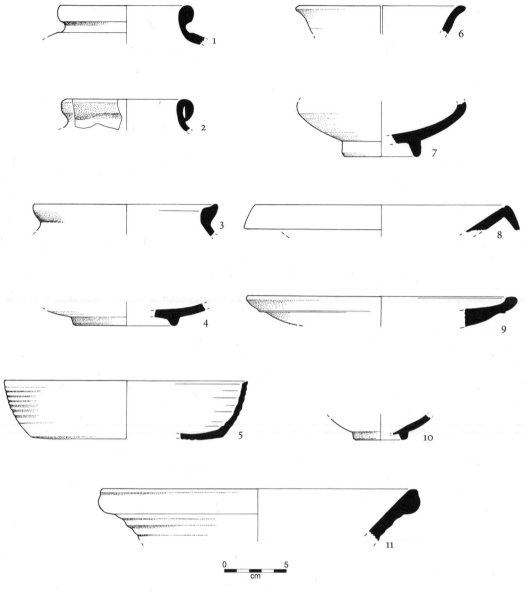

No.	Reg. No.	Form	Description
1	23/1	storage jar	Hard, sandy red clay 10R 5/8, rough texture, and few grits.
2	23/2	storage jar	Hard, red clay 2.5YR 6/6, rough texture, and numerous grits of reddish brown to grey.
3	1001/10	cooking pot	Burned, plastered for re-use.
4	10/3	bowl	Hard, pink fabric 5YR 7/4, smooth texture, few inclusions.
5	0046/1	casserole	Light red, high iron content, crystallized clay.
6	1001/8	bowl	Soft pink to reddish clay 7.5YR 8/4 to 8/6, and black gloss.
7	C009	bowl	Silty pink clay 7.5YR 7/4, well levigated, weak black slip.
8	C010	fish plate	Reddish yellow fabric 7.5YR 7/6, heavy lustrous black gloss, Attic.
9	C005	bowl	Reddish yellow clean clay 5YR 7/8, lustrous black gloss.
10	1014/2	bowl	Red clay with exterior black gloss.
11	12/3	mortarium	Extremely coarse, hard, pale yellow clay 2.5Y 7/3, rough texture and large dark grey grits.

Fig. 11.   *Surface ceramics: Persian and Hellenistic (1–2, 6–11); Byzantine (3–5).*

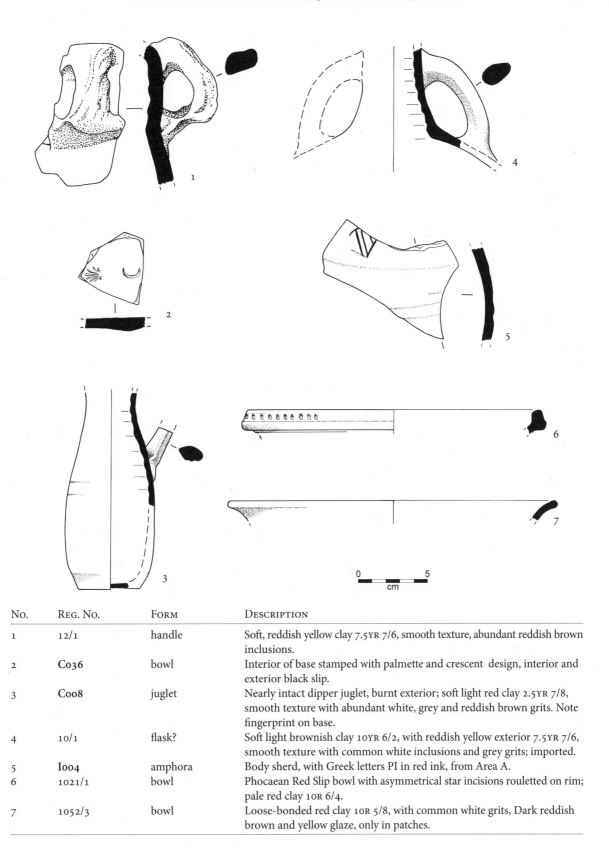

No.	Reg. No.	Form	Description
1	12/1	handle	Soft, reddish yellow clay 7.5YR 7/6, smooth texture, abundant reddish brown inclusions.
2	C036	bowl	Interior of base stamped with palmette and crescent design, interior and exterior black slip.
3	C008	juglet	Nearly intact dipper juglet, burnt exterior; soft light red clay 2.5YR 7/8, smooth texture with abundant white, grey and reddish brown grits. Note fingerprint on base.
4	10/1	flask?	Soft light brownish clay 10YR 6/2, with reddish yellow exterior 7.5YR 7/6, smooth texture with common white inclusions and grey grits; imported.
5	I004	amphora	Body sherd, with Greek letters PI in red ink, from Area A.
6	1021/1	bowl	Phocaean Red Slip bowl with asymmetrical star incisions rouletted on rim; pale red clay 10R 6/4.
7	1052/3	bowl	Loose-bonded red clay 10R 5/8, with common white grits, Dark reddish brown and yellow glaze, only in patches.

Fig. 12.   *Surface ceramics: Persian and Hellenistic (1–4); Byzantine (5–6); Crusader (7).*

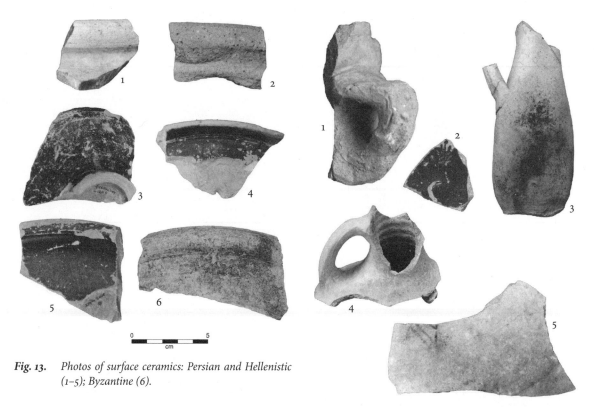

Fig. 13.   *Photos of surface ceramics: Persian and Hellenistic (1–5); Byzantine (6).*

Fig. 14.   *Photos of surface ceramics: Persian and Hellenistic (1–4); Byzantine (5).*

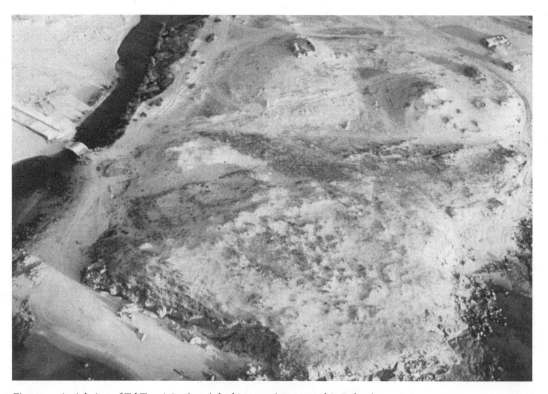

Fig. 15.   *Aerial view of Tel Tanninim (1974), looking east (courtesy of A. Raban).*

During the 1997 season, while excavations continued in Areas A and B, the excavation of Area D was undertaken. In 1998, the work went on in Area A, and a new area, named B2, was opened in order to explore the region to the west of Area B. One of several ceramic pipelines originating from the Area B reservoir led to this area, while there were also surface indications suggesting the presence of structures in this location. In the 1999 season, excavations resumed both in Areas A and B2.

When we began the excavations in Area A, the topsoil was uncovered under an aeolian sand cover of about 80 cm. During the third excavation season in 1998, bedrock was reached in Area A, in one of the squares (B1), at an elevation of about 2.75 m above sea level. This was the only square where the excavation had reached bedrock. As we had started digging at Area A, near the summit of Tel Tanninim (the datum for Area A was on the surface near the summit of the mound, at an elevation of +9.10 m), we now had a complete cross-section of Tel Tanninim in this location. The fourth TAP excavation area—Area A2—was opened east of Area A in 1999, because a substantial rectangular structure was discernable in the aerial photograph, and some wall outlines were visible on the surface (fig. 15).

2. The Stratigraphy and Architecture (Areas A and A2)

by A. Asa Eger

The highest region on a tel exhibits the full stratigraphic cross-section of settlement. Implicit in stratigraphic deposition, however, is a reality that overlying occupations are (1) rarely continuous, (2) destroy and transform preexisting spatial and architectural features, and (3) cannot all be classified as settlements. Areas A and A2 of Tel Tanninim exemplify this reality. An analysis of stratigraphy merged with a discussion of architectural features should illuminate the erratic composition of tel occupations over prolonged time periods. The synthesized approach of stratigraphy and architecture will reveal the complicated and non-continuous chronology and history of Tel Tanninim from its earliest occupation, just above bedrock, in the fifth century B.C.E. (Stratum VIII) through the latest phase, the Late Ottoman period (Stratum I).

The low-lying Areas B, B2, and D, situated around the base of Tel Tanninim, will not be discussed because they only exhibit one major period of occupation. Structures in Areas B, B2, and D were found just under the surface sand cover that continued in some areas to a depth of four meters. In Areas A and A2, major architectural features and construction activity were discerned in the Persian to Hellenistic, Early Byzantine to Early Islamic, and Crusader eras, demonstrating a punctuated settlement pattern on the site. Temporary living surfaces, robbing trenches, altered preexisting architecture, and material culture all point to transient occupations between the major settlement phases, as evidenced by the finds from the Roman Period, Early Islamic II to Middle Islamic I, and Mamluk to Ottoman periods.

It is the challenge of the excavator to attempt to piece together the continuous but erratic occupational sequence in a logical and cogent manner that accurately depicts the history of the site. However, a punctuated settlement pattern interspersed with robbing and quarrying activities complicates this task. In addition, inherent and logistical problems such as unconnected excavation seasons and the destructive nature of fieldwork provide further obstacles. Invested in the analysis is another host of issues revolving around the methodology and presentation of the stratigraphy of the site. The goal of an archaeological dig report is to provide enough information that would permit a re-creation of the features of the excavations. A stratigraphic analysis should be readable by a wider audience who does not require the specifics of the excavation, but would benefit by a broad synopsis of the occupational sequences of the site. The decision to combine the stratigraphic presentation of the entire site of Tel Tanninim with the architectural features found in Areas A and A2 is a deliberate connection, because no stratigraphy for more than one major occupation period occurs in the low-lying areas around Tel Tanninim. Phasing and chronological assignments for these areas were, as a result, determined from the material culture associated with the architecture, which belong to Strata IV–VI (Early Byzantine to Umayyad). These areas are presented below, in Chapters II.3 (Areas B and B2) and II.4 (Area D).

The first part of our analysis deals with the relevant loci (architectural features and levels) from all excavated grid squares in Areas A and A2. These are presented by strata and ordered from bottom to top, that is, chronologically. The loci are tied within a larger discussion of the architecture of each period. It is important to note that unstratified mixed fill loci impart little evidence to the overall picture and will not be discussed. It should also be emphasized that the individual material culture reports were not used, as the stratigraphic and architectural analysis is based on information from excavated loci alone. Exceptions occur with numismatic evidence that supplements the stratigraphy. We seek to impart objectivity to the analysis, as the stratigraphy of the site should stand independently.

The discussion in the second part of this chapter will deal the history of the site in light of the finds and relevant parallels from other excavations. The parallels are introduced to obtain a contextualized view as well as link together the various elements of Tel Tanninim.

AREA A (fig. 16)

The excavated Persian and Hellenistic remains at Tel Tanninim provide only a very small window into the earliest settlements at the site and were only reached in Area A in three squares (A1, B1, and B2, where bedrock was reached). The architecture was scanty, but several walls and living surfaces, combined with a large amount of local and imported ceramics, as well as fish and animal bones, suggest a domestic occupation. It is important to note that the stratified levels in squares A1 and B1 were disturbed by the foundation of the Byzantine church apse wall that cut down into these layers. As such, while the pottery was essentially Persian/Hellenistic, a few Byzantine sherds that were waterworn and rolled appeared in these lower levels and so, strictly speaking, the Persian/Hellenistic levels excavated were not completely sealed contexts.

Stratum VIII—Persian (450–332 B.C.E.)

Bedrock

A layer of irregular *kurkar* gravel was found over the entirety of Square B1, particularly in the center, with associated patches of brownish sand. Directly below, a "paving layer" of extremely dense local strong brown soil known as *hamra*, with many shell and sea concretions was laid down at +2.90 m, over a mixed fill of yellowish brown sandy soil at +3.10 m and a layer of aeolian light yellowish brown sterile sand at +3.35 m. This was done in order to level the uneven bedrock that ranged from a hight of +2.70 m to its lowest level in the square at +1.85 m. These three sublevels lying over bedrock (L 1244) were a phenomenon also seen in Area A2, Square AA7.

Living Surface

The earliest settlement on the site was only reached in Square B1, in a small area, which was situated directly over bedrock at about +3.40 m. Locus 1234, the only undisturbed Persian-Hellenistic surface excavated, was located in the SW corner of Square B1, below the juncture of W 1135 and W 1138 (the Byzantine apse, see below). It resembled a living

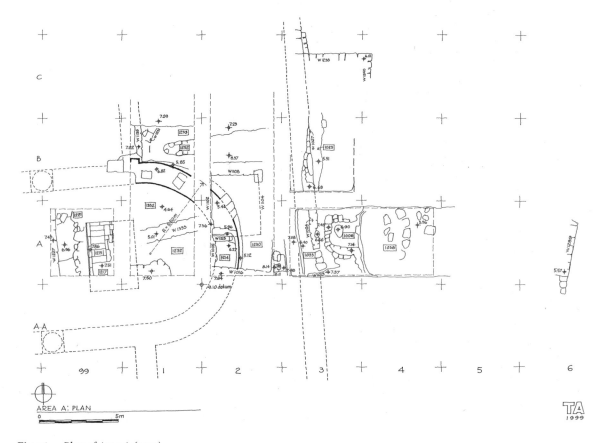

Fig. 16. *Plan of Area A (1999).*

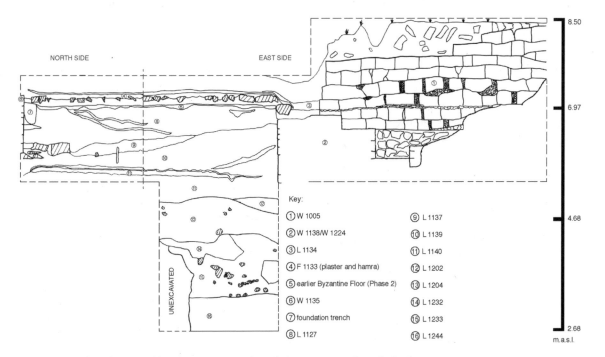

Key:

① W 1005
② W 1138/W 1224
③ L 1134
④ F 1133 (plaster and hamra)
⑤ earlier Byzantine Floor (Phase 2)
⑥ W 1135
⑦ foundation trench
⑧ L 1127
⑨ L 1137
⑩ L 1139
⑪ L 1140
⑫ L 1202
⑬ L 1204
⑭ L 1232
⑮ L 1233
⑯ L 1244

Fig. 17. *North and east profiles of Squares A1 and B1, showing stratigraphy to bedrock.*

surface and was composed of a dark brown compact sandy soil with plaster and charcoal pieces, a brick fragment, and large amounts of pottery, 99 percent of which was Persian. The ceramics included two lamp fragments (L043, L044) and a painted sherd from an Attic red figure *lekythos* (C035), later joined to two additional sherds from this vessel found in L 1233, immediately above L 1234 (see Chapter IV.4.B1).

Over the bedrock and around the living surface in the northern half of Square B1 appeared a slightly undefined thick mixed reddish sand fill (L 1233) at +4.50 to +4.00 m, with charcoal, shell, chalk inclusions, as well as several large stone inclusions (fig. 17). The layer continued at lower levels to the south with the exception of three pockets. At these lower levels appeared many sherds lying on top of each other. Locus 1233 was mainly characterized by a dominance of locally produced Persian pottery (some 175 diagnostic pieces), with many basket handled amphorae, and a mix of imported Greek wares, including two more fragments of the *lekythos* found below in L 1234. Also in the matrix of L 1233 were many fish and animal bones, two more Persian lamp fragments (L038 and L049, perhaps from the same lamp; see Chapter IV.2, fig. 145:1), and all three types of dye-producing purple shells, at about +3.75 m. L 1233 was a mixed foundation fill of the Persian level, which had been disturbed at a later date, most likely during the succeeding Hellenistic settlement. In the SE corner, was a grouping of nearly 50 *Murex brandaris* shells, two fish vertebrae, and a large part of an intact cooking pot filled with chicken bones. They were found in a brownish yellow sandy fill (L 1235/L 1242) in the SE corner beginning at +4.04 m.

Stratum VII—Hellenistic (332–ca.100 B.C.E.)

Walls

Architectural remains from the Hellenistic settlement were revealed in Squares B1 and A1. The surfaces and walls were poorly preserved, stripped down to their lowest courses, and left *in situ* because they did not interfere with the placement of the massive church apse wall during the Byzantine era. In Square A1, a poorly constructed wall (W 1333) was preserved running east–west, made up of loose rubble stones and clay. It was the lowest course, or perhaps a foundation, for a Hellenistic wall. The top elevation was +5.01 m, the bottom +4.94 m. To the north, in Square B1, outside the overlying apse, were two more very poorly preserved wall remains. These were at the bottom of the thick and dense foundation fill (L 1204) for the early Byzantine church (see below). One was a wall running SE–NW consisting of one course of 2–3 stones, cutting off the NW corner of the square at +4.70 m (W 1231). The second, at +4.97 m, was possibly the scanty remains of two walls (L 1232), intersecting at a 90-degree corner, in the middle of the east wall of the square. On one of these stones was a threshold-type cutting at +4.77 m. These were the remains of buildings from the Hellenistic era (fig. 18).

At +4.64 m in Square A1 was a layer composed of densely packed, slightly moist strong brown clay with small stones (L 1335). It sloped down gradually from south to north, toward the northern part of the apse wall. The slope indicated its disturbance by Byzantine construction directly upon it. At its southern end, the layer was abruptly cut in a straight line by the overlying foundation fill for the church (L 1332). The pottery from this surface was predominantly Persian with several Hellenistic sherds, exhibiting a multitude of ware types. A pestle and a Hellenistic ceramic loom weight (Chapter IV.3.B) were among the interesting finds. Excavation ended at +4.51 m, some 10 cm into the layer.

The majority of the Hellenistic (and Persian) material culture came from later deposits such as the foundation fills for the church apse wall (L 1204, L 1129, L 1205, L 1241, L 1323), and its foundation trench (L 1331–1332). Although from Byzantine deposits, two Seleucid bronze coins (N90 and a second-century B.C.E. type) attest to occupation. The pottery assemblage was characterized by large quantities of locally produced light-greenish Persian basket handled amphorae, imported glazed, painted, and stamped Hellenistic fine ware, and buff blackened cooking pot sherds approximating 260 total diagnostic pieces. In addition, the

Fig. 18.   *Hellenistic wall remains in Square B1.*

discovery of bone (primarily fish), Murex shells, a mortar and pestle, and lamp fragments suggest a domestic context for the Hellenistic (and perhaps Persian) remains. At the very bottom of L 1204, a peculiar faunal object was unearthed, which may be a calcified and worked piece of crocodile hide (see Chapter IV.3.F, fig. 158). The object strongly suggests that these reptiles lived in the vicinity of the site, and were associated with the Persian/Hellenistic settlement appropriately named *Krokodeilon polis*.

Gap—Late Hellenistic through Roman (ca. 100 B.C.E. –324 C.E.)

No settlement existed at Tel Tanninim from Late Hellenistic times through the Roman period. Several lamps and coins dating to this period were found in unstratified mixed fills and Late Byzantine floor foundation fills. These attest to a Roman presence; however, no discernible stratigraphic horizons were found in the excavated areas. The heavy construction and building activities undertaken at the site in the Byzantine period would have obscured and disturbed most of the earlier levels on the site, accounting for the lack of a visible aeolian sand cover during the abandonment period.

Stratum VI—Early Byzantine (324–450 C.E.)

The Church—Phase 1

At the top of Area A were the remains of a large Byzantine church. The northern half of a massive semicircular, east-facing, external apse foundation (W 1138) was traced in four squares. This foundation was attributed to the first phase of church building in the late fourth–early fifth centuries. They lay beneath a thick layer of dune sand accumulated during an abandonment period, suggesting that the church was left unfinished and not actually used until its second phase.

Apse Wall. The apse had a radius of 5.5 m, enclosing a space approximately 8.5 m wide and 4.2 m deep (fig. 16). Its highest point, in Squares A1/B1, was preserved at +6.82 m. In all areas the apse was leveled and robbed. This was evidenced particularly in the curved east section (W 1225) that was preserved at the elevation of its first footing at +5.83 m. The construction was of header stones roughly measuring 34 × 53 × 17 cm. The wall ranged from 1.3 to 1.6 m wide. Above and between these stones was a thick, dark gray mortar that left header marks atop the robbed wall. Near the head of the apse, the apse wall was robbed to a lower level, at +5.46 m.

Fig. 19.   *East wall (W 1135) and apse of church in Probe B99.*

Footings. The mortar footing on the exterior of the apse foundation in square B1 projected out irregularly at +5.85 m. The footing consisted of a line of stones (W 1119) covered with dark gray plaster, and bonded by ash and chalk plaster particles. A lower apse footing appeared at +5.12 m, some 70 cm below W 1119, which was most likely constructed to accommodate the downward east slope of the bedrock upon which the structure was built. In Squares A2/B2, three rectangular *kurkar* ashlars, bonded with dark gray mortar, extended from the apse footing (W 1128) at +5.50 m. This was added later to widen the curvature of the apse, although it is difficult to date this addition. Two footings were found on the interior of the apse, one at +5.81 m, 19 cm wide, evenly cut, and matching the exterior footing, and a lower footing, extending under the upper one and widened in the opposite direction (westward), at +5.47 m. The foundation below the footing projected out and was made up of sand with large amounts of Kabbara clay.

Other Walls. North of the apse foundation was the eastern closing wall of the church. It was a leveled concrete north–south wall foundation (W 1135), partially robbed on its upper course at the southern end, where it would have bonded with the

apse wall. The wall was of two phases, the earliest directly connected with the apse (fig. 19). At the bottom of the foundation trench for the later wall appeared courses different from its upper part at +6.70 m. They were characterized by larger ashlars bonded by dark gray mortar, similar to that in the apse foundation. At about +6.17 m, the bottom of two superimposed sandy fills (L 1127 and L 1137), W 1135 and the apse were bonded together. Their plaster footings were approximately matched at +5.71 m.

Foundation Trench. A compact, dark yellowish brown soil layer (L 1331 and L 1332) with scattered rubble formed part of the foundation trench for the apse at +5.16 m. The trench sloped towards the apse wall from west to east. The large volume of mainly Hellenistic wares was small and fragmented; however, a bronze coin dated to the late fourth century C.E. provides a probably fifth century date for the construction of the apse wall. Between this layer and the Hellenistic living surface below (L 1335) was a 30 cm layer of virtually sterile light yellowish brown sand (L 1334), possibly the bottom of the foundation trench for the apse, which rested on the living surface at +4.64 m. Another possibility is that this sand layer is what is left from the long period of the major gap in the settlement history, beginning with the Late Hellenistic period and extending through the Roman period.

Foundation Fills. The apse was built directly on the Persian-Hellenistic levels. Thick foundation fills were placed both on the exterior and interior of the wall during construction. On the exterior of the head of the apse in Square A2 was a dark, compact, yellowish brown clay layer (L 1230), sloping down sharply eastward. It was part of the church foundation, extending from +4.88 m to + 4.50 m, placed to buttress the foundation and level the surface. The pottery predominately consisted of Persian/Hellenistic wares from the cut Stratum VII with very few intrusive Byzantine sherds. The lowest point of excavation at this level reached +4.50 m. Heavy buttressing was necessary east of the apse foundation, as the bedrock below drops down significantly towards the east. However, in contrast to the foundation fills in other areas, the fill east of the apse was quite thin and preserved to a lower elevation. This is a result of erosion caused by the gradient change of the bedrock. A deeper covering of aeolian sand during the abandonment of the structure after Phase 1 further emphasizes this phenomenon (fig. 20).

The foundation fill was detected in Square B1, above the disturbed Persian fill L 1233. The thick layer (L 1204) was uneven, composed of dark compact clay with charcoal flecks, shell bits, sand pockets, and stone inclusions. The clay became less and less compact towards the bottom of the level. L 1204, while excavated as one locus, was found to consist of six slight matrix variations in the post-excavation examination, also evident in the east balk profile (fig. 17). This further shows that the locus was a mixed fill. L 1204 was higher in the center of the square and sloped down gradually toward the south, north and apse foundation at +5.07 m. The level terminated at approximately +4.48 m. Unlike the foundation fill in Square A2 to the east, its slope interestingly descended toward the apse. The layer was rich in Persian/Hellenistic material culture, with few Byzantine sherds, indicating the fill was a disturbed earlier horizon that was re-deposited and packed against the exterior of the apse in the

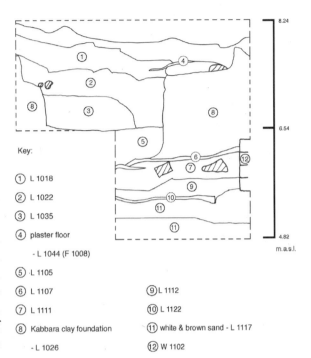

Key:

① L 1018
② L 1022
③ L 1035
④ plaster floor
  - L 1044 (F 1008)
⑤ L 1105
⑥ L 1107
⑦ L 1111
⑧ Kabbara clay foundation
  - L 1026
⑨ L 1112
⑩ L 1122
⑪ white & brown sand - L 1117
⑫ W 1102

Fig. 20. *South profile of Square A2, showing abandonment after Phase 1 of church.*

Early Byzantine Period. A Scythian bronze arrowhead (**M080**) and a bronze coin (**N055**) dated to Late Hellenistic–Early Roman times were among the notable finds.

The foundation fill within the apse, in Square A1, was thicker and constituted of semi-compact uneven fills. The layers (L 1129, L 1205, L 1241 and L 1323) sloped sharply away from the apse wall southward and towards the west. They began at average elevations of +6.18 m, nearly a meter higher than those on the apse's exterior. As seen on the exterior foundation fills, the soils became less compact and sandier at lower elevations. A bronze *minimus* from the fourth century C.E. provides a *terminus ante quem*. Pottery was predominately Persian and Hellenistic, but yielded also some abraded Byzantine fragments. Most interesting among the finds was a smoothly cut and polished hematite weight with a bronze handle (**S066**; see Chapter IV.3.C).

A parallel for this construction type occurs at the similar coastal Byzantine church at Shavei Zion, north of Akko. The wall foundations also revealed a fill over bedrock of "dark-brownish hardened clay soil that contained numerous sherds of the Roman and Hellenistic periods" (Prausnitz, Avi-Yonah and Barag 1967: 19). Prausnitz dated the first phase of the church to the early fourth century. The initial phase of the Tel Tanninim church, from numismatic evidence, must be dated at the earliest to the very end of the fourth or beginning of the fifth century.

Gap in the Phase 1 Occupation

Two thick layers of predominately sterile aeolian sand recorded in every square indicated a period of abandonment following the initial construction of the church. These layers do not corroborate the gap in the Roman period, as they were deposited *following* the Byzantine church foundation and blanketed the area very evenly. Moreover, the presence of sporadic stray and heavily abraded Byzantine sherds within the layers and foundation fills below cannot be ignored. The layers consisted of white/very pale brown dry sand with a top elevation of +5.51 m, over a damper and slightly darker sand, lying over the Early Byzantine foundation fills. It is also likely that the two sand levels, though not displaying the characteristics of foundation fills, were used to level the surface for the placement of a sixth century church mosaic floor (fig. 17). In Square B1, one bronze coin was discovered (**N053**), dated to 383–395 C.E. In Squares A2 and B2 on the eastern exterior of the apse wall, the sand layers were thicker and more numerous owing to the effects of erosion and natural processes on the slope of the tel (figs. 20–22). They were all abandonment deposits.

Stratum V—Late Byzantine (450–ca. 600 C.E.)

The Church—Phase 2.

Following the erection of the apse foundation and a period of abandonment, building activity resumed with placement of the walls and floor of the church. An extended eastern exterior wall inscribed the church apse and created additional rooms to either side and behind it (*pastophoria*). In this second phase, the church began to be utilized.

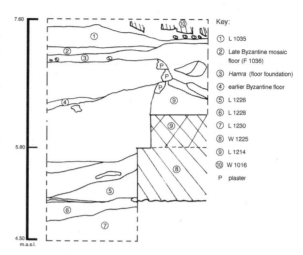

Fig. 21.   *North profile of Square A2.*

Key:
1. L 1035
2. Late Byzantine mosaic floor (F 1036)
3. *Hamra* (floor foundation)
4. earlier Byzantine floor
5. L 1226
6. L 1228
7. L 1230
8. W 1225
9. L 1214
10. W 1016
P plaster

Apse Wall. Traces of the apse's upper courses were found between Squares A1 and B1. An east–west wall (W 1208), jutting out from the western edge of the square, was composed of three large stones (40 × 35 × 20 cm). Atop the stones was a dense layer of red *hamra* and a thin layer of mortar, indicating that the wall was most likely robbed. Below this wall was the top of the curved apse in B1 (W 1138). The top of the apse wall, similarly robbed, had a thin layer of black mortar at +6.82 m.

Other Walls. A probe (B99) was sunk to further expose the relationship of the apse wall and the north wall (W 1135) perpendicular to it. At their juncture was a square of stones with empty spaces where some stones may have been pried loose in the later dismantling of the church (fig. 23). This also correlates with a robbing trench on the eastern part of W 1135. Over the robbed stones, as seen in the apse wall in Square B1, was a thin blackish mortar. The apse wall extended towards the west past W 1135 at the juncture, on a course shifted slightly north. This may not be the continuation of a proper wall, but rather the extended apse may have terminated as a pier, or side aisles, jutting into the nave of the church. In this phase, a new eastern exterior wall for the church (W 1042) was constructed that extended beyond the apse and was parallel to W 1135. The north–south wall lay approximately 3.5 m east of the head of the apse, thereby inscribing it. The top of the wall was in Square A3, at +6.47 m.

Fig. 22. *South profile of Square A2, showing sand layers deposited after Phase 1.*

Its eastern face was heavily plastered and its stones were square and large.

Apse Floor. Within the church apse, a series of floors were excavated. The lowest floor (F 1115) consisted of a crushed *kurkar* surface and white/cream plaster at +7.33 m, spread out over the entire Square A1. It was laid over a pavement (L 1114) of large well dressed blocks imbedded in thick clayish *hamra* comprising a 20 cm thick floor foundation, and ending at about +6.87 m. This floor corresponds to the lowest level of L 1221—a series of superimposed floors and floor foundations in Square A99 that were excavated as one locus. The floor consisted of red *hamra* clay and small fieldstones with pockets of yellow sand, small stones, and chalky powder over a red *hamra* clay with larger semi-cut fieldstones at +7.13 m. The stones in this last level appeared to have been arranged in a purposeful SW–NE axis in the northern part of the square. The bottom of this level was +6.96 m. Below the floor pavements was a fill of brown sand, unexcavated, at +6.89 m.

Expanded Church Floors. In square B1, evident only in the northern profile, was a thin, light gray plaster floor at +6.87 m, lying beneath the *hamra* clay foundation for the Phase 3 floor (fig. 17). A

Fig. 23. *Juncture of east wall and apse of church in Probe B99.*

Fig. 24.   *Remains of plaster and stone feature on apse wall and Crusader vault wall in Square A2.*

foundation trench for W 1135 cut the early floor. The foundation trench, plaster layer, and W 1135 were covered by the Phase 3 floor foundation. From this evidence, it appears that the thin white plaster layer was an earlier floor and did not correspond with the upper part of W 1135, but rather coexisted with its lower courses. Traces of the same thin, light gray plaster floor with shells and marble chips were seen in Square A2, in the south profile at +6.70 m. The layer was badly preserved and sloped down and away from the apse head. It is likely that the plaster layers in Squares A2 and B1 comprised the flooring behind the apse (fig. 24). A square pillar composed of two dressed stones (fig. 25) associated with this floor was embedded within a later floor foundation in Square B1.

The western face of the eastern exterior wall (W 1042) abutted a floor composed of pebbles and sherds imbedded in mortar (approximately +6.47 m). Excavation terminated at this floor and was not continued. It is interesting to note that the floor level beyond the apse is 40 cm lower than the traces of an early floor in Square B1. The two floors are different and the relationship between them was not discerned. It is likely that seismic activity caused the floor to subside, particularly as it is situated where the underlying bedrock descends sharply.

Remains of Plaster and Stone Feature. At the head of the semicircular apse was a raised feature (L 1214) built directly on top of the apse wall. Two small courses of stones (one row was removed for placement of the later Crusader vault) demarcated the northern part of the construction at +5.84 m, and spanned the width of the apse wall plus 17 cm, most likely because this was the widest part of the apse. An even plaster footing, 6 cm wide, extended from the easternmost stone. South of it was the main foundation area. Its top was at +6.27 m, but about 40 cm of mortar were resting over it (fig. 20). On top of it was a poorly preserved thin partition of irregular large plaster chunks that separated it from the floor behind the apse (see below). The identification of this feature is problematic. The possibility that this was a bishop's seat seems unlikely, as it would seem that a plaster foundation, preserved 60 cm below the floor of the *bema*, would not be necessary (figs. 22, 24, 26).

Fig. 25.   *Mosaic floor foundation incorporated in F 1133 in Square B1.*

Fig. 26.   *Foundation wall for the* bema *step in Square A99.*

The Church—Phase 3

In the third phase, the *bema* floors within the apse were raised. The floors of the *pastophoria* to either side and behind the apse were also raised

and paved with mosaics, fragments of which were preserved. During this period, the second phase of the wall adjacent to the apse foundation (W 1135) was raised to a higher level. The change is indicated by the difference in construction style,

Fig. 27.   *Mosaic floor foundation (F 1017) and church wall in Square A3.*

matching the elevation of the floor foundation fill, which also served as a foundation trench for the wall, and by the association with the later mosaic floor. The preserved top of W 1135 was at +7.15 m and it was 95 cm wide.

A second phase to the eastern exterior early wall W 1042 in Square A3 was constructed directly over the earlier wall and plastered to it (fig. 27). Wall 1024/W 1027 consisted of foundations and two lower courses of *kurkar* ashlars (31 × 39 × 21 cm) bonded with gray, sandy mortar, resting on a course of headers (30 × 15 × 10 cm) and rubble stone. Its overall length was about 9.5 m, spanning Squares A3 and B3, with its eastern face nicely preserved and its top elevation at +6.66 m. At the northern edge of the wall, in Square B3, was a similar foundation course of a perpendicular east–west wall (W 1028) made of well dressed *kurkar* ashlars. The connection between the two walls was not established, as excavation did not continue here, however, the two were probably contemporary based on their similarities in elevation and construction. This would strongly suggest that W 1028 was the northern exterior wall of the church.

A surface probe in the northern part of Square C3 was done to investigate the partially exposed

foundation remains of a wall resting on sand. The east–west wall (W 1238) consisted of two to three courses of fine *kurkar* ashlars, measuring 6 m along its lowest course. At the eastern end, it turned a corner and abutted the start of a north–south wall (W 1240). The stones were approximately 60 × 30 × 20 cm each. The elevation at the corner was +6.01 m. In the west, at an elevation of +6.85, were several flat stones sitting on brown, sandy soil. These were not removed nor excavated further. The walls, Byzantine in construction, were possibly related to the newly expanded church structure together with W 1027, W 1028 (Square B3) and W 1024 (Square A3), or they formed part of another structure situated further down the slope of the tel.

Apse Floors. In Phase 3 of the church construction, a stone pavement (F 1113) was laid over the earlier floor at an average elevation of +7.47 m in Square A1. It was of a different composition, made up of large pebbles and flat slabs. Into the pavement an L-shaped row of dressed stones (W 1116) was incorporated along the western edge, whose top elevation was +7.59 m. The stones were differentiated slightly due to their regularity and evenness and their central location within the apse, approximately 5 m from the eastern head and 3 m from the northern base of the wall. This is under the precise location of the later altar (see below). The single long cornerstone of the L-shape was curved slightly rather than perpendicular. It is possible that this feature might have been an altar built within the floor pavement of the *bema* with an apsidal shape. Within the floor were Byzantine sherds predominately dating to the sixth century. In Square A99, two pavements of L 1221 corresponded with this floor. These were constructed of red *hamra* clay with large fieldstones and a cut reused ashlar over a red *hamra* clay with small stones and chalky white plaster, with larger stones and plaster on the northern edge. In the latter pavement, an octagonal cut stone of porphyry was found, suggesting that the *bema* was covered, at least partially, with an *opus sectile* floor.

Above F 1113 was another floor (F 1041) at +7.56 m, composed of white plaster over stone slabs imbedded in compact *hamra* soil (fig. 28). On top of the floor was a thin, even scattering of small marble chips. The upper pavement of L 1221 in Square A99 matched this floor, and was made of red-brown *hamra* with small stones and marble chips. The presence of scattered marble chips may indicate marble craftsmen working on site adjusting the marble elements of the church structure. A large number of marble and mosaic fragments indicated that the floor was tessellated and/or decorated with *opus sectile*.

Expanded Church Floors. In the sixth century, mosaic floors were laid uniformly around the church outside the apse, corresponding with the extended exterior walls. The floor remains were exposed in virtually every square. In Square B1, the mosaic floor (F 1133) abutted W 1135, indicated by a plaster line that clearly demarcated the floor from the actual wall. The floor also may have covered the apse wall. A small section of the apse, found where the apse wall and Byzantine floor were cut for the placement of a later Crusader wall (W 1005), was covered with the red *hamra* foundation. The plaster feature and small partition wall on the head of the apse were similarly covered with *hamra* above its preserved height. For the most part, the mosaics

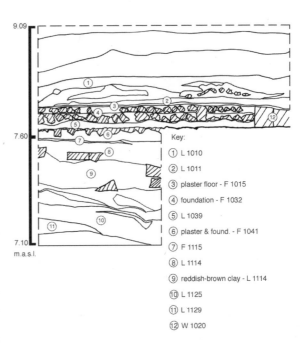

Key:
① L 1010
② L 1011
③ plaster floor - F 1015
④ foundation - F 1032
⑤ L 1039
⑥ plaster & found. - F 1041
⑦ F 1115
⑧ L 1114
⑨ reddish-brown clay - L 1114
⑩ L 1125
⑪ L 1129
⑫ W 1020

Fig. 28.   *South profile of Square A1.*

were either robbed or destroyed. The mosaics were set into plastered bedding over a compact reddish-brown *hamra* foundation, with pebble inclusions over a sandy fill. The floor elements will be discussed individually from top to bottom.

A mosaic floor fragment (F 1036) was found at the southern edge of Square A2, at about +7.11 m, embedded in gray chalky plaster and poorly preserved (figs. 20, 29). The mosaic consisted of a white fringe and a border design of connected individual double-locked inner guilloches. This specific border pattern is not very commonly seen in Byzantine mosaics. A large medallion depicting a nautical scene in the northern side aisle of Horvat Beit Loya was encircled with this pattern. Unfortunately, the excavators could only broadly date the pavements and church to the sixth–eighth centuries (Patrich and Tsafrir 1993: 265–72 and Pl. XIXa). Only a fragment of the west end survived, indicating that the mosaic continued toward the east probably until the eastern exterior wall W 1024/W 1042. The fragment consisted of a vine pattern suggesting to the excavator a possible larger pattern with figurative medallions and vines emerging off an amphora (Yankelevitch, personal communication). The western wall of the mo-

Fig. 29.   *Mosaic floor (F 1036) behind the apse in Square A2.*

saic room was robbed, as evidenced by a robbing trench. A later Crusader vault wall (W 1014), and a pit (L 1035) cut 20 cm into it, destroyed the mosaic's center, but F 1036 was spared. Several other patches of mosaic fragments were found *in situ* in Squares B1 and B2. One part contained a single line of black *tesserae* on a white background. Another section, about 30 cm to the north and disappearing into the balk, exhibited the end of a circular pattern of black color with two gray lozenges. The tesserae size was 2.5 cm. On the NW edge, fragmentary very small tesserae were found. In Square B1, a small patch *in situ* consisted of 1.5–2 cm tesserae in white, black, yellow, and red (fig. 30). They were similar in size and style to those surveyed in 1979 on the southern edge of the tel and just 20 cm higher in elevation.

A dark gray plaster Byzantine floor was the bedding for the mosaic outside the church apse. The floor foundation (F 1133, F 1017, F 1124) consisted of a thin, white, hard, chalky surface on black ash and plaster, and imbedded with pebbles, shells, sherds, marble chips, and tesserae. Its elevation descended very slightly from west (+7.27 m, Square B1) to east (+7.08 m, Square A3). This also occurred in the earlier expanded floors in these squares. A fifth century *minimus* was found in its

excavation. Beneath the mosaic floor and bedding was a floor foundation layer of compact *hamra* clay with pebbles.

Foundation fills were laid down to level the surface for the mosaic floor, thus destroying the early floor. The sand fills (L 1127 and L 1137) were differentiated from the dune sand accumulation of the post-Phase 1 gap because, in stark contrast to those windblown sterile layers below, they were full of material culture, thus resembling more the foundation fills for the apse wall in Phase 1 of the church. A pit hoard of objects was placed beneath the floor and the early plaster flooring. It was located in the southern center of Square B1, near the apse wall at elevation +6.61 m. Around these finds were the scanty remains of a pit formed with *kurkar* stones arranged in a circle at elevation +6.58 m. About 30 coins were discovered in the pit hoard, dating to the fifth–sixth centuries C.E. Additionally, there was a cache of 12–15 oil lamps in various stages of preservation, but mainly intact, including two Late Byzantine oil lamps bearing a cross/rosette (fig. 154:7–8) and an intact oil lamp resting within a Gaza jar missing its neck and rim. All were of the Late Byzantine Tel Tanninim type "Ba" (see Chapter IV.2), with the interesting exception of two

Fig. 30.   *Mosaic floor foundation and pieces* in situ *behind the apse in Square B1.*

examples of Roman first–third- century C.E. lamps (**L016, L017**). There was also a fine glass vessel in fragments. Most unusual among the hoard finds were two *Glycimeris* shells inscribed in cursive Greek (Chapter IV.3.A1–2).

Stratum IV—Final Byzantine to Umayyad (600–750 C.E.)

The Church—Phase 4

In Phase 4 of the church, the *bema* floors within the apse area (Squares A1 and A99) supporting the altar were raised considerably. This was most likely to give further prominence to sacredness as the church expanded in size and importance. Thus, a successive series of floors were built, one over the other, to raise the altar and *bema*.

Apse Floors. At approximately +7.85 m in Squares A1 and A99 was a floor 12–15 cm thick (F 1032 and F 1216), very badly preserved and composed of thin soft white plaster atop a bedding of small stones, marble, and clay, in gray ash mortar and *hamra* with small, embedded, and eroded sherds and shells. The floor was mosaic bedding similar to the expanded floors in Phase 3. Within the makeup of

the floor were five corroded small bronze *minimi*. At elevation +7.77 was the matrix foundation for the floor, excavated as the same locus, F 1032, made of large rubble stones (20 × 15 × 10 cm) imbedded in very hard compact ash mortar (fig. 20). Below was a level of red-brown compact *hamra* with small stones and marble chips (L 1039). Small *opus sectile* slabs not *in situ* were in the layer, as well as a concentration of homogenous Byzantine bag-shaped amphorae in the NE corner of the square. These clay layers served as the foundations for both the altar platform (L 1215) and the mosaic floor. A second floor (F 1015), made up of white chalky plaster composed of small marble angular fragments like concrete, lay over F 1032 and was the latest floor encountered in Square A1. The floor's top elevation was +7.94 m. Nothing significant rested upon the floor. Interestingly, this latest floor was attached to the eastern edge of the altar but was not found in square A99 in association with the altar's western edge (fig. 28). Thus, the floor between the altar and the apse of the church was raised even higher still by this latest phase.

Bema *Step.* The western edge to the raised *bema* rested about 4 cm under the plastered floor (F 1216) in Square A99. This wall or *bema* step (W 1227),

Fig. 31.   *Raised* bema *of church, Phase 4, in Square A99.*

incorporated into the *bema* floors, was parallel to the altar table and 1.9 m west of it. The wall was mortared on top with thin fragments of compact soil plastered to the stones; plaster also appeared on the outside eastern face. The top elevation of the wall was +7.43 m and the bottom was still not reached below +6.96 m. It is possible that this step may have supported a chancel screen, as a marble chancel pillar was found in previous explorations at the site. However, no slots were found on top of the wall that might firmly indicate the presence of a chancel screen. The *bema* step enclosed an area for the *bema* 10 m long (until the head of the apse) and 8.5 m wide. It projected approximately 5.7 m beyond the chord of the apse creating a presbytery.

Altar/Reliquary. Part of the altar (L 1215) was revealed in Square A99. It was a platform constructed of large flat *kurkar* slabs bordered by thin stones. The total unearthed dimensions of the platform were 3.2 × 2.5 m, but the abrupt break in the balk between A1 and A99 suggested that the altar continued into A1. The center of the platform was damaged and slabs were removed, suggesting the presence of a reliquary within the altar platform.

In the first season of excavations, remnants of the altar foundations, originally thought of as a north–south wall attached to the floor (W 1020/W 1218), were visible in Square A1; however, an Umayyad (Early Islamic I) robbing pit (L 1010, see below) cut through most of them. A marble fragment of an *akroterion* was found within this pit, probably associated with the marble reliquary found on the surface of the site. The foundations on either side of the robbing pit were built of dressed *kurkar* blocks measuring 35 × 25 × 20 cm, with a foundation course composed of headers (fig. 28). Its top elevation was +7.87 m and the bottom was at +7.62 m (fig. 31). It was 1.9 m from the *bema* step (W 1227). The flat slabs on top of the altar platform contained a small indentation on their tops at the western edge, where marble would have been attached. No postholes were discovered on the top of the feature to suggest a supported altar table. Along the eastern balk, there was a broken groove cut into the stones, 1.1 m long and 4–7 cm wide. It may have served to delineate the place for the reliquary holding bones of a saint, or as a drain for the altar. Several parallels for altar platform/reliquaries exist in Jordan and Israel including one at the coastal site of Ostrakine on the Sinai Peninsula.

Fig. 32. *Abbasid period robbing pits (L 1010) within the church.*

The church, also furnished with an inscribed apse, had a raised rectangular platform of slabs on the *bema* with a stone reliquary and was dated to the early fifth century (Oren 1993: 308–13). An altar of similar proportions (3.25 × 3.4 m) was found in the church at Zahrani, dating between 535–541 C.E., according to the mosaics around it (Donceel-Voûte 1988: 436).

Stratum III—Abbasid to Fatimid Periods (750–1099 C.E.)

Black ash layers with burnt Byzantine architectural fragments and pottery indicated that the church finally went out of use and was destroyed in the middle of the eighth century. The Abbasid (Early Islamic II) period at Tel Tanninim was scantily represented and not characterized by any settlement. Rather, the site was quarried for construction materials, as evidenced by the appearance of several robbing trenches and pits placed in Area A to remove the floors and building stones of the Byzantine church.

Destruction

Layers of black ashy dirt with charred bones and sherds (L 1030) were found in Squares A1 (L 1011) over the floor F 1015 at +7.94 m and A3 (L 1030) at +6.47 m. Most of the artifacts found at the bottom of these layers consisted of fragments of the Byzantine church floors and roof, as well as some Early Islamic sherds. Further evidence along the interior of the apse foundation in A1 showed traces of burning and charred pottery and shell within several darker clayish soil lenses and ash pockets, attesting to the destruction layer. Among the mixed assemblage was an Islamic rim of the tenth century, providing a date for the destruction level and robbing trench above.

Robbing Pits and Trenches

Most activity was detected in Square A1, within the apse. Three pits were excavated (fig. 32). In the SE part of the square, a sandy pit (L 1004) near the surface was excavated mechanically. The pit continued as a brown *hamra* layer (L 1010) with some gray ash and mortar that sloped downward from west to east, cutting the eastern and northeastern

Fig. 33.   *Robbing pits (L 1010) cutting though the* bema.

edges of the grayish-black destruction level (L 1011). Pit L 1010 widened as it deepened and assumed a rectangular shape when the bottom of the Early Byzantine floor foundation (L 1039) was reached at +7.54 m. On the northern edge of the square, the destruction level (L 1011) was cut in a straight line by the *hamra* (L 1010) in a robbing trench fashion. Below these, several centimeters of *hamra* at +7.70 m, another pit in the center of the western edge (L 1010) defined itself more clearly and was lined with stones in a circular shape. As it deepened, the pit became wider and was lined with small stones of about 10 cm and the bottom was filled with the same stones and Early Islamic buff ware sherds of the tenth–eleventh centuries. In addition, a marble *akroterion* from a Byzantine reliquary or sarcophagus was found in the pit's section. This pit cut through the successive floors throughout the square and the eastern edge of the altar/reliquary (L 1215) in A99, most likely in an attempt to retrieve it. The pit terminated on the lowest floor (F 1115) at +7.33 m (fig. 33). The NE pit (L 1034) was smaller, rounded, and lined with stones.

On the northern edge of A1, an E–W robbing trench (L 1021) of golden sand cut through the highest Late Byzantine floor and removed an east–west wall, probably the later apse wall (W 1208) and/or part of the earlier apse foundation (W 1138/W 1224). The robbing trench terminated at about the same elevation as the top of the robbed apse wall, +6.87 m. While W 1208 lay partially preserved and was built over the apse foundation, courses between the two walls were robbed out. In addition, both walls exhibited the red *hamra* layer and a thin layer of blackish mortar on the top surfaces where stones were removed. This was most evident on top of the apse foundation, where the outline of missing stones was apparent. Also within the apse in Square A99 a pit was found in the southeast corner, within the altar created from removed or damaged stones.

In Square B1, just on the other side of the apse foundation and to the north, more evidence of the same robbing activity was found. At the southern edge of the square an east–west robbing trench (L 1134) cut through the Late Byzantine mosaic floor and was filled with loose *hamra*, windblown sand and huge blocks evidently from the robbed apse wall. The bottom elevation was +6.81 m. Another robbing trench (L 1132), whose bottom elevation was +7.15 m, ran north–south on the west side of the square and perpendicular to the previous one, and also cut through the mosaic floor foundation. This was further seen in the west section of the balk, clearly showing the *hamra* level cut by a robbing trench. The object of this trench was the north–south wall (W 1135/W 1212) running north from the apse base. A 1 × 1 m probe was placed in Square B99, just west of this robbing trench at the juncture of W 1135/W 1212 and W 1138/W 1224, and above the juncture an Abbasid coin associated with the remains of a sheep/goat was found. The remains were in unstratified dune sand.

Another robbing trench (L 1037/L 1209)—60 cm wide— in the SW corner of Square A2 at +7.06 m ran north–south, and contained reddish *hamra* soil and a small number of Abbasid sherds. Its placement was for the removal of the apse wall. It also cut through the mosaic floor (F 1036) of the Byzantine church.

In the center of Square A3 was a robbing trench of brown/beige sand (L 1031). It cut through an earlier plastered floor (F 1017) of the Byzantine church adjacent to wall W 1024, whose stones (and removal) were the object of the trench. The trench also cut into the lower burnt layer at a bottom elevation of +6.73 m.

Stratum IIB—Crusader (1099–1265 C.E.)

A fairly well preserved Crusader structure with at least two rooms joined by a threshold and supported by a barrel vault substructure was excavated in Squares A2, B2, and A3. The Crusader construction style was characterized by the use of large, well dressed ashlars, unmortared and set into a foundation of extremely dense Kabbara clay. The heavy black silt came from the nearby Kabbara swamps and acted as a mortaring compound, filling in the foundation trenches of unmortared walls; a regional style indicative of Crusader construction and detected throughout the site. This structure was oriented almost exactly along the north–south cardinals, parallel to the Crusader tower structure in Area A2. The architectural elements and associated levels will be discussed from west to east.

Building Walls

Square A2 was situated exactly over a Crusader building and vault. The western closing wall of the building, appearing immediately under the aeolian sand, was built into the Byzantine apse foundation wall. This north–south Crusader wall (W 1005), on the western edge of the square separating Squares A1 and A2 (figs. 17, 34), consisted of eight courses that were broken down into four sublevels. The upper level was only preserved on the southern portion of the wall, and these two courses are what remained of the actual wall above the foundation. The well dressed ashlars averaged 30 × 30 × 20 cm. The second sublevel (courses 3–4) was the top of the foundation and constructed of very solidly cut ashlars (reused from the Byzantine church), many of which still had traces of plaster facing on their west or north sides. The north face of the wall showed that the width of the fourth course consisted of one large ashlar (about 90 cm). A third sublevel (courses 5–6) was offset about 11 cm from the upper courses. This lower level consisted of well dressed ashlars chinked with small rubble and *kurkar* in a heavy sand content mortar. The lowest sublevel (courses 7–8) was separated from course 6 by a thin layer of stones. The bottom courses were truncated, because they were built into and over the apse wall (W 1138), which was cut deliberately to accommodate them. Course 8 rested on a layer of fieldstones and heavy Kabbara silt. To accommodate the curvature of the apse wall and at the same time utilize its foundational support, a wedge shape in front of the wall cut through the upper courses of the apse in a step fashion (20–26 cm deep) and was filled with the silt and rubble. The apse ashlars were removed for the placement of the bonding clay and stones, in order to firmly anchor the Crusader wall (fig. 35). Although the apse wall was used to support the Crusader wall, the two walls are not bonded to each other, even though the mortar on top of the apse continues right up against the later wall. The same construction process presumably occurred on the other side of the apse further south; however, no excavations were conducted in Square AA1. The top of the wall was at +8.32 m, and its base at +6.94 m. Further north, the wall cut through the

Fig. 34. *Crusader structure built over the apse wall.*

Fig. 35. *West face of Crusader wall built over the apse wall.*

Late Byzantine mosaic floor (F 1133) that was extant amorphously around the northern face, just a few centimeters away. Plastering on the north face of some of the stones and the presence of undamaged Byzantine floor indicated that this point was the northern extent of the wall, lining up with the closing wall of the vault (W 1108) underneath. As a whole, W 1005 was built quite sturdily and about 1.5 m of it would have been subterranean. A large foundation trench of Kabbara clay (L 1026) was associated with the construction of W 1005.

Walls found to the south and east enclosed a room. At the southern end of W 1005 ran W 1016/ W 1013, an east–west wall 3.5 m long, which con-

Fig. 36. *East wall of Crusader structure in Square A6.*

tinued into square A3. Its preserved top and base elevations were +7.84 m (+7.57 m in Square A3) and +6.99 m, respectively. To the east, W 1014 divided both east and west rooms in Squares A3 and A2, and included a threshold allowing access between the rooms. Its preserved top elevation was +7.62 m. Walls W 1016/W 1013 and W 1014 were preserved just to their foundations and built on top of the Late Byzantine mosaic floors associated with the church (F 1017, fig. 24). Their foundation courses were composed of small rubble *kurkar* stones bonded with Kabbara silt. The foundation trench of Kabbara silt with inserted pebbles (L 1026) for the Crusader walls (fig. 21) was seen in various parts along the edges of Square A2 at +7.59 m. The extensive compact clay/rubble layer may also very well have been a platform laid down purposely for the foundation of the room, leveling the space over the barrel vault below. Excavation revealed Late Islamic thirteenth–fourteenth century pottery. The level terminated at +6.40 m. At the southern end of W 1014, a threshold sat on the foundation courses. The threshold was made of three flat dressed *kurkar* slabs with a drainage channel built underneath. It was at an elevation of +8.11 m. The enclosed room would have been roughly 5.5 × 4 m.

Further east, in the only partially excavated Square A4, scattered building stones of the Crusader structure were found, including several that were well dressed and quite large (60 × 40 × 20 cm). Two stones that were cut in a gabled fashion with angled corners may have been part of the Crusader superstructure of the building. The location of the eastern closing wall of the Crusader building was not determined. A probe in the center of Square A6 exposed a massive, well built, north–south exterior Crusader wall (W 1239) that corresponded to W 1005 to the west (fig. 36). The well preserved wall segment measured 3.75 m long. The large unmortared ashlars were 95 × 26 × 31 cm. There were two visible courses plus one remaining *kurkar* block from the third upper course. The elevation at this topmost stone was the datum point of +5.75 m. Some 30–40 cm from the wall's southern end was a demarcated change in the stone arrangement from headers to footers turning west. This may suggest either a break in the wall, an addition, or a pillar base. All along the eastern front of the wall were piles of cut stones in a cascading collapse, presumably from the wall; however, the collapsed stones were of varying sizes. These may have come from within the structure west of the

Fig. 37.   *West wall of Crusader vault.*

wall. Also found was a large and well cut keystone (54 cm long at its longest side; 37 cm long at its shortest; 35 cm wide; 22 cm thick) that is likely to have come from the Crusader vault in Square A2. Wall 1239 was within one degree of parallel with the Crusader tower (L 1300) in Area A2.

Building Floors

In the main Crusader room were two patches of a thin beaten earth floor (F 1008) with a crushed shell and pebble surface. The floor was segmented and found at the top of W 1016/W 1013, nearby at W 1005, and at the threshold of W 1014. The floor yielded glazed Crusader pottery and animal and fish bone. It was at an elevation of +8.07 m, four centimeters below the threshold. In the north wall section, a light gray thin layer (L 1044) appeared to correspond to this layer (fig. 21). A floor foundation lay beneath F 1008, consisting of 5 cm of Kabbara clay bedding (L 1025) and containing several brown glazed cookingpot sherds (thirteenth–fourteenth centuries).

Vault Walls

Attached to the foundations of the east face of W 1005 was the west vault wall (W 1102), fairly well preserved and built from dressed *kurkar* (fig. 37). The vault sprung out roughly below the second course of the lower layer (course 6) of W 1005. The top of the preserved vault was +7.65 m and its bottom was at +5.75 m. In between the two walls was the Kabbara silt and rubble stone bonding (L 1026), placed to fill in the gap and most likely continuing over the top of the vault, leveling the surface. White plaster remains appeared on the interior vault stones with marble slabs attached, indicating their reuse from the Byzantine church. Associated fallen stones with plaster in pit L 1035 were from the vault structure. Closing the vault to the south side was W 1103/W 1213, consisting of three well dressed stones (37 × 23 × 22 cm) bonded with clay in an east–west row of two courses coming out from under the western vault wall (W 1102), about 1.6 m from the south balk. The western vault wall was clearly built over the last stone of this wall, indicating that this end wall (W 1103/W 1213) was built first, and that W 1102 was built into and over it (fig. 24). Its top elevation was +6.28 m and its

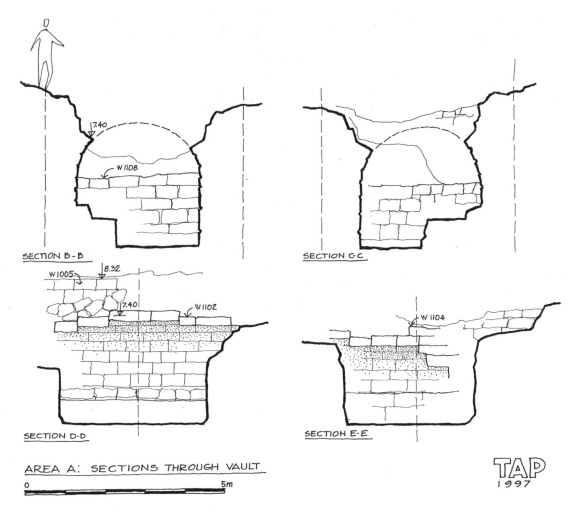

SECTION B-B

SECTION C-C

SECTION D-D

SECTION E-E

AREA A: SECTIONS THROUGH VAULT

0   5m

Fig. 38. *Four sections through the Crusader vault.*

bottom was at +5.84 m. The eastern vault wall was W 1104, also preserved up to the springing point of the vault, but not as high as W 1102. Its top elevation was +7.25 m, and it terminated at +5.62 m.

Just to the north of the vault, a foundation trench or, more accurately, a workspace (L 1123) on the north side of W 1108 was created for the construction of the vault in Square A2. It was about 1 m wide and cut through the Late Byzantine church mosaic floor. The bottom of this sandy pit was at +5.42 m and contained many plaster and mosaic fragments most likely fallen from the disturbance of the floor into the trench. The trench spanned the width of the vault. It yielded sherds from all periods and an iron blade.

The barrel vault was built within the Crusader building and used its sturdy ashlar walls as support

and to give the vault lateral thrust protection. The solid apse foundation would have provided additional support on the west and south sides. The interior space of the vault was roughly 3.5 × 3 m. Its projected height would have been 3 m, cutting through the Byzantine mosaic floor (fig. 38). It would have lined up with the threshold on top of W 1014 and was most likely utilized to support the Crusader floor, as well as to provide space within the vault for storage or other activities.

Stratum IIA—Mamluk (1265–1400 C.E.)

Mamluk (Middle Islamic II–III) occupation on Tel Tanninim was confined to the Crusader building and vault in Area A and the Crusader tower in Area A2. The nature of the settlement was temporary,

Fig. 39.   *Northern wall of vault in Square C2, constructed in the Mamluk period.*

reusing the preexisting buildings. Several living surfaces were identified with Middle Islamic pottery and a large quantity of bone, predominately from local fish. Robbing activity was evident in the SW corner of Square A2, where a square pit of sand (L 1019; roughly 88 × 69 cm) was situated between the building walls (W 1005 and W 1016) and the Kabbara silt foundations (L 1026). The pit cut through the silt and rubble layer down to the foundations of the walls. It contained sherds of a Middle Islamic green glazed jug from the thirteenth–fourteenth centuries. At +7.38 m, dune sand appeared in the pit.

Occupation was detected within the Crusader vault, consisting of one or more living surfaces and some minor architectural features. The closing wall to the vault (W 1108) to the north was made of *kurkar* blocks of different dimensions with clay cemented between them. The wall, unlike W 1103 to the south at the other end of the vault, was not bonded to W 1102 to the west, but attached to it and not quite perpendicular to either of the sidewalls (fig. 39). It was a later wall built into the vault. Its top elevation was +7.20 m and its bottom was +5.60 m. In the NE corner of the vault, a pile of stones was pushed up against W 1104, functioning

as a makeshift supporting buttress when the vault was reused.

Beneath a mixed fill (A2-L 1105, B2-L 1106) was a 10 cm accumulation of soft white plaster and ash beginning at +6.18 m (A2-L 1107, B2-L 1109). Present within the layer was a large amount of charred wood pieces. Sifting produced glass fragments and some three dozen nails and hooks, indicating that the matrix was a collapsed wooden ceiling with plaster, supporting the original vault, or built after it had collapsed. Few Islamic potsherds were present, but many fish bones and scales, turtle bones, olive pits, top shells (*Monodonta turbinata*) and *M. trunculus* appeared, suggesting a living surface occupied temporarily. At +5.98 to +6.01 m, a light beige wet sand fill with dark brown pocketing appeared (A2-L 1111, B2-L 1110). Pottery from the twelfth–thirteenth centuries included a strainer, fragments of a *dolium* type container, and large pieces of an unribbed jar with an *omphalos* base (thirteenth century). There was also a Byzantine cooking pot. Many pottery sherds were "rusted" due to the damp consistency of the matrix, suggesting that the vault was covered while it was re-used. Below was a grayish beige sandy fill (L 1112) at about +5.70 m, upon which the *ad hoc* buttress for the vault rested. At the bottom stone of the buttress a small intact cooking pot was found. Just west of it another—smashed—cooking pot was found. The level became grayer and more clayey with plaster fragments, resembling another surface (L 1122), at about +5.50 m. At this height, a nearly whole Mamluk yellow glazed jug with a trefoil lip was found. A brown/purple glazed cooking pot and an unglazed cooking pot, both fragmented, were also among the finds. These glazed cooking pots and jugs dated to the thirteenth–fourteenth centuries. A bronze coin and an iron key, iron fragments, glass, pumice, slag, and bone were also associated, further indicating that this was an actual surface dating to the Mamluk Period within the reused vault.

Stratum I—Mamluk to Late Ottoman (1400–1917 C.E.)

There were no architectural features firmly attributed to this stratum. An oval lime kiln installation (L 1006) was discovered just under the aeolian sand in Square A3 (fig. 16). It measured 183 × 140 cm and was 57 cm deep, with three roughly dressed stone courses and a stone paved floor with burn marks. The kiln rested on a sandy base at +6.90 m. The eastern edge of the kiln and the square were situated on the slope of the tel and damaged by erosion. No pottery was associated with the kiln, but a marble slab was found inside. The kiln cut into a reddish/brown soil mix fill and a lower sandy layer. This fill, seen throughout the Area A, was post-depositional Crusader and most likely created by the dismantling and robbing activities of the Crusader Period buildings and the accumulation of debris during the Mamluk and Ottoman phases. This would postdate the kiln to the last few centuries when seasonal deposition of sand and fills from the dismantling of the site were already in place. The lime kiln indicated the continuation of these activities demonstrated by the burning of marble fragments. While stratigraphically it appeared of recent construction, a large cache of marble fragments in a Mamluk layer in Area A2 suggested similar activities in earlier periods. A few Late Islamic/Ottoman sherds were found in surface fills in Areas A and A2. Of particular note

were a Late Ottoman plate, found in several pieces (C011; Chapter III.3, fig. 125), and an Ottoman ceramic tobacco pipe bowl (C022; Chapter IV.3.B5, figs. 160–61). The latter was found between the rocks of the added northern vault wall (W 1108) in Square B2.

While the majority of the material culture inside the vault indicated Mamluk reuse, it is likely that the vault was still open and fairly undamaged or re-penetrated between the seventeenth and nineteenth centuries. Several post-depositional and unstratified Crusader and Mamluk levels were discerned that lay within the now destroyed structure and vault. Two superimposed sandy fills appeared under the surface layers that extended deeper in the middle of Square A2. These layers (L 1018, L 1022) yielded mixed period pottery and smaller finds and cut through the Crusader floor (F 1008) and foundation trenches of the Crusader building (L 1026; fig. 21). These two levels contained no medieval pottery and were post-Crusader and Mamluk deposits within the structure. The central slump was due to the collapse of the Crusader vault below. From the evidence, Ottoman occupation of the areas was quite sparse and confined to the eighteenth and nineteenth centuries. It is possible that this intermittent presence was related to the quarrying and dismantling of building materials from the site (an activity attested from earlier periods) and/or connected with a military outpost on top of the tel, as seen in many other sites in the Levant.

AREA A2 (fig. 40)

Strata VIII to VII—Persian to Hellenistic (450–ca. 100 B.C.E.)

No significant architecture or soil layers were found attributed to these strata. A probe sunk in the NW corner of Square A7 revealed two layers over bedrock: (a) strong brown sand, (b) dark reddish brown clay, and bedrock at +1.47 m. These were all excavated as L 1327 and were similar to the clay and sand leveled bedrock (L 1244) in Area A, Square B1. Within them were found Persian sherds and a bronze fishhook. The bedrock in Area A2 is

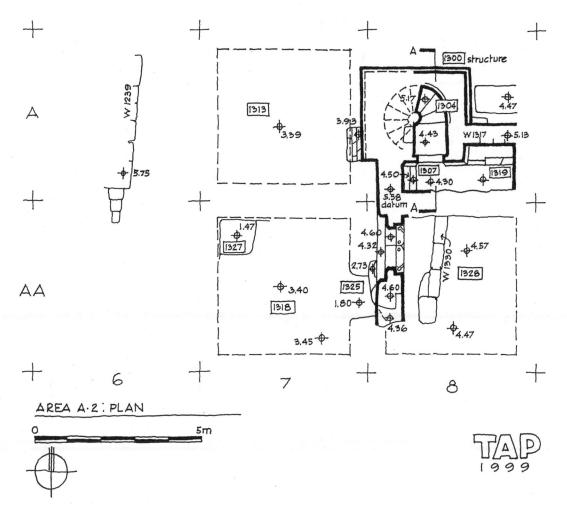

Fig. 40.   *Plan of Area A2 (1999).*

0.4–1.2 m lower than in Area A, demonstrating a significant drop.

Stratum VI—Early Byzantine (324–450 C.E.)

The Early Byzantine Tower

Another probe between Squares AA7 and AA8 revealed an earlier construction phase below the Crusader tower and beneath a Late Byzantine building corresponding to Phase 1 of the church construction (fig. 41). The wall of the Early Byzantine building was rounded and composed of two courses of matching large ashlar stones bonded with Kabbara clay and curving underneath the later foundations. The lack of mortar in the Early Byzantine structure shows that it was leveled to

its foundation before being built upon. The top of this foundation was at +2.82 m. The east wall probe section showed a large foundation trench to the south associated with the structure and composed primarily of a yellowish-brown sandy fill with *kurkar* pebbles, shells, clay and mortar (fig. 42). The north section of the probe showed no foundation trench, but white sand (L 1324) where the foundation wall curved under the structure. In this sand were several pieces of worn Byzantine pottery plastered on one side. The Early Byzantine foundation sat on a layer of Kabbara clay and dark moist sand covering a crushed *kurkar* surface (L 1325) at +2.10 m; directly below this is bedrock. A probe to trace the footing of the Crusader tower just west of L 1304 in A7 showed no evidence of the Early Byzantine foundations. This is due to the fact that the Early Byzantine structure with its curved foundation walls was probably a rounded tower. Unfortunately, the size of the probe did not allow further insights into the building's dimensions or orientation.

Above the bedrock in the probe in the NW corner of Square A7, L 1325 continued at approximately +1.8 m, where large and unworn pieces of flat lying Byzantine pottery and bag-shaped amphorae of the fourth–seventh centuries with concretions came out of the wet yellowish-brown sand layer with many irregular *kurkar* stones. L 1325 was similar to the crushed *kurkar* surface built over sand on bedrock in Area D, which possibly supported a coastal road moving up the tel from the Nahal Tanninim bridge.

Strata V to IV—Late Byzantine to Umayyad (450–750 C.E.)

The Late Byzantine–Early Islamic Building

The Late Byzantine phase consisted of three excavated elements, all belonging to the same building (fig. 40). Just north of the Crusader tower a mas-

Fig. 41. *Probe in Area A2, showing Byzantine structural remains below Crusader tower.*

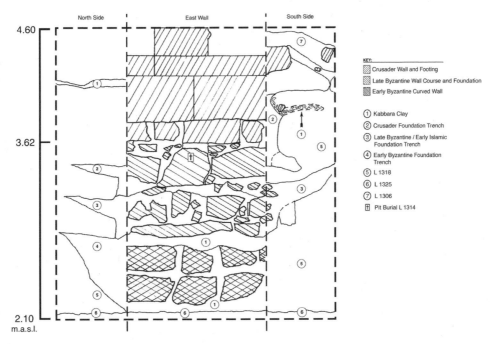

Fig. 42. *East profile of Square AA7, showing Crusader and Byzantine foundations.*

sive *kurkar* foundation (W 1336) was discovered, extending 1.23 m and 28 cm away from W 1317, and 1.38 m east and 19 cm from L 1304. The foundation was composed of 3–5 mortared layers of stones, rectangular in shape with irregular tops. This wall foundation rested on a larger, flat platform of rubble stones. From its massive size and 90-degree orientation to a Late Byzantine wall in AA8 (W 1330), and its low elevation at +4.47 m, it is clear that W 1336 was part of an earlier fortification wall belonging to a Late Byzantine structure.

A thin interior wall (W 1330) was perpendicular to this foundation and built within the Crusader floor foundation. It ran north–south, but was askew to the Crusader wall orientation (fig. 43). The wall was at least 1.2 m high and composed of two courses of dressed ashlars over at least three foundation courses of irregular rubble stones and clay. In the section profile, remnants of a Byzantine floor were seen at the same elevation as the top of the foundation stones on W 1330 at +3.90 m (fig. 44). The wall was part of the Late Byzantine structure underneath the Crusader tower.

Under W 1316 of the Crusader tower, as revealed in the east wall probe of Square AA7, were the exterior wall foundations of the Late Byzantine structure, composed of two courses of irregular *kurkar* stones chinked with smaller ones and unmortared, showing that the wall was leveled to its foundation before being built upon (figs. 41–42). The elevation for the top of this foundation was approximately +3.62 m. The foundation trench for this wall was evident in the section. Foundations for the Late Byzantine structure under W 1316 were also evident under the footing on the west face of the squared tower projection (L 1304). Two courses of stones, headers over stretchers, descended about one meter. They sat on a 30 cm thick Kabbara silt foundation sloping under the tower. The lower courses projected out slightly. The strategic location of the building, the massive fortification style construction of the exterior walls, and the use of the structure as a tower or similar fortified building in its previous Early Byzantine phase and subsequent Crusader phase all suggest that the building was used in a similar fashion during the Late Byzantine Period.

Fig. 43. *Interior wall of Byzantine building and threshold of Crusader tower in Square AA8.*

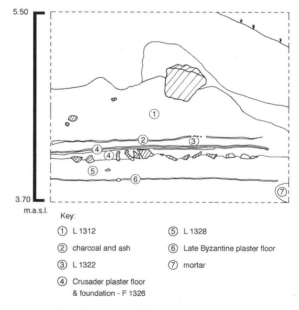

Fig. 44. *Final destruction layer, Crusader and Late Byzantine floors in east profile of Square AA8.*

Stratum III—Abbasid to Fatimid Periods (750–1099 C.E.)

Burials

Three pit burials were found within a locus of dune sand that continued down in the middle of Squares A7 and AA7 at +4.08 m. The very pale brown sand (L 1313/L 1318) over the entire square was similar to the surface sand, but differentiated from it in that it was virtually sterile except for rolled and water-worn Byzantine pottery and bone. The best preserved of these burials (L 1314) was oriented with its head pointing west and in the east balk (fig. 45). Initial analysis shows that it was a young male, who was buried in a Christian fashion with arms folded across the chest, one palm down, one palm up. The top of his head was at +3.45 m. The burial was about 40 cm below the bottom of the rubble collapse around the Crusader tower (L 1306), thereby predating the structure. The tarsal and metatarsal bones of the skeleton were not found and were most likely disturbed when the foundation of the tower (L 1300) was placed. Although Late Byzantine sherds, *tesserae*, and glass were scattered around the body, the elevation of the body in dune sand between the Crusader and Late Byzantine/Early Islamic building phases indicates that the burial likely belongs to the abandonment phase between these two periods. An iron arrowhead directly above the burial (L 1314) may have been associated with the body. Within the locus two more disarticulated pit burials appeared; one reburied in the northern balk (L 1320) at +3.33 m, and one reburied in the eastern balk (L 1321) at +3.09 m. In L 1321 an iron spear/arrow head was found on the left humerus and a mark of discoloration on the bone where it may have entered. The remainder of the square continued with the aeolian sand (L 1313) to +2.8 m.

A thick layer of fine yellow sand (L 1328) with some marble chips and kurkar pebbles surrounded the Late Byzantine wall (W 1330) in AA8. The aeolian sand accumulated after the Late Byzantine structure went out of use and before the Crusader structure was erected. It continued quite deep and excavation stopped before reaching its bottom at +3.07 m.

Fig. 45. *Late Byzantine burial, perpendicular to foundations in Area A2.*

Stratum IIB—Crusader (1099–1265 C.E.)

The Crusader structure (L 1300) in Area A2 was a massive, well built square tower that included a square tower projection, walls, and floors. These comprised the NW corner of a large structure, the rest of which remains unexcavated (figs. 40, 46).

The Crusader Tower

The best preserved section was L 1304, the square tower fortification, with a circular staircase and stairwell in its center in Square A8 (fig. 47). The north side of L 1304 consisted of two well cut *kurkar* ashlars, 75 cm long, with their upper outer corners cut in a beveled edge at a 45-degree angle. The tops of the stones had small marble fragments imbedded in plaster, suggesting that the stones were originally part of the Byzantine church. The NE ashlar was a cornerstone and turned south following the same

Fig. 46. *The Crusader tower in Area A2.*

Fig. 47. *Northwest corner of Crusader tower with circular stairwell.*

beveled edge. The lower course was also made up of large cut ashlars (90–100 × 53 cm). The NE cornerstone was about 91 × 53 cm and not beveled as the above course was. The W side of the squared tower projection was similarly constructed with no styled edge. In a small section along its western face, a footing of slightly irregular stones (+3.93 m) was discovered projecting 15 cm away from the wall. Thus, the squared tower fortification was approximately 3.1 m × 2.8 m.

The interior of L 1304 contained a remarkably well preserved spiral staircase with the three bottom steps *in situ*, measuring 24 cm wide at the center (figs. 48–49). The turning post had a diameter of 36 cm. At the bottom of the stairs was a small hallway (90 × 84 cm) that was also plastered on the interior. The hallway ended at a raised threshold (22 cm wide) that opened to a large southern room, whose north interior wall comprised evenly cut ashlar projections with sloped beveled extensions reaching the floor, 10 cm away from the wall. The beveled edge turned a corner between L 1304 and the east–west wall, W 1317, delineating a possible column base or other support for a vaulted ceiling. Within this room were the remains of a poorly preserved pitted plaster floor. At the western end was a small installation of a row of squared stones (W 1310) in line with the stairwell walls, heading south. The irregularly topped stones had only one course and were plastered on their interior face and to the floor 15 cm away from the west wall, W 1316, creating a narrow niche. The top elevation was +4.50 m. This enclosed niche may have been an addition used as a storage space for weapons or a shaft to install a rope lift to the upper stories.

Walls

Two main walls enclosed the structure to the north (W 1317) and west (W 1316). Running east from the squared tower projection was a thick fortification wall (W 1317), possibly built in two phases. The outer portion consisted of three visible courses of stretchers, whose stones varied considerably, suggesting reuse. This wall was built over the Late Byzantine/Early Islamic W 1336. In this earlier wall, stones were removed for the Crusader structure creating gaps to the west and south. These gaps were filled in with Kabbara clay and small stones, and the foundation platform was also covered with the clay to bond this earlier wall to the Crusader wall. Another line of stone strengthened the wall and formed a bonded 90-degree corner with the beveled ashlars of the squared tower fortification. An even, well cut ashlar footing projected 12 cm out at this corner at +4.22 m. South of this wall were three irregular *kurkar* stones in 1–2 courses,

Fig. 48. *Detail of circular stairwell in Crusader tower.*

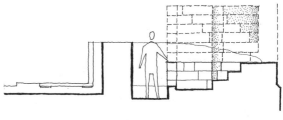

AREA A·2: SECTION A-A
0   3m

TAP
1 9 9 9

Fig. 49. *Section through Crusader tower, with the entrance to the structure on the left.*

continuing east and abutting the beveled edge of the column base near L 1304. These stones (53 × 17 cm, 40 × 30 cm) extended into the floor. Between the outer fortification walls and the inner wall was a mortar and rubble fill that bonded both walls together creating a solid 1.2 m wide wall. The interior wall could have been a secondary addition, because it abutted the beveled projection of the room. This later addition and mortar/rubble fill may have been constructed to further fortify the walls. Another alternative is that the interior south course (+4.49 m) that was preserved much lower than the north course (+5.13 m) was intended for use as a bench in the tower room.

W 1316 to the west ran south into Square AA8, bordering the main room to the west, and was pierced by the entranceway. The wall consisted of 2–3 courses of very well preserved and dressed ashlars. On the north side of AA8, two abutting and slightly offset ashlars (25–27 cm wide), whose tops were plastered, had their SW edges trimmed vertically in a chamfered style. The chamfered edges were 8 cm wide and were usually employed in a heavily trafficked area. The chamfered blocks were repeated symmetrically south of the door at a lower course, and the wall eventually broke off at the southern edge of AA8. The threshold was 1.29 m wide with a central cutting possibly used as a drain or spillway. Doorposts, both outer and inner for bolting and locking, were cut into the stones implying a wooden door that swung inward (fig. 43). Based on the cuts in the stone, the doors were not of equal size, but one was wider than the other. The threshold was at +4.60 m and there was a lower front step at +4.32 m. A probe underneath W 1316 revealed the Crusader wall foundations and footing. The foundations consisted of two courses of massive well dressed ashlars over a thin irregular footing. These rested on a Late Byzantine foundation (see fig. 42). Associated and seen in the north and south sides of the section was the foundation trench for the Crusader tower, consisting of a compact light yellowish-brown sandy fill over a pale brown fill.

Floor

To the south of Square AA8, the entrance threshold to the tower led into a room with a damaged plastered floor (F 1326) at +4.27 m that extended throughout the square in varying stages of preservation and continued south into the balk (figs. 44, 50). Within the Crusader floor, a *kurkar* weight with a drilled hole, an iron bolt imbedded in the floor, and glazed pottery were found. Under the 10-cm-thick plaster floor was a layer of rubble stones, plaster, and Kabbara clay constituting a floor foundation of equal size, whose bottom elevation was at +4.08 m. It was built over the Late Byzantine/Early Islamic W 1330 that was leveled and bonded to the Crusader foundation with large amounts of Kabbara clay, typical of Crusader construction.

Stratum IIA—Mamluk (1265–1400 C.E.)

The Crusader building was destroyed, as evidenced by a destruction layer consisting of collapse and conflagration. However, living surfaces and material culture throughout the interior of the Crusader tower and on the exterior attest to a temporary reuse of the structure in the Mamluk period *before* the destruction of the building (fig. 40). This was most clearly discerned in square AA8 within the building.

Mamluk Occupation

Several rows of large rubble stones were used to seal the threshold entrance of the structure in a secondary phase. The ashlars placed along the threshold to seal it in the thirteenth century cut in and under the Crusader floor. Associated with the stones was a brown soil (L 1315) along the interior of the threshold that contained brown glazed sherds, fish and other bone, and an almost complete curved scythe blade. A living surface (L 1322) rested on the Crusader tower's damaged plaster floor (F 1326) at +4.33 m. It was a locus of light beige sandy soil (L 1322) that was compact and contained many glazed brown cooking pot sherds laying flat, as well as fish, turtle, and other bones, broken *Glycimeris* shells, and metal nails including an iron blade.

This locus continued north of the balk in A8, excavated as two loci (L 1307, L 1319), where numerous fish bones were revealed by sifting. These two other thin very pale brown fine sand levels lay adjacent to each other, at +4.46 m and +4.28 m, respectively. Below these layers, at +4.30 m and +4.22 m, was the damaged plastered Crusader floor, the same as F 1326 in AA8, but 10 cm lower. This was accounted for by the thin beige layers above, which were comprised of the disintegrated floor. These layers contained brown glazed Mamluk sherds and fish bone. Also under L 1305, in the northwestern corner of the room, was a yellowish-brown sandy soil (L 1309), somewhat moist, with plaster chunks confined in the small niche/installation created by stones plastered to the floor. The soil continued deeper than the floor level and excavation stopped at +4.11 m. Out of it came glazed pottery (Crusader/Mamluk) and fish bone.

Fig. 50.   *Detail of Crusader floor, Mamluk living surface, and final destruction layer in tower.*

An amorphous living surface of brown compact soil (L 1311) extended outside the building's west wall (W 1316) to the north at +3.73 m. It contained much glazed cookware, painted black *Proto-majolica* Mamluk ware (thirteenth century), three coins tentatively dated as Mamluk, decorated glass, oil lamp fragments, bone, and worked chert. The living surface could be confidently identified as a thirteenth-century temporary Mamluk occupation associated with the Crusader tower, and also corresponding to similar occupation within the tower. The blocking of the threshold and the living surface loci represented the period in the Crusader tower's final reuse, prior to its eventual destruction during the Mamluk Period, when it was dismantled and reused for building material until the Ottoman Period.

Destruction

A thick sloping black ash/burn layer (L 1312) lay above the Crusader floor and Mamluk living surface in Square AA8, at an average height of +4.57 m (figs. 44, 50). The silty ash with charcoal bits and sandy patches yielded mainly Mamluk glazed sherds, a Crusader yellow glazed sgraffito sherd, and fish and other bones. Above it was the

highest feature in the structure, consisting of a sizeable rubble and ashlar collapse and associated Byzantine/Late Islamic mixed fill of dark brown semi-compact soil with some plaster chunks that spilled out into AA7. Collapse continued to the north within the building. In the squared tower fortification (L 1304), three loci consisting of grayish brown sandy mixed soil fills were located within the stairs (L 1302), stairwell hallway (L 1303), and southern room (L 1305; top at +5.07 m). Within these fills were also thin lenses of gray ash. The fills contained many large rubble stones and pieces of the spiral stairs at various depths and orientations. Mixed pottery characterized the material culture of the fills, including a Mamluk brown glazed cooking pot and oil lamp fragments. Also present were large quantities of fish and other bone, obtained through sifting, iron nail fragments, and a nearly complete Mamluk oil lamp (see Chapter IV.2, fig. 156:5). A cache of about 200 marble pieces of varying thickness lay in the fill, perhaps being amassed for burning in the nearby lime kiln. Other Byzantine architectural elements, such as a marble acanthus capital fragment, a marble cross, and a basin probably originated from the church atop Area A.

The aeolian surface sand outside the tower was very thick and full of building stones and architectural fragments from both the Crusader tower and the Byzantine church above. A rough semicircle of stones, possibly from a fallen archway, lay in the sand. Beneath and within the surface sand was a large rubble collapse spilling out from the tower and into Squares A7 and AA7. The general nature of the collapse showed a concentration of stones falling outward from the SW area of the exposed Crusader tower. A dark brown compact soil layer with plaster chunks (A7-1308, AA7-1306) lay beneath the collapse in uneven patches. In both squares, the layer continued deeper with an increasing sandy content and large ashlars. Most of the pottery was Crusader/Mamluk glazed ware, including sherds of a celadon glazed vessel.

DISCUSSION

Strata VIII–VII

Stratified deposits and architectural remains of Persian-Hellenistic date were found only in the lowest levels of Squares A1 and B1, just above bedrock that had been paved and leveled with *hamra* soil. Material culture from these periods appeared in every occupational stratum, fill, and surface collection in the area. No pottery dating before the fifth century B.C.E. was found. These Persian-Hellenistic levels were disturbed by the construction of a large Byzantine church that cut into the layers. The pottery in the lowest strata was to 99 percent Persian-Hellenistic, with stray Byzantine sherds, water-worn and abraded. One small living surface was attributed to the Persian period, while the Hellenistic period just above revealed thin foundational courses of 2–3 walls. The Persian and Hellenistic stratigraphy and pottery were not sharply delineated, suggesting a continuous occupation without break. Persian wares were predominately local, mainly storage jars and cooking pots. Hellenistic wares generally consisted of imported fine wares. Associated with the ceramics were many Murex shells and fish bone, alluding to dyeing and fishing activities at Tel Tanninim. The relatively large quantity of Persian/Hellenistic material culture (approximately 260 diagnostic sherds) and the domestic nature of the assemblage

recovered suggested that this small area may have been a residential part of the settlement. Dating from lamps and coins encompassed a wide chronological range from the sixth–second centuries B.C.E. for the strata. From this small area of excavation, it is possible to hypothesize that: (1) earliest occupation was confined to the Area A mound, because Persian and Hellenistic material culture was found only there and not at all in Areas A2, B, B2, and D, but the coast south of Tel Tanninim may have been part of the earliest settlement, as indicated by surface pottery; (2) Persian-Hellenistic occupation, while probably continuous, ended at the beginning of the Roman period; and (3) the settlement was involved in dyeing and fishing activities.

Gap—Late Hellenistic to Early Roman

No Roman ceramics were found in the excavated areas and surface collections, except for two cases in Late Byzantine fills. They consisted of: (1) several stray third-century sherds, and (2) seven oil lamp fragments datable to the Roman era, six in Area A and one in Area B. When compared with the high percentage of material culture from other periods, the excavated Roman materials exhibit a significant dearth of evidence. However, while Roman settlement on Tel Tanninim did not occur, Roman presence can certainly not be discounted. Building activity on the nearby high and low level aqueducts that fed Caesarea and at Caesarea itself suggests a Roman presence in the immediate vicinity of Tel Tanninim. It is also, perhaps, the focus of these major constructions that detracted the establishment of a new settlement over the ruined small coastal site of Tel Tanninim. It is interesting to note that at Shavei Zion, a similar small coastal site north of Akko with a comparable church, second century C.E. evidence was notably absent from the early pottery under the Byzantine levels (Prausnitz, Avi-Yonah and Barag 1967: 40–41).

Stratum VI

In the Byzantine period, a large basilica church was erected on the summit of Area A, and a round tower was built in Area A2. The church underwent a series of four phases from the very late fourth/early fifth century to the early eighth century (ca. 500–750 C.E.). Only 7 squares were excavated in the central and northern *chevet* of the church, limiting a full architectural discussion of the church. In the first phase, a massive east-facing apse and perpendicular eastern wall were erected, indicating an intended basilica-style church with an external apse, nave and side aisles. The chord of the apse had a radius of 5.5 m and was 8.5 m wide and 4.2 m deep. The width of the wall ranged from approximately 1.3 to 1.6 m at the head of the apse. The deep foundations of the structure cut through the early levels of the site and came to rest on the Persian and Hellenistic surfaces just above bedrock. Soil with large amounts of domestic material culture from these early periods was used extensively as foundation fills around the walls. Another example of foundation fills dominated by earlier material culture, with contemporary sherds, was noted at Shavei Zion (Prausnitz, Avi-Yonah and Barag 1967: 19). This phase was dated to the very late fourth/early fifth century C.E. by the architectural plan, Early Byzantine pottery, and numismatic evidence. Excavation showed that construction on the church was halted for a period of time, resuming most likely in the mid-fifth century. In Area A2, a probe beneath the Crusader tower structure showed two curved foundational courses for an Early Byzantine tower that was not excavated.

Gap

A period of abandonment on the church building project followed the initial placement of the apse foundation walls in Area A. This was shown by thick, horizontal, undisturbed layers of dune sand blanketing the foundation fills in all of the excavated areas on the summit of the tel. The halt of church construction, however, does not necessarily indicate site abandonment. It could be that only the large church project was temporarily stopped due to financial, political or religious factors. Such a large edifice, subsequently ornamented with glass wall mosaics and marble capitals, would surely have demanded strong financial backing and physical labor.

Strata V–IV

Building activity on the church resumed and can be divided into three phases. In Phase 2, the apse and other walls were raised and the *bema* floor was laid down. The apse was then inscribed, when an eastern exterior wall was built east of it, enclosing a plaster floor approximately 4.2–4.3 m long. A *pastophorium* or sacristy to the north of the inscribed apse bore traces of this same thin plaster flooring. Presumably, the same would be true for the other half of the church. A pillar base was found resting on the floor in the side chamber. In Phase 3, the *bema* and *pastophoria* pavements were further raised and a mosaic floor (sixth century) was laid around the outside of the apse. A hoard of Roman and Byzantine lamps and other objects was buried in a pit beneath this floor in the north *pastophorium*. Other walls to the north of the church may have been an extension of the building or part of an adjacent structure. In the final Phase 4, the *bema* was again raised with two additional superimposed floors. A step marked the western edge of the *bema*, enclosing a chancel 10 m long and 8.5 m wide. No grooves for a chancel screen were detected. The *bema* extended into the nave, creating a presbytery 5.7 m beyond the chord of the apse. An altar platform was situated on the *bema* floor, just beyond the chord, 1.9 m from the step. No slots for altar table posts were found. However, heavy damage and robbing of slabs from its center, a marble *akroterion* found in an Early Islamic robbing pit, and a reliquary fragment found on the surface suggest the presence of a reliquary within the altar platform.

The church was significantly expanded in the successive building phase, during the fifth–sixth centuries. The apse, perhaps originally intended as external, was inscribed within the projected walls and floors of the church. Basilica churches with inscribed rectangular transepts were uncommon in Palestine (Avi-Yonah, Cohen and Ovadiah 1993: 305). Only one example, at Tabgha (Heptapegon), was listed as belonging to this type. It too was initially dated to the late fourth/early fifth century with sixth century additions to the *bema* floor. The fifth-century churches of SS. Sergius and Bacchus

(North Church) and St. Mary (South Church) at Nessana featured inscribed apses; however, these differ in that they are completely free standing. In later phases, short walls connected them to the exterior walls (Colt 1962: 10–13). The space behind the apse in the inland churches at Tabgha and Nessana consisted of narrow walkways, unlike the larger room (4.2–4.3 m) with a mosaic pavement at Tel Tanninim. The Church at Gerasa, formerly a synagogue, was reoriented, so that the space behind the free-standing apse was paved over the atrium of the synagogue. An inscription in the chancel dated it to 530/1 C.E. (Piccirillo 1993: 291).

Closer parallels for Tel Tanninim occur further north along the coastline. The early church (église inférieure) at Khan Khaldé, a settlement on the *Via Maris* located just south of Beirut, exhibited a 6 m space behind the apse, containing a room with mosaic pavement. On either side were *pastophoria*. The eastern exterior wall of the apse created an irregular space due to the sloping topography. The apse was about half as wide and deep as that at Tel Tanninim. The church was dated to the middle of the fifth century and was superseded by the later church (église supérieure) in the second half of the sixth century (Duval and Caillet 1982: 320–46; Donceel-Voûte 1988: 385–92). The church at Zahrani, further south along the coast between Beirut and Tyre, was only partially preserved on its apse end. In its second phase, the floors in the *pastophoria* and around the apse were raised (Donceel-Voûte 1988: 424). Additionally, the church was furnished with an altar extending into the nave. A succession of mosaic floors dated the church, revealing several building phases from its first phase in 389–390 C.E. to its final phase in 541 C.E. The church at Shavei Zion also had a possible inscribed apse, surmised from the fact that a *pastophorium* was found outside the apse. The reconstructed apse measured an 6.5 m wide and just over 4 m deep, approximating the Tel Tanninim church closely. While initially dated to the early fourth century by the excavator (Prausnitz, Avi-Yonah and Barag 1967: 72), Ovadiah (1970: 162) redated it to the late fourth/early fifth century, closer to its second phase, dated by an inscription to 485/486 C.E. Lastly, parallels can be drawn from the site of Ostrakine on the northern

coast of the Sinai Peninsula near Rhinocolura (al-ʿArish). Of the three basilicas discovered, two exhibit inscribed apses and external rooms similar to Tel Tanninim. A basilica uncovered during the North Sinai Expedition had *pastophoria* and a small room behind the apse, about 2.5 m long. The apse itself was also similar in its proportions (7 m wide, 4 m deep). Furthermore, a *bema* projected into the nave with a small altar at its center. Another basilica church excavated by Clédat in 1914 was also very closely arranged. These churches were dated to the fifth century and continued until the seventh (Oren 1993: 305–14). In these last two examples, the churches were linked with coastal industrial activities, a central feature of Tel Tanninim. Remains of a related wine industry directly associated with the Shavei Zion church indicated that it was also a monastic complex (Aviam 2001: 9). Ostrakine was also famous for its salting and fishing industries (Oren 1993: 306).

Donceel-Voûte (1988: 497–98) assembles several of these churches in the regional typological category of "maritime Phoenicia." These coastal churches (Khan Khaldé, Zahrani, Beit Mery, Shavei Zion, Nahariya and ʿEvron) are grouped in clusters around larger bishopric cities (such as Beirut and Akko). According to her, they are characterized as (1) generally medium to small churches with (2) shallow semi-circular apses, and (3) rooms around the apse (*pastophoria)* that are not always aligned and vary. The church at Tel Tanninim fits into this category architecturally and as a satellite of Caesarea. The regional type should be expanded somewhat as a southern Levantine coastal group to include the close parallel of Ostrakine. These sites would have functioned as way stations for pilgrims traveling to Jerusalem on the *Via* Maris. Primarily, these churches were constructed in the late fourth to early fifth centuries and underwent floor repairs in the mid-sixth century.

Returning to Tel Tanninim, successive building phases of floors with increasing ornamentation attested to the further prominence of the church. The later floors had tessellation, colored mosaics and *opus sectile* pavements. The walls were decorated, as shown by the abundance of glass tesserae and bronze clips for fastening marble panels.

Fragments of marble, a basin and a reliquary were found near the church. The number of excavated and known column capitals from the site suggests an arcade with at least seven columns per side. The secondary phases at virtually all of the parallel churches resembled these latest phases at Tel Tanninim and support the general dates suggested by the stratigraphy and architecture: Phase 1: late fourth/early fifth century C.E.; Phase 2: mid/late fifth century C.E.; Phase 3: early/mid sixth century C.E.; Phase 4: late sixth/early seventh century C.E. The estimated proportions of the church would have to be based on the other parallels. Within the coastal group, three churches follow a basilica ratio of 1:3 (Zahrani, Beit Mery, and ʿEvron) and four are roughly 1:6 (Khan Khaldé, Shavei Zion, Ostrakine, Nahariya). Given the excavated portions of the apse and *pastophorium* at Tel Tanninim, the width would approximate 20 m. Based on the number of column capitals found, the large flat area on top of the Area A summit (nearly 90 m W–E) and the closer parallels of the 1:6 churches, the estimated size of the Tel Tanninim church is 30 × 20 m. In Area A2, foundations and two walls of a Late Byzantine structure below the Crusader tower and over the Early Byzantine tower were probably parts of a similar fortified structure also rebuilt in this later phase.

A large basilica church, a fortification tower along the road and a *castellum* for obtaining water are key elements for pilgrim stations. The Early Byzantine monastic complex of St. Peter (Qasr ʿAli), a pilgrim station of the mid-fifth century on the Jerusalem–Jericho road, and Khirbet al-ʿAmed offer parallels, as they feature a combination of church and reservoir, roadside tower and living quarters (Hirschfeld 1990). Such pilgrim stations were not uncommon in Byzantine Palestine. Thus, the church becomes part of a larger complex dominating the entire site. The existence of an extensive aquaculture industry coupled with the large richly ornamented basilica church suggests that Tel Tanninim in the fifth and sixth centuries was a Christian community, possibly monastic or pilgrim based, that relied on marketing fish for its economy. The church continued to function well into the Early Islamic period. Pottery and other material culture on the site confirm continuity into the eighth century (Umayyad period), just as Caesarea continued after the Arab conquest of 641, albeit in a diminished state. Tel Tanninim continued for another century or so, maintaining its church and perhaps its fish industries, substantiating the observation that the Early Muslims were not interested in dismantling monotheistic communities and erected their new state around existing sites.

Stratum III

Following the Final Byzantine/Umayyad transitional period, the church complex fell into disuse. Destruction layers found at the bottom of robbing trenches further sealed the church's fate in the middle of the eighth century. Small quantities of material culture of the Abbasid, Tulunid, and Fatimid periods were usually associated with pits or robbing trenches that cut into earlier levels. These and later such activities led to the dismantling of virtually all structures excavated in Area A. Only the foundations remained. Robbing activities of this period were not detected in Area A2. Although it is known that new Early Islamic settlements were frequently placed on the margins of the site, as seen throughout the Near East (and at Caesarea), these were generally Umayyad and surface survey did not provide any evidence to support this. From the excavations and surface survey of the site, it would seem that Tel Tanninim was abandoned about 750 C.E. This is in stark contrast to the efflorescence of nearby Qaysâriyah (Caesarea) in the Abbasid, Tulunid, and Fatimid periods.

Stratum IIB

The Crusader site of Tel Tanninim, known as *Turris Salinarum* (see Chapter I) was confined to Areas A and A2. Occupation was found in two buildings oriented along the cardinal directions. In Area A, a building with at least two adjacent rooms, separated by a threshold and built over a subterranean vault, was excavated. The western room (ca. 22 m²) was built over a barrel vault, laid within the church foundations, whose top was leveled by Kabbara clay. The floor was of beaten earth. The vault (interior 10.5 m², projected height 3 m) provided support for a superstructure and storage space. It appears to have been open to the north. The eastern exterior wall of the entire structure was delineated in Square A6. Assuming the structure spanned from the western wall of the west room in A2 to the eastern exterior wall in A6, the building was elongated with a total length of roughly 30 m. Rubble collapses indicate the building was extensive. It may have been a hall-house, described by Pringle (1997: 11) as a hall with one story built over a vaulted basement. The one at Calansue (Qalansuwa), on the coastal plain south of Caesarea, was part of a group of buildings including a tower. The Calansue hall-house was 30 m long and 16.5 m wide.

In Area A2, a large rectangular Crusader tower was erected, with an estimated area of 170 m². The ruin is visible in an aerial photo (fig. 15), indicating a structure roughly 10 × 17 m; however, probes along the northern slope of the mound did not reveal its walls. The NW corner tower projected past the structure walls and had a well preserved circular staircase within it. The entrance into the structure, marked by a threshold with pivot holes, was to the west. The walls were made of well dressed ashlars reused from Byzantine structures and laid 0.9–1.2 m thick without mortar. Their foundations were of *kurkar* fieldstones and limestone blocks of varying sizes, embedded in black Kabbara clay. Chinking with small rubble stones was common in wall foundations. The foundation trenches were also stabilized with Kabbara clay. The floor of the main room was plastered. Three additional towers on the coastal plain south of Tel Tanninim had varying areas (Montdidier 102 m², Caco 124 m², and Tour Rouge 169 m²), thicker walls (1.7–2.0 m, 2.8 m, and 2.2 m, respectively) and two parallel barrel vaults, either in the basement or on the first floor (Pringle 1997: 38, 67, 83–84). These were all rectilinear structures and did not exhibit the castle-like fortified projection with circular stair as at Tel Tanninim.

The Crusader *Turris Salinarum* may have functioned as a lookout post or road station, like Destroit Tower east of Athlit (Pringle 1997: 6). The Crusader structures at Tel Tanninim were probably erected prior to the mid-twelfth century, when sources say that the Tower "together with the hill on which it was built" was given by Lord Hugh of Caesarea (1154–1168) to the Hospitallers, a grant confirmed by Lord Walter in 1182 (Tibble 1989: 115, 151). The village (*castel*) of Calansue, with its hall-house and tower, offers a close parallel. Small fortifications in the twelfth century Latin Kingdom of Jerusalem were frequently erected by vassal knights as residences and were usually square two-story (15 m) towers with two floors, barrel vault basements, and an undefended entrance at the ground level (Kennedy 1994: 33; Pringle 1997: 7). These towers were well placed geographically and strategically near roads, beside towns, and within visual sight of larger castles. The tower and attendant building at Tel Tanninim fall among similar fortifications in the area, such as Calansue, Destroit, Montdidier, Caco and Tour Rouge.

Stratum IIA

The archaeological evidence for a Mamluk occupation demonstrates an intermittent settlement with no new construction, but reuse of the Crusader buildings, at least temporarily. This fleshes out the evidence from the documentary sources that say that Crusader sites along the Palestinian coast were totally destroyed in 1265 by Sultan Baybars. In Area A, some robbing pits were cut into the Crusader structure. Both the vault and tower showed a continued and defensive use, albeit temporary. The vault was sealed off with a northern skewed wall and the door of the tower was blocked. Living surfaces in the vault, tower stairwell and rooms contained fairly intact Mamluk vessels, and many fish bones, olive pits and shells showed occupation prior to the destruction of the vault and tower. Upon the living surface in the main tower room was further evidence for the destruction of *Turris Salinarum*, seen in a thick layer of ash with burnt marble, roof tiles, and Crusader and Mamluk ceramics. A possible explanation for this may be that the Hospitaller owners abandoned it or were killed during the Mamluk sieges, whereupon it was used as a temporary encampment or post by the troops of Sultan Baybars.

Stratum I

The Ottoman Period is distinguished by sporadic and intermittent habitation in various areas of the site. Late Islamic/Ottoman ceramics, while few and far between, were found unstratified near surface fills in Areas A and A2. A lime kiln just under the surface in Square A3 may have belonged to this period, or perhaps earlier. The presence of the kiln alludes to various robbing activities on the site that would have continued into the Ottoman Period. Dismantling and collapses of the structures are only associated with this final phase based on their existence just below the surface. The Ottoman ceramics and pipes provide a late date, corresponding to a house built within the Byzantine reservoir in Area B and the Ottoman bridge in 1898. It is possible that the Crusader structures in Area A and A2 were also re-used as military outposts during this period.

3. Hydraulic Installations
(Areas B and B2)

by Diane Everman

While discussion of Tel Tanninim's hydraulic installations is divided here into two areas, Areas B and B2, in reality they are parts of the same whole. Staff and volunteers conducted all excavations stratigraphically; however, remains discovered and excavated in this area immediately north of Caesarea Maritima are basically buried beneath successive layers of beach sand. Sadly, even with numerous wet sieved samples sent to analysts, not much evidence about the type(s) of fish being raised in these areas has been revealed. It can be stated without hesitation, however, that the water-related elements discussed here date to the Byzantine period. Almost without exception, the material culture retrieved from the excavation of all loci fell between the dates of the fourth through eighth centuries C.E. Thus, the presentation of the hydraulic installations here is done to offer the reader a glimpse into the multifaceted and changing elements of the water elements of these areas of the site, rather than an analysis of the stratigraphy as presented in Chapter II.2.

It must also be noted that, while currently there is not much evidence available to offer a more precise date for these installations, it can be stated with relative confidence that the major elements appear to have gone out of use in the eighth century C.E. Although it is known that Tel Tanninim's dates of occupation precede this date by centuries and even postdate it by several more, the particular installations presented here offer no insight into earlier and later water elements. A well on the site has yet to be explored, and its role in providing water for the site and its dates of usage are unknown. Other known water installations, such as those found in Area D, are discussed elsewhere in this volume, although they too appear to date to the Byzantine period.

The water supply system of Tel Tanninim contained a great mix of elements, including wells, a water-wheel, fishponds (*piscinae*), a reservoir (*castellum*), and an aqueduct pipeline that intersected one of the main aqueduct channels that fed nearby Caesarea Maritima. There were also a large number of pipes, both ceramic and lead, to move the water from one place to another. Not all of these elements operated at the same time, but many of them were interrelated and depended on each other to function fully. While no pipeline to or at Tel Tanninim has been excavated from beginning

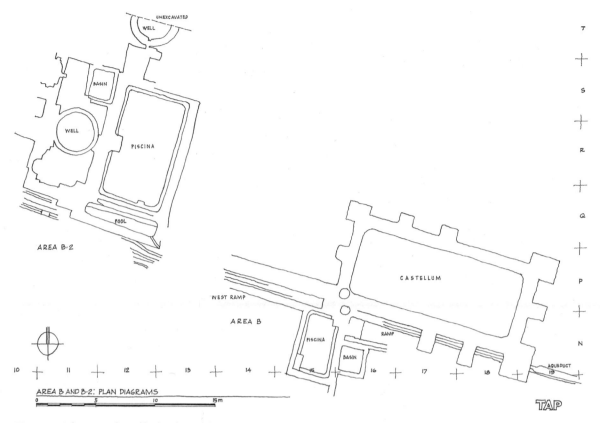

Fig. 51. *Schematic plan of hydraulic installations in Areas B and B2.*

to end, it is possible to generate a picture of the hydraulic installations over a period of time, albeit mostly during the Byzantine period. Discussion of the water-related structures from Area D can be found in Chapter II.4.

While excavation on the tel itself indicated activity as early as the Persian period, no excavated remains of the site's water-related installations dated earlier than the Byzantine period. In fact, no water-related structures, conduits, or receptacles were found on Tel Tanninim itself. Rather, the excavation by the Tanninim Archaeological Project (TAP) revealed all such entities at the foot of the tel to the northeast near the river (Area D), and on the hillock to the east (Areas B and B2), where a complex of hydraulic installations was unearthed (fig. 51).

Most tourists visiting Caesarea Maritima have seen that city's High-level aqueduct and its Low-level companion water line approaching the city from the north. Many of the details of those structures, however, have only recently come to light, due to the tireless efforts of several archaeologists and scholars. While this chapter is not about Caesarea's aqueducts, information about which can be found elsewhere, it is necessary to present some information here, because one of Caesarea Maritima's High-level channels appears to have also supplied water to Tel Tanninim. The date of Caesarea's High-level aqueduct channels is still somewhat in debate, but in general it can be stated that the first High-level channel, the easternmost one called Channel A, is the earliest and lasted the longest in service to the city. It operated at least until the mid-seventh century C.E. The E-Field Bath at Caesarea, which received its water via a pipeline off Channel A, provides a closing date for this earliest channel. Porath (1993: 28) noted that the tunnel beneath Jisr az-Zarqa served at least Channel A only to the end of the Byzantine period, and not after the Islamic conquest of 640 C.E.

Channel B, which is probably datable to Hadrianic times, followed and abutted the first aqueduct, mirroring its route but gathering its water from a greater distance. Channel C, the third conduit, rested upon the abutting walls of Channels A and B, at least along the extant southern section of these channels, and dates from the late fourth to early fifth century C.E. It was poorly built and leaked profusely. Understandably, it had a short period of use. Caesarea's Low-level aqueduct, which dates to the same period as Channel C, was a terrain-hugging channel, the water from which was probably not potable.

Most of this has been known since the survey of Conder and Kitchener in the nineteenth century, but there were gaps in our knowledge, particularly in the aqueduct's hidden, subterranean sections. One of those areas was the underground section beneath the village of Jisr az-Zarqa, northeast of Caesarea and east of Tel Tanninim. Excavation of this portion of Caesarea's elevated aqueducts expanded our knowledge about those water conduits and their route, and offered new information about several of its aspects, including the pipeline leading toward Tel Tanninim that drew from the water supply intended for Caesarea Maritima.

Porath's discovery of this pipeline, now called Channel E, countered the earlier belief that Tel Tanninim extracted water from Caesarea's Low-level aqueduct. Makhouly, a British Mandate antiquities inspector, noted in 1934 that the ruined building on the eastern edge of Tel Tanninim had water brought by built canal branching from the Low-level aqueduct (see Chapter I). This was certainly believed by the author (Everman 1992; 1997) and others, including Porath (1988: 175), who had thought that a pipeline ran from Caesarea's Low-level aqueduct to Tel Tanninim. Porath's later work at Jisr az-Zarqa changed all that.

The breach in the subsurface aqueduct section beneath Jisr az-Zarqa was in the north side of the tunnel, ca. 1.42 m above sea level, or 0.94 m above the floor of the channel. Although somewhat difficult to picture, the excavation team related that the opening led into Channel E by means of a regulating device to a small basin with a clay pipe, which had a diameter of 10.5 cm. Porath and his team found additional remains of Channel E in a probe ca. 200 m west of the opening in the subterranean tunnel. At its departure from the subterranean tunnel, Channel E was about 25 cm wide and a little more than half a meter deep (Porath 1993: 28). The remains that Porath and his team found of Channel E were of two types, which, he believed, represented two periods of construction. One was an open conduit made of small stones and mortar covered with horizontal stone slabs. The open conduit had a pink-tinged hydraulic plaster lining that Porath noted was typical of the third to fourth centuries C.E. (Porath 1993: 29). The other conduit was a pipeline.

In 1988, the Caesarea Combined Excavations North Coast Survey, a field survey of the coastal area north of Caesarea around that city's aqueducts up to the Nahal Tanninim, found parts of both of these conduit types (NC56). Most of the remains, however, were along the south bank of the Nahal Tanninim, angling toward the Low-level aqueduct. The section closest to the tel was the pipeline type, encased in *kurkar* blocks and concrete and resting on a *kurkar* shelf, which projected beyond the pipe ca. 26.5 cm on each side. The encased pipe lay in a 40 cm deep trench. The total width of this pipeline section was up to 1.55 m. Pipe sections were ca. 45.5 cm in length, and the pipes had an interior diameter of 12.5 cm (fig. 52). The North Coast Survey also recorded a similarly built tap line to nearby Tell Tadwira, which sits between Tel Tanninim and Caesarea and west of the High-level aqueduct. There the pipe was encased in small stones and concrete and laid on a *kurkar* foundation, and the entire pipe was covered with large flat stones. The Tadwira pipe sections were 47.5 cm in length with the familiar 12.5 cm interior diameter. At Tel Tanninim, the North Coast Survey also found an open channel in the vicinity of the closed one (NC55), although its direct correlation to the pipeline could not be discerned. The open line, built of *kurkar* slabs, was 40 cm wide (26 cm interior) and ran in a southeastern–northwestern direction. The Survey also recorded another open channel section that ran east–west about 90 m from the then northern edge of the Jisr az-Zarqa cemetery. Both open channel sections had been destroyed by the time the area was revisited in 1991.

The date of the Tanninim pipeline that led from Caesarea's High-level aqueduct was most clearly

Fig. 52.   *Encased ceramic water pipe in Channel E.*

demonstrated by the presence of a cross made of shells set into plaster just above the subterranean juncture of the main line and the tap (Porath 1993: 29). Those who built this junction, therefore, were Christians, or at least construction was done after the acceptance of Christianity in the empire. Small finds from within the mud at the bottom of the Jisr az-Zarqa tunnel indicated that the tunnel functioned into the Late Byzantine period. Excavators reported that the tunnel was certainly out of use before the ninth/tenth centuries c.e. (Porath 1996: 127). Tapping into a civic aqueduct was no small feat—technically or politically—and indicated that the decision to construct Channel E and to provide running water to Tel Tanninim was made by someone of importance, whether official or not.

Water reached the eastern ramp of Tanninim's water reservoir via a 13 cm-diameter ceramic pipe, set at an elevation of 2.35 m above sea level. A settling tank rested at the highest point of the ramp (5.54 m above sea level) that conveyed the pipeline along the south side of Tanninim's reservoir. The ascending ramp on the south face of the reservoir had a gradual rise, while that from the settling basin and western ramp toward the tel was even gentler.

The elevation of Caesarea's High-level aqueduct in the vicinity of Tel Tanninim is ca. 10.75 m above sea level, while the Low-level aqueduct is 5.50 m above sea level. The eastern ramp of the Tanninim reservoir's highest elevation of 5.54 m means that it could probably not have received water from the Low-level aqueduct. Porath's discovery of a pipeline off the subterranean tunnel suggests that the High-level aqueduct was indeed the source for Channel E, although excavation along the pipeline from Porath's probe to sections of the line close to Tel Tanninim would be necessary to prove the case. The intended target for the Tel Tanninim pipeline was the reservoir in Area B, as well as other structures on the site. While no hydraulic remains have been found on the tel proper (summit = 9.66 m above sea level) it is not out of the question that water from the High-level aqueduct could have provided water to that point.

AREA B

The Reservoir (L 2043)

Like parts of the pipeline toward Tel Tanninim, the upper reaches of a large hydraulic feature (L

Fig. 53.   *Ruins of reservoir in Area B.*

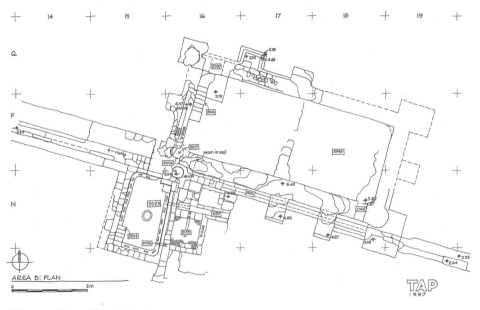

Fig. 54.   *Plan of Area B (1997).*

2043) had been known and visible for many years. The ruins stood ca. 1.50 m above the surrounding sand dunes, but the size, construction, and usage of the structure were not revealed and clarified until the TAP's 1996 and 1997 excavation seasons (fig. 53). This structure was a large construction, 15 × 7.5 m (13.60 × 5.44 m internal dimensions), built of unhewn *kurkar* stones. Builders constructed its north (W 2007) and south (W 2009) walls thicker than the other two. The structure was designed specifically to collect, hold, and channel water. Excavations revealed that the interior wall height was at least 2.75 meters; the floor elevation was at 3.75 m above sea level. To counter the water pressure's outward thrust on the walls, both at the top and bottom, the builders erected external buttresses at the corners and along the walls (fig. 54). The southern wall had three buttresses, the northern had at least two and the western had one. The full extent of the eastern wall has not been excavated, but it too probably had a mid-wall buttress. The southern wall of the reservoir (W 2009) was intricately built, since it served not only as an outer wall, but the aqueduct pipeline and its ramp abutted it. No doubt

Fig. 55.   *Stone ramp along south wall of reservoir.*

this necessitated additional support and construction. Excavators cleared only the northwestern buttress to its foundation, revealing two footings—one beneath the entire north wall and the other lower footing only beneath the buttress itself. The lower footing rested on bedrock (Stieglitz 1998: 58).

Builders constructed the ramp (L 2020) of mortared hewn stones along the reservoir's southern wall to carry the 13 cm ceramic pipeline upward, at a 40-degree slope, through two of the buttresses (figs. 55–56). A layer of mortar surrounded the pipe, and flat rectangular *kurkar* blocks encased it. Near the southwest corner of the reservoir, the pipeline conducted water into a terracotta tank (L 2017). This roughly round tank, 0.9 m in diameter, had a preserved wall height of 32 cm and a pebble floor with a plaster coating. Calcium carbonate covered the entire internal surface of this tank up to 5 cm thick (Stieglitz 1998: 61). A 15 cm-long ceramic pipe built into the reservoir's western wall, and now filled with ca. 3 cm of calcium carbonate, fed an open plaster-lined channel (L 2011) along the top of the wall that fed the water into the reservoir. Examination of both the tank and the pipe indicated lengthy accumulation of calcium carbonate, as evidenced by several layers of the material. Not all water, however, was diverted through this terracotta tank and into the reservoir. Water also passed through the tank and was conducted along the remainder of the southern wall, descending via the western ramp toward the mound of Tel Tanninim.

Another terracotta tank (L 2004), this one squared with rounded corners, ca. 0.75 m wide, existed at the highest point along the ramp with its base at an elevation of 5.54 m above sea level. It too had a pebble floor with a plaster coating. The plaster channel atop the reservoir's western wall also received water from here. Both tanks then served not only as junctions, but also probably as settling basins. The squared tank was bonded to the ramp and attached to a rebuilt wall section, which was indicated by a visible seam. The rebuilt area beneath the squared tank (L 2004), hewn versus unhewn stones elsewhere, implies that it was built later than the original wall of the reservoir. It probably means that it was more recent than the round tank (L 2017). The rebuilding of the tank and the wall seam suggests repairs made to the reservoir, perhaps as a result of damage by earthquakes. Such tanks probably served as distribution boxes, with pipes leading from them to other elements in the area.

Fig. 56.   *Stone ramp leading westward from the reservoir.*

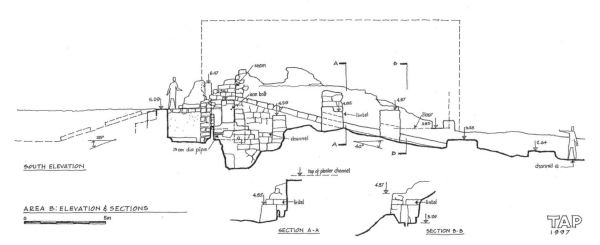

Fig. 57.   *Elevation and sections of Area B.*

The pipeline ramp that led westward from the reservoir (fig. 57) descended at a 35-degree slope, then leveled off a little more than six meters from the walls of the structure (Stieglitz 1998: 62). This water line, along with others, probably fed some of the hydraulic structures in nearby Area B2, as well as leading water on toward the tel (fig. 56).

Excavation of the reservoir revealed plastered walls, inside and out, and exterior plaster on the buttresses. The interior plaster was applied in two layers, totaling ca. 6 cm in thickness. The upper layer had the characteristic pink hydraulic plaster with a backing of large sherds, the latest dating to the sixth century C.E. This represents the final plastering of the structure, indicating that Caesarea's Channel A probably did not convey water to Tanninim much longer after that period. The lower layer was gray with inclusions of ash and burnt organic material. According to Porath (1988: 22), this type of plaster was characteristic of the Late Byzantine/Early Umayyad period, but Constantinian coins found in the southeast corner

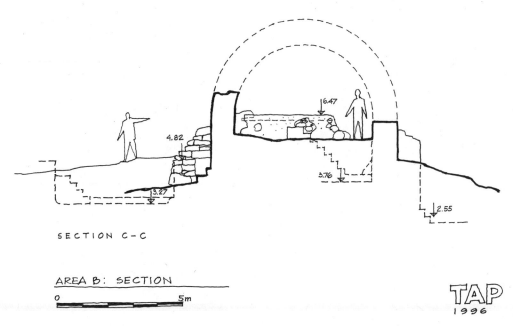

SECTION C–C

AREA B: SECTION

0   5m

TAP
1996

Fig. 58.   *Section C–C of the reservoir.*

of the reservoir indicated that the tank was in use earlier than this last plaster indicates (Stieglitz 1998: 58).

Calcium carbonate on the interior plaster of the reservoir indicated the maximum water depth at 2.72 m. This depth, in conjunction with the overall size of the building, gave it a balanced proportion of 5:2:1 (Stieglitz 1998: 58 n. 11). If water was kept constantly at that depth, the reservoir provided a ready-to-use water volume of a little more than 200 cubic meters. According to Peleg (2000: 242) this water volume and water depth probably meant that Tel Tanninim's reservoir really served more as a settling basin than a storage reservoir. While this may be true, it is also possible that Tel Tanninim's reservoir served as a type of mid-point water tower/reservoir from Caesarea's High-level aqueduct to some structure(s) at the lower slopes of Tel Tanninim. As shown by the watermarks in Caesarea's High-level aqueduct channels, it is highly unlikely that the Channel E aqueduct provided water to the reservoir at a consistent rate and/or volume.

Excavation also revealed a stairway (L 2016) leading along the western wall (W 2008) to the reservoir's floor, beginning about mid-wall and continuing north. These seven heavily plastered treads of hewn stones, ca. 75 cm wide, abutted the western wall. The current state of remains suggests that someone would have to step over the open plastered channel that runs atop this wall to access the stairs, presenting a somewhat problematic arrangement, even if the stairs only provided access for those who periodically cleaned the structure. A splash platform at the foot of the stairs indicated that water dropped from the plastered channel directly into the reservoir. Plaster covered the reservoir's stone and cement floor (F 2026) that sloped slightly downward east to west. Because the entire floor of the water tank has not been excavated, it is unknown whether there was an additional sunken settling basin or pipelines leading out closer to the floor. The remains of the reservoir's northern and southern walls curved inward at the top, indicating that the structure was roofed, probably by a barrel vault, while the thick calcium carbonate deposit on the interior walls indicated a relatively long period of use without cleaning (fig. 58).

At some time in its operational life, probably by the eighth century C.E., the reservoir ceased to serve its original function and became a dry structure, most likely a residence. This was clearly indicated by the creation of doors cut into the walls near the southeastern (L 2042) and northwestern (L 2057) corners and the insertion of a north–south

Fig. 59. *The southern fishpond (L 2023).*

wall that divided the tank into two rooms. In fact, the local fishermen reported a family living in the structure as recently as the mid-twentieth century. A 2 × 2 m probe in the northwestern corner of the reservoir produced a quantity of modern material culture, including Ottoman ceramic tobacco pipes (see Chapter IV.3) and even modern ammunition casings.

The Southern Fishpond (L 2023)

Immediately south of the reservoir, and bonded to its southwest corner and the eastern edge of the western/downward ramp, excavators found a 4.5 × 5.5 m fishpond (L 2023) oriented north–south, with internal dimensions of 2.75 × 5 m (see plan, fig. 54). Water from the southernmost round settling tank atop the reservoir wall appeared to feed this installation. Although the ceramic pipe descending from the tank into the fishpond is no longer extant, the idea that it existed is supported by the presence of a ca. 40 × 50 × 10 cm *kurkar* step (L 2040), a splash platform, plastered to the floor (F 2036) in the northwestern corner of the pond.

The *kurkar* stone walls of this fishpond varied in thickness, although all were half a meter or less. The interior hydraulic plaster of the walls, preserved to a height of 1.6 m, suggested a water volume of ca. 22 cubic meters for this fishpond. In the southwestern corner, a short flight of five plastered steps (L 2034), ca. 0.5 m wide, descended along the western wall northward to the floor (ca. 3.25 m above sea level). Excavation also revealed an off-centered elliptical settling basin (75 × 35 cm) in the fishpond floor. The presence of sixteen complete Gaza amphorae, each 72 cm long and embedded in a mortar casing at the junction of the walls and floor, clearly indicated that this structure was a fishpond and not a fountain or ornamental pool (fig. 59).

The amphorae, which served as individual cells (*speci*), were set lengthwise with the toe of one set into the mouth of the next. The rectangular opening cut into the side of each amphora allowed fish to enter and exit. Columella (*De Re Rustica* 8.17.6) was one of the first to recommend the creation of a series of "cells" within a fishpond that could protect the fish from the heat yet be open enough to allow water to circulate. He also recommended the erection of lattice gratings near outlet drains to keep fish from escaping. Fishponds with arrangements similar to that in Area B can be found in

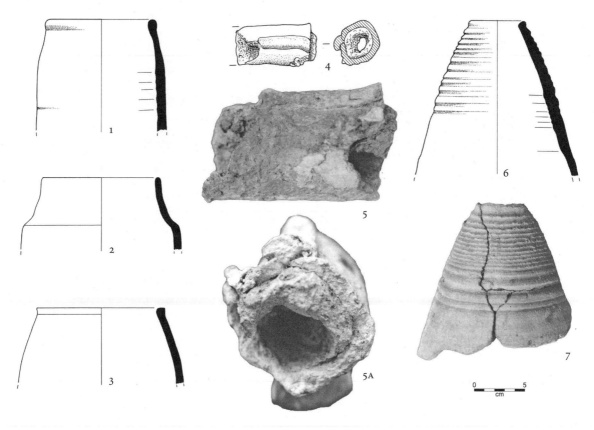

No.	Reg. No.	Locus	Description
1	0049/3	2000	Ceramic pipe rim; dark gray core between reddish yellow exterior surface (5YR 6/8), common white grits.
2	0057/1	2023	Ceramic pipe rim; light yellowish brown fabric (10YR 6/4).
3	0061/2	2031	Ceramic pipe rim; reddish brown clay (5YR 5/3, common spread of white inclusions.
4	M047	2100	Lead pipe fragment, 7.4 cm long; outside diameter 3.73 cm; heavily encrusted travertine deposit on interior; molded lengthwise lead ridge on exterior..
5–5A			Photographs of above.
6	0104/7	2041	Gaza amphora base fragment; broad ribbed walls to toe, which is missing; edges rounded for re-use as funnel(?); reddish yellow clay (5YR 5/8).
7			Photograph of above.

Fig. 60. *Water pipe fragments (1–5A) and funnel (?) (6–7).*

Caesarea's E-Field bath (Horton 1996: 177 n. 6), at Khirbet Sabiya and at Sataf (Ayalon 1979).

   A short section of an east-west ceramic pipe (L 2056) in the pond's eastern wall, about 20 cm above the floor, drained the structure. Iron bolts found near the western end of the pipe suggest the presence of one of Columella's recommended grates. Although excavators found no remains of the screens or grates in Area B, they recovered a large number of stone grates with drilled holes in Area B2. Higginbotham (1997: 13, 234 n.13) noted that stone grates were the best for all fishponds, because they do not corrode, warp or swell. Another interesting find from within the debris excavated inside the fishpond was a Gaza amphora base fragment cut to be utilized as a funnel (?) (fig. 60:6–7).

Fig. 61.   *Pool (L 2103) adjoining the southern fishpond.*

Although it is not possible to say exactly when this fishpond at Tanninim went out of use, the presence of Byzantine amphorae sherds on the floor, dating as late as the mid-seventh century C.E. (L 2031, Baskets 83–86), indicated it was open at least to that time. Whether it still functioned as a fishpond then is not clear.

Attached Pool (L 2103)

The ceramic pipe mentioned above joined the southern fishpond to a smaller pool (L 2103) to its east (fig. 61). This structure had none of the typical fishpond features. The 1.8 m square pool was built of *kurkar* ashlars with walls 0.5 m thick or less, and had a preserved wall height of approximately half a meter. Three phases of plaster on this small pool's southern wall indicated a relatively long period of use, at least into the Late Byzantine period, the date of the latest sherds within the backing. The floor of this pool was tessellated; the center stones were set on an angle, while several rows of stones around the border were not. The ceramic pipe that pierced the eastern wall of the southern fishpond (L 2023) entered the western wall of this small pool at an elevation of 3.62 m. The presence of this pipe above the floors of both the fishpond (at a height

of 39 cm) and of the small pool (at 31 cm) indicated that the water within both installations had to be at least that deep, and that it flowed from the fishpond into the pool. A small plastered step or platform rested along the southern wall, ca. 25 cm wide and ca. 75 cm long.

Excavators found fragments of ceramic water pipe sections (13 cm interior diameter) in the excavated area immediately near and inside the fishpond (L 2023; fig. 60:1–3). A 13 cm ceramic pipe (interior diameter), found in the center of the attached pool's northern wall at floor level, drained the water from it northward into a stone channel (L 2107). The floor immediately in front of the pipe was concave to assist in funneling the water from the pool into the pipe and the channel. The plaster-lined stone channel (L 2107) sloped west to east and carried a relatively shallow amount of water. A 7.4 cm-long lead pipe fragment with an exterior diameter of 3.75 cm and a wall thickness of 0.29 cm (fig. 60:4–5A), found in the rubble southwest of the pool, suggested that the attached pool might have been a fountain basin (Stieglitz 1998: 65). While this is certainly possible, it is more likely that it served as a place for fry or other fish that needed to be separated from the rest of the fish population. Regardless of its relationship to the pool, the lead

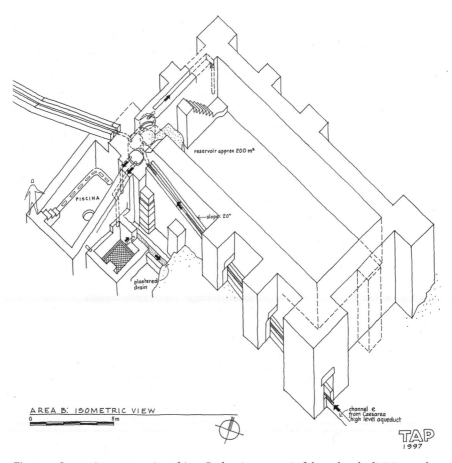

Fig. 62.   *Isometric reconstruction of Area B, showing reservoir, fishpond and adjoining pool.*

pipe fragment was probably related in some way to the reservoir or the pipeline from the Caesarea aqueduct, because it was completely filled with calcium carbonate deposits.

Outside the eastern wall (W 2105) of the Tel Tanninim pool, excavators found remnants of another tessellated surface, possibly indicating another pool or a paved surface. Eger (1998: 15–19) has noted a similar fishpond with smaller side pools at Caesarea. The pairing of a fishpond and an adjoining pool was also found in Area B2 at Tel Tanninim. The excavations in Area B thus revealed a well planned architectural hydraulic unit. It consisted of a substantial reservoir, fishpond and adjoining pool, all connected to the running water supply provided to Tel Tanninim via a tap line connected to Caesarea's High-level aqueduct (fig. 62).

AREA B2

The Large Fishpond (L 2251)

The biggest surprise during the excavation of Area B2 was the discovery of a beautifully preserved large fishpond (L 2251), 9.05 × 5.35 m and about 1.75 m deep, on a north–south orientation (fig. 63). Two parallel plastered lunettes, thought at first to be partially exposed plastered pipes, on the lip of the fishpond formed a channel of sorts between them around the top. The *kurkar* cobble and concrete walls of this man-made pond had a well preserved interior covering of hydraulic plaster, consisting of a thin white skim coat, a hydraulic layer, another white layer and finally a backing of large sherds. The *speci* for this pond were just below the bow of the walls, which are slightly convex. As in the southern fishpond in Area B, these Gaza amphorae were set into the wall lengthwise, toe-to-mouth, with the toes to the north. But unlike that smaller fishpond, these amphorae were offset in two rows at about mid-wall. The upper row of *speci* was at 2.79 m above sea level, the lower row at 2.57 m. The 14-cm openings into the embedded amphorae were round, rather than the rectangular openings of the amphorae in the southern fishpond of Area B. The amphora openings were precisely 61 cm apart (fig. 64).

The amphorae set in the southern end of the pond lay according to which side of a small pier they were placed. The toes of the amphorae on the east side of the pier pointed east, while those on the west side pointed west. Excavators uncovered the floor of the fishpond in the northwest corner and the southern end, revealing that the pebble and mortar floor (F 2310) sat upon a bedding of sand and pebbles. Like the walls of the pond, the floor showed little, if any, calcium carbonate accumulation. Strangely enough, there were also no readily visible watermarks on the pond walls. Excavators retrieved numerous ceramic pipe fragments and worked *kurkar* stones in various shapes and sizes from the sand within the fishpond, including several that had possible channel cuts. Winter weather between the 1998 and 1999 field seasons uncovered remains of a large pier (L 2301), half way along the western wall of L 2251, the top of which rested just below the lip. Made of *kurkar* cobbles and concrete, the pier (1.39 × 0.81 m) was built against the interior wall and then plastered at the same time as the fishpond (fig. 65).

Excavation revealed another internal buttress, or pier (L 2308), near the southeastern corner of the fishpond, although this one was much narrower than that found along the western wall. This element seems to have served a different purpose than its counterpart. Although it abutted the fishpond wall and was plastered like its counterpart, it was hollow vertically and had a square floor-level opening that went through the pond wall. Not far above this opening was a small cross shape modeled into the plaster surface (fig. 66). It is interesting that both the subterranean connection of Caesarea's aqueduct channel and Channel E, as well as this element had crosses adorning their junctures. It

is unclear at this time why the pier was hollow, particularly because it had been intentionally filled with cobbles and concrete. The opening at floor level led to a short pipe that allowed water to flow between the fishpond and an adjoining trapezoidal pool (L 2325) situated to its south.

A tessellated area (L 2302), possibly a pavement, topped the remains of the junction wall that joined the large fishpond to its attached pool, apparently providing a walkway or platform for those who maintained the ponds. This pavement had approximately the same elevation as the walls surrounding the fishpond. Unlike the pier of the buttress along the fishpond's western wall, this pavement was probably not meant to be at or slightly below the water level of the pond. Just above the small pier within the pond (L 2251), where the tessellated surface was missing, volunteers found the impression of a pipe. Perhaps this was in some manner associated with the vertical hollow of the pier. The trapezoidal pool's northern wall was lower than the tessellated surface and provided a stair step of sorts into that structure.

The Trapezoidal Pool (L 2325)

The pairing of a fishpond with a smaller pool, found in Area B, was thus repeated in Area B2. The trapezoidal pool (L 2325) associated with the large fishpond measured ca. 6 × 0.50–1 m (fig. 67). Unlike the fishpond and pool combination in Area B, those in Area B2 did not share a common wall. Also unlike the complex in Area B, in Area B2 the water appeared to flow from the pool to the pond, rather than the opposite. The elevation of the large fishpond's floor and that of its adjoining pool, as well as the elevation of the pipe through the hollow pier, indicate that water flowed south to north. Like the basin that adjoined the southern fishpond in Area B, the trapezoidal pool's floor (F 2330) was tessellated. Interestingly, the opening and pipe through the pier on the Area B2 fishpond's southern wall aligned perfectly with an opening found in the southern wall of the attached pool.

The southern wall (W 2336) of the trapezoidal pool was pierced not only by this "continuing" pipe but also by a north–south channel (L 2350) atop

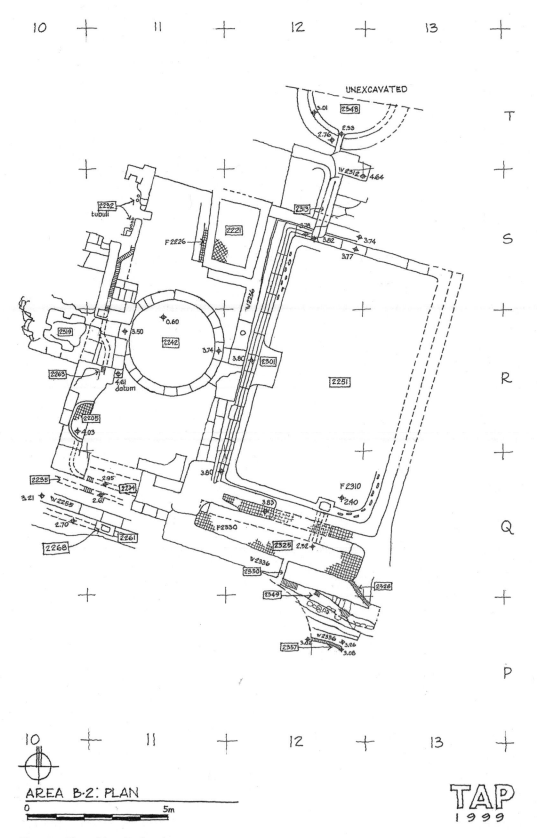

Fig. 63.   *Plan of Area B2 (1999).*

Fig. 64.   *General view and detail of the* speci *in the large fishpond (L 2251), Area B.*

Fig. 65.   *Pier (L 2301) in the large fishpond.*

Fig. 66.   *Inner buttress (L 2308) in the large fishpond; note modeled cross.*

the wall, and by a pipe leading from the basin's southeastern corner (L 2328). A channel, associated with the severed end of another pipe (L 2349), appeared to drain into the pool. The ceramic pipe in the southeastern corner of the pool was 13 cm in diameter (exterior), constricting to 10 cm (exterior) at a bend that turned the pipe eastward. This pipe drained water out of the basin and into an unexcavated area. Cuts in the stone wall in the corner of the pool accommodated this pipe, perhaps indicating a later phase. The one-meter thick eastern wall of the trapezoidal pool was much thicker than other walls in the complex, but because this area was not completely excavated, the reason for that thickness is currently unknown.

The excavators retrieved a surprising amount of material culture, concentrated around the sides and particularly heavy in the western end, from the trapezoidal pool. Primary loci within this pool (L 2304, 2326 and 2327) yielded numerous nails, bone fragments, an unreadable coin, pipe fragments, several Murex shells, a lamp fragment (**L059**) and various roof tile fragments. Although there was a variety of material culture, volunteers recovered an unexpectedly large quantity of glass, including pane glass. While this material cannot be related directly to the pool, and was probably refuse depos-

Fig. 67.   *The trapezoidal pool (L 2325).*

Fig. 68. *General view and detail of parallel ceramic water pipes south of the trapezoidal pool.*

ited into it, it is unlikely that the material had been carted a long way from its source. Ayalon (1979: 178) commented in his discussion of the material culture retrieved from Khirbet Sabiya that most of it was deposited after the basins were no longer used for their original purpose(s), and, therefore, does not tell much about the original use of the structure. However, it does tell something about what was built or went on around the structures being investigated.

The Southern Zone

South of the large fishpond and its associated trapezoidal pool in Area B2, excavators uncovered a series of pipes, channels and ledges all oriented in an east–west direction (fig. 68). One of the pipe fragments (**I006**), found in the upper matrix of the southern part of Area B2 (L 2227), was inscribed in Greek with the word "(of) Hesiod." To the right of the name was what appeared to be an animal figure, possibly a ram. This may be the sign of the pipe fabricator or possibly a waterworks official (see Chapter IV.3.A4). The pipe fragment was made of a dark gray/brown fabric and found in a hard packed locus that included pebbles, shells, burnt plaster and mortar.

An extremely thick sand overburden covered the elements in this southern zone, which possibly ties Areas B and B2 together. The excavation of this area, unfortunately, began late in the 1999 field season and thus excavators cleared only a small portion. Enough was uncovered, however, to further complicate the picture of water distribution and use. Adjacent to the southern wall of the trapezoidal pool, excavation revealed sections of an east–west 16.5 cm-diameter ceramic pipe (L 2349) *in situ*. These somewhat curved sections revealed that water flowed westward through this pipe, its water source possibly the reservoir or the aqueduct pipeline itself. The pipe rested on a plastered ledge and abutted a wide stone and cement channel (ca. 17 cm) to its south, which had a lower elevation than the pipe. South of the channel was another plastered ledge, which was adjacent to Wall 2356, which in turn was adjacent to another smaller (10 cm diameter) ceramic pipe (L 2357) that was also oriented east–west and had a westward flow. This pipe had a slight arc with the western end bending south.

The Well (L 2242)

Another surprising discovery in Area B2 was the presence of a large, 3 m-diameter well (L 2242) west of the large fishpond. Built of well hewn *kurkar* mortared stones and unlined except for a plaster lip on the top course, this water supply element appeared to be a separate water source for the fishpond, at least at some period of use. Unfortunately, time and manpower prevented excavators from reaching the bottom (water level) of the well. It appears from the alignment of the walls east and west of the well, which have an almost true north–south orientation, that they were constructed at a different time than the large fishpond. The latter's alignment was actually off a few degrees east of north. This realignment indicates that the large fishpond and the well were probably not built at the same time.

The wall immediately west of the fishpond (L 2251) and east of the well was actually a series of walls butted against one another that were of different thickness and construction. These walls, however, did not run the full length of the pond, but were of various lengths. A small gap between the lip of the pond at its southern end and its abutting wall to the west (W 2320) flared slightly at its northern end. Another gap between the wall assemblage east of the well, including W 2257 and the northern end of the fishpond's western wall (W 2247) also existed. There the space was much larger and filled with stone and concrete. Excavation revealed a small vertical posthole, 7.5 cm square, near the juncture of the wall (W 2256) and the well platform, approximately even with the northernmost edge of the fishpond's western pier (L 2301). This hole appeared to be associated with the water-wheel mechanism. Wall 2256, associated with the well and not the large fishpond, appears to have been in place when a small basin (L 2221, discussed below) and W 2262 were installed.

It is probable that at an early phase the large fishpond received water from a source other than the reservoir or the well (L 2242). This was suggested by the presence of a stone-cut plastered channel (L 2313), ca. 22 cm wide (narrowing to 9 cm), and a marble spout at the northwestern corner of the fishpond that sloped inward toward the pool. The slab's alignment with the channel formed by the two parallel plastered lunettes around the pond's western wall and northwestern end, suggested that water came along the fishpond wall and then dropped into it via the marble slab (fig. 69). The presence of the north–south channel immediately north of and also adjoining the marble slab, however, suggested that the pond was fed by some water source to the north. Elevations of the channels and the marble slab complicated the situation somewhat, although it can be stated that it was more likely that water came via the northern source. While clearing the northern end of the fishpond (L 2251) and the zone immediately to its north, excavators removed a large channel piece (0.33 × 1.4 × 0.44 m), unlike any *in situ* pieces, that had been intentionally filled with concrete, cobbles and pottery sherds. The slightly arced channel had 11- to 14-cm widths. The piece was so heavy that it took more than six volunteers and staff to shift it out of the area. Although not found *in situ*, this element probably also played a role in the water supply of this area (fig. 70).

Water-Wheel Mechanism

Several elements found near the fishpond suggest the existence of a water-wheel mechanism for well L 2242. The pier (L 2301) inside the western wall of the large fishpond was probably associated with the mechanism, as was the posthole found in the wall abutting the large fishpond's western wall. Niches on the eastern and western side of the well apparently accommodated vertical posts that supported the water-wheel. A 1.25 × 1.5 m stone pier (L 2319) on the western edge of the excavated area in B2, reinforced with bricks along its northern and western faces, braced wooden poles also associated with the mechanism (fig. 71). Locus 2322, immediately above the pier, included a Gaza amphora sherd that dated from the fifth to the mid-seventh centuries C.E. The final confirmation of the use of an water-wheel in Area B2 was the recovery of several water-wheel jar fragments from the loci around the well.

The most complete water-wheel jar fragment recovered from Area B2 (**C045**), from L 2240 in the

Fig. 69. *Northern inlet to large fishpond in Area B2.*

Fig. 70. *Filled channel fragment from earlier phase of large fishpond in Area B2.*

area between the well and the northern basin (L 2221), contained the entire mouth, the externally-ribbed neck and part of the body. The mouth had a 7.88 cm exterior diameter (6.36 cm interior), then constricted at the neck (Chapter III.2.B). Based on Ayalon's chronology, this jar is unquestionably Byzantine (Ayalon 2000: 222, No. 4). The locus in which this fragment was found also yielded six coins, most of which dated from the fifth and sixth centuries. Fragment **C058**, a water-wheel jar from

Fig. 71.   *Pier (L 2319) for the water-wheel mechanism.*

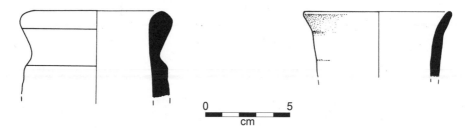

Fig. 72.   *Two rim fragments of water-wheel jars.*

the heavy sand layer (L 2222), appears to have been reused. It had an 8-cm mouth, a ribbed neck and a 0.9 cm-thick body. Plaster and mortar covered the exterior of this fragment, while calcium carbonate filled its interior. Two other fragments, sherds **0048/15** from the surface (L 2000) and **0095/3** from the mass of debris inside the southern fishpond of Area B (L 2023), are probably also from Byzantine water-wheel jars (fig. 72). Fragment **0048/15** (7.5 YR 8/4) has a mouth diameter of 9.2 cm with a rim 1.4 cm-thick and a body 1.08 cm-thick. In general, the water-wheel jars in Israel appear to date from end of the second/beginning of the third century C.E. through the early Islamic period, although Ayalon has also found examples that dated to the Crusader and Mamluk periods. Those found at Tel Tanninim appear to be Byzantine in date.

The use of a water-wheel mechanism, attested in Talmudic sources of the Byzantine era, allowed its builders to utilize the well to supply water for the large fishpond. This particular water-lifting device is known by many names, including the Arabic name *saqiya*, pot garland, chain of pots and Persian wheel, among others. In Spanish, a device on which the pots are tied directly to the wheel was called *noria* (from Arabic *na ʿurah*).

Water-wheel jars, or *saqiya* pots, have been found throughout the Middle East, and indeed continue to be manufactured and used in India, Egypt and elsewhere. John Oleson (1984: 224) stated that these pots, with their characteristic indented necks and knobbed feet, were probably first used in Egypt in the late third/early fourth century C.E. The primary characteristics of these jars are a broad mouth with a slightly everted rim, no handles, a narrowed neck or possibly a narrowed body, and some type of protrusion at the base. Such pots have been found in Israel at Yavne-Yam (Ayalon 1999), Kefar-Manda in the Galilee (Oleson 1984: 217, table 3; Schioler 1973: 100–101), Khirbet Ibreikas south of Hadera (Kletter and Rapuano 1998: 52–53), Dor, Tell Qasile, Horvat 'Uza, Akhziv (Ayalon 2000: 221–23), Kafr ¿Ara, Caesarea, Jalame, Kefar Saba, Nahal Shahaq, Khirbet Sabiya, and Abu Suwwana, along with numerous unpublished examples. The work of Ayalon (2000) on these water-wheels, and others in Israel, provides a typology and chronology.

Although the water-wheel was typically associated with irrigation, at least at Tel Tanninim it was associated with aquiculture. Several well, water-wheel and pool combinations have been found in Israel, including those at Kefar Saba (Ayalon 1998: 9) and Yavne-Yam (Ayalon 1999: 73). The work at Kefar Saba uncovered a waterwheel, well, sedimentation basin and large reservoir that were part of an industrial section of the community. All components, including a winepress, pottery kiln, and the water-lifting grouping dated to the Byzantine period. Ayalon noted that residents intentionally placed the industrial zone, just like today, outside and downwind of the settlement. At Yavne-Yam, the well and an earlier pool dated to the fourth century C.E., while the waterwheel mechanism was added at the end of the fifth century and was out of use by the mid-sixth century. Unlike the situation with the well in Tel Tanninim's Area B2, the bottom of which was still not reached, the 5.5 m-deep Yavne-Yam well yielded pottery dating from the Byzantine to the Mamluk period. Like the situation at Tel Tanninim, however, there was also a shallow basin and a water reservoir nearby. The Yavne-Yam waterwheel did not supply water to a fishpond (Ayalon 1999: 72–73). Water-wheels described elsewhere also provided water for baths, fishponds and industrial installations (Ayalon 2000: 219).

Animal power, probably a mule, donkey or ox, provided the propulsion for the wheel mechanism. Although there were, and are, examples of two animals yoked to turn the mechanism, it is more likely that only one was needed (Venit 1988:

74 n.15). At Tel Tanninim, the animal(s) probably walked in a counterclockwise direction west of the excavated region of Area B2 (fig. 73). One of the wall paintings from the Wardian painted tomb in Egypt studied by Venit (1987: 71–91; 1988: 219–222) clearly shows a water-wheel mechanism being turned counterclockwise by two oxen. It is likely that the Tel Tanninim system was a later development in the machinery, because of the closeness of the animal (power) and the horizontal wheel (gearing) to the well, which made it more efficient. More uncertain is whether the wheel within the well turned north–south or east–west, although the niches in the eastern and western walls of the well suggest the former. The biggest unknown, however, is whether the Tanninim water-wheel jars were lashed directly to the wheel or suspended from a rope/chain attached to the wheel. Based on the diameter of the well, its unknown depth (more than 2.5 m) and other research, we have chosen to reconstruct this water-wheel with a chain of pots (fig. 74). Hill (1997: 135) has remarked that the "chain of pots" is the most common way to draw water from wells and is the most effective method to raise water to a greater height.

The Second Well (L 2348)

The excavations also unearthed a second well (L 2348), situated north of the large fishpond (fig. 63). Part of the opening of this well was discovered in the final days of the 1999 season below a wall that supported the north–south channel that fed the large fishpond. The instability of the wall (W 2312), made of *kurkar* blocks, bricks, mortar and plaster and partially resting on sand, caused it to collapse during excavation. Upon removal of the wall debris, volunteers uncovered the well cut mortared *kurkar* blocks that formed the well rim immediately north of the wall. A *kurkar* platform (L 2345) surrounded this 2.5 m-diameter well, while a layer or course of mortared cobbles faced with plaster rested just inside the lip of the well. Five interior courses of the well were exposed to a depth of about 1 m. Many of the stones within showed an accumulation of calcium carbonate, possibly from a leak in the nearby channel (L 2313). The most

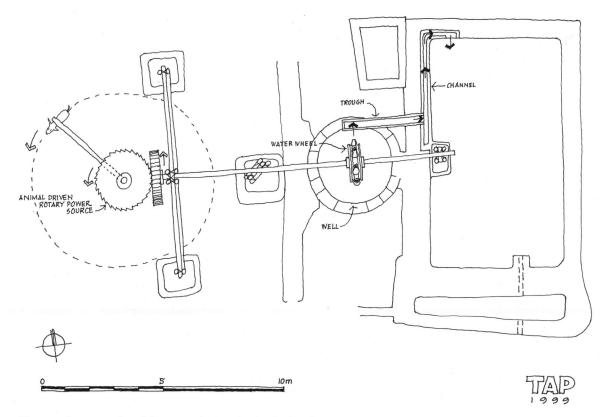

Fig. 73. *Reconstruction of the water-wheel mechanism in Area B2.*

perplexing aspect of this water feature was that it appeared to have been intentionally filled with concrete, like several other elements discovered through excavation. The entire well rim was not excavated, nor was the interior of the well totally revealed. A partially filled channel (L 2351), cut into the lip of the well, sloped southward toward the previously mentioned north–south channel (L 2313). Based on the current evidence, this well probably provided water for the large fishpond at an early phase, predating the well L 2242 and its water-wheel mechanism. Excavation of this area did not reveal any material associated with a water-wheel, thus it is unknown how the well supplied water for the fishpond.

The Northern Zone

Further excavation of the northern zone of Area B2 will undoubtedly clarify mechanisms for the water flow in this area, but at this time the picture is not completely clear. The elevation of the marble slab

(3.82 m above sea level) is crucial to how the water flowed in the fishpond by this method, namely, not via the water-wheel mechanism that raised water from well L 2242. The problem lies with the channel along the western wall of the fishpond, which has an elevation varying between +3.80 and +3.78 m, i.e., slightly lower than that of the marble slab. The north–south channel feeding the pond from the north, however, could definitely have brought water from north of the fishpond. Its northern elevation was +3.87 m and dropped to +3.84 m closer to the marble slab. In addition to these elements, this excavation zone also included a possible east–west sewer line (L 2354), as well as several ledges, platforms, and a *in situ* 13-cm pipe section curving northwest–southeast. Water definitely flowed through this area over a period of time, as indicated by the accumulation of calcium carbonate at the extant southern end of the pipe mentioned above, the western face of channel of L 2313, and the northern face of W 2324. Excavation began on a north–south wall to the west of this

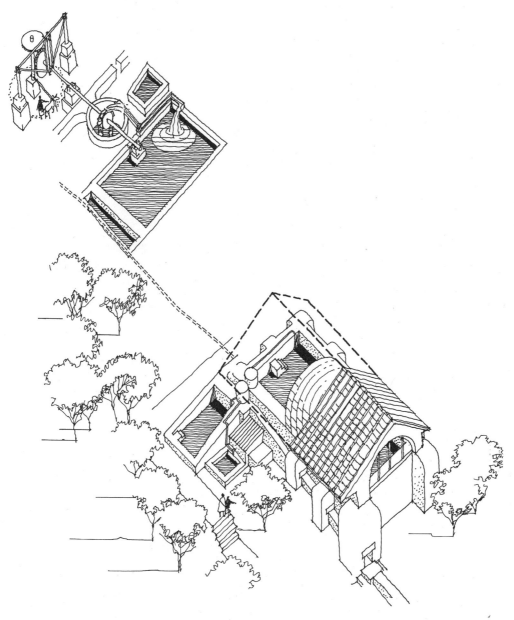

Fig. 74. *Isometric reconstruction of Areas B and B2.*

water-conducting northern zone in the final days of the 1999 field season. This wall, only three courses high, rested on a soil layer heavy with material culture. Unfortunately, time did not allow for the further excavation of this area.

The Western and Southern Zones

The wall west of the well L 2242 had several roles in the water system and the use of the area in gen-

eral. Most noticeable on this wall abutting the well was its prominent arched niche, with a stone sill between two wall sections (W 2203 and W 2215). This niche and its counterpart on the other side of the well were associated with the water-wheel mechanism. Excavators recorded that the stones were set differently in the wall associated with the niche, indicating that it appeared to be rebuilt. South of the niche, just above the well opening was an arced plaster shadow (L 2245). Its distinct lines

Fig. 75. *Imprint of plaque above the well (L 2242).*

hinted at the possibility of some sort of plaque or attached element (fig. 75).

South of the niche was an entire array of water-related elements. Wall 2203 had several jogs as it proceeded south. A 13-cm closed pipe (L 2263) near the top of the wall angled down to the south, although not enough of it was extant to determine its role in the overall water system. The end of the pipe, as well as the wall, seemed to end at a pit at the northern end, the bottom of which was never reached. The eastern face of the wall near the pipe was covered with a calcium carbonate cascade; at least at some time water dripped in this area from a not-so-well-sealed pipe. A ground-level stone platform (L 2248) rested in the corner created by the junction of well L 2242 and Wall 2203. The exterior faces of the wall in this area were plaster covered.

Farther along the wall south of the closed pipe was the western half of an intentionally cut basin (L 2205). Hydraulic plaster with a backing of large Byzantine sherds coated the basin's walls; its floor was tessellated. It is likely that this basin, like the nearby pipe, was intentionally filled at some time. Excavators found a solid concrete/mortar deposit (L 2238) above the tessellation, particularly in the southern end of the basin. The height of the basin's

floor in relation to what could possibly be a walking surface beside it implied that eastern access to whatever was inside had to be done while standing. The area to its west was not excavated.

South of the half basin, on the other side of a possible east–west wall (W 2231) that was also severed, was a series of pipes and ledges similar to those south of the trapezoidal pool, which was directly east of this zone. Interestingly, the two main pipes found in this area also appeared to be intentionally severed like the basin mentioned above. Excavators found an additional remnant of both pipes beyond the resulting gap of 63–70 cm (fig. 76). An ashlar and plaster surface (F 2230) encased and surmounted the northernmost and higher of the two pipes (L 2234). The pipe had a top elevation of 2.95 m above sea level, and water flowed through it in a westward direction. The pipe, however, was almost completely clogged with calcium carbonate, suggesting that it received water from the aqueduct tap pipeline via the reservoir. The more southern and lower of the two pipes (L 2235) was 10 cm in diameter (interior) and, unlike L 2234, was not encased. Instead it rested on a concrete platform (L 2237) and was covered by a layer of flat stones. This pipe's greater visibility showed its 40-cm sections, and had a top elevation of +2.67 m

Fig. 76.   *Pipes and severed basin west of the large fishpond.*

above sea level. Like its counterpart, it also flowed westward, but unlike L 2234 it was not filled with calcium carbonate. The extant western end of the higher elevation pipe (L 2234) appears to curve to the north. Perhaps its water supplied the severed half basin (L 2205), a relatively short distance from it, although it would have had to go upward almost one meter to reach the basin floor.

The platform and stone covering of pipe L 2235 were reminiscent of the aqueduct pipeline east of the reservoir and its remnants on the descending ramp. Unfortunately, the distance between these pipes (L 2234 and L 2235) and those found late in the 1999 field season south of the trapezoidal pool has not been excavated. They do not appear to line up exactly with one another, either horizontally or vertically, but only excavation can reveal their precise relationship with each other and the tap pipeline on the ramp. In his work on water-lifting devices for the UN Food and Agriculture Organization (FAO), Frankel (1986:14) makes sure to point out to his readers, and those who might want to build various devices, that water pipes do not really need "accurate leveling and grading." Landels (1980: 37) reminded his readers that a pipe "can slope up or down at any angle, provided that it does not rise at any point above the level of the intake," i.e., the

point of origin. Thus, the fact that the pipes south of the trapezoidal pool (L 2325) and pipes L 2234 and L 2235 do not appear to align horizontally does not mean that they are not part of the same pipelines.

Additional water-related elements lay south of the severed east–west pipes, including another pipe (L 2261) covered with a relatively thick layer of small stones and mortar. The plastered rounded top of this covering was pierced with a circular opening (L 2268) that led to the pipe (L 2261) below. Excavators uncovered the remains of a tessellated floor on the western end of this pipe or drainage line. Some of the tessellated pavement was *in situ,* while others segments were found upside down.

In the opposite direction, north of the well (L 2242), but still west of the large fishpond, another pipe (L 2263) sat atop the north–south wall (W 2215), its southern end resting on a marble slab *in situ* (fig. 59). This pipe ran south to north along the wall for about two meters before it made two 45-degree turns and angled down 34 cm onto a stone shelf. Unlike the closed pipe to its south, this 10.25 cm-diameter (exterior) pipe had extremely thin walls and showed no accumulation of calcium carbonate. Its appearance was more reminiscent of an air pipe than a water pipe. A series of stepped stones

Fig. 77.   *Remains of* tubuli, in situ *west of the large fishpond and north of well L 2242.*

led from the extant top of Wall 2215 to the surface adjacent to the well below. The possibility that this wall-top pipeline was actually an air conduit was furthered by the presence of six vertical *tubuli* (L 2232) found to its north (fig. 77). Four *tubuli* remained west of the pipeline wall, south of a gap in that wall; the other two were on the opposite side of the gap. Four brick columns were found in the area of the *tubuli*, two abutting the vertical air ducts and two others not far to the west. The extremely fragile, thin-walled *tubuli* were 8–9 cm in diameter (interior); not all were made of the same fabric. A floor pavement stone bridged the gap between the two *tubuli* groups.

The presence of a probable air pipe, the *tubuli*, and the brick piers suggest that a bath-house may be found in the area northwest of Area B2. Excavators encountered a hard packed dark brown layer (L 2225) in the area east of the *tubuli* and north of the well. This locus lay on an almost direct line from W 2215 to the nearby basin (L 2221) and was filled with square, rectangular and round bricks, thin cut marble pieces and construction debris, including four L-shaped *kurkar* stones. The nature of this locus suggested to excavators that a massive brick column fell in a northeasterly direction after the area went out of use. This column fell upon

a tile surface (L 2272), the impressions of which were extant. The matrix for this surface consisted of pebbles and plaster, and abutted the platform (L 2262) that supported the nearby tessellated basin (L 2221). Excavation revealed several surfaces on the west side of the tessellated basin (L 2221), including a tessellated surface (F 2226) at the base of the basin's western wall, as well as a lower stone surface that curved inward. Each surface was covered with a thick sand layer (L 2222), indicating some period of disuse before the next surface was erected. The tessellated floor (F 2226) appears to have been destroyed (or replaced) before the sand layer (L 2222) accumulated.

Tessellated Basin (L 2221)

The small tessellated basin (L 2221) in this zone was a poorly constructed element, with highly friable walls made of rubble held together primarily by the plaster facings. The basin was ca. 2.25 m north–south and 1.25–1.5 m east–west. Plaster was extant on all interior wall faces, as well as on the outside face of the western wall. All had a coating of calcium carbonate, particularly the interior face of the eastern wall (28 cm). White *tesserae*, set on the diagonal, covered the floor that sloped about three degrees to the north, particularly in the northeast corner. Unlike the walls, however, the floor had no calcium carbonate accumulation. Excavation revealed no water outlet, or inlet, for this feature, although the heavy calcium carbonate on the interior eastern wall perhaps suggests a possible direction of a water inlet. The western and southern walls of basin L 2221 rested on a platform, perhaps indicating that it was a later addition to the complex of installations in this zone. The basin's placement and relationship to the large fishpond in Area B2, the platform beneath the southern and western walls, and the series of possible surfaces beneath its western wall suggested that basin L 2221 was constructed at a different time, probably later than the large fishpond.

DISCUSSION

It is clear from the installations uncovered in Areas B and B2 that water-related operations dominated this region of the site. It was in this area that water traveled from the reservoir toward the tel, and it was also here that someone endeavored to store, raise and possibly breed fish. The reservoir at the eastern edge of the excavated area undoubtedly went through several phases, two of which involved the actual movement of water, while the last one changed it from a hydraulic installation to one of habitation. Certainly by the time the second settling tank (L 2004), which either replaced or supplemented the first one, was built atop the southern wall of the reservoir, the plan involved the creation of the adjoining southern fishpond (L 2023). The large quantity of Late Byzantine/Early Islamic pottery found crushed upon the floor of the southern fishpond suggests that the structure had been built by that time. It is unknown whether a collapse necessitated the repair of the wall beneath the second reservoir tank or if the wall was simply altered as a result of the new building. The reservoir, while operational, however, always received water from Caesarea's Channel A, via Channel E, and some portion of that water went into the southern fishpond.

Although it is possible that the southern fishpond's adjoining pool was a later addition, the presence of the same combination in Area B2 and elsewhere suggests that it was part of the regular building practice for fishponds. It has been suggested that the tessellated pool in Area B was a fountain, but the relatively small amount of water that came from the pond, under almost no head, indicates otherwise. It is more probable that the adjoining pool served as a receptacle for fry or other fish that needed to be kept separate from those in the fishpond.

Porath (1996: 127) recorded that Caesarea's Channel A probably operated into the Late Byzantine period and was out of use by the ninth or tenth century C.E. He also noted that the hydraulic plaster lining within Channel E, which conducted water from Channel A toward Tel Tanninim, dates to the third–fourth centuries C.E. This information suggests that water was first conveyed toward Tel Tanninim in the fourth century C.E., and water continued to flow through that pipeline possibly into the Islamic period. This would fit with the fact that the latest hydraulic lining of the reservoir in Area B dated to the sixth century. It is, however, difficult to believe that the lining continued in use, without repair or replacement, for an extended period. While it is somewhat speculative to use fill material to assist in dating a structure or an installation, the material culture recovered from within the reservoir suggests that it went out of use by the eighth century C.E. Even this date, which required the latest hydraulic plaster lining to function for two centuries, is pushing the limit.

It is reasonable to assume that the southern fishpond and its attached pool were built after the reservoir. However, the southern pond did receive water from the reservoir through one of the distribution box settling tanks. Pottery sherds on the floor of the southern pond suggest that this structure was open until the seventh century C.E., although it is unknown if it still operated as a fishpond at that time.

The connection and the sequencing of the water installations and related elements in Area B2 are more complicated. It appears that the multitude of east–west oriented pipes found throughout the southern zone of this area indicate that water flowed from the reservoir toward the tel. Whether it reached the top of the tel via one or many of these pipes, or was used for some other purpose in the area between B2 and the tel, has yet to be revealed. As with Area B, there was little pottery predating the Byzantine period retrieved from the Area B2 excavations. In fact, only a few pieces of material culture retrieved from either Area B or B2 predate the fourth century C.E. For example, of the 13 lamps recovered from Areas B and B2, only one (**L002**) was Hellenistic (second–early first century B.C.E.), and only one (**L055**) was known to be Roman (end of the first to early third century C.E.). All others were Byzantine. Ten of the lamps were classified as Type Bb, which at nearby Caesarea date from the fourth–seventh centuries, including the Byzantine-Islamic transition period of the second half of the seventh century. Six of the recovered lamps came from the trapezoidal pool (L 2235) and another six from the area immediately south of it.

The presence of numerous fish-related objects—everything from fishhooks (**M003**) and lead net weights (**M028, M107, M112, M127, M130**) to a bronze net mender (**M075**) and a large number of stone grate pieces (18 pieces from B and B2), used to keep fish from escaping through the fishpond inlets and outlets—indicates the prominence of the fish industry. Providing water for the freshwater fishponds, however, seems to have presented a bigger challenge and one that changed throughout the period of operation.

The presence of fishponds in this area is not surprising, because of its ecological location, i.e., its proximity to the Nahal Tanninim and the latter's confluence with the Mediterranean, as well as the site's location beside, or maybe astride, a major north–south road. Whether the fish, possibly tilapia, were all for local consumption, i.e., area residents and travelers, or available to a wider population, is not known. The number of saltwater, freshwater and brackish water fishponds found on the site, however, hint at providing them to a greater populace, including that at Caesarea.

It is possible that at some time water came to the large fishpond in Area B2 via a pipe, or pipes, from the reservoir and channeled around the western side and northwestern corner of the fishpond. However, the lack of calcium carbonate within that channel and the relatively small amount found on the walls of the fishpond indicates that if this water source was used, it was not used for long. It is fairly evident that the water conveyed via Caesarea's High-level aqueduct pipelines, having come through and from karstic terrain, contained a large amount of calcium carbonate.

The remains of the filled channel segment found during the excavation of the large fishpond in Area B2 indicate that at some time another channel provided water, but that means of conveyance was intentionally halted. Because this segment was filled and discarded, it is likely that it represents an early method of water conveyance either to the large fishpond or to some other nearby water installation.

It is likely that the large fishpond received most of its water through the years from wells, either the one to its west or that to its north. Unfortunately, the northern zone has not yet been excavated fully enough to determine when or how it furnished water to the pond, or if and when, in fact, it was intentionally filled as it currently appears. It does seem that the large fishpond and the trapezoidal pool, which were part of the same construction phase, were not built at the same time as the well and the facilities to the west. The difference in orientation and the necessity to fill in the space between the fishpond's western wall and the series of walls east of the well support the proposal that the pond predated the digging of the well and the construction of the water-wheel mechanism.

It is known from an inscription along Caesarea's High-level aqueduct, near the area known as the diversion, that Flavius Florentius, proconsul of Palestine in 385 C.E., repaired the aqueduct. Choricius tells us that in the sixth century C.E. the proconsul Flavius Stephanus not only repaired the Caesarea aqueduct, but also built a new bath and water supply system for his native town of Gaza. Choricius tells that the flow through Caesarea's aqueduct had slowed so much that some of the city's fountains failed and others dropped in yield (Mayerson 1986: 269–72). Either incident could have prompted the inhabitants of Tel Tanninim to find new means by which to provide water for their fish industry installations. A well with a water-wheel mechanism would do just that.

The trapezoidal pool (L 2325), built at or near the same time as the large fishpond, probably played an integral role in the latter's use. Unlike the fishpond/pool combination south of the reservoir in Area B, the water in Area B2 flowed into the fishpond at one time from the trapezoidal pool, which appears to have had both water inlets and outlets. Like the other adjoining pool, it too could have been for fry or fish that needed to be separated from the others for some reason.

Finally, there was an abundance of material culture retrieved from Areas B and B2. Although these items do not necessarily have anything to do with the activities that occurred in the areas, they must have served a role somewhere on the site. Beside the large number of fish and fishing-related items, there was a large number of roof tiles, both pan and *imbrices*, marble floor tiles, *opus sectile* tiles, including some that had been reused, iron nails and spikes and plenty of building material. There was even an Umayyad flask (**R002**; see Chapter IV.3.B4), found in the early days of the excavation of Area B, with a parallel from Pella, dated to about 720 C.E. (McNicoll, Smith and Hennessey 1982: 169:1). The most unexpected material culture, however, was the large amount of glass, including pane glass, retrieved from the excavations (see Chapter IV.1).

Phasing and dating the elements found in Area B2 remains difficult. Not enough was gleaned from the few sherds retrieved from beneath the floor of any of the installations or elements to give a more precise date of construction. It is unfortunate that much of the evidence still rests on dating the fill material of the loci within those installations and elements. However, it can be stated that the water-wheel jars retrieved from the excavations appear to date to the fifth–sixth centuries C.E. Several architectural elements have sherds, to which a Byzantine date has been assigned, utilized as part of their hydraulic lining. While the sherds have a wide range of dates (fourth–seventh centuries), the coins suggest that the early phases date to the fourth–sixth centuries.

The excavation of Areas B and B2 at Tel Tanninim clearly indicates that this area served as the site's industrial area, one that focused on fish. It is also clear that many of the hydraulic installations there supported this endeavor. While it is true that the initial undertaking, that of bringing water to Tel Tanninim, could not have been accomplished without tapping Caesarea's civic aqueduct, the presence of wells provides proof that there was subsurface water available on the site. Because of the importance of the reservoir in water distribution on the site, it must have been among the first hydraulic installations constructed during the Byzantine period. Thus, evidence in Areas B and B2 points to a Byzantine date for construction of these hydraulic installations, probably in some way associated with the renewed habitation on the site of Tel Tanninim beginning in the Early Byzantine period (fourth century C.E.), and possibly a result of it. There is little doubt that this renewed settlement on the site took place as a result of the municipal expansion of Caesarea.

The full extent of the fish industry at Tel Tanninim, indeed, of all the water structures and elements on the site, is not yet known. The region of Tel Tanninim, however, was extremely active and flourishing, at least in the Byzantine period. After the site was reoccupied, probably in the fourth century C.E., the need for water continued to grow along with the site. Over time the needs for and the means of providing water changed, as did the hydraulic installations. Only further excavation of the northern area of B2, the area between Areas B and B2, and west of Area B2 can, hopefully, clarify many of the questions posed by the Tanninim Archaeological Project excavations.

4. A Fishpond and Bath-House
(Area D)

by Robert R. Stieglitz

Remains of several rock-cut installations were situated on the beach, below the northeast edge of Tel Tanninim, some 20 meters west of the terminus of the Ottoman bridge (fig. 15). The ruins included a well preserved fishpond with an outlet to the sea and were obviously connected with marine and/or riverine fishing activities. The area had been previously surveyed, as noted in Chapter I, particularly after winter storms in the early 1990s had removed some of the sand cover and had exposed parts of rock-cut installations.

In 1996, the TAP explored this region of the beach, which we named Area D, beginning with the remains of a tessellated floor of a small tank found under a shallow sand layer. In 1997, TAP began excavations in Area D and soon discovered that to the south there was also a long wall and a bath-house situated south of the shore remains. The wall extended from the foot of the Ottoman bridge, running to the northwest, and terminating at the edge of the mound, a distance of some 35 m. The bath-house was situated immediately south of this wall.

A BRACKISH WATER FISHPOND

The most prominent feature unearthed at the water's edge, north of the wall (W 4007) that separated the rock-cut installations from the bath-house, was a large trapezoidal fishpond (*piscina*), cut into the bedrock at an elevation of 0.2 to 0.5 m above sea level (fig. 78). When its edges were first exposed, it was found to be completely filled with clean sand. Most of the sand was removed mechanically to enable drawing the structure, and to explore any architectural features within the pool. No ceramics, nor any other material culture, was found within the fishpond (L 4010) and its immediate vicinity. The only exception was a badly worn small bronze

coin found just below the surface within the sand of the pond. The coin was evidently washed down from the nearby edge of the mound. The lack of pottery sherds was doubtlessly due to the constant exposure of the area to the sea, whose waves removed any ancient materials that may have been inside the fishpond. Indeed, within a fortnight of the fishpond excavation, the wind and waves had re-filled the entire excavated area with sand.

The outside dimensions of the fishpond (L 4010) measure 8.4 × 6.6 m, and its average depth was 0.75 m, as measured from the top of its northern wall. A narrow ramp was cut into the bedrock along the interior of its south wall, sloping downward to the southeast into the pond. On the northern wall of the pond, two roughly square postholes were hewn into the rock, each of them about 10 cm wide (fig. 79). Presumably they held posts for an awning, or perhaps for a device used in handling the fish inside the pond. About 5 m west of the fishpond's southwest corner, the remains of the small rock-cut tank (L 4014), first explored in 1996, were found. Some 7 m southeast of the pond were situated three segments of a large structure, preserved to a height of about 0.7 m. They are aligned with the ruins of the Ottoman bridge and are apparently the remnants of the bridge's western end (fig. 80).

The fishpond is situated about 5 m south of the river mouth, with the sea a few more meters to the northwest. During high tide, seawater covers the entire area of the pond. It is possible that during the Byzantine period the sea level was somewhat higher than at present, but independent tectonic movements due to the many earthquakes in this region may have cancelled the change. It seems likely that the height of the pond's edges above sea level during the Byzantine era was approximately the same as it is today. The flushing of coastal fishponds by the waves was a desirable action, as it

Fig. 78. *The fishpond (Area D) at the foot of the mound; the river outflow is at left.*

Fig. 79. *One of the rock-cut holes in the northern wall of the fishpond.*

eliminated stale water within the pond (Columella, *De Re Rustica* 8.17).

The fishpond was connected to the river by means of a curved rock-cut channel, about 1 m wide. Along the southern edge of the channel were remains of a low partition, built of small ashlars that were mortared in a curve along the channel's edge and led to the southeast. This was a reinforcing partition for the curved channel leading to the river. The course of the channel then turned and proceeded northward, ending with its opening at the river (fig. 81). This connecting channel allowed for the circulation of river water in the fishpond, and was no doubt equipped with a metal or stone grate to prevent the exit of fish from the pond. As the pond was periodically also flushed by sea water from above, the water within it must have been brackish.

Fig. 80. *The fishpond, with tessellated basin left, and Ottoman bridge at upper right.*

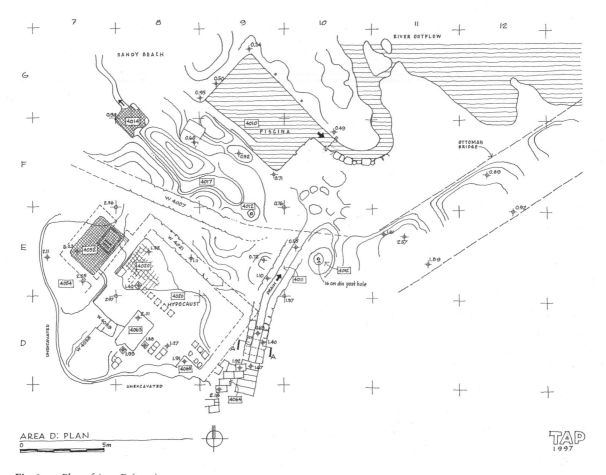

Fig. 81. *Plan of Area D (1997).*

Fig. 82. *Tessellated floor of the basin west of the fishpond.*

The fishpond in Area D was clearly constructed at this location to take advantage of the area where river and sea meet. namely, a region of brackish water that is rather significant for mariculture, a fact which was well known in antiquity (Varro, *De Re Rustica* 3.17). The local fish farmers of Kibbutz Maʿagan Mikhael, who visited the TAP excavations, remarked about the advantages offered by this particular coastal spot. It seems that the resulting water mixture in a maritime-riverine confluence constituted an optimal salinity blend for promoting the growth of certain euryhaline fish species.

Fishponds situated in such a location could easily be stocked with young fish after spawning and then be utilized as holding tanks during the other seasons of the year. Two smaller fishponds hewn in the rock, in the shallow waters off the mound, were found in the survey conducted by Spier in 1993 (see Chapter I). Unlike the large fishpond in Area D, these smaller ponds utilized only sea water. They could have served to stock surplus fish or the purple producing species of shellfish (Columella, *De Re Rustica* 8.16.7).

As noted above, west of the fishpond we unearthed remains of a hewn tank with a mosaic floor (L 4010). It measured 1.5 m square and was cut into the rock to a depth of about 30 cm (namely, 1 Byzantine foot; officially 31.25 cm). The tessellated floor of the tank (L 4014), situated at an elevation of +0.70 m, was composed of large white *tesserae* (fig. 82). The original height of the tank is unknown. Along the bottom of the tank's walls were remnants of hydraulic plaster 3 cm-thick, composed of two layers. The inner layer, about 23 mm thick, was grey, while the outer, 7–9 mm thick, was pink (fig. 83). A rock-cut drain, about 20 cm wide, lead from the tank to a collecting area, hewn into the bedrock to the southeast. The tank could also be drained to the north (fig. 81). The tessellated tank was clearly built to handle liquids. No ceramics were found in the tank or its immediate vicinity. The few badly worn bronze coins recovered from the surface sand near the tank appear to have been washed down from the mound above.

The installation appears to have been an industrial tank, utilized in connection with the fishpond, probably in processing fish and fish products such as fish sauces. It is also possible that small-scale production of sea purple took place at this site, as numerous shellfish remains were found here. The plain mosaic pieces of the tank's floor have a rather wide date range, from the fourth to tenth centuries, but the grey and pink hydraulic plaster limits the range considerably. The plaster seems to be a variant of aqueduct plaster Type II 2–3 of Porath (1989), dated to the third–fourth centuries. Its date is almost certainly pre-Islamic, and the tank was likely to have been constructed in Early Byzantine times.

Between the tank and the fishpond there were poorly preserved remains of three smaller rock-cut basins, and two additional depressions, now eroded, that had been cut into the bedrock. Two of the basins were rectangular, each measuring 62 × 124 cm (2 × 4 Byzantine feet), and were joined by a shared wall. The floor of the southern basin was at +0.60 m and was higher than that of its northern neighbor by about 23 cm. Adjoining them to the west was the third basin, triangular shaped, measuring about 1.5 m along its sides. East of the southern basin was an irregular depression in the rock, whose sides were completely eroded, that had probably served as a catch basin. Another depression, southeast of the latter, with its floor at +0.32 cm, apparently served as another catch basin. While the area is now severely eroded by the sea, it appears that the three adjoining upper basins, and the two catch basin associated with them, were utilized to handle liquids and/or fish products. The cleaning or processing of these materials involved liquids used in the three hewn basins and the two catch basins situated below them. This work area was connected to the fishpond by the sloping ramp built along its interior southern wall (fig. 81).

If we consider the entire complex of the hewn coastal installations found within Area D and its vicinity, namely, the large fishpond utilizing brackish water, the two smaller salt water *piscinae* in shallow water, a square basin with hydraulic plaster and a mosaic floor, as well as two smaller basin and catch basins all designed to handle liquids, the impression gained is that we are dealing with installations for one or more marine industries. Among the likely candidates are one or more of the following: a facility for fish farming (raising, processing, salting); a fish sauce (*garum*) or other fish preserves factory, and/or a facility for small-scale sea purple manufacture (Stieglitz 1998a).

The latter is suggested by the recovery of numerous shells used in producing sea purple, also

Fig. 83. *Detail of basin corner showing preserved hydraulic plaster.*

Fig. 84. *Purple shells from various excavation areas of Tel Tanninim.*

known as royal purple or Tyrian purple (fig. 84). The two fishponds utilizing seawater would have been well suited to serve as storage for shellfish, which are retrieved by fishing and diving in shallow waters. The purple shells found at Tel Tanninim are common finds at coastal sites, but not all three types of shellfish used to manufacture the sea purple dye are always attested in excavations. The two most common types are *Murex trunculus* and *Murex brandaris,* and both are edible. These remains may be connected with diet and not with the dye. The third type, *Purpura haemastoma,* is not edible and was used only in the dye manufacture process. When all three types are found together, as they were at Tel Tanninim (fig. 85), they provide evidence that they are likely to be refuse not only from the diet, but also from dye manufacture.

THE BATH-HOUSE

When the excavation proceeded southward along the long wall (W 4007) that formed the boundary for the fishpond complex, parts of a large structure emerged. The area was also found to be overlaid by several sandy soil layers, deposited above a level of *kurkar* gravel that had been mixed with mortar sandy soil and some red loam fill (fig. 86). In the gravel layer were some Late Byzantine sherds. Below the gravel, there was a thick grey ash level with a few Byzantine sherds, deposited over a massive collapse of brick and tile rubble from a ruined structure below (fig. 87). The debris was in various states of preservation. Some pieces were hard baked, others were moist and extremely brittle. After the floor of the ruined structure was reached, it became apparent that the materials were the rubble from a destroyed fire chamber (*hypocaustum*). The chamber was a low subterranean room for heating the floor of a hot-room (*caldarium*) in a bath-house

(*balneum*). The hypocaust system was also utilized to heat other areas of the bath-house by means of ceramic pipe flues and tubes (*tubuli*) that circulated the hot air directly from the fire chamber to other parts of the structure (see Chapter II.3 for the remains of another bath-house in Area B2).

The floor (F 4016) of the hypocaust (L 4020) was hewn out of the bedrock. It was not leveled, as

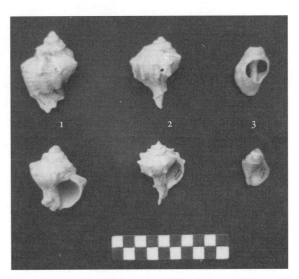

Fig. 85. *The three shell types used for dye manufacture: (1) Murex trunculus; (2) Murex brandaris; (3) Purpura haemastoma.*

Fig. 86. *Strata above the burnt destruction layer of a structure below.*

Fig. 87. *Destruction debris above the hypocaust floor.*

its elevation ranged from +1.40 to +1.32 m. Near the floor's center, a large rectangular column, measuring 1.25 × 2.5 m, was carved out of the rock and left as a support for the ceiling of the fire chamber and the floor laid over the ceiling. The top of the column was at +2.01 m. The fire chamber was roughly rectangular, with internal dimensions of the excavated area being 5.5 × 7.25 m. The room was originally larger, as its southern sector and wall were not excavated. The eastern wall of the fire chamber was not preserved at all, due to the subsequent construction that had rebuilt the area directly above that sector of the bath-house (fig. 81).

On the bedrock floor and lower sections of the hypocaust walls, rows of square ceramic tiles had been mortared into place. The grey mortar on the walls was 4 cm thick, with organic and shell tempers. The vertical wall tiles measured 23 × 23 × 2 cm, while the floor tiles were somewhat smaller at 17 × 17 × 2 cm. The average space between the preserved rows of tiles, both on the floor and on the walls, was 1 cm (fig. 88). The tiles had evidently covered the entire floor and at least the lower portions of the hypocaust walls. Built atop the tiles were remnants of small square pillars (*suspensurae*), constructed of fired bricks that had survived only in some parts of the chamber. The little pillars were arranged in a

grid pattern and preserved to varying heights, up to 50 cm. At their base, some pillars measured 23 × 23 cm, while others were 31 × 31 cm. The distance between adjacent pillars in the chamber was 31 cm, presumably one Byzantine foot.

Most of the individual bricks composing the pillars measured 23 × 23 × 4 cm. In some of the larger *suspensurae*, smaller bricks measuring 19 × 19 × 4 cm were used, and on these pillars they were supplemented by small bricks that were attached alongside. In the southern sector of the chamber, a few round bricks were found, placed atop the square pillars. The round bricks had a diameter of 20 cm and were 3 cm thick. The use of diverse sizes and shapes of bricks suggests that the bath-house was in use for an extended period and had undergone maintenance and repairs.

The debris layer above the floor of the chamber also contained fragments of some very large bricks. They were of two sizes: (1) 40 × 55 × 5 cm, (2) 41 × 41 × 5 cm. These large bricks had been placed over the tops of four adjacent pillars and were supported on the corners of the pillars.

It appears likely that some of these large bricks were also attached to the walls. One brick was found intact *in situ*, next to the west wall of the chamber (W 4019), where it had been cemented

Fig. 88. *Ceramic tiles on the hypocaust floor and lower portion of its walls.*

Fig. 89. *Detail of hypocaust floor showing large ceramic tiles cemented over floor tiles.*

above the floor directly atop the floor tiles adjacent to the wall (fig. 89). The large bricks are most likely further indications of different phases in the use of the structure.

Other architectural ceramics found within the hypocaust debris included several sections of ceramic pipes, either box-like rectangular shaped, or cylindrical with a spout at one end. These pipe sections were the remains of the flues that conducted the hot air from the fire chamber to other part of the bath-house. The rectangular flue sections measured 12 × 17 cm with a length of about 22 cm and a wall thickness of 1.5 cm. Their inside dimensions were about 9 × 14 cm. One well preserved flue section had a large hole punched in the middle of its wide wall to facilitate its attachment to the wall of the room (fig. 90). The cylindrical flue section (**A042**) was 13 cm in length, with a ribbed body. Their inside diameter was 5.5–6 cm and their wall thickness varied between 0.6–0.85 cm. At one end, the tube had a ledge or rim, from which projected a curved cone narrowing to form a small circular opening with an inside diameter of 2.5 cm (fig. 91). The specialized form of the cylindrical tube sections (known as venturi tubes when used for liquids) suggests that these flues were designed to circulate the hot air at higher speed and over longer distances than the rectangular flues. The only other material culture found within the debris of the fire chamber floor were a few Byzantine sherds.

West of the hypocaust, and attached to its western wall, were remains of a small rectangular entrance room measuring about 2 × 3 m. It had a doorway opening to the northeast and a tessellated floor sloping to the southwest from +2.08 to +1.99 m, perhaps as a result of subsequent earthquakes. The floor was situated above the remains of the hypocaust's western wall. All that remained of the antechamber was its well preserved mosaic floor (F 4052), laid directly on the bedrock, which had a brief Greek inscription embedded near the doorway. The mosaic was composed of large white *tesserae*, within which was laid a framed two word inscription situated in the northeast corner of the floor facing the doorway. The letters were executed in red stones, set within a simple rectangular red stone border (fig. 92). The message is only partially preserved, but may be restored as follows:

$$\text{Ε Ι Σ Ε [Λ Θ Ε]}$$
$$\text{Ε Π Α [Γ Α Θ Ω]}$$

The welcoming words are ἔισελθε ἐπ' ἀγαθῷ "come in, for the good." The message here is likely to be a shortened version of a formula, such as preserved in the Byzantine period House of Eustolios at Kourion (Christou 1996: 26): "enter [ἔισαψε], for the good luck of the house." A similar mosaic greeting to ours, with the message "come in, enjoy, and [...]," is known from the baths at Ashkelon (Stager 1991: 28). From the entrance room, stairs would lead the guest to the dressing room (*apody-*

Fig. 90.   *Rectangular ceramic flue section from the hypocaust debris.*

Fig. 91.   *Two views of a cylindrical ceramic flue section from the hypocaust debris.*

terium) and to the bathing facilities in the rooms directly above the hypocaust (Lucian, *Hippias* 5).

The excavated area of the bath-house in Area D totaled 82 square meters. It is likely that additional sections of the bath are preserved in the region above and south of the partially exposed south wall of the hypocaust (W 4059). This area was not excavated, but a section of wall running southward (W 4058) and perpendicular to the south wall of the hypocaust indicates the likely presence of other sections belonging to the bath-house buried under the edge of the mound.

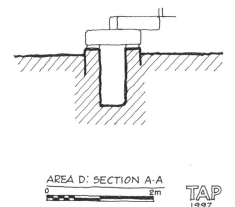

Fig. 92. *Two views of the inscribed mosaic mat in the antechamber of the bath house.*

East of the hypocaust, a substantial and well built stone drain (L 4011) was found. It was 0.4 m wide, constructed of two parallel rows of large *kurkar* ashlars that had been mortared unto the bedrock and were covered by flat rectangular blocks (fig. 93). The drain originated in the area south of the hypocaust, where the rest of the bath-house would have been. It drained its liquids from south to north, past the northeast corner of the hypocaust, and terminated less than five meters southeast of the fishpond, at an elevation of +0.70 m. At its terminus, there were remains of a circular stone ring, about 2 m in diameter, in whose center the channel of the drain came to an end.

We may have here a structure that, at high tide, permitted the seawater to enter the lower portion of the drain and flush it. This feature, if it is correctly interpreted, brings to mind the description by Flavius Josephus of the seawater flushing system provided for the major sewers in Roman Caesarea (*Antiquities of the Jews* 15.340). In any event, the large drain for the Area D bath-house serves as a reminder that one would expect to find the terminus of a ceramic water pipe in the southern region of the bath. In our case, the bath-house water sup-

AREA D: SECTION A-A

0   2m

TAP
1997

Fig. 93. *Section of the drain L 4011 in Area D.*

ply would most likely be delivered by one of the parallel water pipelines found in Area B2. These pipes derived their water from the water reservoir in Area B. It is also possible that the water supply to Area D came not directly from the reservoir in Area B, but via the water pipeline on the ramp (L 2022) leading westward from the terminus tank of Channel E (L 2004; see fig. 54, Chapter II.3).

Between the drain and the southeast corner of the hypocaust were found remains of a stone pavement (L 4064), constructed of large ashlars. Only a

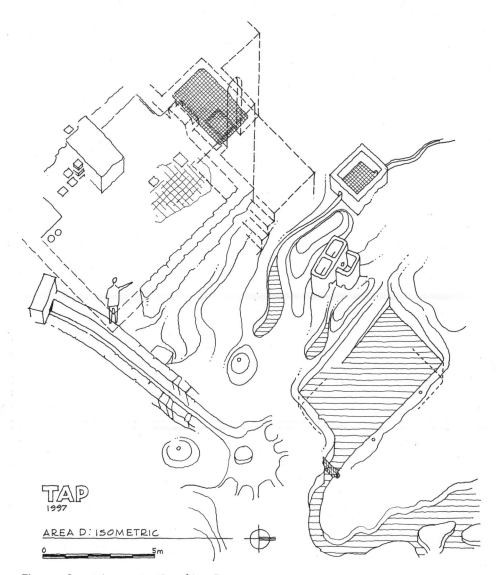

Fig. 94. *Isometric reconstruction of Area D.*

small segment of this pavement was unearthed. It was oriented precisely on a north–south axis and was laid at an elevation of +2.18 to + 1.92 m sloping northward. The pavement stones had been laid over an uneven white layer (10 YR 8/2) of crushed gravel, composed of *kurkar* and mortar, with an average thickness of 10 cm, that also contained small Byzantine sherds. The layer served as a bedding for the stone pavement, and extended over the ruins of the hypocaust, indicating it had been laid over the bath-house after the latter had gone out of use and was in a ruined state. This can clearly be observed in the stratigraphic sections of the south

balk, over W 4059, and in the west balk, over W 4019, in Square E8. In the north, the gravel layer terminated at the long wall W 4007.

DISCUSSION

It is likely that the stone pavement was laid in the seventh century, after the Muslim conquest of Caesarea. The paved road probably led from the contemporary Crocodile River bridge to the top of Tel Tanninim, where a sizeable church was situated at the summit of the mound. Another branch of this road, probably not paved, traversed the site from north to south to the edge of the settlement, some 125 m south of the bridge. From there, the road continued along the coast to Caesarea Maritima.

The Byzantine bath-house and its associated fishpond complex in Area D (fig. 94) are datable to a period when similar facilities existed at Caesarea and its suburban sectors. The sixth century bath, unearthed in 1974–1978, one kilometer north of Caesarea, featured a freshwater fishpond adjoining the bath-house (Horton 1996: 178). Evidence for a similar complex was also unearthed at Tel Tanninim in Area B2 (see Chapter II.3). The situation of the bath-house in Area D, to be dated to an earlier phase in the Byzantine era, was different. This bath provided the guests not only with the usual bathing amenities, but with the additional option of swimming, either in the nearby river or

the sea. The scant material culture recovered in this sector of the site permits only a rough Early Byzantine date for the origin of the structures in Area D. It is possible that the Bath-house complex was in use until the Muslim conquest of the region.

The Romans delighted not only in taking their baths but also in varieties of seafood delicacies, particularly those derived from artificial fishponds. By the Late Roman era, these elements of their culture had been diffused to many of their provinces, including Byzantine Palestine. In the first century C.E., Martial (*Epigrams* 10.30:21–24, tr. W.C.A. Ker) vividly portrayed the Roman attraction to, and their fondness for, the varied produce derived from fishponds very much like those excavated at Tel Tanninim:

piscina rhombum pascit et lupos vernas,
natat ad magistrum delicata muraena,
nomenculator mugilem citat notum, et
adesse iussi prodeunt senes mulli.

The fishpond feeds turbot and home-reared bass;
to its master's call swim the dainty lamprey;
the usher summons a favorite gunard, and,
bidden to appear, aged mullets put forth their heads.

Chapter III

The Pottery

1. Iron Age, Persian and Hellenistic

by Shalom Yankelevitch

Until the TAP excavations, there was a lack of any sign of occupation prior to the Persian period. This was surprising, as one would expect a close link between Tel Tanninim and the adjacent Tel Mevorakh. In a personal communication in 1978, the late Prof. M. Dothan informed me of finding a few Iron Age sherds on Tel Tanninim. Indeed, while analyzing the excavation ceramic finds for publication, several of them could be assigned to the Iron Age IIC.

Persian and Hellenistic pottery was collected from all the excavation areas, but the strata of these periods were exposed in restricted and most of their loci were disturbed. Area A revealed Persian and Hellenistic levels, but very few loci were free of Late Roman or Byzantine intrusions. As a result, we shall analyze the Iron Age, Persian and Hellenistic pottery typologically and not stratigraphically.

In the vicinity of Tel Tanninim are some key sites to these periods. The latest and most detailed publication is that of Tel Dor. Others are Tel Michal, Tel Mevorakh, Shikmona and Tell Keisan. Typological and chronological discussion of the Tel Tanninim materials will be based, therefore, mainly on the comparison with the finds from these sites.

Some of the sherds shown in the figures are quite small, thus preventing a secure attribution to the specific type of vessel. The discussion of the pottery will proceed in the usual order, beginning with open vessels and continuing to the closed types.

IRON AGE POTTERY

Bowls

Five bowl sherds were noticed, which may be divided into two types. Both are carinated and belong to the period Iron IIC (700–586 B.C.E.).

Type A. Carinated bowl with red paint on rim and below (fig. 95:1–3)

Small to medium bowls made of pale, very well levigated clay and very well fired. The carination appears in the middle of the vessel and the walls above it are flared. The rims are everted, triangular in section and painted red. The paint may be inside and outside the rim. These bowls are very common from the seventh century B.C.E. onward and most common at the end of the Iron Age. They are considered to be a Phoenician vessel type (Mazar 1985: 109).

Parallels are numerous, among them from Tell Keisan Stratum IV, seventh century B.C.E. (Briend and Humbert 1980: Pl. 30:1–4), where the type continues to the sixth century (*ibid.*, fig. 20:9); Dor Stratum 3a, Type 26a–b (Gilboa 1995: 5 and

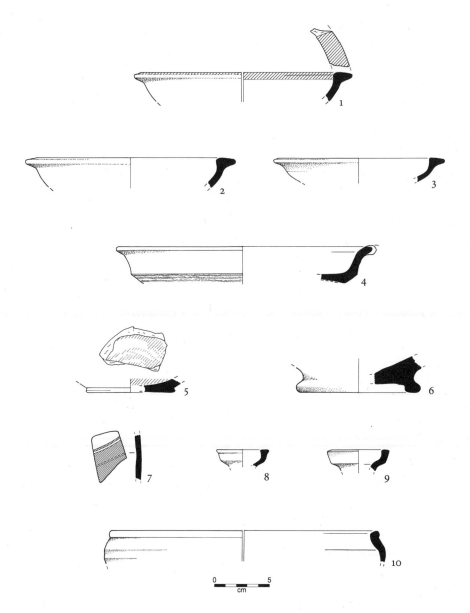

No.	Reg. No.	Locus	Form	Description
1	1054/19	1232	bowl	Pale pink clay 5YR 7/4 with very few grits. White slip 10YR 7/4; red slip 5YR 6/4 on rim.
2	1066/22	1234	bowl	Same as previous.
3	1067/12	1233	bowl	Same as previous.
4	1057/2	1129	bowl	Reddish brown clay 5YR 5/6, few small dark grits. Self slip.
5	1044/9	1232	bowl	Light red clay 2.5YR 7/6, few medium size grits. Red 10R 4/8 irregular wheel slip interior.
6	C014	1007	bowl	Poorly bonded crystallized clay. Hard, silty light red fabric 10R 6/6; many large white inclusions.
7	C029	1204	jug?	Fine levigated clay.
8	1075/23	1233	decanter	Light reddish brown 5YR 6/4; red slip 2.5YR 6/6 on lip. Very well levigated.
9	1067/11	1233	decanter	Reddish yellow clay 7.5 YR 7/6, tiny red grits.
10	1028/9	1007	bowl	Red clay 10R 5/6, self burnished. Core dusky red 10R 3/4, few gray and white specks.

Fig. 95.   *Iron Age pottery.*

fig. 1.3:18–19); Tell Qasile (Mazar 1985: fig. 55:25); Samaria, not earlier than seventh century B.C.E. (Crowfoot, Crowfoot, and Kenyon 1957: fig. 32:8); Kabri, seventh century B.C.E. "Phoenician Fine Ware" (Lehman 2002: 194 and fig. 5.76:20–21). Although in our bowls the bases are missing, the usual ones are disk or shallow ring bases. The base in our fig. 95:5 is possibly such a base, but differs by the red burnish throughout the interior.

Type B. Carinated bowl, partly burnished, with bar handles (fig. 95:4)

A medium sized vessel, carinated at about two thirds of the bowl. Flaring rim ending in a slightly inverted lip, where there is a bar handle. Burnished at the bottom, interior and exterior. The base is missing, but there are traces of a ring base. Parallels: Akhziv Type B6I, tenth–eighth century B.C.E. (Dayagi-Mendels 2002: 115 and figs. 4.7:1; 5.2:6); Hazor Stratum VI (Yadin, Aharoni, and Amiran 1961: Pl. 67:8); Tel Michal Stratum XII, eighth century (Singer-Avitz 1989: 183 and fig. 7.4:3).

Kraters

One rim sherd could be defined as a *krater* (fig. 95:10). Carinated below the rim, which is slightly inverted and thickened outside. Parallels have two handles from rim to carination (Stern 1978: fig. 13:9), or are without handles (Stern 1978: fig. 13:6). The base is usually round, but ring-bases appear as well. This vessel type begins in the tenth century B.C.E., as evident from Tel Mevorakh, Tel Michal, Jatt (Porath, Yannai, and Kasher 1999: 17 and fig. 10:10–12), among others. A coarse ring-base fragment (fig. 95:6) could be from a plain Iron Age krater, or cooking pot, due to the clay.

Jugs

Three sherds represent two jug types.

Type A. Phoenician Bichrome (fig. 95:7)

A small piece of body sherd of a closed vessel, decorated with alternating black and red bands of identical width, over a white slip. This pottery family is attributed to Iron Age I–II contexts. Gil-

boa (2001: 367–88, esp. 383), in the latest and most comprehensive discussion of this type, points out that Iron II pottery of this type is exclusively found in Phoenicia.

Type B. Rims of decanter jugs (fig. 95: 8–9)

Two decanter rims, both of the same very well fired ware. The clay is similar to the bowls in fig. 95:1–3. They too are painted red on the lip. No. 8 has an everted thickened rim, while No. 9 has a straight rim. Decanters are common in Iron II. The earliest known examples are from Megiddo Stratum IV (Megiddo I, Pl. 4; Megiddo II, Pl. 91:1) and the latest are found in Persian period assemblages, although quite rarely (Singer-Avitz 1989: 119 and fig. 9.2:6).

THE PERSIAN PERIOD

Bowls

It was already noticed by Stern (1995: 51) that ordinary bowls are poorly represented at the coastal sites of the Persian era. This phenomenon is even more salient at Tel Tanninim. We could actually detect less than a dozen bowl rims that fit into our Persian period repertoire. In our opinion, this stems from the very limited area of excavation into the levels of that era, or, that Tel Tanninim's inhabitants preferred the imported ware on their tables (see below), an argument already advanced by Elgavish (1968: 60). The sherds consist of two types.

Type A. Bowl with rounded walls (fig. 96:1)

Small bowl with rounded wall and sharply inverted rim. Base is missing, but it could have been a disk or ring-base. Undoubtedly an imitation of Attic bowls, this type was very common in the period. Some examples are from Shikmona (Elgavish 1968: Pl. 56:125–26); Akko (Dothan 1976: fig. 27:2); Tell Keisan (Briend and Humbert 1980: Pl. 20:6); Tel Michal (Singer-Avitz 1989: fig. 9.16:4); Dor (Stern 1995: 52 and fig. 2.1:8). A few similar bowls were found with the pottery of the Ma'agan Mikhael shipwreck (Artzy and Lyon 2003: 184 and fig. 1:4–5), where they are classified as "galley" ware. All examples date from the mid-fifth century to the end

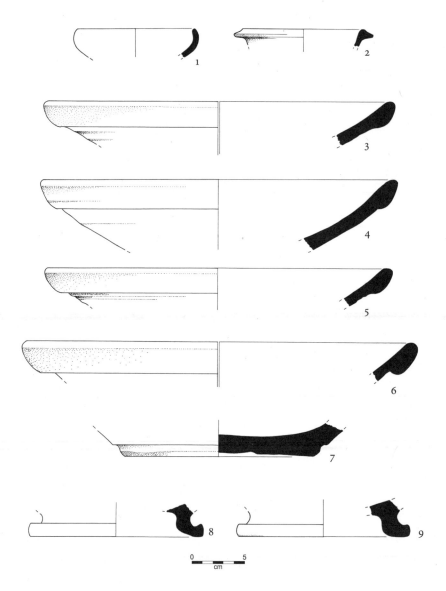

No.	Reg. No.	Locus	Form	Description
1	1075/3	1233	bowl	Reddish yellow clay 7.5YR 6/8, well levigated and fired. Exterior slip pinkish white 7.5YR 8/2.
2	1049/13	1230	bowl	Reddish yellow clay 5YR 7/6, few very small white and red grits. Exterior slip pinkish white 7.5YR 8/2.
3	1075/6	1233	mortarium	Light reddish brown clay 5YR 6/4 with many medium white, black and red grits. Interior/exterior pink slip 7.5YR 8/3.
4	1075/8	1233	mortarium	Very hard metallic clay, very pale brown 10YR 7/3, common white and gray grits. Pale yellow 2.5Y 8/3 slip; surface smoothened.
5	1075/7	1233	mortarium	Very coarse pale yellow clay 2.5Y 7/3. Rough texture and common large dark gray grits.
6	1075/12	1233	mortarium	Like No. 4.
7	1075/9	1233	mortarium	Like No. 5.
8	1075/5	1233	mortarium	Very coarse very pale brown clay 10YR 7/3, with many large black grits. Surface light gray 2.5Y 7/2.
9	C051	1220	mortarium	Like No. 8.
–	12/3	surface	mortarium	See Chapter II.1, fig. 11:11

Fig. 96. *Persian period bowls and mortaria.*

of the fourth century B.C.E. The date given by Artzy and Lyon (ibid. 197) to the shipwreck assemblage is about 400 B.C.E.

Type B. Bowl with ledge rim (fig. 96:2)

A small bowl with straight flaring walls and triangular projecting rim. Stern (1995: 53 and fig. 2.1:6) accepts the opinion that this bowl is a local imitation of the Attic fish-plate, thus appearing later than the prototype (Singer-Avitz 1989: 130 and fig. 9.10:7). At both sites and at Tell Keisan they date to the second half of the fourth century. The base is missing, but the reference bowls from Dor and Tel Michal have ring-bases.

Mortaria

These are large and heavy open vessels (fig. 96:3–9; also fig. 11:11, Ch. II.1). The *mortarium* is also commonly referred to as a "Persian bowl" because of its frequent appearance in Israel in Persian period strata (Stern 1982: 96). These bowls appear predominantly, but not exclusively, in Levantine coastal sites. Since Stern's fundamental study of 1982, numerous additional examples have been published, from Tel Michal (Singer-Avitz 1989: 115–44); Tell el-Hesi (Bennett and Blakely 1989: 46–59); Tell Qasile (Mazar 1985:128 and fig. 58:3–5); Tell Keisan and Dor (Stern 1995: 53–55 and fig. 2.2), among others. Although subtypes were defined by Stern (1982: 96–98), it is clear that they have no chronological significance and they all appear simultaneously. All six examples come from the same locus and basket. The differences in the treatment of rims and bases appear throughout the period. As to their function, Artzy and Lyon (2003: 187) concluded that they were used as secondary grain grinders, to achieve finer grain, after the primary grinding with basalt grinders.

The chronological range of these vessels extends beyond the Persian period. The earliest examples in Israel are from the seventh century, from various sites, among them Tell Qasile Stratum VII (Mazar 1985: 128 and fig. 58:3–4) and Tell Keisan Stratum IV (Briend and Humbert 1980: Pl. 31), where they have exclusively flat bases. The mortaria continue into the Hellenistic era at Tel Anafa (Berlin 1988: 107–10); Dor (Guz-Zilberstein

1995: 295 and fig. 6.91:8), where they are dated to 275–125 B.C.E., and Tell Keisan Stratum II (Briend and Humbert 1980: Pl. 12:1–3).

Kraters

Two types of kraters were observed (fig. 97:1–2). The fragments are small, so no complete shape could be reconstructed, nor the presence of handles, if any, detected.

Type A. Small krater with everted rim (fig. 97:1)

It has some resemblance to Stern's Type 4 (1982: fig. 126), dating from the sixth–fourth centuries B.C.E., and some examples from the later Persian period at Dor (Stern 1995: 55 and fig. 2.3:1–3).

Type B. Medium krater with straight neck and out-turned projecting rim (fig. 97:2)

Parallels come from Tel Mevorakh Stratum IV (Stern 1978: fig. 5:7, a large krater); Dor (Stern 1995: 55 and fig. 2.3:1–3) and Tell Keisan Stratum III (Briend and Humbert 1980: Pl. 20:22).

Cooking Pots

The cooking pots from Tel Tanninim (fig. 97:3–7) fit well into the common types of the period. They are globular with a short vertical or blunt angled neck. The rims are triangular in section, or straight and thin. At Tel Michal, it was noticed that the thinner straight rims are later than the triangular ones (Singer-Avitz 1980: 130), while at Dor both rim forms continue throughout the period (Stern 1995: 55).

The handle fragment (fig. 97:3) is part of the typical handles extending from rim to shoulder. The pots in fig. 97:4–5 have triangular projecting rims. Complete examples of such vessels have two handles from rim to shoulder. At Tel Michal Strata XI–VIII (525–400 B.C.E.), they appear in the early part of the period (Singer-Avitz 1989: figs. 9.1:3–4; 9.2:4; 9.5:12). At Tel Mevorakh, they are dated to the last phases of the period (Stern 1978: 32 and fig. 5:14–16); at Dor, they date from the fifth–fourth centuries B.C.E. (Stern 1995: fig. 2.26:12–13); at Tell Keisan, throughout the period (Briend and Humbert 1980: 123 and fig. 21:9–10).

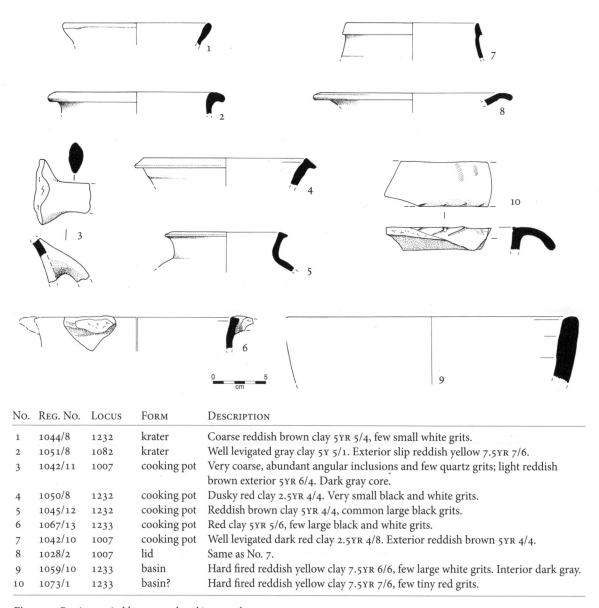

No.	Reg. No.	Locus	Form	Description
1	1044/8	1232	krater	Coarse reddish brown clay 5YR 5/4, few small white grits.
2	1051/8	1082	krater	Well levigated gray clay 5Y 5/1. Exterior slip reddish yellow 7.5YR 7/6.
3	1042/11	1007	cooking pot	Very coarse, abundant angular inclusions and few quartz grits; light reddish brown exterior 5YR 6/4. Dark gray core.
4	1050/8	1232	cooking pot	Dusky red clay 2.5YR 4/4. Very small black and white grits.
5	1045/12	1232	cooking pot	Reddish brown clay 5YR 4/4, common large black grits.
6	1067/13	1233	cooking pot	Red clay 5YR 5/6, few large black and white grits.
7	1042/10	1007	cooking pot	Well levigated dark red clay 2.5YR 4/8. Exterior reddish brown 5YR 4/4.
8	1028/2	1007	lid	Same as No. 7.
9	1059/10	1233	basin	Hard fired reddish yellow clay 7.5YR 6/6, few large white grits. Interior dark gray.
10	1073/1	1233	basin?	Hard fired reddish yellow clay 7.5YR 7/6, few tiny red grits.

Fig. 97. *Persian period kraters and cooking vessels.*

The vessel shown in fig. 97:6 is a type with straight rim and two handles. Parallels at Tell Keisan Stratum IV are of early date (Briend and Humbert 1980: fig. 34:1, 10); Late Persian at Tel Michal Stratum VII (Singer-Avitz 1989: fig. 9.7:3), and mid-fifth century B.C.E. in the Maʿagan Mikhael shipwreck (Artzy and Lyon 2003: 186 and Pl. 3:5).

A cooking jug (diameter 14 cm), shown in fig. 97:7, has a very slightly out-turned and triangular ridged rim, convex inside. Although it has a parallel at Dor, dated to the late Persian era (Stern 1995: fig.

2.31:2), a closer parallel is an Iron Age vessel from Dor, Type CP6 (Gilboa 1995: 7 and fig. 1.1:18–20).

Lids

Lids are quite few in the Persian era, but are frequent in the Hellenistic period and onwards. Our example (fig. 97:8) is shown here because of its orange-red clay and wheel made grooves on the rim, a type noted at Tel Michal, dated by coins to the end of the fourth century B.C.E. (Singer-Avitz

1989: 135–36 and fig. 9.13). Similar lids appear at Dor in the fourth century (Stern 1995: 58 and fig. 2.4:1), Tel Mevorakh (Stern 1978: fig. 5:13), and an Athlit tomb, fifth–fourth centuries (Johns 1933: 97, fig. 79).

Basins

These are quire rare in the Persian period ceramic repertoire. One example is known from Tel Michal (Singer-Avitz 1989: 129 and fig. 9.7:8), and another from Dor (Stern 1995: 66–67 and fig. 2.13:1). Our first specimen (fig. 97:9) generally resembles the examples mentioned. The vessel in fig. 97:10 is unique and was assigned to this type because of its straight square walls. It has a wide everted ledge rim and traces of incised decoration.

Storage Jars

The Tel Tanninim jar assemblage (figs. 98–99; also see figs. 11:1–2; 13:1, Ch. II.1). contains most of the known types from the period and they may be divided into four types.

Type A. Jars with cylindrical neck (fig. 98:1–3; see also fig. 11:1–2)

These jars have thickened rounded rims atop of a cylindrical neck and slanted shoulders. When complete, they have a bag-shaped body and a convex to pointed base. Most of these vessels come from the Sharon coast to the north of the country. Many jars of this type have been salvaged from the sea. References come from Tel Michal, where five complete specimens were found in a kiln (Singer-Avitz 1989: 100–3 and fig. 8.14; Pls. 30–32; 63:1–5). At this site, they served both as storage and burial jars throughout the Persian period (*ibid.* 139–42 and fig. 9.17:1; Pls. 61–63); Shikmona, second half of the fourth century B.C.E., with coins of Alexander the Great (Elgavish 1968: Pl. 59:142); Tel Mevorakh (Stern 1978: fig. 7:1–4); at Tell Keisan, the group is conspicuously dated to two different times: one group from Stratum II is fourth century to Hellenistic (Briend and Humbert 1980: Pl. 8), while the other group, from Stratum IV is seventh–sixth century B.C.E. (*ibid.* Pl. 25: 6, 9); at Dor it was found in late fourth century context (Stern 1995: fig. 2.6).

Type B. Jars with basket handles (fig. 98:4)

Only a few sherds could be assigned to this type. Body sherds are not shown. The handle shown is too fragmentary to attribute to any sub-type. The basket handle jar must have been a major vessel in marine trade, as it is found throughout the Levantine coasts, including Cyprus and Rhodes (Sagona 1982: 106–8; Zemer 1977: 31). The find of this type as the main cargo of the Maʿagan Mikhael ship accentuates this assumption. As to their origin and date, Artzy states that its Cypriot origin is attested by several factors: their early appearance there, the general Cypriot character of the ship's cargo, and Cypriot syllabic signs incised before firing on such a jar found at Amathus (Artzy and Lyon 2003: 195). The same cargo lead Stern to look for an East Greek provenance for these jars (Stern 1982:11; 1995: 63). Vessels from Tell Keisan, Tel Michal, and Tell Sukas on the Syrian coast prove the existence of local imitations to these jars. The earliest jars of this type were found in Cyprus, about 600–475 B.C.E., for the early sub-type, and fifth–fourth centuries for the later (Artzy and Lyon 2003:195). The same time frame is valid for the finds from Israel (Briend and Humbert 1980: 136–41 and Pls. 23–24; 27). Similar jar handles to the one shown in fig. 98:4 come from Tel Mevorakh, dating to the later sub-type of the basket handle jars (Stern 1978: fig. 8:12–14); Tel Michal, fourth century B.C.E. (Singer-Avitz 1989: 135 and fig. 9.13:18–19). The Dor examples come from all the Persian period levels (Stern 1995: 63 and fig. 2.10).

Type C. 'Torpedo' jar (fig. 98:5)

Only one rim fragment could be attributed to this type. It has a short round neck and everted thick rim. The complete jars are characterized by a conic slanted shoulder, short round neck, thick everted rim and a long cylindrical body. They are very common along the coast and inland in Phoenicia, Mesopotamia and especially in Cyprus (Stern 1995: 62; Raban 1976: 55–57). Parallels come from Tel Mevorakh, Athlit and Tel Megadim from the whole period (Stern 1982: 105 and fig. 146, Type G). At Dor, they are dated from the fifth century to the first half of the fourth century B.C.E. (Stern 1995: 62 and fig. 2.9:1).

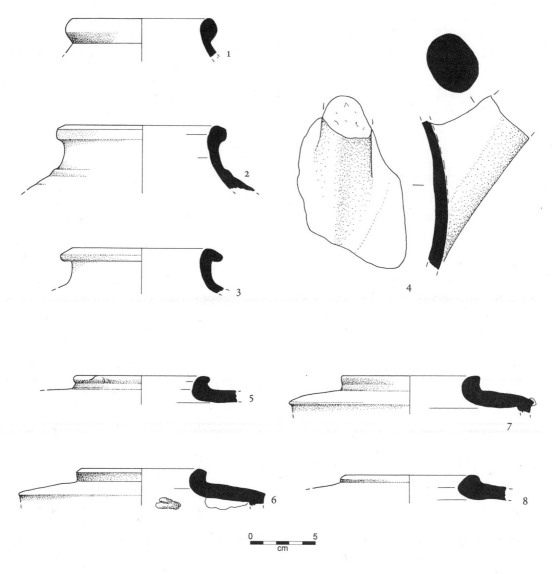

No.	Reg. No.	Locus	Form	Description
1	1025/3	1007	storage jar	Soft, pink clay 7.5YR 8/3, common reddish brown and white grits.
2	1050/2	1232	storage jar	Light brown clay 7.5YR 6/4, common white, black and red grits. Ext. slip very pale brown 10YR 7/6.
3	1050/4	1232	storage jar	Same as previous.
4	1059/19	1233	handle	Light reddish brown clay 5YR 6/4, large white grits. Exterior slip very pale brown 5YR 7/4.
5	1059/3	1233	storage jar	Light brown clay 7.5YR 6/4, very few red brown small grits.
6	1060/1	1234	storage jar	Like No. 5, large lime chunks.
7	1055/1	1233	storage jar	Like No. 5, few medium white and small red grits.
8	1050/7	1232	storage jar	Same as previous.
–	23/1	surface	storage jar	See Chapter II.1, fig. 11:1.
–	23/2	surface	storage jar	See Chapter II.1, fig. 11:2.
–	12/1	surface	handle	See Chapter II.1, fig. 12:1.

Fig. 98. *Persian period storage jars.*

Type D. Flat shouldered jars
(figs. 98:6–8, 99:9–18; see also fig. 12:1, Ch. II.1)

The flat-shouldered storage jar is the most common pottery vessel and appears at almost every site of the period, along the Levantine coasts and in the Punic settlements in the Western Mediterranean. They are found in the hinterland and about half of the specimens were recovered from the sea off the Israeli coast (Zemer 1978: 25). The jar has a broad flat shoulder set at a right angle to the body, a wide mouth with a very short neck that is sometimes missing, and a very short rim. The handles are twisted and attached from shoulder to body. They were previously described as poor workmanship and carelessly attached, but Artzy (1980) showed that the handles were purposely twisted to make them easier to lift and transport.

The jars shown in figs. 98: 6–8 and 99 are classified by Stern as Sub-type H-6, with a relatively high rim, horizontal shoulders and biconical body (Stern 1982: fig. 152), and Sub-type H-8, a bag-shaped body with slanted shoulders sometimes overlapping the walls (*ibid.* fig. 154). These two sub-types show chronological development: H-6 is earlier and dates to the sixth–fifth centuries, while H-8 dates to the fifth–fourth centuries (Singer-Avitz 1989: 141 and fig. 9.17:3; Stern 1995: 62 and figs. 2.7; 2.8; Onn 1999: 61 and fig. 14).

Our examples of the H-6 variants are shown in fig. 98:5–8, while these in fig. 99:9–18 can be assigned to the variant H-8. An interesting feature is found in fig. 99:10, which has very poor traces of red paint on the shoulder. Such a feature was published only from two sites, Tel Mevorakh (Stern 1978: 34 and fig. 6:4) and Tel Michal (Singer-Avitz 1989: 122 and fig. 9.3:7), both dating to the fifth century B.C.E.

Jugs

Only a few rim fragments and one base could be assigned to jugs and the examples are difficult to identify. They may be divided into three types (fig. 100:1–4).

Type A. Jug with concave neck
and simple everted rim (fig. 100:1)

The complete body is bulky and balloon-like. It is most probably Stern's Class G or H (1982: fig. 117:171–72). References: Tel Mevorakh Type 2, the most common at the site, dated late fifth and fourth century (Stern 1978: 36, fig. 9: 2–3); Athlit (Jones 1933: 92 and Pl. 21:819); Dor (Stern 1995: 63 and fig. 2.11:7); Tell Keisan (Briend and Humbert 1980: fig. 19:6), all dating in the same range.

Type B. Jug with concave neck
and thickened everted rim (fig. 100:2)

When complete, it has a globular or bulky body (Stern's Class H). References: Tel Michal Stratum IX (525–490 B.C.E.), but most common in Stratum VI, dated 350–300 B.C.E. by coins (Singer-Avitz 1989: figs. 9.1:9; 10:9). At Qadum, of the same date (Stern and Magen 1984: 190 and fig. 4:5); Dor, fourth century B.C.E. (Stern 1995: figs. 2.11:10; 2.37:13).

Type C. Jug with simple flaring rim and handle
stretching down from it (fig. 100:3)

This form falls into Class E (Stern 1982: 116 and fig. 169). The example from Tell Abu Hawam is of fifth–fourth century date. The base shown in fig. 99:4 is a ring-base typical to the globular jugs of the period. References: Shikmona (Elgavish 1968: Pls. 32:2–3; 48:86); Tel Mevorakh (Stern 1978: 37, fig. 9:6), dating to the fifth–fourth centuries B.C.E.

Juglets

Three types of juglets from the period were unearthed (fig. 100:5–10; also see fig. 13:3, Ch. II.1).

Type A. Elongated dipper juglet with flat or
pointed base (fig. 100:5–7; 10; and fig. 12:3, Ch. II.1)

The juglets in fig. 100:5–6, as well as fig. 13:3, have a sack-shaped body with flat base, wide neck and out flaring rim. A loop handle extended from rim to mid-body. These are Stern's Type 2b dipper juglets (1982: 119). Parallels: Shikmona (Elgavish 1968: Pls. 30; 33:11); Tel Michal Stratum VIII, 430–400 B.C.E. (Singer-Avitz 1989: fig. 9.5:14). The rim shown in

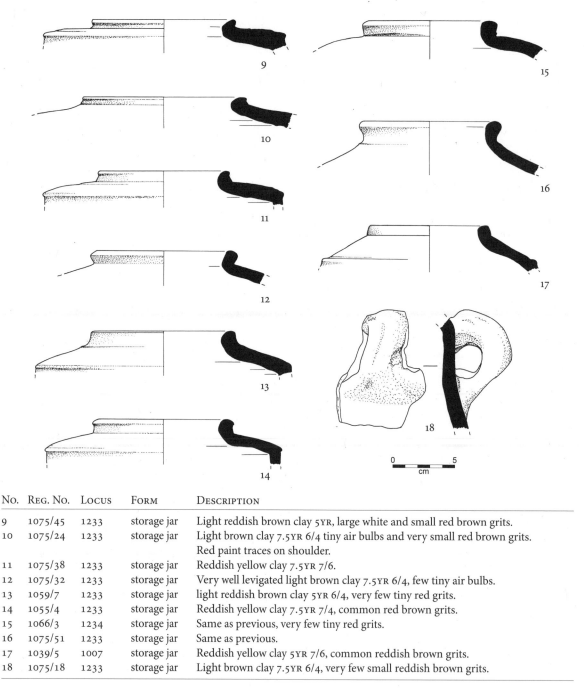

No.	Reg. No.	Locus	Form	Description
9	1075/45	1233	storage jar	Light reddish brown clay 5YR, large white and small red brown grits.
10	1075/24	1233	storage jar	Light brown clay 7.5YR 6/4 tiny air bulbs and very small red brown grits. Red paint traces on shoulder.
11	1075/38	1233	storage jar	Reddish yellow clay 7.5YR 7/6.
12	1075/32	1233	storage jar	Very well levigated light brown clay 7.5YR 6/4, few tiny air bulbs.
13	1059/7	1233	storage jar	light reddish brown clay 5YR 6/4, very few tiny red grits.
14	1055/4	1233	storage jar	Reddish yellow clay 7.5YR 7/4, common red brown grits.
15	1066/3	1234	storage jar	Same as previous, very few tiny red grits.
16	1075/51	1233	storage jar	Same as previous.
17	1039/5	1007	storage jar	Reddish yellow clay 5YR 7/6, common reddish brown grits.
18	1075/18	1233	storage jar	Light brown clay 7.5YR 6/4, very few small reddish brown grits.

Fig. 99. *Persian priod storage jars.*

fig. 100:7 seems to be a close sub-type to Type 2a, with a cylindrical body. It has parallels at Shikmona (Elgavish 1968: Pl. 33:12); Yokneʿam (Ben-Tor et al. 1979: 83 and fig. 7:8). It appears that the origin of these types is Cyprus, where hundreds were discovered and classified as Plain White V–VII, dating to the sixth–fourth centuries B.C.E. (Gjerstad 1960: fig. 9:11). The base in fig. 100:10 differs only by the pointed or convex form (Stern 1982: 119 Type 1). Parallels: Tel Mevorakh, fourth century (Stern 1978: 37 and fig. 9:9–10); Givʾat Yasaf, Persian period (Rochman-Halperin 1999: 105 and fig. 18:5).

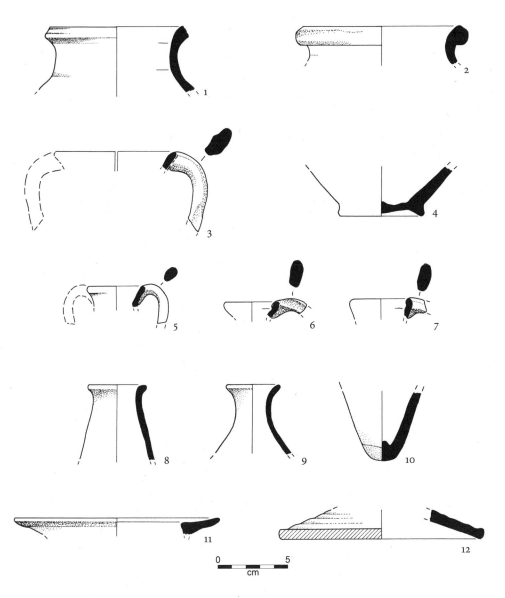

No.	Reg. No.	Locus	Form	Description
1	1078/4	1018	jug	Light red clay 10R 7/8, abundant white grits.
2	1045/27	1232	jug	Reddish yellow clay 5YR 6/4, common white grits.
3	1032/7	1117	jug	Light brownish gray clay 10YR 6/2, few tiny black grits. Exterior slip very light gray 2.5Y 7/2.
4	1075/5	1233	jug	Yellow clay 10YR 7/4, fine exterior slip 10YR 8/2.
5	1067/41	1233	juglet	Very fine levigated, very pale brown clay 10YR 7/4, self slipped.
6	1075/16	1233	juglet	Very fine levigated light red clay 2.5YR 7/6.
7	1045/23	1232	juglet	Light red clay 2.5YR 7/6 with gray core. Exterior white slip 2.5Y 8/3.
8	1075/29	1233	juglet	Reddish brown metallic ware 5YR 7/6, self slipped.
9	1081/9	1331	juglet	Very pale brown clay 10YR 7/4, self slipped.
10	1075/1	1233	juglet	Light brown clay 7.5YR 6/4, common white and reddish brown grits.
–	12/4	surface	juglet	See Chapter II.1, fig. 12:3.
11	1067/21	1233	chalice	Very fine reddish yellow clay 5YR 7/6.
12	1054/41	1232	chalice	Same as previous. Red band on lip.

Fig. 100. *Persian period jugs, juglets and chalices.*

Type B. Juglet with trefoil rim (fig. 100:8)

No exact parallels.

Type C. Globular juglet (fig. 100:9)

This form has the rim and neck of Type B2/4 (Stern 1982: 120 and figs. 182–84). Our specimen could be a sub-type with a short concave neck and handle from rim to shoulder (Type B2), or a long concave neck with handle from mid neck to shoulder. Parallels: Athlit (Jones 1933: Pl. 29:781); Tel Megadim Stratum II, fifth century B.C.E. (Stern 1982: fig. 184).

Chalices

Chalices are not frequent vessels of the period, and the two illustrated specimens could be of earlier date (fig. 100:11–12). As a matter of fact, the clay of fig. 100:12 as well as the red band on its rim fit well into the Iron Age pottery characteristics. However, a few chalices in the Persian period are known, namely from Shikmona (Elgavish 1968: figs. 130, 183) and Tel Michal (Singer-Avitz 1989: 119 and fig. 9.1:19).

IMPORTED FINE WARES

Considering the very limited excavation area at the lower levels of Tel Tanninim, the quantity of imported wares relative to the local pottery is quite impressive (figs. 101–2; see also figs. 11:8; 12:2, 149:5; 150:5). The imported ceramics may be divided into Athenian and East Greek wares. As in the nearby coastal sites of Tel Michal, Tel Mevorakh, Dor and Shikmona, the bulk of imported ceramics at Tel Tanninim is Athenian, with a small quantity of East Greek imports.

Athenian Imports

Type A. Bowls with thickened incurved rims (fig. 101:1–2)

These bowls, completely black glazed, are the most common of Attic wares. They appear in the fourth century B.C.E. at Dor (Marchese 1995: 127 and fig. 4:1). Other parallels, at Tel Michal (Marchese 1989:

147 and fig. 10.2:1–3); Tel Mevorakh (Stern 1978: Pl. 29: 7, 19); Shikmona (Elgavish 1968: Pl. 56:125–26) are only a few among the vast number of examples known from this period.

Type B. Bowls with projecting rims (fig. 102:6–7; also fig. 11:6, Ch. II.1)

These bowls have a convex outer profile and a rounded or tapered rim. The type is known from the third quarter of the fourth century in the Athenian agora (Sparkes and Talcott 1970: 803), where it continues until the end of the fourth century B.C.E. (Rotroff 1997: Pl. 59: 866, 868). At Tel Michal, they date to the fifth century (Marchese 1989: fig. 10.2:5), while at Dor to 475–450 B.C.E. (Marchese 1995: figs. 4.2:2–3; 4.3:3).

Incised and impressed bowls or cups (fig. 101:3–5; also fig. 12:2, Ch. II.1)

As we have only fragments, no attempt is made to assign the sherds to specific bowl or cup types. Figure 101:3 has alternately linked palmettes around a central inscribed circle, surrounded by a double circle of impressed dots. The parallel from Dor (Marchese 1995: fig. 4.7:6) is dated to 375–350 B.C.E. Figure 101:4, with linked palmettes attached to ovules that surround a double incised circle, dates to ca. 425–400 B.C.E. (Marchese 1995:150 and No. 46560/3). Figure 101:5 has a similar design, but instead of impressed dots, double rouletting surrounds the palmettes. The surface sherd in fig. 12:2 (Ch. II.1) is relatively thin and has a floating palmette over a central inscribed circle. It may be from a stemless cup base, as may be the sherd in fig. 102:8.

Fish plate (fig. 11:8, Ch. II.1)

The fragment has a broad almost horizontal floor and a sharply down turned triangular rim. Fish plates are usually fourth century in date, but at Tel Michal some were dated to the fifth century B.C.E. (Marchese 1989: 147).

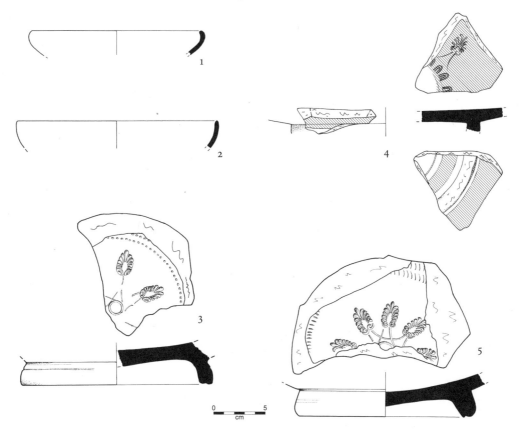

No.	Reg. No.	Locus	Form	Description
1	1051/2	1018	bowl	Reddish yellow clay 5YR 6/6, no grits. Black lustrous glaze.
2	1075/41	1233	bowl	Same as previous.
3	Co55	1229	bowl	Same clay. Underside of base and ring totally black lustrous. Int. red lustrous 2.5YR 5/8.
4	Co31	1204	bowl	Same clay. Int./ext. lustrous black glaze. Thick concentric black lustrous and reserve bands under base.
5	Co53	1241	bowl	Same clay. Int./ext. totally black matt glaze.

Fig. 101. *Persian period imported Athenian fine wares.*

Skyphoi (fig. 102:9–12)

These were the most popular drinking vessels in Athens during the sixth–fourth centuries B.C.E. The examples here are of Type A, with horseshoe handles attached to the rim, straight walls and painted exterior on the ring base. All these elements are typical to the second-third quarters of the fifth century B.C.E. Parallels: Dor (Marchese 1995: 131 and fig. 4.4:3–4, 6–7); Akko, mid-fifth century (Dothan 1976: fig. 27:3–4).

White lekythoi (fig. 102:13–14)

These two fragments probably are from white lekythoi. They probably are the White Ground types, black banded and painted (Type 17). This type is dated to the fifth century B.C.E., with the nearest site parallels at Tel Michal (Marchese 1989: fig. 10.2:27–28); Dor (Mook and Coulson 1995: fig. 3.9:1–2) and Shikmona (Elgavish 1968: 42 and Pl. 52:113), all dated to the fifth century.

Red Figure lekythos

See Chapter IV.3.B1, and figs. 157:5; 158:5, below.

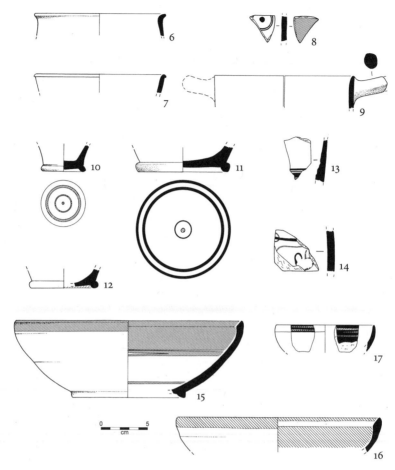

No.	Reg. No.	Locus	Form	Description
6	1051/4	1018	bowl	Same clay and glaze.
7	1073/27	1233	bowl	Same clay and glaze.
8	C039	1233	bowl	Same clay. Int. black lustrous glaze. Ext. base underside reserved, thin concentric red circles 2.5YR 5/8.
–	C036	surface	bowl	See Chapter II.1, fig. 13:2.
–	1001/8	surface	bowl	See Chapter II.1, fig. 11:6.
–	C010	surface	fish plate	See Chapter II.1, fig. 11:8.
9	1066/34	1234	skyphos	Red clay 2.5YR 6/6. Interior black lustrous, exterior dark gray glaze.
10	C066	1323	skyphos	Same clay. Int./ext. lustrous sepia glaze. Base underside: reserved, thin concentric yellowish red circles 5YR 4/6.
11	C050	1233	skyphos	Reddish yellow clay 5YR 6/6. Int./ext. black lustrous glaze. Base underside reserved with thin black concentric circles.
12	1066/17	1234	skyphos	Light reddish brown clay 5YR 6/4. Interior sepia lustrous glaze. Exterior black lustrous glaze, reserved at walls and base junction. Base underside matt red slip 2.5YR 5/8.
–	C035	1233+34	lekythos	See Chapter IV.3, figs. 149:5, 150:5.
13	1075/8	1233	lekythos	Reddish yellow clay 5YR 6/4. White ground, black lustrous stripes.
14	C056	1233	lekythos	Same. Traces of fragmentary black painted design.
15	C043	1233	bowl	East Greek. Very fine reddish yellow clay 5YR 6/8. Self ext. burnish. Matte sepia paint. Knife shaved exterior.
16	1054/43	1232	bowl	East Greek. Fine reddish yellow clay 5YR 7/6. Black to dark reddish paint.
17	1037/2	1118	bowl	East Greek. Fine light reddish brown clay 5YR 6/4. Self slip. Black to brown paint.

Fig. 102. *Persian period imported Athenian and East Greek fine wares.*

East Greek Imports

The East Greek imported wares consist of banded bowls (fig. 102:15–17). These are shallow hemispherical bowls. When complete, they have one or two horizontal loop handles and ring bases. The exterior is always decorated with a band at the rim, and often a second band below it. The top of the interior is decorated with a broad band and narrower bands are found near the bottom. They are dated from the seventh through sixth centuries to the end of the fifth century B.C.E. (Mook and Coulson 1995: 93–94). The bowls presented here are of two sub-types:

Type A. Wide bowls (fig. 102:15–16)

Diameters 22 and 25 cm, with a ledge rim overhanging the interior, slanting downwards. Parallels: Dor, Type C and others, sixth century (Mook and Coulson 1995: fig. 3.3).

Type B. Small bowls (fig. 102:17)

With a diameter of 10 cm, this may have been a cup. It has an almost concave rim tapering up to a pointed lip. While considered to originate in East Greece, most examples have come from other Mediterranean sites. The earliest parallels to this vessel come from Mersin, seventh century B.C.E. (Barnett 1940: 120–21). An early example from Tell Keisan dates to 575–550 B.C.E. (Briend and Humbert 1980: 126 and Pl. 22:6). The Dor parallels are dated to late fifth century (Mook and Coulson 1995: 94 and fig. 3.1:14–18).

A few very small red painted sherds (not illustrated) may belong to East Greek juglets.

HELLENISTIC POTTERY

Bowls, Cups and Plates

In the Hellenistic period, the imitations of imported types prevail in the bowls and cups repertoire (figs. 103–4; also figs. 11:4, 7, 10; Ch. II.1). Most of the bowls continue to have the shapes of the Attic prototypes, and imitate the black lustrous slip of the Athenian pottery of the Persian period. Small numbers of imported wares are also found.

Type A. Small bowls with incurved rim (figs. 103:1–5, 104:18–21)

These have a ring base and curved walls, and are covered by a matt slip, black, red to brown, or all mottled together. These are the most popular bowls in the Hellenistic era in the country. Parallels are known from almost every excavation in Israel and outside: Ashdod (Dothan 1971: fig. 98:7); Tel Michal, throughout the Hellenistic era (Fischer 1989: 177 and figs. 13.1:3–5; 13.2:6–9; 13.3:1–3, 9–19, 23); Tel Mevorakh, third–second centuries B.C.E. (Rosenthal 1978: 23 and fig. 3:10–12); Akko, second century (Dothan 1976: fig. 30:4–6); Tell Keisan Stratum II (Briend and Humbert 1980: Pl. 13:1–7); Shikmona, second century (Elgavish 1974: Pl. 33:300); Dor, from the second half of the fourth to the mid-first century B.C.E. (Guz-Zilberstein 1995: 289–90 and fig. 6.1:1–24).

Type B. Large bowls with incurved rim (fig. 103:6)

They have the same profile and lip as Type A, but a larger diameter. Found at Dor, all Hellenistic phases (Guz-Zilberstein 1995: 290 and fig. 6.1:25–29). A similar bowl comes from Tell Keisan, third–second centuries B.C.E. (Briend and Humbert 1980: fig. 13:7).

Type C. Miniature bowls with incurved rim (fig. 103:7; also fig. 11:7, 10, Ch. II.1)

They have the same profile and brown wash. At Dor, these bowls are identified as cosmetic mixing bowls, end of the fourth century (Guz-Zilberstein 1995: fig. 6.1:30–32); Samaria, early Hellenistic (Hennessy 1970: fig. 11:10).

Type D. Flat rolled grooved rim bowls (fig. 103:8–9)

A flat and shallow bowl, derived from the Athenian West Slope Ware. The bowls are black slipped, and there are traces of white paint on the interior. Parallels: Tell Keisan (Briend and Humbert 1980: Pl. 13:25–25a); Dor, where like our examples ware and slip are very similar to the original eastern-made West Slope technique (Rosenthal-Heginbottom 1995: 223–31). They date to the third–second centuries B.C.E.

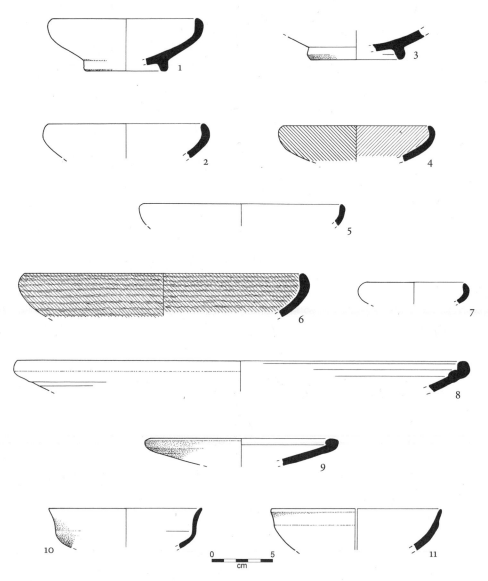

No.	Reg. No.	Locus	Form	Description
1	C028	1205	bowl	Red clay 2.5YR 5/6, tiny red and black grits. Matt black interior and exterior slip.
2	1042/15	1106	bowl	Light reddish brown clay 5YR 6/4. Interior black lustrous slip, exterior dark gray matt slip.
3	1042/1	1107	bowl	Very well levigated clay, pink 7.5YR 8/4 to reddish yellow 75.YR 8/6. Interior rouletted, red weak glaze 2.5YR 5/8, exterior weal black glaze.
4	1044/18	1204	bowl	Yellow soft clay 10YR 8/6, many tiny black and white grits. Interior matt slip weak red 10YR 4/4, exterior red.
5	1014/27	1207	bowl	Hard, fine light red clay 10R 6/6, dark gray gloss.
6	1047/13	1123	bowl	Brown clay 7.5YR 5/4, exterior brown burnished.
7	1019/14	1007	bowl	Pinkish gray clay 7.5YR 7/2, traces of brown slip.
8	1044/16	1204	bowl	Fine light brown clay 7.5YR 6/3. Matt black glaze. White paint, not shown.
9	C067	1312	bowl	Fine red clay 2.5YR 6/6, matt sepia glaze.
–	10/3	surface	bowl	See Chapter II.1, fig. 11:4.
10	C042	1233	cup	Fine levigated red clay 2.5YR 6/6. Interior and exterior lustrous black glaze
11	1054/46	1232	cup	Same as previous. Attic?

Fig. 103. *Hellenistic bowls and cups.*

Cups (figs. 103:10–11, 104:17)

They have a smoothed out-turned rim and carinated body. The walls are thin and slipped by a high gloss grayish black slip. The walls of cup no. 11 are somewhat thicker than those of no. 10, pointing to a possible Attic origin. Parallels: Dor, dated to the end of the fourth century (Guz-Zilberstein 1995: 338 and fig. 6.69:8). Rotroff (1997: 57–58) suggest that the smaller vessels were also used in Athens for serving olives, shelled nuts and other dry food. Our fig. 104:17 shows a bowl or cup with straight walls and tapered rim.

Fish plates (fig. 104:12–16)

They are the hallmarks of the period. The bowls feature everted, down-turned rims, and walls sloping down towards a central depression. They are covered with a black, brown, red dull slip, unlike the early Attic prototype with the black lustrous slip. They prevail throughout the period. Our examples nos. 13–14 should be assigned to Dor Type BL 4d, dated to the third century, but especially to the second century B.C.E. (Guz-Zilberstein 1995: 292 and fig. 6.3:22–27). Other parallels come from Samaria, third–second centuries (Crowfoot, Crowfoot and Kenyon 1957: fig. 54:11–12), Akko, second century (Dothan 1976: fig. 30:2); Tell Keisan, third–second centuries (Briend and Humbert 1980: Pl. 13:12–12a). The base in our no. 15 has a raised ring surrounding the central depression. Parallels: Samaria (Crowfoot, Crowfoot and Kenyon 1957: 262 and fig. 54:5, 14, 17, 20); Tel Michal (Fischer 1989: fig. 13.2:15); and Dor (Guz-Zilberstein 1995: fig. 6.3:10, 12), all dating to the second century B.C.E.

A surface locally made bowl, with a central depression and a disk base (fig. 11:4, Ch. II.1), probably derives from the fish-plate tradition. The base is string cut. Parallels: Ramat Aviv, third–second centuries (Gorzalczani 2000: fig. 4:5); Tel Michal, first century B.C.E. (Fischer 1989: fig. 13.3:8).

Skyphoi (fig. 104:22–24)

The fragment shown in no. 22 is a spurred handle, while nos. 23–24 are the ring bases of the Hellenistic skyphos. They have relatively thick walls, shallow ring bases and are covered by a dull reddish brown slip. Unlike the horizontal handle of the early Attic period, this skyphos has two outward extending handles, turning sharply downwards and spurred at the turn. At Samaria, they date to the first century B.C.E. (Crowfoot, Crowfoot and Kenyon 1957: fig. 39:4); at Tell Keisan, beginning of the second century (Briend and Humbert 1980: pl. 13:26), while at Dor they are found from the end of the fourth century to the end of the second century B.C.E. (Guz-Zilberstein 1995: 294 and fig. 6.6:3–9).

Krater

Only one rim fragment (fig. 105:1) could be assigned to a krater, a rare type, with an out-flaring, wide curving rim. The type resembles Athenian West Slope technique kraters (Guz-Zilberstein 1995: 296, and the parallel from the beginning of the second century, fig. 6.12:7). Another possible parallel is the bowl from Samaria, dated to the Late Hellenistic era (Hennessy 1970: fig. 9:24).

Cooking Pots and Casseroles

The cooking vessels of the period are of two categories: globular cooking pots, of several types (figs. 105:2–6, 106:7–8), and casseroles (fig. 106:9–12).

Globular cooking pots with vertical necks (fig. 105:2–3)

These pots continue the Persian period tradition: globular body, straight to angled neck, and two handles from rim to shoulder. Manufacture in the Hellenistic period is much better and the clay is well fired to metallic. Slight ribbing appears on the body. Our fig. 105:2–3 illustrates cooking pots with a straight vertical neck and simple rim. Number 3 is metallic fired, slightly ribbed, with strap handles. Parallels: Tel Michal Stratum IIIa, first century B.C.E. (Fischer 1989: fig. 13.3:18–19); Tell Keisan, second century B.C.E. (Briend and Humbert 1980: Pl. 11:3a–b); Ashdod, second century (Dothan 1971: figs. 10:7; 80:3–4). At Tel Anafa and Jatt, they are dated as Early Hellenistic (Berlin 1997: 85 and Pl. 21:184–86; Porath, Yannai and Kasher 1999: fig. 13:7).

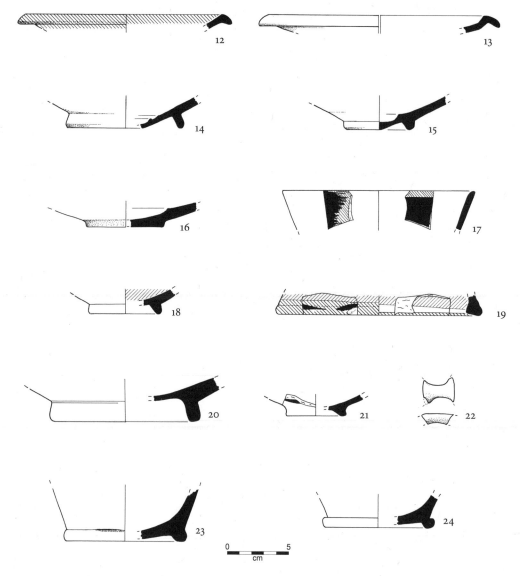

No.	Reg. No.	Locus	Form	Description
12	1045/45	1232	fish plate	Very fine levigated red clay 2.5YR 6/6. Interior and exterior matt black glaze.
13	1049/112	1230	fish plate	Reddish yellow clay 7.5YR 6/6, black gloss slip.
14	1049/8	1018	fish plate	Pink 7.5YR 8/4 to reddish yellow 7.5YR 8/6 clay. Interior exterior red and black gloss.
15	1049/16	1018	fish plate	Reddish yellow clay 5YR 7/6. Exterior red gloss 2.5YR 5/8.
16	1067/8	1233	fish plate	Reddish yellow clay 5YR 7/6, common red grits.
17	1059/32	1233	cup	Fine levigated reddish brown clay 5YR 5/4, lustrous sepia glaze.
18	1044/3	1204	bowl	Very fine levigated red clay 2.5YR 6/6. Interior red gloss 10R 5/8.
19	1044/4	1204	bowl	Red clay 2.5YR 6/6. Int./ext. metallic sepia glaze.
20	1057/3	1129	bowl	Same as previous.
21	1044/23	1204	bowl	Pale yellow clay 2.5Y 8/4, many tiny white grits. Int./ext. metallic black glaze. Reserved ext. base.
22	1051/9	1018	skyphos	dark gray gloss.
23	1073/4	1233	skyphos	Very fine red clay 2.5YR 5/6. Int./ext. black gloss. Reserved under base.
24	1075/3	1233	skyphos	Same as previous.

Fig. 104. *Hellenistic bowls and cups.*

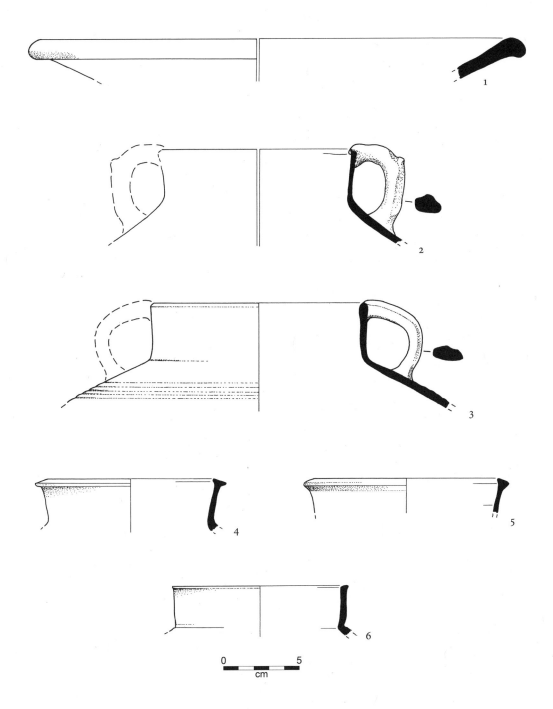

No.	Reg. No.	Locus	Form	Description
1	1049/6	1018	krater	Sandy pale yellow clay 2.5YR 7/3, many tiny black and white grits.
2	1032/14	1204	cooking pot	Red clay 2.5YR 5/6. Few large white grits, many tiny black grits.
3	1044/1	1204	cooking pot	Dark red clay 2.5YR 4/6, common white grits.
4	1067/38	1233	cooking pot	Yellowish red clay 5YR 5/8. Abundant tiny black and white grits.
5	1032/23	1204	cooking pot	Same as previous.
6	1045/7	1232	cooking pot	Dusky red clay 5YR 4/3. Few tiny black and white grits.

Fig. 105. *Hellenistic krater and cooking pots.*

Cooking pots with triangular thickened rims (fig. 105:4–5)

These are derived directly from the Persian period. Parallels: Tell Keisan, end of the fourth century (Briend and Humbert 1980: Pl. 11:1–2); Tel Michal, Persian period (Fischer 1989: figs. 9.1:3–4; 9.2:4); Dor (Guz-Zilberstein 1995: 298–99); Tel Anafa, dated 95–75 B.C.E. (Berlin 1997: 90 and Pl. 24:208–9).

Pots with a straight to concave neck, fitting a lid (figs. 105:6, 106:7–8)

This is a new type, without a local prototype, and may be of Greek tradition (Dothan 1976: 30, fig. 30:13, Early Hellenistic). Parallels: Dor, they begin in the third century, continuing to the second century (Guz-Zilberstein 1995: 299 and fig. 6.19:2, 5, 11). The same dates are given at Tel Anafa (Berlin 1997: 86 and Pl. 21:187–90). At Ashdod (Dothan 1971: 48, 144 and figs. 10:7; 80:3–4), Tel Michal (Fischer 1989: 184 and fig. 13.3:17), and Tell Keisan (Briend and Humbert 1980: Pl. 11:3) they are dated to the first century B.C.E.

Casseroles are shallow cooking vessels with lid receptors, usually with two strap handles from rim to shoulder. This vessel type is Greek, and is known from Greek assemblages as early as the fifth century B.C.E. In Hellenistic Greece, they are very common and in some case the prevalent type of cooking vessel found (Berlin 1997: 94). In the Levant, they appear during the Hellenistic era at sites with Greek influence.

A handleless casserole, with curved body and everted rim is shown in fig. 106:9. There is a lid device ridge inside the rim. Parallels: Akko, Late Hellenistic (Dothan 1976: fig. 30:12); Tell Keisan, end of fourth century to end of second century (Briend and Humbert 1980: Pl. 11:9); Dor, from third century to end of second century (Guz-Zilberstein 1995: 300 and fig. 6.21:12).

Casserole with flaring concave rim (fig. 106:10–11)

When complete, they have a rounded body and a pair of handles, either vertical straps or horizontal loop handles. Parallels: Tell Keisan (Briend and Humbert 1980: Pl. 11:5d, 8); Dor, beginning in the third century, but mainly dated to the second century (Guz-Zilberstein 1995: 299 and fig. 6.20:6–7); Tel Anafa, end of second century to early first century B.C.E. (Berlin 1997: Pl. 28:236, 238).

Casserole lid (fig. 106:12)

This form is the typical lid from the Hellenistic period onwards.

Storage Jars

The Hellenistic period storage jars are divided into two types: bag-shaped (fig. 107:1–7) and flat shouldered (fig. 107:8). The former type is the most common and is actually found in every excavated Hellenistic site on the coast or in the northern part of Israel. When complete, these jars have elongated bodies, round shoulders and two opposite handle attached from shoulder to the body. The rim is always everted, and sometimes serves as a neck. In our examples, the rim treatment may be divided as follows: A. Nos. 1, 4–5 have well modeled rims; B. Nos. 2–3 rounded thickened rims; C. Nos. 6–7 simple everted rims, narrowing towards the top. When complete, they are usually ribbed.

Sub-types A and B have parallels throughout the period at Dor (Guz-Zilberstein 1995: 311 and fig. 6.36); Tell Keisan (Briend and Humbert 1980: Pl. 8:3–7); Tel Michal, second century (Fischer 1989: fig. 2:20); Shikmona, second century (Elgavish 1974: Pl. 27:269); Samaria (Hennessy 1970: figs. 9:1, 11; 10:10–11, 13; 11:12–13, 16).

Sub-type C is later than the previous two, and at Dor they first appear in the last quarter of the second century B.C.E. (Guz-Zilberstein 1995: 311 and fig. 6.37:1–5); Shikmona, same date (Elgavish 1974: Pl. 27:268); Tel Michal, second century (Fischer 1989: fig. 13.2:21); Samaria, Late Hellenistic (Hennessy 1970: fig. 9:10). At Ramat Aviv, they are dated to the third–second centuries B.C.E. (Gorzalczani 2000: fig. 4:14–16).

The flat shouldered storage jar (fig. 107:8) has a conical, down-sloping shoulder, short neck and a rounded thickened rim. When complete, they have two twisted handles from shoulder to body. The body is wider at the bottom and is usually ribbed. It continues the flat shouldered jar of the

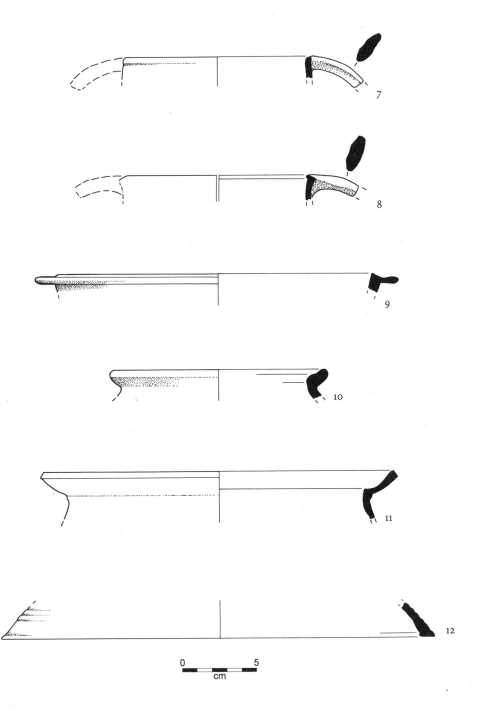

Fig. 106. *Hellenistic cooking pots, casseroles and lid.*

No.	Reg. No.	Locus	Form	Description
7	1045/32	1232	cooking pot	Same as previous.
8	1045/1	1232	cooking pot	Same as previous.
9	1049/2	1230	casserole	Yellowish red clay 5YR 5/8. Few white grits.
10	1073/5	1233	casserole	Same as previous.
11	1048/3	1204	casserole	Same as previous.
12	1028/3	1007	lid	Burnt black.

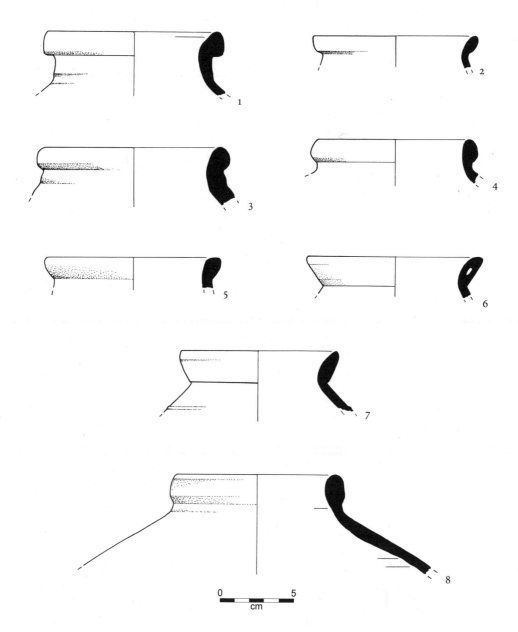

No.	Reg. No.	Locus	Form	Description
1	1045/8	1232	storage jar	Very fine levigated pale brown clay 10YR 6/3. Int./ext. yellow slip 2.5YR 7/3.
2	1108/9	1035	storage jar	Light red clay 2.5YR 7/8. Few white inclusions.
3	1028/1	1007	storage jar	Reddish yellow clay 5YR 6/8, gray core 7.5YR 6/1. Common black and white grits. Exterior pink slip 7.5YR 8/3.
4	1067/1	1233	storage jar	Very fine levigated pale brown clay 10YR 6/3. Exterior yellow slip 2.5YR 7/3.
5	1059/12	1233	storage jar	Pale brown clay 10YR 6/3. few large white inclusions. Ext. very pale brown slip 10YR 7/3.
6	1016/1	1007	storage jar	Light red clay 10R 7/8, few grits. Ext. very pale brown slip 10YR 8/3.
7	1060/3	1018	storage jar	Pink clay 7.5YR 7/4, few tiny white inclusions. Exterior pale yellow slip 2.5Y 8/3.
8	1045/10	1232	storage jar	Light brown clay 7.5YR 6/4 with few large white chunks. Ext. very pale brown slip 10YR 7/3.

Fig. 107. *Hellenistic storage jars.*

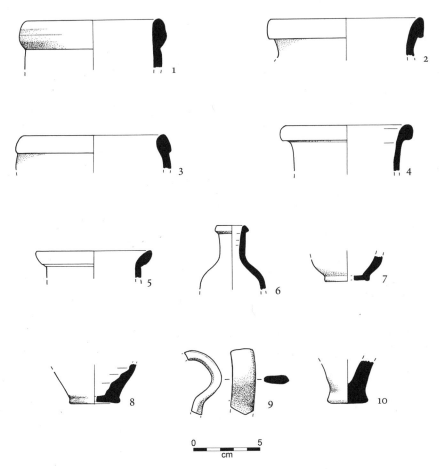

0 _____ 5
cm

No.	Reg. No.	Locus	Form	Description
1	1028/8	1007	jug	Reddish yellow clay 5YR 7/8, many black and white grits.
2	1028/12	1007	jug	Light red core 10R 7/8, surrounded by pink outer surface 7.5YR 7/4. Few medium size white grits.
3	1080/1	1010	jug	Fine levigated reddish yellow clay 5YR 6/8.
4	1045/38	1232	jug	Light reddish clay 5YR 6/4, few large white inclusions.
5	1106/9	1038	jug	Same. Ext. slip very pale brown 10YR 8/4.
6	C040	1204	bottle	Light yellowish brown clay 10YR 6/6. Very few tiny red grits.
7	1051/10	1009	bottle	Very fine levigated reddish yellow clay 7.5YR 8/6.
8	1039/4	1007	juglet	Fine levigated reddish yellow clay 5YR 7/6. Exterior slip very pale brown 10YR 8/4.
9	1028/3	1007	juglet	Reddish yellow clay 5YR 7/6, smooth texture, few grits. Red gloss 7.5R 5/6.
10	1049/14	1018	juglet	Sandy very pale brown clay 10YR 8/4. Self slipped.
–	10/1	surface	amphoriskos	See Chapter II.1 fig. 12:4.

Fig. 108. *Hellenistic jugs, bottles and juglets.*

Persian period. Parallels: Shikmona, mid-second century (Elgavish 1974: Pls. 10:211; 17:235 (inscribed); 23:251–52). At Dor, these jars are earlier, most of them dated to the end of the fourth to third century, except for one specimen from the second century B.C.E. (Guz-Zilberstein 1995: 312 and fig. 6.38:1–2, 4).

Jugs

There are five specimens (fig. 108:1–5). The examples in fig. 108:1–3 are of the globular type. They have a wide cylindrical neck and thickened everted rims. When complete, they have a widening bag-shaped body and a loop handle from rim to shoulder. This type continues the Persian era type. Parallels: Dor, Early Hellenistic through second century B.C.E. (Guz-Zilberstein 1995: 309 and fig. 6.30:1–5); Samaria, Late Hellenistic (Hennessy 1970: fig. 9:15); Tell Keisan, fourth century B.C.E. (Briend and Humbert 1980: Pl. 9: 3–11).

The walls of the vessels in fig. 108:4–5 are thinner than the previous and they have flaring rims. When complete, they have piriform bodies and a shallow ring-base. These are very common in the period. Parallels: Shikmona, second century (Elgavish 1974: Pls. 15:228; 33:301); Tel Keisan, end of fourth century to third century (Briend and Humbert 1980: Pl. 9:12); Dor, similar dates (Guz-Zilberstein 1995: 309 and fig. 6.31:3–8); Ashdod, first half of the first century B.C.E. (Dothan 1971: figs. 11:4–5; 100:3).

Bottles and Juglets

These vessels are represented by several types (fig. 108:6–10; also figs. 13:4; 14:4, Ch. II.1). The most common type of bottle is the *unguentarium* (fig. 108:6–7). The thin walls with a relatively short neck date it to the end of the third century to the second century B.C.E., as was noted at Dor (Guz-Zilberstein 1995: 304–5 and fig. 6.26), where it is a transitional sub-type between the heavier early types and thinner and longer later bottles. The bases in fig. 108:8 and 10 are of deeper juglets, as is the slipped handle (fig. 108:9).

A surface find (figs. 13:4; 14:4, Ch. II.1) has walls too thin to be an *amphoriskos*. It is probably a flask. The presence of vertical wheel ribbing on the interior point to a double bowl vessel. Flasks with a long narrow neck are common in the southern part of the land from the second century B.C.E., while the northern ones have shorter necks are more massive. The parallel from Dor fits well the form and date (Guz-Zilberstein 1995: 310 and fig. 6.34:2), as does that from Tirat Yehuda (Yeivin and Edelstein 1970: fig. 7:21–23).

DISCUSSION

The typological analysis of the Tell Tanninim pottery reveals a succession of habitation from the end of the Iron age to the end of the Hellenistic period. The new finds of the Iron Age pottery, dated to the seventh century B.C.E., link Tel Tanninim to the contemporary settlement at Dor. Since Tel Mevorakh experienced a gap in occupation during these times, it is possible that Tel Tanninim took its place, exploiting the anchorage at the mouth of the Tanninim River.

The presence of this natural anchorage is probably the *raison d'être* for the settlement of the Persian period. It must have been established as early as 550–500 B.C.E., on the evidence of the East Greek banded bowls, with a large number of sherds from the fifth century onward, as is also evident at most coastal sites in the region. The dated pottery shows that there was no break in the occupation of the site until the end of the second century B.C.E. Although some types could be assigned to the end of the second century and the first century B.C.E., the lack of prominent types, such as the Megarian bowls and the sigillata wares, indicates that the site was deserted after the end of the second century B.C.E.

More than at nearby sites, the Tel Tanninim excavated household repertoire is very limited, with actually no local bowls, kraters and very few jugs and juglets. On the other hand, the fact that storage jars are abundant during both Persian and Hellenistic periods raises the possibility of a trading station and depot. The presence of relatively large quantities of imported wares may add weight to this argument.

Although no quantitative measurements were done on the pottery, it seems that the Persian period pottery surpasses the Hellenistic. Does it tell about the size of each period's settlement? It is important, though, to bear in mind the very limited area that was excavated. It is likely that larger scale excavations in the relevant levels will change the picture depicted here.

2. Byzantine

by Michal Oren-Paskal

The pottery assemblage discussed below derives from selected loci of Areas A, B and B2 at Tel Tanninim. Pottery is classified on the basis of form typology within the groups of fine ware, cooking ware and amphorae. The types are arranged and discussed in the following order: bowls, jugs and flasks, closed and open cooking pots, lids, local and imported amphorae. The catalogue provides a description of each piece, indicating form, fabric, date range and parallels. Each ceramic in the catalog is designated by its registration number (= basket number) and locus. The color of the ware is taken from Munsell Color Chart 1994. The pottery is dated by comparative research to other sites, however, in some cases, it is impossible to draw exact parallels to vessels of the same type.

RED SLIP WARE BOWLS

Three major groups of Red Slip Ware are represented here: African, Phocaean, and Cypriot. The bowls were imported from three manufacture centers. African Red Slip was manufactured in North Africa, Phocaean Red Slip came from Asia Minor and Cypriot Red Slip came from Cyprus. The vessels are characterized by a hard red fabric and slip. The most common group belongs to the African Red Slip, while only two vessels represent the Phocaean Red Slip and Cypriot Red Slip. The assemblage suggests a date between the late fifth to early eighth century.

African Red Slip Ware (fig. 109:1–8)

African Red Slip is the leading fine ware in most parts the Mediterranean region over a period of several centuries. The clay is fairly coarse and orange-red to brick-red in color. The slip is of good quality and commonly a shade or two deeper in tone than the clay of the body. African Red Slip ware is represented by one type (nos. 1–5), which may be compared to Hayes' Form 104C, that consists of number of variants. This type occurs between the late fifth to the early eighth century. These variants mainly differ by the number of grooves. Number 5 bears an unidentified stamp. Stamped decoration is a characteristic feature of the ware. This is usually found on the floors of bowls, mainly of the larger varieties.

1. 2044/18, L 2327. Rim d. 31.8 cm, surface: light red slip 10R 6/6, core: red 10R 5/8; hard clay with few small white grits. Rounded knobbed rim, a groove below the rim. Date range: late fifth to early eighth century. Refs: Lechaion, Greece, mid-sixth to early seventh century (Hayes 1972: 163–66 and fig. 30:23); Khirbat al-Karak, coins 491–518 and 730/731 C.E. (Delougaz 1960: 32 and Pl. 53:11:3); Jerusalem, first half of sixth century (Tushingham 1985: 193 and fig. 62:14–15); Yoqneʿam, late sixth–seventh century (Avissar 1996: 66 and fig.XII.1:7); Tell Keisan, seventh century (Landgraf 1980: 54 and fig. 14a: Form 10b); Kursi, early seventh to early eighth century (Tzaferis 1983: 31 and fig. 4:1); Beth Sheʿarim, second half of sixth to early seventh century (Vitto 1996: 128 and Fig. 22:2); Shavei Zion, fifth–sixth centuries (Prausnitz, Avi-Yonah and Barag 1967: 42 and fig. 12:3); Pella, second quarter of sixth century (Smith, McNicoll and Watson 1992: 176 and Pl. 111:12).

2. 2063/15, L 2340. Rim d. 33 cm, surface: red slip 10R 6/8, core: red 10R 5/8; hard clay with few small white grits. Rounded knobbed rim, a groove on internal wall. Date range: fifth to early eighth centuries. Refs: see no. 1.

3. 2037/9, L 2304. Rim d. 34.2 cm, surface: light red slip 10R 6/6, core: red 10R 5/8; hard clay with few small white grits. Rounded knobbed rim, a groove on internal wall. Date range: fifth to early eighth centuries. Refs: see no. 1.

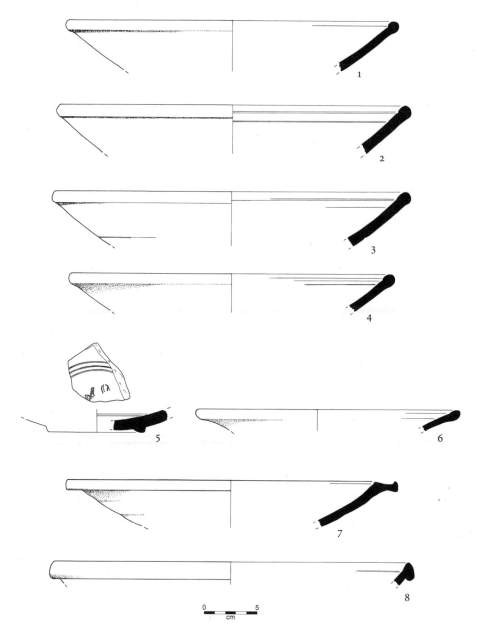

Fig. 109. *African Red Slip Ware.*

4. 2035/5, L 2304. Rim d. 31 cm, surface: red slip 10R 5/8, core: red 10R 5/8; hard clay with few small white grits. Rounded knobbed rim, a groove on internal wall. Date range: fifth to early eighth centuries. Refs: see no. 1.

5. 0054/2, L 2031. Base d. 9.2 cm, surface: light red slip 10R 6/8, core: red 10R 5/8; hard clay. Ring base. Unidentified stamp surrounded by three concentric grooves on floor. Date range: fifth to early eighth centuries. Refs: see no. 1.

6. 0077/6, L 2031. Rim d. 27.2 cm, red clay 10R 5/8 with a few white grits. Refs: see no. 1.

7. 0047/5, L 2023. Rim d. 32 cm. Wide overhanging horizontal rim with a slightly concave lip summit. Red clay 2.5YR 6/6. Date range: sixth–eighth centuries. Refs: Capernaum Stratum V (Peleg 1989: 37 and fig. 14.16); Carthage, coins until early seventh century (Riley 1981: 98 and fig. 4.9); En Boqeq, coins until 571 (Gichon 1993: Taf. 35.31); Khirbat al-Karak, coins 518–731 C.E. (Delougaz 1960: 51–52

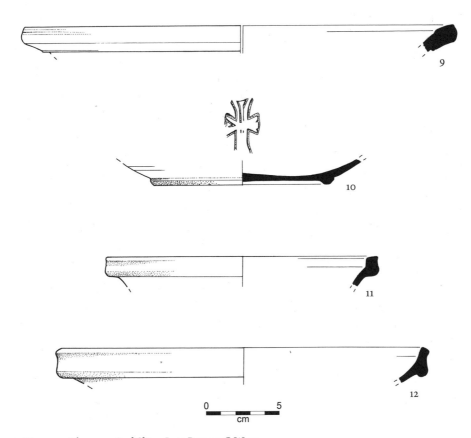

Fig. 110. *Phocaean Red Slip – Late Roman C Ware.*

and Pl. 52.65); Shavei Zion, fifth–sixth centuries (Prausnitz, Avi-Yonah and Barag 1967: 71 and fig. 13:2–3).

8. 1020/1, L 1001. Rim d. 35.2 cm. Bulbous rim overhanging body wall. Light red clay 2.5YR 7/8. Date range: sixth–seventh centuries. Refs: Capernaum Stratum V, early seventh century to 650 (Peleg 1989: 35, No. 2); Carthage, coins almost entirely mid-sixth century to 607 (Riley 1981: 98, 101–2 and fig. 4–5); Jerusalem Form 99a–b (Hayes 1985: fig. 62.9); Pella Stratum 3a, 525–550 (Smith, McNicoll and Watson 1992: 166 and Pl. 111:14).

Phocaean Red Slip – Late Roman C Ware (fig. 110:9–12)

This group was common throughout the Eastern Mediterranean during the fifth–seventh centuries, and the main manufacture centers were in Phocaea (Hayes 1980a: 525). At Khirbat al-Karak and Hammat Gader, the Late Roman C is dated up to

the eighth century (Delougaz 1960: 31–32; Ben-Arieh 1997: 359). Our nos. 9–10 can be compared to Hayes' Form 10 and bear a cross with double outline. This is the most common cross type on Late Roman C (Hayes 1972: 365). The ware is fine-grained brownish-red and hard-fired. The red slip, which covers the entire surface, is a thin layer and usually integrated with the ware.

9. 2015/5, L 2211. Rim d. 28 cm, surface: dark red slip 2.5YR 4/6, core: red 2.5YR 5/8; hard clay and many small white grits. Flattened rim with a small offset at junction with wall. Date range: late fifth–eighth centuries. Refs: Emporio, Chios, early to mid-seventh century (Hayes 1972: 343 and fig. 71:11); Hammat Gader, sixth–eighth centuries (Ben-Arieh 1997: 359 and Pl. VII:2); Tell Keisan, mid-sixth to mid-seventh century (Landgraf 1980: 54–65 and fig. 14a:8–11); Khirbat al-Karak, late fifth and early sixth to early eighth century (Delougaz 1960: 31–32 and Pl. 52:46); Yoqne'am, late sixth–seventh century (Avissar 1996: 66 and fig. XII:11–12); Sumaqa, fifth–seventh centuries (Kingsley 1999: 278 and fig. 2:9); Caesarea, early seventh century (Bar-Nathan 1986: 168 and fig. 4:9); Caesarea, late sixth to mid-seventh century (Magness 1995: 134 and fig. 1:3); Jerusalem, sixth century (Tushingham 1985: 193 and fig. 64:16).

10. 2015/4, L 2211. Base d. 13 cm, surface: red slip 10R 5/8, core: red 10R 5/8; hard clay, smooth texture. Low ring base stamped with double-outlined cross in the center. Date range: sixth to early seventh century. Refs: Lechaion, early sixth century (Hayes 1972: 365–66 and fig. 79:71e); Ramat Hanadiv, sixth century (Calderon 2000: 112 and Pl. X:69).

11. 0060/4, L 2033. Rim d. 19.2 cm. Shallow concave outer rim with a low offset ridge. Red clay 2.5YR 5/8. Refs: Hayes' Form 3F, sixth century.

12. 0039/3, L 2024. Rim d. 25.6 cm. High thin rim with a shallow concave outer plane. No offset ridge. Red clay 2.5YR 6/8. Date range fifth–seventh centuries. Refs: Hayes' Form 3C, 450–500; En Boqeq, latest coin 571 (Gichon 1993: Taf. 31.2); Horvat Castra, sixth–seventh centuries (Siegelmann 1996: 62 and fig. 7.16); Jerusalem Form 3B–C (Hayes 1985: 193 and fig. 63.10).

Cypriot Red Slip Ware (fig. 111:13–18)

Cypriot Red Slip ware is the third common group of red slip ware in the east. The precise source of the ware is unknown, but according to Hayes it was manufactured in Cyprus (Hayes 1972: 371), where a large quantity of these bowls has been found. The vessels closely resemble the Early Roman Cypriot Sigillata ware. The fabric varies between orange to brown and is entirely covered by a thin slip. The typical decoration on this ware is coarse rouletting, either of the whole wall or narrow bands. No. 13 assigned to Hayes' Form 9, Type B, dates to the late sixth until the end of the seventh century. This bowl is a common type during the Byzantine period in many sites throughout Israel and is one of the popular forms at Jalame.

13. 2040/10, L 2240. Rim d. 23 cm, surface: dark red slip 2.5YR 4/8, core: 2.5YR 6/6; hard clay. Inward curved rim, overhanging the body wall. Roulette decoration over the body wall. Date range: sixth

to mid-eighth centuries. Refs: Emporio, late sixth–seventh century (Hayes 1972: 379–82 and fig. 81:9); Jalame (Johnson 1988: 163 and fig. 7–16: 287); Caesarea, sixth–seventh centuries (Adan-Bayewitz 1986: 111–12 and fig. 5:8); Yoqne'am, late sixth–seventh century (Avissar 1996: 67 and fig. XII.3:5); Tell Keisan, mid sixth–seventh century (Landgraf 1980: 55 and fig. 15:9a); Ramot Nof, sixth–seventh centuries (Ustinova and Nahshoni 1994: 168 and fig. 7:9); En Boqeq, sixth–seventh centuries (Gichon 1993: 194–95 and Taf. 34:5–20); Dhiorios, Cyprus, mid-seventh to mid-eighth century (Catling 1972: 40 and fig. 5).

14. 0039/6, L 2024. Rim d. 24 cm. Incurving rim with a rounded outer plane. Very eroded clay, discolored by burning.

15. 0067/1, L 2018. 3 percent of rim fragment. Inward curving rim, grooved on outer plane. Incised striations over body, sub-triangular gouges on rim. Reddish yellow clay 5YR 6/8 with red gloss 2.5YR 5/8. Date range: late fifth to eighth centuries. Refs: Anemurium, late fifth to early sixth century (Williams 1989: 30 and fig. 11.164); Caesarea Hippodrome, 500–550 (Riley 1975: 37, No. 46); Capernaum Strata IV–V, early seventh century (Peleg 1989: 39, No. 35); Dhiorios, 650–750 (Catling 1972: 23 and fig. 5); Horvat Castra, sixth–seventh centuries (Siegelmann 1996: 83 and fig. 8.9); Khirbat al-Karak, coin range ca. 500–731 (Delougaz 1960: 51–52 and Pl. 52:29–30); Tell Keisan, *terminus ante quem* 638 (Landgraf 1980: 53, 59).

16. 1028/10, L 1007. Short rim, flattened on summit and incised with linear rouletted striations. Very eroded clay, climatically degraded. Date range: sixth–seventh centuries. Refs: Hayes' Form 7, second half of sixth to early seventh century; Capernaum, early seventh century (Peleg 1989: 41, No. 42); En Boqeq, latest coin 571 (Gichon 1993: Taf. 35.37a); Tell Keisan Form 7, until 638 C.E. (Landgraf 1980: 53, 59).

17. 1039/2, L 1007. Rim d. uncertain. Incised elongated oval incisions directly above the rim. Reddish yellow clay 5YR 7/8. Refs: Anemurium, late sixth to seventh century (Williams 1989: 31 and fig. 12.171).

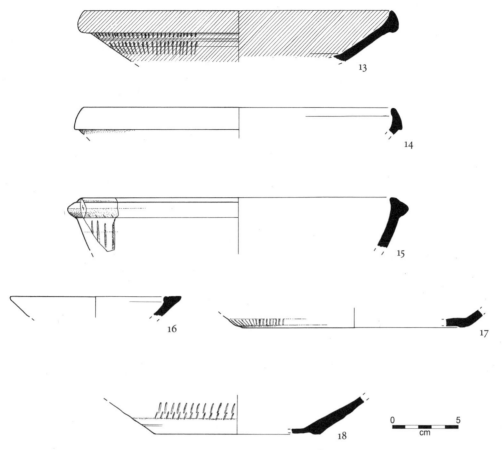

Fig. 111. *Cypriot Red Slip Ware.*

18. 0090/3, L 2038. Base d. 12.8 cm. Two lines of oblique, narrow oval striations directly above the base. Red clay 2.5YR 6/6. Date range: sixth–seventh centuries. Refs: Caesarea (CCE Field Report 1993: 20 and fig. 36B.2); Carmiel, latest coin 641–668 (Yeivin 1992: fig. 23.15).

JUGS AND FLASKS

Nos. 19–21 are representative of a jug with a strainer and spout. The ware is red and well-fired. The vessel is characterized by a strainer, sited at the transition between the neck and the body. Generally the body is covered with fine ribbing. The type is well known throughout Israel, Egypt and Cyprus and dated to late Byzantine and early Islamic periods. The water-wheel jar, no. 26, was attached to a wheel utilized to draw water from a well. The hard clay is red and contains many white grits. The vessel was connected to a wheel by a rope which was attached below the rim. This type of jar is dated from the Late Byzantine to the beginning of Islamic periods. Number 27 is a pilgrim flask made of hard red clay. The form is characteristic by a body created of two parts, as one is usually more concave than the other. Similar vessels are known from many sites in Israel and dated from the Late Byzantine to the Early Islamic period.

19. 2044/9, L 2327. Jug; body fragment, surface: red 10R 5/8, core: red 2.5YR 6/8; hard clay with many small white grits. Flaring neck with interior ribbing, remains of strainer at bottom of neck. Date range: sixth–eighth centuries. Refs: Sumaqa, early fifth to early seventh centuries (Kingsley 1999: 282 and fig. 12:8); Ramat Hanadiv, sixth–seventh centuries (Calderon 2000: 110 and Pl. VIII:53, 55); Caesarea, first half of the sixth century (Magness 1992: 147 and fig. 64:13); Caesarea, sixth to mid-seventh

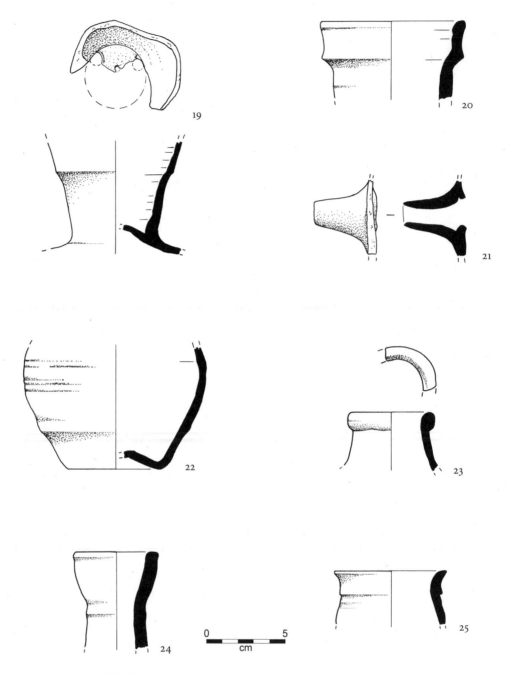

Fig. 112. *Jugs and Flasks.*

century (Magness 1995: 136 and fig. 3:16); Horvat Hermeshit, sixth–eighth centuries (Greenhut 1998: 135 and fig. 26:9); Ramot Nof, sixth–seventh centuries (Ustinova and Nahshoni 1994: 162 and fig. 6:32); Kellia, sixth–eighth centuries (Egloff 1977: 129 and Pl. 71:3); Dhiorios, sixth century (Catling 1972: 13 and fig. 5:P141).

20. 2037/5, L 2102. Jug; rim d. 9 cm, surface: red 2.5YR 6/6, core: red 2.5YR 5/8; hard clay with many small white and few small black grits. Slightly everted collar rim. Date range: sixth–eighth centuries. Refs: see no. 19.

21. 2021/1, L 2252. Jug; spout, surface: red 2.5YR 6/6, core: red 2.5YR 6/8; hard clay with many small white

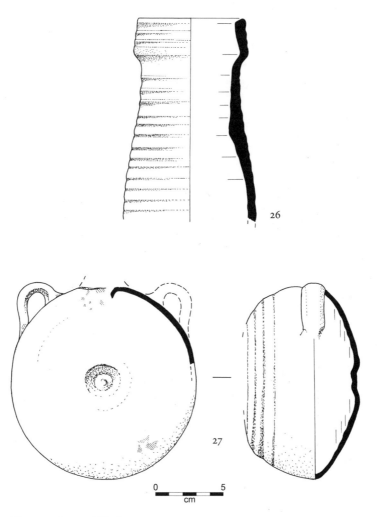

Fig. 113. *Jugs and Flasks.*

grits. Date range: sixth–eighth centuries. Refs: see no. 9.

22. 2090/1, L 2222. Jug; base d. 6.8 cm, surface: 5YR 7/6, core: red 2.5YR 6/8; medium-hard clay with many small white grits. Shallow ribbed wall attached to an omphalos base. Date range: sixth–eighth centuries. Refs: Horvat Hermeshit, sixth–eighth centuries (Greenhut 1998: 125 and fig. 10:4); Pella, mid-eighth century (McNicoll, Smith and Hennessy 1982: 170 and Pl. 142:1); Kellia, sixth–eighth centuries (Egloff 1977: 129 and Pl. 71:3).

23. 1005/5, L 1002. Rim d. 5.9 cm. Everted, semi-circular beaded rim lip. Silty light brown clay 7.5YR 6/4. Early Islamic.

24. 0039/1, L 2024. Rim d. 5.8 cm. Funnel-shaped water jar neck with simple rounded lip. Very soft, smooth lime-rich pale yellow clay 2.5Y 8/2, with few grits. Early Islamic.

25. 1060/5, L 1018. Rim d. 8 cm. Outwardly folded lip summit. Hard clay with abundant white shell grits, pale yellow 2.5Y 8/3. Early Islamic.

26. 2072, L 2240. Water-wheel jar (C045); rim d. 8 cm, max. height 14.6 cm, surface: light brown 7.5YR 6/4, core: yellowish red 5YR 5/6; sandy clay and few tiny white grits. Inverted ribbed rim, ribbing over entire body. Date range: sixth–eighth centuries. Refs: Sumaqa, early fifth to early seventh century (Kingsley 1999: 282 and fig. 12:18); Jalame (Johnson 1988: 214 and fig. 7-51:754); Ramat Hanadiv, sixth–seventh centuries (Calderon 2000: 147 and Pl. XXV:73); Caesarea, mid seventh–eighth century (Lenzen 1983: 393 and Pl. 42); Caesarea, mid to late sixth century (Riley 1975: 35, No. 38).

27. 1023/1, L 1007. Pilgrim flask; surface: light red 10R 6/6, core: red 10R 4/8; hard metallic clay with few small white grits. Round body composed of two parts; one part is ribbed and two loop handles are attached to the shoulder. Date range: sixth to mid-eighth century. Refs: Hammat Gader, sixth to mid-eighth century (Ben-Arieh 1997: 377–80 and Pl. XV:4–6); Kursi, early to mid-eighth century (Tzaferis 1983: 34 and fig. 8:20); Ramot Nof, sixth–eighth centuries (Ustinova and Nahshoni 1994: 162 and fig. 5:10); Khirbat al-Karak, sixth–seventh centuries (Delougaz 1960: 36 and Pl. 57:5–6); Rehovot-in-the-Negev, sixth–seventh centuries (Rosenthal-Heginbottom 1988: 88 and Pl. III:140); Pella, late seventh century (Watson 1992: 243 and fig. 14:118).

COOKING WARE

The vessels comprise closed cooking pots and open cooking vessels (casseroles, frying pans and lids). All the vessels are characteristic of the Byzantine period.

Closed cooking pots (fig. 114:28–33)

These comprise the largest group, which dominates the cooking ware, and is subdivided into vessels with neck (nos. 28–29) and without neck (nos. 30–32). The former type is characterized by a concave neck, thin wall and inward pointed rim. The clay is hard and contains few white inclusions. Cooking pots of similar type are known from Cyprus (Catling 1972: 95) and Kellia (Egloff 1977: 103), as well as from many sites in Israel. Number 30 is well represented in Caesarea, Jalame, Khirbat al-Karak, Yoqneʿam and Pella in the Byzantine layers. Vessel No. 31 usually has vertical handles and, according to Smith and Day (1989: 110), may have been manufactured in the region of Pella. This has to be tested by further analysis since many vessels of this type were found in sites in Israel.

28. 2031/24, L 2304. Rim d. 14 cm, surface: light red 10R 6/6, core: red 2.5YR 5/6; hard metallic clay, with few tiny white grits. Inward pointed rim, concave neck. Date range: mid-fourth to mid-eighth century. Refs: Caesarea, seventh century (Adan-Bayewitz 1986: 108 and fig. 4:4); Caesarea, mid-seventh century (Blakely 1993: 65 and fig. 134:5); Caesarea, late fourth to mid-eighth century (Oleson, Fitzgerald, Sherwood and Sidebotham 1994: 38 and fig. 8:K22); Caesarea, sixth to mid-seventh century (Magness 1995: 135 and fig. 1:16); Khirbet ʿOvesh, sixth to mid-seventh century (Aviam and Getzov 1998: 69 and fig. 9:11); Ashqelon, sixth–seventh centuries (Nahshoni 2000: 103 and fig. 5:12); Kellia, seventh century (Egloff 1977: 103 and Pl. 52:1–2, 4); Dhiorios, mid-seventh to mid-eighth century (Catling 1972: 95 and fig. 7:P96); Anemurium, sixth to seventh centuries (Williams 1989: 68 and fig. 37:406).

29. 2040/12, L 2240. Rim d. 9.5 cm, surface: dark gray 7.5YR 4/4, core: red 2.5YR 5/8; hard metallic clay with many small white grits. Inward pointed rim, concave neck, ribbed shoulder. Date range: mid-fourth to mid-eighth century. Refs: see no. 27.

30. 2063/19, L 2340. Rim d. 13.4 cm, surface: pale red 10R 6/4, core: red 2.5YR 5/8; hard clay with many small white grits and little quartz. Outward folded rim with a recess for a lid, no neck, heavy ribbing on shoulder. Date range: late fourth to mid-seventh century. Refs: Khirbat al-Karak, seventh century (Delougaz 1960: Pl. 53:37), Yoqneʿam, late sixth to seventh century (Avissar 1996: 72–73 and fig. XII:6–8); Jalame, late fourth century (Johnson 1988: 200 and fig. 7-42:628); Caesarea, mid-sixth century (Magness 1992: fig. 62:8); Pella, mid-seventh century (Watson 1992: 235 and fig. 2:14).

31. 1028/6, L 1113. Rim d. 19 cm, surface: reddish gray slip 10R 5/1, core: pale red 10R 6/4; sandy clay with many minute-small white grits. Folded beveled rim. Date range: fourth–eighth centuries. Refs: Hammat-Gader, sixth–eighth centuries (Ben-Arieh 1997: 371 and Pl. XII:19); Yoqneʿam, late sixth to seventh century (Avissar 1996: 73 and Pl. XII.6.9); Sumaqa, early fifth to seventh century (Kingsley 1999: fig. 9:8); Ramat Hanadiv, sixth to beginning of seventh century (Calderon 2000: 140 and Pl. XXII:45); Caesarea, late fourth to early fifth cen-

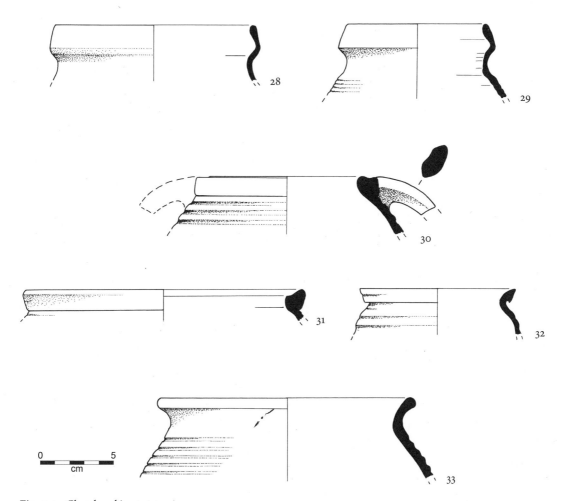

Fig. 114. *Closed cooking pots.*

tury (Tomber 1993: 319 and fig. 7:116); Pella, sixth century (Watson 1992: 235 and fig. 2:11); Pella, sixth to early seventh century (Smith and Day 1989: 110 and Pl. 51:8); Kellia, seventh century (Egloff 1977: 101 and Pl. 48:3).

32. 2063/5, L 2340. Rim d. 11 cm, surface: white slip 10YR 8/2, core: red 2.5YR 5/6; hard fine clay with few minute white grits. Outward folded rim with a groove on exterior lip, no neck, heavy ribbing occurs on shoulder. Date range: sixth–eighth centuries. Refs: Hammat Gader, sixth–eighth centuries (Ben-Arieh 1997: 371 and Pl. XII:16); Jerusalem, beginning of third quarter of sixth century (Tushingham 1985: 92 and fig. 28:28); Pella, mid-seventh century (Watson 1992: 235 and fig. 2:13).

33. 0087/1, L 2038. Rim d. 17.6 cm. Outward rolled rim; ribbed shoulder and upper body. Silty poorly

bonded red clay 2.5YR 5/8, with high iron content, common white inclusions. Date range: sixth–seventh centuries. Refs: Caesarea, 630–660 (Adan-Bayewitz 1986: fig. 127.2); Capernaum, 600–650 (Peleg 1989: 65, No. 18); Jalame Form 27 (Johnson 1988: 199, No. 623); Jerusalem Phase IIIa (Tushingham 1985: fig. 30:27); Pella, 500–525 (Smith, McNicoll and Watson 1992: 164 and Pl. 110:3).

Open cooking vessels (fig. 115:34–39)

Number 34 is a cooking bowl, covered entirely by ribbing, with horizontal handles. This type is characteristic of the Byzantine period and continuing into the Islamic period with few changes. At Khirbet ed-Deir this open form is more common than the closed vessels (Calderon 1999: 138). The frying pan (no. 37) has a "wishbone" handle and

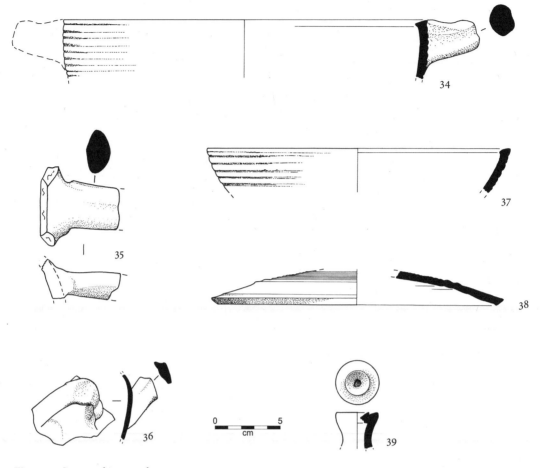

Fig. 115. *Open cooking vessels.*

a beveled rim. The type is characteristic to the Jerusalem region and southern Israel in the late Byzantine period (Magness 1993: 171, 213). This type of lid (no. 38) was used to cover the open cooking bowl. The handle is absent however the lid is well known in numerous sites throughout Israel during the Byzantine period. At Caesarea this lid was found in layers of the late forth and early fifth centuries (Tomber 1999: 300). The lid together with the cooking bowl originates in the late Roman period and continues into the Abbasid period (Watson 1992: 235).

34. 2037/3, L 2304. Casserole; rim d. 28 cm, surface: light red 2.5YR 6/6; core: yellowish red 5YR 5/6; hard clay with common small white grits. Slightly beveled rim, ribbed wall, two horizontal thick handles. Date range: fifth–seventh centuries. Refs: Khirbet Shema, fifth–seventh centuries (Meyers, Kraabel and Strange 1976: 189 and Pl. 7.13:8); Sumaqa, fifth–

seventh centuries (Kingsley 1999: 282 and fig. 9:4); Ramat Hanadiv, sixth–seventh centuries (Calderon 2000: 140 and Pl. XXIII:47); Caesarea, sixth–seventh centuries (Magness 1992: 132–33 and fig. 68:5); Jerusalem, first half of sixth century (Magness 1993: 211, 212:3); Ramot Nof, sixth to mid-seventh century (Ustinova and Nahshoni 1994: 162 and fig. 6:7); Rehovot-in-the-Negev, sixth–seventh centuries (Rosenthal-Heginbottom 1988: Pl. V:201).

35. 0072/5, L 2031. Casserole handle; th. 1.67 cm, body th. 0.78 cm. Hard clay, light red 10R 7/6 to reddish yellow 7.5YR 8/6 fabric; smooth texture, few grey grits.

36. 0034/3, L 2005. Casserole handle, burnt; th. 0.98 cm, body th. 0.29 cm. Local sand-rich red clay 10R 5/8.

37. 2037/2, L 2102. Frying pan; rim d. 23 cm, surface: burnt, core: red 10R 5/6; hard clay with common minute white grits and quartz. Slightly beveled rim, ribbed wall. Date range: sixth to early eighth century. Refs: Ramat Hanadiv, sixth–seventh centuries (Calderon 2000: 142–43 and Pl. XXIII:58); Caesarea, sixth–seventh centuries (Adan-Bayewitz 1986: 107 and fig. 3:22); Caesarea, sixth to early eighth century (Oleson, Fitzgerald, Sherwood and Sidebotham 1994: 109 and fig. 35:K46); Jerusalem, sixth–seventh centuries (Magness 1993: 213, Form 2); Ashqelon, sixth–seventh centuries (Nahshoni 1999: 103 and fig. 5:13).

38. 0104/10, L 2041. Lid; rim d. 22.4 cm, surface: red 10R 5/8; core: red 2.5YR 4/8; hard clay with common small white grits. A lid with beveled edges, convex shape. Dense ribbing occurs on the upper surface and becomes wider toward the lip. Date range: mid-fourth to early eighth century. Refs: Hammat Gader, sixth to mid-eighth century (Ben-Arieh 1997: 371 and Pl. XII:3); Caesarea, sixth to mid-seventh century (Adan-Bayewitz 1986: 108–9 and fig. 4:8); Caesarea, late fourth to early fifth century (Tomber 1999: 300 and fig. 3:64); Ramat Rahel, sixth–seventh centuries (Aharoni 1964: 38 and fig. 8:2); Ras Abu Ma'aruf, sixth to early eighth century (Rapuano 1999: 179 and fig. 6:93); Ramot Nof, mid-fourth to mid-seventh century (Ustinova and Nahshoni 1994: 162 and fig. 6:23); Rehovot-in-the-Negev, sixth century (Rosenthal-Heginbottom 1988: 90–93 and Pl. V.217); Pella, sixth–seventh centuries (Watson 1992: 235 and fig. 1:1).

39. 1062/4, L 1011. Casserole lid handle; d. 3.2 cm. Dark red ware 2.5YR 4/6. Plaster encrusted. Date range: sixth to mid-seventh century. Refs: Caesarea (Magness 1995: 136, 145 and fig. 3.10); En Boqeq, latest coin 570/71 (Gichon 1993: Taf. 43.43).

LOCAL AMPHORAE

Two forms are mainly known among the local amphorae, and although no statistics have been done, it seems that these types dominate the Tel Tanninim material. The first type is the bag-shaped amphora, which appears in many variants of form and fabric (gray, red) and leads most assemblages in sites of the Byzantine period throughout Israel. At Sumaqa, this vessel type accounts for 90.7 per-

cent of the site's total amphorae during the Roman and Byzantine periods (Kingsley 1999: 264). At Caesarea's hippodrome it accounts for 64 percent of the vessels.

Although no petrography and neutron activation analysis tests have yet been done, it is possible to determine from a visual study the nature of the local fabric of the bag-shaped amphora. This hard fired fabric is characterized by a reddish-yellow to gray color and contains average size white grits and occasionally quartz grits. During these periods, although some features vary, the shape of the body and the loop handles remain the same.

The second type is the well-known Gaza jar, very common in the southern region and along the coast of Israel, but also throughout the Mediterranean region. This type was the most common jar at Ramat Hanadiv (Calderon 2000: 126) and the second most common amphora at Caesarea. We can distinguish typological development of the body and rim, but the fabric is usually brown (5YR 5/6) and contains white grits.

Gray bag-shaped amphorae (figs. 116–17:40–52)

The amphora has a bag-shaped body and the shoulder has a pronounced ridge at the transition to body. Number 40 has a sharp ridge at the bottom of neck. The type is hard fired and the walls are thin. The gray color of the ware, that is characteristic to this type, sometimes varies in the firing to red. The clay has many white grits. Nos. 51–52 have a decoration of white wavy lines. Based on the fabric, the contexts in which it has been found and the distribution pattern, Adan-Bayewitz assumes that oil was the content of this amphora. This vessel is especially common at sites in the Galilee and the Jordan Valley, areas known for their olives and oil production (Adan-Bayewitz 1986: 100–101). Landgraf calls these amphorae "Beth Shean Jars" and indicates that by reason of the thinner and harder fabric they are less porous (Landgraf 1980: 69–76). These amphorae were found in Istanbul, Carthage and Cyprus. A workshop producing amphorae of this type has been discovered at Uza (Avshalom-Gorni 1998: 58). Although the examples from Jalame suggest a late Roman date, at most of the

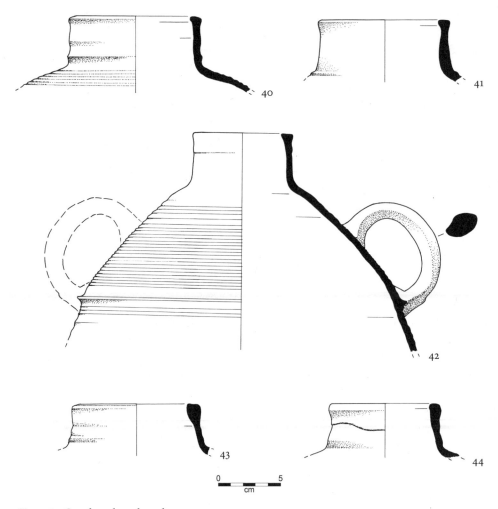

Fig. 116. *Gray bag-shaped amphorae.*

sites these amphorae occur during the Byzantine period. The variants exposed at Tel Tanninim can be typologically distinguished by the shape of the rim. The shapes range through slightly flat on top (nos. 40–47), round (no. 48) and square (no. 49). The ware is hard metallic and varies from gray to red. Amphorae nos. 40–47 have similar rims with the exception of no. 40 that has a sharp ridge at the bottom of the rim.

40. 2044/1, L 2327. Rim d. 9.3 cm, surface: gray 5YR 6/1, core: gray 2.5YR 5/1 to red 5YR 5/6; hard metallic clay with many small white grits. Slightly flat rim. Date range: mid-second to mid-seventh century. Refs: Hammat Gader, sixth–eighth centuries (Ben-Arieh 1997: 357 and Pl. VI:4); Capernaum, fourth

to mid-seventh century (Loffreda 1974: 43–44 and fig. 8:2, 4); Kursi, until mid-eighth century (Tzaferis 1983: 35 and fig. 7.13); Tell Keisan, sixth–seventh centuries (Landgraf 1980: 69–74 and fig. 21:17); Khirbet Shema, fifth to mid-seventh century (Meyers, Kraabel and Strange 1976: 227 and Pl. 7.21:22); Khirbet ʿOvesh, sixth to mid-seventh century (Aviam and Getzov 1998: 70 and fig. 9:13); Jalame, mid-fourth century (Johnson 1988: 218 and fig. 7-53:805); Horvat Castra, sixth–seventh centuries (Siegelmann 1996: 87 and fig. 12:15); Pella, sixth–seventh centuries (Smith and Day 1989: 107 and Pl. 48:6, 9).

41. 0094/1, L 2038. Rim d. 9.8 cm. Vertical rim with significant reduction in thinness toward lip. Broad horizontal rib at rim base. Hard clay, bluish

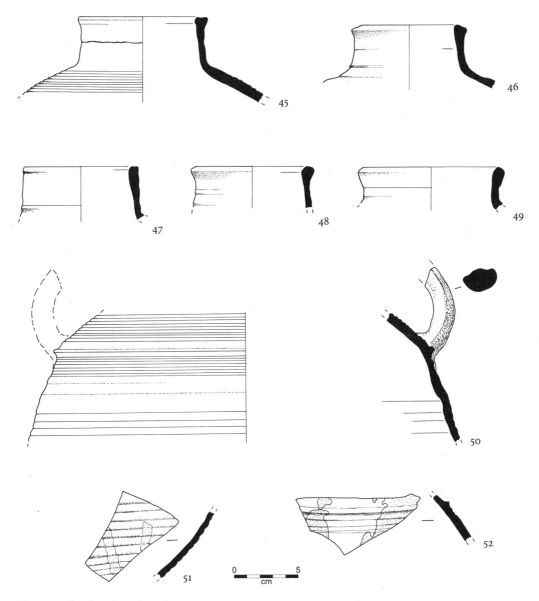

Fig. 117. *Gray bag-shaped amphorae.*

gray, of metallic resonance with common white inclusions.

42. 0099/6, L 2041. Rim d. 9.5 cm. Tall. Vertical rim widening at lip, flattened at apex. Wide handle narrow in section. Two incisions 2 cm. Long and 0.4 cm wide, cut into unfired clay on underside of lower handle, which rests on horizontal ridge. Narrow band of combing from upper shoulder. Body wall has narrow corrugations. Hard metallic clay, cleanly levigated. Smooth texture and small white inclusions and larger gray grits. Date range: sixth–eighth

centuries. Refs: Caesarea, mid-seventh century destruction layer (Lenzen 1983: Pl. 14); Horvat Castra, sixth–seventh centuries (Siegelmann 1996: 87 and fig. 12.15); Khirbat al-Karak, coins range 518–731 (Delougaz 1960: Pl. 55.2); Khirbet Shema, 419–640 (Meyers, Kraabel and Strange 1976: Pl. 7.21, No. 22); Kursi, up to mid-eighth century (Tzaferis 1983: 35 and fig. 7.13); Pella, 525–550 (Smith, McNicoll and Watson 1992: 166 and Pl. 111.4).

43. 2032/8, L 2326. Rim d. 10.4 cm, surface: reddish yellow 7.5YR 7/6, core: gray 7.5YR 5/1; hard clay with many tiny white grits. Slightly flat rim. Date range: fifth to mid-eighth century. Refs: see no. 40.

44. 2040/11, L 2240. Rim d. 9 cm, surface: gray 5YR 5/1, core: dark gray to red 2.5YR 5/6; hard clay with many minute-small white grits. Slightly flat rim. Date range: fifth–eighth centuries. Refs: see no. 23.

45. 2063/7, L 2340. Rim d. 10.8 cm, surface: gray 5YR 5/1, core: red 2.5YR 5/6; hard clay with many minute-small white grits. Slightly flat rim. Date range: fifth to mid-eighth century. Refs: see no. 40.

46. 0059/2, L 2031. Rim d. 9.6 cm. Vertical rim with shallow, concave profile. Single rib at rim base. Hard clay with rough texture and abundant small white grits. Light red clay 10R 7/8, with reddish gray exterior slip 5YR 5/2. Refs: see no. 42.

47. 2034/1, L 2102. Rim d. 8.8 cm, surface: gray 5YR 5/1, core: red 2.5YR 5/6; hard clay and many minute-small white grits. Slightly flat rim. Date range: fifth to mid-eighth century. Refs: see no. 23.

48. 2013/2, L 2204. Rim d. 9.8 cm, Surface: gray 7.5YR 6/1, core: gray 7.5YR 5/1; hard metallic clay with few small white grits. Round rim. Date range: mid-second to mid-seventh century. Refs: Capernaum, fourth to mid-seventh century (Loffreda 1974: 43–44 and fig. 8:4); Jalame, mid-fourth century (Johnson 1988: 218 and fig. 7-53).

49. 2062/9, L 2342. Rim d. 10.5 cm, surface and core: gray 2.5YR 5/1, hard clay with few small white grits. Everted rim, short neck. Date range: mid-second to early seventh century. Refs: Capernaum, fourth to mid-seventh century (Loffreda 1974: 43–44 and fig. 8:2); Jalame mid-second to early fourth century (Johnson 1988: 216 and fig. 7-52:794); Ramat Hanadiv, sixth to early seventh century (Calderon 2000: 130 and Pl. XVIII:19).

50. 0084/1, L 2038. Body fragment, surface: grayish brown 10YR 5/2, core: reddish yellow 5YR 7/8; hard metallic clay with many small white grits. Ribbed, pronounced ridge occurs on the shoulder, ring handles attached to shoulder. Date range: fourth–eighth centuries. Refs: Capernaum, fourth to mid-seventh century (Loffreda 1974: 43–44 and fig. 8:5); Tell Keisan, fifth–eighth centuries (Landgraf 1980: 69–81 and fig. 22); Horvat Kav, late fifth to sixth century (Avshalom-Gorni 1998: 63 and fig. 5:2);

Caesarea, seventh century (Adan-Bayewitz 1986: 99–101 and fig. 2:1); Ramat Hanadiv, sixth–seventh centuries (Calderon 2000: 130 and Pl. XVIII:16).

51. 2080/2, L 2038. Body fragment, surface: gray 7.5YR 6/1, core: red 2.5YR 5/6 to gray 7.5YR 5/1; hard metallic clay with many small white grits. Decoration: very pale brown 10YR 8/4 diagonal lines. Date range: mid-second to mid-seventh century. Refs: Jalame, mid-second to early fourth century (Johnson 1988: 218 and fig. 7-53:807); Caesarea, fourth to late fifth century (Riley 1975: 31, No. 31:18); Caesarea, mid-fourth to seventh century (Magness 1995: 144 and fig. 3:8).

52. 2031/14, L 2304. Body fragment. Surface: dark gray 2.5YR 4/1, core: very dark gray 2.5YR 3/1 to light red 2.5YR 6/8; hard clay with few tiny white grits. Horizontal sharp ridge occurs between the shoulder and the body. Sharp ribbing below the ridge and white lines on exterior wall. Date range: fourth–seventh centuries. Refs: Uza, fourth to mid-seventh century (Avshalom-Gorni 1998: 57–58 and fig. 3:7); Tell Keisan, sixth to mid-seventh century (Landgraf 1980: 68–80 and fig. 21:1); Caesarea, seventh century (Adan-Bayewitz 1986: 99–101 and fig. 2:1); Caesarea, sixth–seventh centuries (Magness 1995: 144 and fig. 3:8); Ramat Hanadiv, sixth–seventh centuries (Calderon 2000: 130 and Pl. XVIII:16); Pella, seventh century (Watson 1992: 238–39 and fig. 9:72).

Bag-shaped amphorae (figs. 118–19:53–72)

This vessel is characterized by a vertical low neck, bag-shaped body, and a very narrow combed shoulder compared to its grooved body. A plain zone separates the grooved shoulder from the body. Sandy fabric and accretions of clay are found below the rim. Some of these may be attributed to the manufacturing process (Adan-Bayewitz 1986: 91). The color of clay varies between light red and light reddish brown. This type can be divided into a number of variants according to the shape of the rim. Vessels 53–61 have an everted rim and a convex neck; nos. 63–64 have an inverted rim, and nos. 66–67 have a thickened rim. Amphora no. 70 was drilled below the shoulder to provide an outlet for

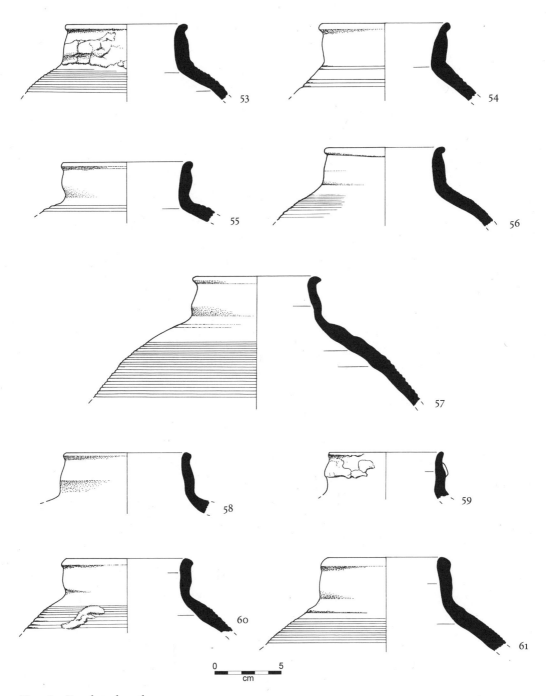

Fig. 118. *Bag-shaped amphorae.*

the escape of carbon dioxide emitted during the continuing fermentation of new wine. This was done to allow pouring without the need to open the stopper (Adan-Bayewitz 1986: 92). Amphorae of this type have a long history in Israel and during the Byzantine period, and this variant is the most

common vessel. In the Late Byzantine Building at Caesarea, this variant accounts for about 39 percent of the rims, handles and bases (Adan-Bayewitz 1986: 91). Throughout the sixth–seventh centuries, this amphora was used as a wine transporter in the Mediterranean region with vessels found at Carthage (Riley 1981: 102), Marseille (Bonifay and Piéri: 1995: 112–13), Histria, Chios and Sardis (Kingsley 1994–95: 49). The low neck of this vessel is the latest form, while the previous amphorae have a long collared neck. This amphora is dated to the sixth and first half of the seventh century, and there are variants that occur until the end of the Early Islamic period.

53. 0054/1, L 2031. Rim d. 9 cm, surface: reddish yellow 5YR 7/6, core: reddish yellow 5YR 7/8; hard clay with few small white grits. Accretions of clay occur on rim. Everted round rim, convex neck and narrow combing on shoulder. Date range: sixth to early eighth century. Refs: Beth Shean, sixth to early eighth century (Peleg 1994: 145 and fig. 13:7); Yoqneʿam, late sixth and seventh century (Avissar 1996:73 and fig. XII.7:4); Ramat Hanadiv sixth–seventh centuries (Calderon 2000: 104 and Pl. VI:7); Caesarea, seventh century (Adan-Bayewitz 1986: 91–97 and fig. 1:6); Caesarea, mid-sixth century (Magness 1992: 152 and figs. 64:2; 68:4); Horvat Hermeshit, sixth to eighth centuries (Greenhut 1998: 125 and figs. 10:11–12; 26:5); Ramot Nof, sixth–seventh centuries (Ustinova and Nahshoni 1994: 161 and fig. 4:5); Jerusalem, late sixth to early eighth century (Magness 1993: 226 and fig. 226:2); Khirbet ed-Deir, sixth–seventh centuries (Calderon 1999: 135 and Pl. 1:2); Tell Fara, sixth–seventh centuries (Tubb 1986: 56–60 and fig. 5:2); Gerasa, sixth century (Uscatescu 1996: 163 and fig. 93:601).

54. 2040/15, L 2240. Rim d. 9.8 cm, surface: light reddish 5YR 6/4, core: red 5YR 5/6; hard clay with few small white grits. Everted round rim, convex neck, narrow grooving on shoulder. Date range: sixth to early eighth century. Refs: see no. 53.

55. 0078/32, L 2035. Rim d. 9.4 cm, Surface: light red 2.5YR 6/6, reddish yellow 5YR 6/6; hard clay with few small white grits. Everted round rim, convex neck, narrow combing on shoulder. Date range: sixth to early eighth century. Refs: see no. 53.

56. 0054/1, L 2031. Rim d. 9 cm. Band of clay accretions on rim, and body combing (5 grooves per cm). Hard, reddish yellow clay 5YR 7/6 with rough texture and few grits.

57. 0080/15, L 2038. Rim d. 9.6 cm. Inward inclined rim, with a bulging wall midway along its length.

Outward twisted, beaked lip. Horizontal band of clay accretions on upper shoulder. Narrow body combing. Soft, reddish yellow clay 5YR 7/8 with smooth texture and few grits.

58. 0080/12, L 2038. Rim d. 9.8 cm, surface: reddish yellow 5YR 6/6, core: reddish yellow 5YR 7/6; soft clay, many small white grits. Everted round rim, convex neck. Date range: sixth to early eighth century. Refs: see no. 53.

59. 2063/23, L 2340. Rim d. 8.9 cm, surface: light red 2.5YR 6/6, core: reddish yellow 5YR 7/6; hard clay with many small white grits. Slightly everted rim, convex neck. Date range: sixth to early eighth century. Refs: see no. 53.

60. 2103/1, L 2270. Rim d. 9.8 cm, rim and shoulder fragment, surface: red 10R 5/6, core: red 10R 4/8; hard clay and common small to large white grits. Everted round rim, convex neck, narrow grooving on shoulder. Accretions of clay occur on the shoulder. Date range: sixth to early eighth century. Refs: see no. 53.

61. 2035/2, L 2304. Rim d. 8.5 cm, surface: reddish yellow 5YR 6/6, core: reddish yellow 5YR 6/8; hard clay, abundant small white grits. Everted round rim, low neck, narrow combing on shoulder. Date range: sixth to early eighth century. Refs: see no. 53.

62. 0093/0, L 2031. Rim d. 11.2 cm. Thick, vertical rim marginally thickened at lip. Clay accretions over rim. Narrow combing over shoulder. Sand-rich, hard, yellowish clay 5YR 5/6 with smooth texture and common white shell inclusions. Date range: seventh–eighth centuries. Refs: Caesarea (Lenzen 1983: 336 and Pl. 15); Capernaum, 600–650 (Peleg 1989: 81, No. 3; 85, No. 32); Carmiel, latest coin 641–668 (Yeivin 1992: fig. 24.2); Pella, 746/7 (McNicoll, Smith and Hennessy 1982: Pl. 146.3); Ramat Rahel, late seventh/early eighth century. (Aharoni 1964: 16).

63. 2062/5, L 2342. Rim d. 10 cm, surface: light red 10R 6/8, core: red 10R 5/8; hard clay with average amount of white grits. Inverted rim, low neck. Date range: sixth–seventh centuries. Refs: Ramat Hanadiv, sixth–seventh centuries (Calderon 2000: 104 and Pl. VI:13); Ramot Nof, sixth–seventh centuries (Ustinova and Nahshoni 1994: 161 and fig. 4:8); Tell Fara, sixth–seventh centuries (Tubb

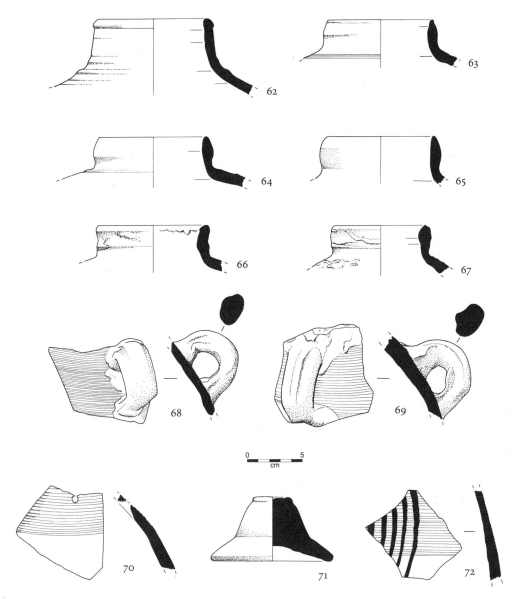

Fig. 119. *Bag-shaped amphorae.*

1986: 56–60 and fig. 5:2); Rehovot-in-the-Negev, sixth–seventh centuries (Rosenthal-Heginbottom 1988: 84 and Pl. 2:55); Pella, early seventh century (Watson 1992: 240 and fig. 10:83).

64. 2029/9, L 2112. Rim d. 10.8 cm, surface: reddish yellow 5YR 7/8, core: reddish yellow 5YR 6/8; hard clay with few small white grits. Inverted rim. Date range: sixth–seventh centuries. Refs: see no. 63.

65. 0059/3, L 2031. Rim d. 10.8 cm. Vertical profile, marginally rounded. Local reddish yellow clay 5YR 7/6.

66. 2092/2, L 2252. Rim d. 10.2 cm, surface: light red 10R 6/6, core: red 10R 5/8; hard clay with many small white grits. Thickened rim. Accretions of clay occur on rim. Date range: sixth–seventh centuries. Refs: Tell Fara, sixth–seventh centuries (Tubb 1986: 56 and fig. 5:9); Ramot Nof, sixth–seventh centuries (Ustinova and Nahshoni 1994: 161 and fig. 4:2).

67. 2044/8, L 2327. Rim d. 9.2 cm, surface: reddish yellow 5YR 7/6, core: reddish yellow 5YR 6/6; hard clay with few small white grits. Thickened rim. Accretions of clay occur on rim. Date range: sixth to mid-seventh century. Refs: Caesarea, sixth century (Riley 1975: 26, No. 3); Caesarea, sixth to mid-seventh century (Adan-Bayewitz 1986: 91–97 and fig. 1:7); Tell Fara, sixth–seventh centuries (Tubb 1986: 56–60 and fig. 4:1); Ramot Nof, sixth–seventh centuries (Ustinova and Nahshoni 1994: 161 and fig. 4:7).

68. 2090/5, L 2222. Handle and shoulder fragment. Surface: light red10R 6/8, core: red 10R 5/8; hard clay with few small grits. Ridged handle attached to the shoulder. Narrow combing occurs on the shoulder. Date range: fifth–eighth centuries. Refs: Caesarea, first quarter seventh century (Lenzen 1983: 90 and fig. 30:41); Caesarea, sixth to mid-seventh century (Adan-Bayewitz 1986: 121 and fig. 1:4); Caesarea, mid-sixth century (Magness 1992: 129 and fig. 58:20); Bet Shean, fifth to early eighth century (Peleg 1994: 145, 147 and fig. 13:7); Khirbet ed-Deir, sixth–seventh centuries (Calderon 1999: 135 and Pl. 1:2); Ashqelon, sixth–seventh centuries (Nahshoni 1999: 108 and fig. 5:19); Ras Abu Ma'aruf, sixth–eighth centuries (Rapuano 1999: 179 and fig. 7:95); Tel Fara, sixth–seventh centuries (Tubb 1986: 59 and fig. 5:10); Ramot Nof, sixth–seventh centuries (Ustinova and Nahshoni 1994: 161 and fig. 4:5); Pella, first half seventh century (Smith, McNicoll and Watson 1992: 168 and Pl. 115:5); Marseille, sixth–seventh centuries (Bonifay and Piéri: 1995: 112–13 and fig. 10:68–71); Carthage Cisterns, early seventh century (Riley 1981: 102 and fig. 8:72).

69. 0125/2, L 2041. Body fragment; surface: light red 2.5YR 6/6, core: reddish yellow 5YR 7/6; hard clay with few small grits. Ridged handle attached to the shoulder. Narrow combing occurs on the shoulder. Date range: fifth to early eighth century. Refs: see no. 68.

70. 0133/4, L 2053. Body fragment; surface: reddish yellow 5YR 7/6, core: reddish yellow 5YR 6/6; soft clay and large amount of white grits. Body fragment is covered by narrow combing. Drilled hole on shoulder. Date range: first–seventh centuries. Refs: see no. 68.

71. 0093/0, L 2031. Bag-shaped amphora stopper (C019); d. 11.2 cm, base width 4.3 cm. Local reddish yellow clay 7.5YR 7/8 with common spread of white shell inclusions.

Bag-shaped amphora with white decoration (fig. 119:72)

This vessel (no. 72) has an identical shape to a bag-shaped amphora but with the addition of painted decoration of parallels lines that intersect at opposite slope and circles. The decoration of lines occurs in very pale brown. The fabric is very sandy and appears in reddish yellow. There are examples in the Athenian Agora from the early sixth century C.E. (Robinson 1959: M329–M330). According to Magness (1995: 135) this vessel belongs to the southern Israel jars. The amphora is dated to the sixth and the beginning of the seventh century.

72. 2103/3, L 2270. Body fragment; surface: red 2.5YR 5/6, core: dark red 2.5YR 4/8; soft sandy clay with common small to large white grits, many common small-large white grits, many quartz grits. White painted lines on exterior. Date range: sixth to mid-seventh century. Refs: Tell Keisan, sixth to mid-seventh century (Landgraf 1980: 76 and fig. 24b:5–9); Ramat Hanadiv, sixth–seventh centuries (Calderon 2000: 128 and Pl. XVII:13); Caesarea, sixth century (Riley 1975: 27 and no. 4); Caesarea, sixth century (Adan-Bayewitz 1986: 97 and Ill. 98); Caesarea, sixth to mid-seventh century (Magness 1995: 135 and fig. 2:14); Athenian Agora, early sixth century (Robinson 1959: 115 and Pl. 32: M329–M330).

Gaza Amphorae (figs. 120–21:73–89)

These vessels have a tall cylindrical body, sloping shoulders and a hollow base that is pointed or flattened. The rim is thickened and varies from inward grooved to everted pointed rim. Two ring handles are attached at the shoulders. Ribbing occurs at the level of the handles and below them. Wide ribbing appears on the base. Accretions of clay are attached below the rim and to the shoulder. The wall is thickened. The ware varies between brown and reddish brown and contains many white grits. The amphora was smeared inside with resin or bitumen. Riley suggests that the amphorae were containers of wine in the fifth and sixth centuries, which seems reasonable, considering the coating inside the amphorae. Adan-Bayewitz (1986:

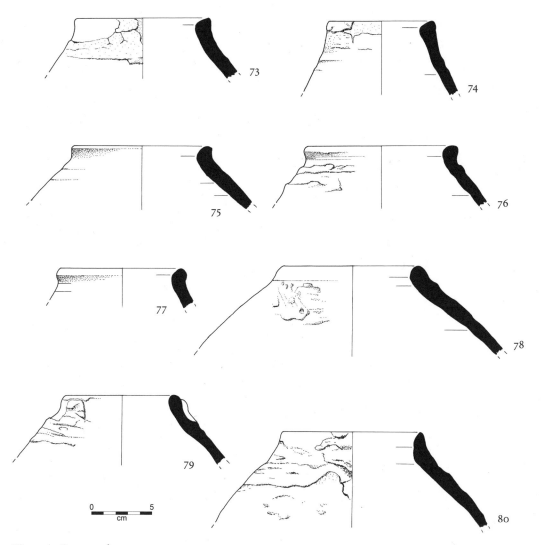

Fig. 120. *Gaza amphorae.*

99) turned down the idea that fish products were packed in this amphora and he strengthens the previous assumption that the trade of Gaza and Ashkelon wine was quite famous in the Byzantine period (Johnson and Stager 1995).

This amphora is recorded on sites throughout the Mediterranean region and dated from the late fourth until the mid-seventh century. Egloff (1977: 116–17) suggested the end of the Umayyad period as the latest production date. Majcherek (1995: 163–69) proposed an outline for the development of the Gaza amphorae by dividing them into four types, according to the amphorae at Kom el-Dikka. In Benghazi (Berenice), the type that is called Late Roman Amphora 3 was recovered at the levels of

early sixth century. According to Riley (1979: 219–22) the type is most frequent in the south-eastern Mediterranean. The amphora began to be imported into the western Mediterranean in the late fourth century. The import of this amphora continued and reached a peak in the middle of the fifth century, then tailed off at the end of the century. The import to Spain had begun at the late fifth century and probably continued until the middle to late sixth century (Keay 1984: 280–81).

In Israel, the distribution is southern and coastal; this type was the most common at Ashdod in the late Roman and Byzantine periods. By contrast, Tel Keisan yielded only one rim sherd (Tubb 1986: 54). Riley (1975: 30–31) suggested the

Gaza region as the origin of the amphora, according to petrologic analysis. At Caesarea, this type comprised 24 percent of all the amphorae in the Byzantine levels. The amphorae found at Tel Tanninim represent a diversity of rim forms: everted beveled rim (nos. 73–77), thickened rim (nos. 78–79), vertical pointed rim (nos. 80–81), vertical round rim (nos. 82–83), inverted beveled rim with an inner groove (nos. 84–85) and inverted beveled rim (nos. 86–87).

73. 2044/7, L 2327. Rim d. 11.2 cm, surface: reddish brown 5YR 5/3, core: light reddish brown 5YR 6/4; hard clay with large quantity of small white grits. Everted beveled rim and accretion of clay on rim and shoulder. Date range: fourth to mid-seventh century. Refs: Caesarea, sixth to mid-seventh century (Adan-Bayewitz 1986: 97–99 and fig. 1:9, 14); Benghazi, fifth to mid-sixth century (Riley 1979: 219–23 and fig. 92:354); Catalunya, fifth–sixth centuries (Keay 1984: 278–81 and fig. 122:12); Tel Ashdod, fourth to mid-seventh century (Baumgarten 2000: 70–73 and fig. 4:9, 12); Tell Fara, sixth–seventh centuries (Tubb 1986: 51–55 and fig. 2:2); Ramot Nof, sixth–seventh centuries (Ustinova and Nahshoni 1994: fig. 4:11); Marseille, fifth–seventh centuries (Bonifay and Piéri 1995: 112 and fig. 9:64).

74. 0101/8, L 2041. Rim d. 12.2 cm. Simple, thickened lip. Clay accretions on lip. Sift, yellowish red clay 5YR 5/6 with few grits. Date range: sixth–seventh centuries. Refs: see no. 74, and Caesarea, mid-sixth century (Magness 1992: 129, 138 and fig. 59:6–8); Jerusalem Phase IIIa (Tushingham 1985: fig. 31.1); Ramat Rahel Stratum IIa (Aharoni 1964: fig. 24); Shavei Zion, fifth–sixth centuries (Prausnitz, Avi-Yonah and Barag 1967: 71 and fig. 11.10); Tell Fara well, sixth–seventh centuries (Tubb 1986: 52, 63 and fig. 1).

75. 0133/2, L 2053. Rim d. 11.4 cm, surface: light brown 7.5Y 6/4, core: brown 7.5YR 5/4; hard clay with few small white grits. Everted beveled rim. Date range: sixth to mid-seventh century. Refs: see no. 74.

76. 1068/5, L 1325. Rim d. 12 cm, surface: reddish yellow 5YR 6/6, core: yellowish red 5YR 5/6; hard clay with many common white grits. Everted beveled rim and clay accretions on shoulder. Date range: fifth–seventh centuries. Refs: see no. 74.

77. 2036/7, L 2304. Rim d. 10.8 cm, surface: reddish brown 2.5YR 5/4, core: red 2.5YR 4/6; hard clay with few small white grits. Everted beveled rim. Date range: fifth–seventh centuries. Refs: See no. 74.

78. 2019/2, L 2218. Rim d: 11.4 cm, surface: light reddish brown 2.5YR 6/4, core: reddish brown 2.5YR 5/4; hard clay with large amount of small white grits. Thickened rim and accretions of clay on rim and shoulder. Date range: fourth–seventh centuries. Refs: Tel Ashdod, fourth to seventh centuries (Baumgarten 2000: 70–73 and fig. 4:8); Tell Fara, sixth–seventh centuries (Tubb 1986: 51–55 and fig. 1:1); Kom el-Dikka, late sixth century (Majcherek 1995: 169 and Pl. 8:2); Pella, beginning to mid-seventh century (Smith, McNicoll and Watson 1992: 168 and Pl. 115:5).

79. 2007/14, L 2207. Rim d. 10 cm, surface: light reddish brown 2.5YR 6/6, core: reddish brown 2.5YR 5/4; hard clay and few small white grits. Thickened rim and clay accretions on rim and shoulder. Date range: fourth–seventh centuries. Refs: see no. 52.

80. 0080/16, L 2038. Rim d. 11.4 cm, surface: reddish brown 2.5YR 5/4, core: reddish brown 5YR 5/4; hard clay with average amount of small to medium white grits. Vertical pointed rim, and accretions of clay on rim and shoulder. Date range: fifth–seventh centuries. Refs: Ramat Hanadiv, sixth–seventh centuries (Calderon 2000: 104 and Pl. XV:4); Caesarea, sixth to mid-seventh century (Adan-Bayewitz 1986: 97–99 and fig. 1:14); Caesarea, sixth–seventh centuries (Magness 1995: 135 and fig. 3:4); Catalunya, fifth–sixth centuries (Keay 1984: 278–81 and fig. 122:13); Tel Ashdod, fourth to mid-seventh century (Baumgarten 2000: 70–73 and fig. 4:6).

81. 2029/8, L 2112. Rim d. 10.3 cm, surface: reddish yellow 5YR 6/8, core: yellowish red 5YR 5/6; hard clay with average amount of small white grits. Vertical pointed rim, accretions of clay on shoulder. Date range: sixth–seventh centuries. Refs: see no. 53.

82. 1068/7, L 1325. Rim d. 11.3 cm, surface: light reddish brown 2.5YR 6/4, core: reddish brown 2.5YR

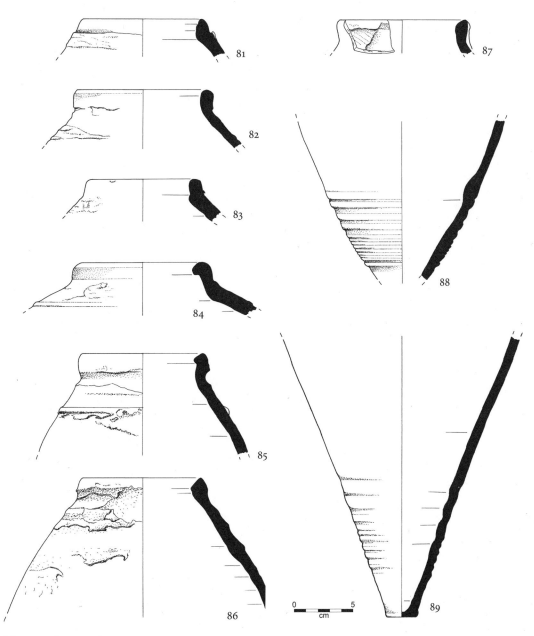

Fig. 121. *Gaza amphorae.*

5/4; hard clay with many small white grits. Vertical round rim and clay accretions on rim and shoulder. Date range: fourth to beginning of seventh century. Refs: Ramat Hanadiv, sixth to early seventh century (Calderon 2000: 126 and Pl. XVI:9); Caesarea, seventh century (Adan-Bayewitz 1986: 97–99 and fig. 1:10); Gerasa, sixth–seventh centuries (Uscatescu 1996: 174 and fig. 95:630); Catalunya, fifth–sixth centuries (Keay 1984: 278–83 and fig. 122:9).

83. 1028/3, L 1113. Rim d. 10 cm, surface: reddish brown 5YR 5/4, core: reddish brown 5YR 5/4; hard clay with common small white grits. Vertical round rim and clay accretions on rim and shoulder. Date range: fourth to early seventh century. Refs: see no. 53.

84. 2016/3, L 2322. Rim d. 9.4 cm, surface: light reddish 5YR 6/4 to 5YR 5/4, core: yellowish red 5YR 4/6 to 5/6; soft clay and few small white grits. Inverted beveled rim with an inward groove. Date range:

fifth to mid-seventh century. Refs: Ramat Hanadiv, sixth–seventh centuries (Calderon 2000: 126 and Pl. XVI:10); Caesarea, sixth–seventh centuries (Magness 1992: 137 and fig. 59:8); Ashqelon, sixth to mid-seventh century (Nahshoni 2000: 106–8 and fig. 5:17); Jerusalem, sixth century (Tushingham 1985: 91 and fig. 27:27); Ras Abu Ma'aruf, fifth–seventh centuries (Rapuano 1999: 179 and fig. 7:108); Gerasa, sixth century (Uscatescu 1996: 174 and fig. 95:627); Kellia, fifth–seventh centuries (Egloff 1977: 116–17 and Pl. 60:3); Catalunya, fifth to mid-fifth century (Keay 1984: 278–81 and fig. 121:8); Benghazi, fifth to early sixth century (Riley 1979: 219–22 and fig. 92:351–52).

85. 2094/6, L 2258. Rim d. 10.6 cm, surface: reddish brown 5YR 6/4, core: yellowish red 5YR 5/6; hard clay with common small white grits. Inverted beveled rim with an inward groove. Date range: fifth to mid-seventh century. Refs: see no. 84.

86. 2094/1, L 2258. Rim d. 10.4 cm, surface: reddish brown 5YR 5/4, core: yellowish red 5YR 5/8; hard clay with common small white grits. Inverted beveled rim and clay accretions on the rim and shoulder. Date range: mid-sixth to mid-eighth century. Refs: Caesarea, sixth to mid-seventh century (Magness 1995: 144 and fig. 3:5); Tel Ashdod, fourth to mid-seventh century (Baumgarten 2000: 70–73 and fig. 4:10); Ramot Nof, sixth–seventh centuries (Ustinova and Nahshoni 1994: 162 and fig. 4:12); Tell Fara, sixth–seventh centuries (Tubb 1986: 51–55 and fig. 2:2); Pella, mid-seventh century (Watson 1992: 239–40 and fig. 10:76); Kellia, mid-seventh to mid-eighth century (Egloff 1977: 117 and Pl. 61:1).

87. 2037/4, L 2102. Rim d. 11.2 cm, surface: reddish yellow 5YR 6/6, core: weak red 10R 5/4; hard clay with many small white grits. Inverted beveled rim. Date range: mid-sixth to mid-eighth century. Refs: See no. 86.

88. 2084/1, L 2249. Base fragment, surface: yellowish red 5YR 5/6, core: reddish brown 5YR 4/4; hard clay with few small white grits. Hollow ribbed base. Date range: fifth to mid-eighth century. Refs: Ramat Hanadiv, sixth–seventh centuries (Calderon 2000: 123–24 and Pl. XV:5); Caesarea, seventh century (Adan-Bayewitz 1986: 97–99 and fig. 1:13);

Caesarea, fifth–sixth centuries (Bar-Nathan and Adato 1986: 132 and fig. 1:9); Caesarea, sixth to mid-seventh century (Magness 1995: 144 and fig. 3:6); Tel Ashdod, fourth to mid-seventh century (Baumgarten 2000: 70–73 and fig. 4:16); Ashqelon, sixth–seventh centuries (Nahshoni 1999: 106–8 and fig. 5:18); Ramot Nof, sixth–seventh centuries (Ustinova and Nahshoni 1994: 162 and fig. 4:12); Tell Fara, sixth–seventh centuries (Tubb 1986: 51–55 and fig. 2:2); Pella, mid-seventh century (Watson 1992: 239–40 and fig. 10:76); Gerasa, sixth–seventh centuries (Uscatescu 1996: 174 and fig. 95:628); Kellia, mid-seventh to mid-eighth century (Egloff 1977: 117 and Pl. 61:1); Catalunya, fifth–sixth centuries (Keay 1984: 278–81 and fig. 123:2).

89. 0087/1, L 2038. Complete base fragment from toe to lower body. V-shaped profile, with a flat toe. Toe d. 2.6 cm. Lower base broadly ribbed. Soft, reddish yellow clay 7.5YR 6/6 with smooth texture and few grits.

IMPORTED AMPHORAE

The forms of the imported amphorae (fig. 122:90–93) vary from a square to an ovoid profile. The rim is thickened and the neck is wide or narrow, short or elongated, and the base is round and has a nipple in the center. The handles are thick and grooved, attached at the top of the neck and to the shoulder. The ribbing is widely spaced on the center of the body, becoming more closely towards the shoulder and the base. There are occasionally red-painted letters on the neck or on the shoulders. These seem to be capacity marks (Riley 1979: 212). The fabric varies from light brown to pale yellow and contains white and black grits and occasional quartz grains.

These are some of the more common amphorae in Byzantine sites throughout the Mediterranean region and are known variously as either Yassi Ada Type 1, Late Roman Amphora 1, British Bii, Type LIII and Beltran 82. The earliest example came from a fourth-century context at Tiritake (Riley 1979: 212). In Catalunya, their earliest appearance is in the late fifth century (Keay 1984: 278). In Carthage, two complete amphorae were found, dated from the beginning of the sixth to the seventh century

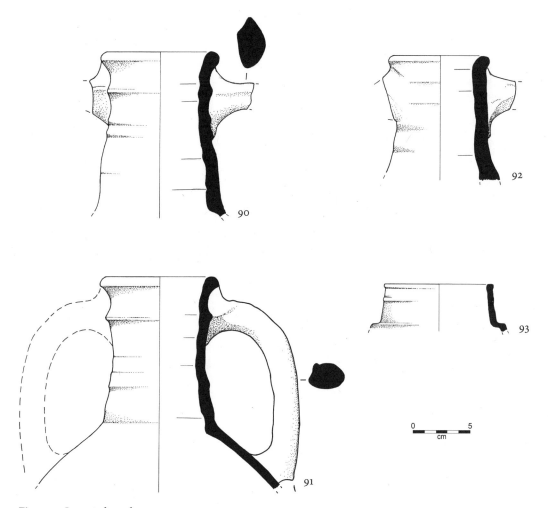

Fig. 122. *Imported amphorae.*

(Peacock 1984a: 119). At Benghazi, the period of greatest diffusion was the early sixth century (Riley 1979: 213). At Kellia, the amphora occurs from the fifth to the end of the seventh century (Egloff 1977: 112–13). The type also occurs at the Athenian Agora in the early sixth century (Robinson 1959: 115).

The variation of fabric suggests more than one production site. An Egyptian origin had been assumed until the petrological analysis done by Peacock (1984: 22) pointed to an origin in an area of ultra-basic volcanic rock. In the Eastern Mediterranean, such small ultra-basic formations are found in central Greece, the Rhodian Peraea, on the western side of the Gulf of Antalya, Cyprus, and around the bay of Iskenderun in eastern Turkey and north Syria (Antioch). Production centers for this type were noticed by Empereur and Picon (1989:

237) along the bay of Iskenderun; three manufacture sites were also found on Cyprus (*ibid.* 242).

According to the amphorae from the shipwreck of Yassi-Ada, the contents of the vessels was wine. One grape seed was found in the only complete amphora that was recovered there, and there was resin lining in several vessels (Van Alfen 1996: 203). If the origin of the amphorae was in the region of Antioch, perhaps the content was oil since there was a marked expansion in olive production from the fourth to the early sixth century (Peacock 1984a: 119).

90. 0083/5, L 2031. Rim d. 10.4 cm, surface: reddish yellow 7.5YR 6/6, core: reddish yellow 5YR 6/8; hard clay with common average black and white grits. Everted round rim, vertical neck with a broad ridge below rim. Grooved handles attached to the rim. Date range: late fourth to mid-seventh century.

Refs: Khirbet 'Ovesh, sixth and early seventh century (Avshalom-Gorni 1998: 81–82 and fig. 10:5); Ramat Hanadiv, sixth–seventh centuries (Calderon 2000: 132–33 and Pl. XIX:20–22); Caesarea, fifth–sixth centuries (Oleson, Fitzgerald, Sherwood and Sidebotham 1994: 22 and fig. 5:A35); Caesarea, sixth to mid-seventh century (Magness 1995: 142 and fig. 2:1); Caesarea, late fourth to early fifth century (Tomber 1999: 319 and fig. 8:130); Rehovot-in-the-Negev, sixth–seventh centuries (Rosenthal-Heginbottom 1988: 86–87 and Pl. III:127); Gerasa, sixth to beginning of seventh century (Uscatescu 1996: 177 and fig. 96:637); Pella, seventh century (Watson 1992: 239 and fig. 10:78); Aqaba, seventh century (Melkawi, 'Amr and Whitcomb 1994: 460 and fig. 10:h); Yassi Ada, first quarter of seventh century (Bass 1982: 155–57 and fig. 8-3:CA5); Athenian Agora, early sixth century (Robinson 1959: 115 and Pl. 32:M333).

91. 0054/5, L 2031. Rim d. 10.2 cm, surface: pale yellow 2.5Y 8/3, core: pale yellow 2.5Y 8/3; soft clay with few average black and red grits. Everted round rim, vertical neck with a broad ridge below rim. Grooved handles attached to the rim to the shoulder. Date range: mid-fourth to mid-seventh century. Refs: Migdal Ashqelon, sixth–seventh centuries (Kogan-Zehavi 1999: 199 and fig. 24:3); Rehovot-in-the-Negev, mid-fourth to mid-seventh century (Rosenthal-Heginbottom 1988: 87 and Pl. II:125); Kellia, fifth–seventh centuries (Egloff 1977: 112 and Pl. 105:164); Yassi Ada, early seventh century (Van Alfen 1996: 200 and fig. 12); Benghazi, fifth–sixth centuries (Riley 1979: 212–16 and fig. 91:237).

92. 0105/1, L 2041. Rim d. 8.6 cm. Entire rim, neck and stump of handle preserved. Tall vertical neck and everted simple lip. Vessel wall thickened at neck/shoulder juncture. Reddish brown clay with abundant gray, red, brown and white inclusions.

93. 0057/3, L 2032. Rim d. 9.6 cm. Hard light clay 10R 7/8 with harsh texture and common white grits. Refs: Dhiorios Kiln VII, probably mid-seventh century at earliest (Catling 1972: 48 and fig. 23).

DISCUSSION

A common sixth–seventh century date has emerged from the typological study. The pottery assemblage comprises local and imported types and is homogeneous in terms of its date. Ordinary household wares, such as cooking vessels, imported bowls, jugs are found together with local and imported amphorae.

Fine wares are represented by three main groups imported from the Mediterranean region. Three main manufacturing centers are known: African Red Slip from North Africa, apparently in Tunisia; Phocaean Red Slip from Phocaea (Asia Minor), and Cypriot Red Slip from Cyprus.

Amphorae of local origin are represented by the bag-shaped and Gaza amphorae: white decorated and gray amphorae from northern Israel and Gaza amphorae of southern Israel. Imported amphorae are represented by the well-known Yassi Ada type.

The forms and the distribution of the pottery types are generally well known even though the centers of manufacture of the various vessels have not yet been established. The imported vessels indicate trade connections with North Africa, Cyprus and Syria.

3. The Late Periods

by Ya'el D. Arnon

The ceramic assemblage of the Late Periods from Tel Tanninim was revealed in Areas A and A2, from various loci, both stratified and unstratified. Area A2 was designated as the "Crusader Tower" (Stieglitz 1999) and the pottery basket reading confirmed this date. Most of the material was exposed in non-stratified loci and a few pieces were found in indicative ones, such as fills below floors, walls or foundation trenches. The sparsity of the specimens caused us to rely on parallel materials for dating data, and as for that, the material was studied typologically and not stratigraphically.

All 223 sherds included in this report, which had previously been sorted in the field, were divided into three categories that yielded the following count: table wares comprised 44.5 percent of the total; cooking wares were 33.5 percent, and containers made up 22 percent of the total. Within these three groups, the pottery was subdivided into glazed and unglazed wares, and then classified according to their types, namely, bowls, jugs, juglets, cooking wares and containers. The 1990 edition of the Munsell soil color charts was used for the clay's hue description.

TABLE WARES

Glazed Bowls

Coarse Ware, monochrome glazed (fig. 123:1–2)

Most of the glazed bowls exposed at the site were from this category. They are characterized by a ring base, an open form and a red-colored, coarsely levigated clay, containing an abundance of small white grits, resembling a cooking pot ware. The inner surface is always white or pinkish slipped under a shining thick monochrome lead glaze in mustard yellow or green. The outer surface is usually smoothed or trimmed by a sharp tool.

This type was designated by Pringle (1985: 177) as "Monochrome glazed slip ware", and is well recorded in Medieval sites all over the Eastern Mediterranean: Yoqne'am (Avissar 1996: 91, Types 34–38); Caesarea (Arnon 1999: 227 and fig. 11:j); Jerusalem (Tushingham 1985: figs. 24–32, 34), Burj al-Ahmar (Pringle 1986: figs. 49–57); St. Mary of Carmel (Pringle 1984: 25–29); Hammat Gader (Boas 1997: 398); Cyprus (Megaw 1972: fig. F:4); Aegean Islands (Armstrong 1991: figs. 7; 19–20) and Tell 'Arqa (Hakimian and Salamé-Sarkis 1988: 12, Type AIII). The suggested date for the type is thirteenth and fourteenth centuries.

Coarse Ware, Sgraffito decorations on monochrome glaze (fig. 124:1)

The main characteristic of this group is an incised decoration on the vessel's surface. The required space is coated, while leather hard, with a white or another light-hue slip, by pouring or dipping. The decorations are engraved or incised through the layer of slip, so that the original hue of the clay is visible and the vessel is then fired. When completely cold, the vase is coated with a monochrome glaze and is then fired for the second time. The final result is an incised decoration in a darker hue.

The origin of this style lies in the fifth–seventh centuries in Egypt, where it was influenced by Coptic art. It was then extended to Mesopotamia and Iran, where it flourished during the tenth–eleventh centuries (Fehervari 1973: 61–62). The so-called *Sgraffito* decorated vessels became very popular in the Byzantine ceramic industry (Papanikola-Bakirtzis 1999) and are well recorded in such sites (Hakimian and Salamé-Sarkis 1988:3, Type AI and fig. I; Thalmann 1978: 24–26, Types C–D; Tushingham 1985: fig. 39:2; Pringle 1985: 183 "Coarse Graffita Ware"; 1986: 150; Megaw 1972: fig. 22). The date ascribed to this type and mentioned in the sites listed above is twelfth–fourteenth centuries.

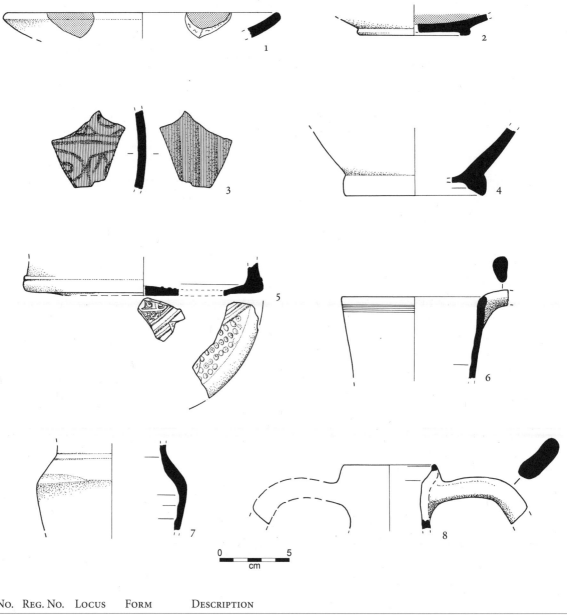

No.	Reg. No.	Locus	Form	Description
1	1008/4	1101	bowl	Red ware 10R 5/8 resembling cooking ware; white slipped under a thick yellow lead glaze.
2	1079	W1238	bowl	Red ware 10R 5/8; white slipped under a thick mustard yellow glaze.
3	1016/6	1301	bowl	Porcelain, grayish stoneware, dull green glaze.
4	1056/6	1315	jug	Red ware 2.5YR 5/6; finely levigated, containing small sized white grits, covered by a thick buff slip.
5	0061/1	2031	jug	Very pale brown ware 10YR 7/3; finely levigated, containing white grits, mica flakes and basalt inclusions. Covered by a thick buff slip.
6	1064/9	1010	juglet	Buff ware 2.5YR 8/3.
7	1041/2	1010	juglet	As the previous.
8	1008/2	1303	amphora	Micaceous light brown ware 7.5YR 7/4; containing basalt inclusions. Very fine ware.

Fig. 123. *Late Islamic and Crusader pottery: table ware (1–7), amphora (8).*

Coarse Ware, Sgraffito *decorations on color splashed glaze (fig. 124:2)*

The manufacture of this type is identical to the previous with one exception. After the first firing and before the glazing, the decoration is enhanced by additional colors. The type's origin lies in the Islamic artistic world with a Chinese T'ang influence from the ninth century onward (Atil 1973: 3). Monochrome *Sgraffito* Ware, as it is called, was extended all over the Byzantine Empire during the twelfth–fifteenth centuries. The style's broad distribution all over the Mediterranean world led scholars to trace the production centers of this style. Workshops were discovered in St. Simeon, the Christian port of Antioch (Lane 1937: 54), on the Greek mainland (Papanikola-Bakirtzis 1999: 158–265) and on Cyprus (Papanikola-Bakirtzis 1989). Boas (1994: 120), in his study of the *Import of the Western Ceramics to the Latin Kingdom of Jerusalem* suggested more than one production center and even a local manufacture. Following his description of the Hamat Gader material (Boas 1997: 394), it seems to us that the Tel Tanninim specimens are of a local or regional production.

Tin glazed, Proto-Maiolica *Ware*

The only tin glazed samples that were exposed at the site were the *Proto-Maiolica* bowls. This type of table ware is characterized by an opacified tin glaze decorated with painted ornaments, usually in blue, manganese, brown and yellow over the glaze. The clay is in a light color, usually buff, due to the relatively iron-free clay source. By definition, this type was imported from South Italy or Sicily and is dated to the twelfth–fourteenth centuries (D'Angelo 1995: 457). Some scholars accepted a twelfth-century date for the appearance of this style (Pringle 1982: 104; 1985: 200; Whitehouse 1967), but a recent study on three well documented churches in the Peloponnese suggests a thirteenth century date for the beginning of the type (Sanders 1989: 19). Such a date is confirmed by excavations in Cyprus (Megaw 1972: fig. F:2), Corinth (Stillwell-Mackay 1967: 257) and Caesarea Stratum II (Arnon 1999: 227). As far as we know, there were no local imitations of this

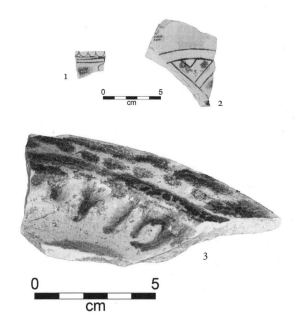

Fig. 124. *Coarse ware with* Sgraffito *decoration (1–2) and Ottoman plate (3).*

type. Based on this data, it seems that the Tel Tanninim bowls were imported from the south of Italy, probably through the port of Acre.

Celadon Porcelain-Chi'ng tz'u *Ware (fig. 123:3)*

Only three sherds, probably belonging to one bowl, were excavated. The precious luxurious porcelain was produced in China. The Tel Tanninim specimen is characterized by a white/grayish stoneware, mold decorated with a floral design under a dull green cracked glaze. Such a description is apt to be Northern Celadon style (Sullivan 1984: 174), produced during the Sung Dynasty (959–1127). According to historical records, this type of ware continued to be manufactured after the conquest of North China by the Chin Dynasty (Sullivan 1984: 175). The Islamic expansion into the western Indian Ocean, the demand for luxurious wares in the West, and the relatively passive openness of the Chinese empire motivated the trade between China and the West (Tampoe 1989: 97). Among the Sung exports, Celadon wares were the most popular (Sullivan 1984: 177). The Lung-Ch'üan workshop was the most popular one. Its products were characterized by grayish stoneware and a cracked, smooth, leaf-green glaze, which fits the Tel Tanninim specimen. This type is dated to the eleventh–fifteenth centuries C.E. and is well distributed in Asia, East Africa, Egypt and the Mediterranean world (Sullivan 1984: 178). A similar example was found in a sealed pit in Fustat, which was dated to 1250–1450 (Scanlon 1984: Pl. 2).

Unglazed Jugs and Juglets

Buff slipped and mold decorated (fig. 123:4–5)

The molded buff vessels are characteristic of the Sassanian/Iranian artistic world. In Susa, they appear in the seventh century and the beginning of the eighth century (Rosen-Ayalon 1974: 193; Kervarn 1984: fig. 27:1), while in the Near East they arrive not before the second half of the eighth century (Baramki 1944: 74; Arnon 1999: 225–26, Stratum VII; Avissar 1996: 158, Type 6). This type was revealed at Ramla with the molds, which might indicate a local production. As far as we know, not even one deposit relating to this type was found in a secure Umayyad context. The decoration style extended into the twelfth–fourteenth centuries, as recorded at Hama and in Jerusalem (Riis and Poulsen 1957: 242–64, Group 518:a–f; Tushingham 1985: fig. 34:20). The Tel Tanninim jugs are attributable to the later category of this type.

Plain Buff Ware (fig. 123:6–7)

This type of jug and juglet is characterized mainly by the hue of the clay, which ranges from light yellowish gray to very light gray or greenish/gray. The ewers are well and relatively thin potted, finely levigated, and well fired. The origin of this style is somewhere in the Sassanian empire (Adams 1970: 95). They already appear in the East in the seventh century (Rosen-Ayalon 1974:205; Adams 1970: fig. 6, Strata IV and V), but arrive at most of the sites in the Near East during the second half of the eighth century, due to the Abbasid expansion (Arnon 1999: 225–26, Stratum VII; Avissar 1996: 155, Types 2–4; Eisenberg and Ovadiah 1998: fig. 15:3; Walmsley 1988: Ill. 9:7–12; Frierman 1975: fig. 72), and became one of the most popular unglazed

wares. Although at some sites this type appears in Umayyad times, earlier in the eighth century (McNicoll, Smith and Hennessy 1982: figs. 144:1; 145:5; Loffreda 1974: 61; Tzaferis 1983: fig. 7:9–15), it seems that the sudden increase occurred sometimes during the second half of the eighth century. As noted above, this type became very popular and is well distributed from Syria in the north, through Transjordan and Palestine, to Egypt in the south and in Mesopotamia and Iran (de Vaux and Steve 1950: 27; Morgan and Leatherby 1987: fig. 47:24; Northedge 1992: fig. 137:2; Sarre 1925: Abb. 6; Rosen-Ayalon 1974: fig. 2–3; Lane 1937: fig. 3:F–G; Pl. 19:2:2B–C; Scanlon 1974: Pl. 15:9).

COOKING WARES

Wheel-made globular cooking pots (fig. 125:1–2)

During the tenth century, the globular cooking pot replaces the open-form casseroles that were common throughout Late Antiquity, in the Umayyad and the Abbasid periods (Arnon 1999: fig. 8:e–j, Stratum V; Avissar 1996: 133, Type 2; Stacey 1995: 167, Stratum III). Its use extends into the eleventh century (Arnon 1999a: 234) and with few examples into the twelfth–thirteenth centuries. The later version of the pot is characterized by a relatively ledged rim smeared with ginger or brown glaze. Similar cooking pots were unearthed at Tell ʿArqa (Thalmann 1978: fig. 32), Cyprus (Megaw 1972: 334 and fig. D), Hammat Gader (Boas 1997: Pl. I), Yoqneʿam (Avissar 1996: 136–37, Types 7–9), Caesarea and Burj al-Ahmar (Pringle 1985: fig. 2:3–8; 1986: 48).

Hand made globular cooking pots (fig. 125:3–4)

These are hand made vessels. The ware is coarsely potted and levigated, containing large quantities of white grits and an abundance of quartz due to sand inclusion. It is unevenly fired, leaving a thick gray core in the section. In several samples, red burnished marks are noticeable. This type of cooking ware appears quite often in Mamluk occupation levels, meaning thirteenth–fourteenth centuries, at such sites as Pella (Smith 1973: 242–43

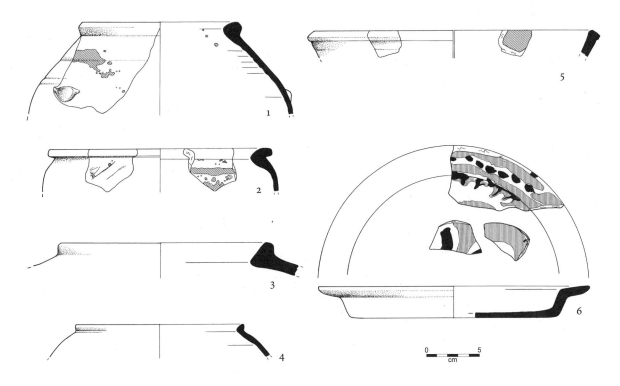

No.	Reg. No.	Locus	Form	Description
1	1003/1	1302	cooking pot	Wheel made, red ware 10R 5/8; small and medium sized white grits. Ginger/brown glazed interior up to the rim.
2	1014/6	1301	cooking pot	As the previous.
3	1055/1	1312	cooking pot	Hand made, coarse pink ware 7.5YR 7/4; gray core containing abundance of white grits and quartz inclusions. Burnished marks on exterior and rim.
4	1051/5	1018	cooking pot	Hard red ware 10R 5/8; smooth texture and common white grits.
5	1071/16	1301	frying pan	Coarse red ware 10R 5/8; containing white grits. Dark brown thick glaze, interior only.
6	C011	1001	plate	Pale yellow ware 2.5YR 8/3; well levigated. Inner surface glazed with strong green shade, interrupted by irregular black spots. Black glaze on lower rim and shoulder, with green glaze dripping onto inner sides of plate. Late Ottoman.

Fig. 125. *Islamic–Crusader pottery (1–5), Ottoman plate (6).*

and fig. 59:1024; Tushingham 1985: fig. 45:16–17; Avissar 1996: 138, Type 11; Pringle 1984: fig. 3:2–4; 1986: fig. 41).

Wheel-made frying pans (fig. 125:5)

Wheel-made frying pans made their first appearance during the tenth century, as recorded at Caesarea and Yoqneʿam (Arnon 1999: 226, fig. 8: a–h; Avissar 1996: 139, Types 13–14). This efficient cooking ware is characterized by its flat base, which is covered with a thick ginger or dark brown lead glaze. The Islamic Period vessels are glazed only

on the bottom, while the Crusader and later types are glazed all the way to the top. Such specimens are well represented in Medieval sites all over the region (Pringle 1986: 48; Thalmann 1978: fig. 31:4–6; Boas 1997: 383; Avissar 1996: 143, Type 18).

Ottoman plates (figs. 124:3; 125:6)

Represents the last occupation horizon at Tel Tanninim, when the reservoir in Area B was converted into a dwelling. All the Ottoman ceramic tobacco pipes (see Chapter IV.3), with one exception, were found in the converted reservoir structure.

CONTAINERS

Most of the samples were body sherds belonging to unidentified storage jars, probably of the "bag shaped" type derived from the Byzantine era. Just one specimen (see below) could be classified as an amphora from sea-borne commerce.

Amphora (fig. 123:8)

This amphora is characterized by its micaceous ware, which could point to a foreign source. Such amphorae were recorded on the Black Sea coast, near the Danube estuary and were dated to the eleventh–thirteenth centuries (Bjelajak 1989: 113 and fig. 3, Type II); on the Greek mainland at Ayios Stephanos (Sanders 1989: 199 and fig. 6), where they were dated to the beginning of the fourteenth century; and in Istanbul (Hayes 1992: 76, Type 63), dated to the twelfth–thirteenth centuries. Taking into consideration the clay's components, one might suggest a Byzantine origin for this vessel, dated to the eleventh–thirteenth centuries.

DISCUSSION

The excavations at Tel Tanninim unearthed 223 potsherds related to the post-Byzantine occupation levels at the site. Of these, 44.5 percent were table wares, 33.5 percent cooking wares and 22 percent were containers. This distribution attests to a normal dwelling occupation during these periods. Most of the vessels could be considered as local production, except for the obvious imported specimens such as the *Proto-Maiolica* bowls, the Celadon porcelain vessel and the Byzantine amphora. The chronological spectrum ranges from the ninth to fourteenth centuries. The ninth–tenth centuries are poorly represented by just five sherds, all of the Buff Ware type. The vast bulk of the pottery related to the thirteenth to fourteenth centuries and probably belonged to the Crusader tower and its adjacent occupation levels (Stieglitz 1999: 7). The extreme range in pottery distribution leaves the Early Islamic era shrouded in mystery, while the Crusader and Mamluk periods are well documented and represented.

Chapter IV

The Small Finds

1. The Glass

by Rachel Pollak

The excavations at Tel Tanninim uncovered hundreds of glass fragments. No intact or complete vessels were found, and the fragments themselves are very small. Thus, although the vessel type can be identified, details of the form are not always known precisely. A total of 784 fragments were counted as indicative parts of identified objects. Hundreds of body fragments were not considered. Of these, 550 fragments are from areas B and B2, the rest are from area A, except for a few from area D. The indicative assemblage fragments contain 372 pieces of windowpanes. The rest consist of table wares that included three major groups: bowls (103 fragments), bottles (153 fragments), and goblets (68 fragments). The remaining pieces are lamps, cups, jugs, juglets jars and few chunks.

The glass is presented by typology, without period division, accompanied by a catalogue. Parallels provide dating. In order to show the whole variety of the glass assemblage from Tel Tanninim, the typology includes vessels not only from sealed loci. The discussion includes assemblies from sealed loci, representing characteristic vessel types

from the various periods on the site. The catalogue provides the basket number of the fragment and its locus. The latter also indicates the area and year of the find (see Note, following Chapter VI, below).

BOWLS

The bowls comprise the third largest group among the indicative fragments. They may be divided into eight sub-types, based on the characteristics of their rims and bases.

Bowls with out-and-down folded rims
(figs. 126:1–7; 127:8–19)

The out-and-down folded rims form the majority within the group of the bowls, about 63 fragments. This is a common type, especially in the Eastern Mediterranean. The distinct characteristic is the out-and-down folded edge of the lip, consequently creating a horizontal tube in most cases. The rims and the folds come in various sizes and forms, ranging from vertical to horizontal and from narrow to wide. The bowls, too, range widely from

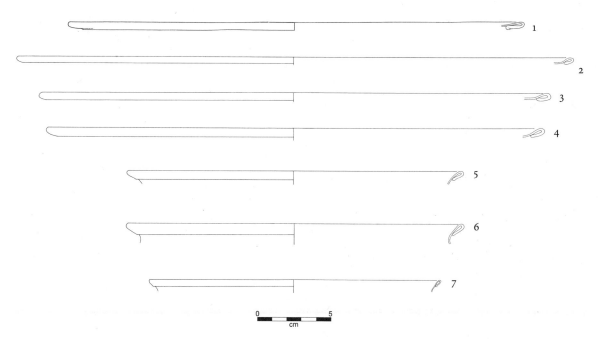

Fig. 126. *Bowls with out-and-down folded rims.*

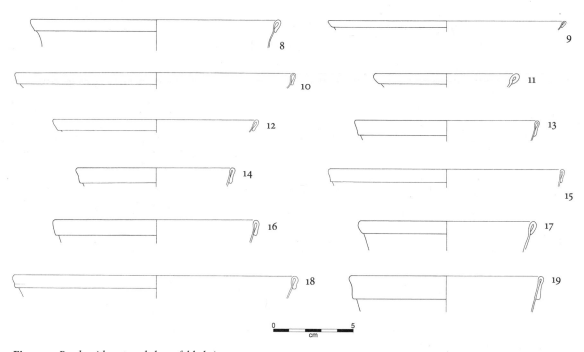

Fig. 127. *Bowls with out-and-down folded rims.*

large to small and from shallow to deep forms. The colors are mostly green and bluish green, a single fragment is of olive green glass. Most of the glass in this category is of bubbly nature.

Rims 1–4 are associated with big bowls with a diameter of over 30 cm. The rims are bent out al-

most horizontally, folded down and back. The side wall probably forms a ledge before curving down. Such bowls first appeared in the second half of the first century C.E., such as Isings' Form 42, and continued in the second and early third century (Isings 1957: 58). The dishes from Tel Tanninim are more comparable to those from Jalame, found in the factory dump dated to the second half of the fourth century (Weinberg and Goldstein 1988: 41–43 and fig. 4-3:20–22). The almost complete profile of the dish from Jalame indicates that it was a shallow dish with convex wall. A smaller intact bowl with similar rim and low, folded tubular base ring from Tomb XV at Hanita was dated to the second half of the third and fourth centuries, but considered to be a continuation of an earlier type, which first appeared during the late first or early second century (Barag 1978: 11–13 and fig. 6:3). Bowls with such rims were not found in Egypt, but they were abundant among the finds in Cyprus, dated to about 300 C.E. (Vessberg 1952: 112–13 and Pl. II:11, 13). A rim similar to no. 4 from Horvat Hermeshit was dated to the Byzantine Period (Winter 1998: 173 and fig. 2:4).

Rims 5–8 are bent out diagonally and the wall curves downward, probably in an S-shape, to form a hemispherical body. Rim fragment 6 may be of a deep bowl, as suggested by its out-curving wall. A similar deep bowl from Tomb XV at Hanita was dated to the second half of the third to mid-fourth century (Barag 1978: 18–23 and fig. 9:31). Rim fragment 8 belongs to a similar type of bowl, but shallower than 6, like a bowl from Hanita. Both the deep and the shallow ones are considered to be variations of the same type (Barag 1978: 11–13 and fig. 6:7–8). Several rim fragments from Jalame have a similar form (Weinberg and Goldstein 1988: 41–42 and fig. 4-3:16, 22, 28).

The identifying characteristic of fragments 9–18 is the in-curving wall below the rim. The rims themselves vary in the size and shape of the fold. Some of the bowls, like 9–12, are shallow, while 13–18 are deeper, similar to rims from Jalame (*ibid.*). Two rims of large, probably shallow bowls from Jerash dated to the Byzantine Period show similarites to bowl 10 (Dussart 1998: 64, Type BI.4121; Pl. 5:11,12).

At Jalame, all the bowls with out-and-down folded rims were classified as one group, although differing in rim and shape. This general group was common in the Syro-Palestinian area, Cyprus and Egypt in the Late Roman Period (Weinberg and Goldstein 1988: 41–44 and figs. 4-3; 4-4). These bowls have mainly pushed-in tubular base rings, except in Egypt, where most of them had tooled base rings (Harden 1936: Pls. XI–XII). Barag's Type 3.17, from Hanita Tomb XV and Cave I from Naharyia, dated to the third and the first half of the fourth century, has a similar rim to 17. Several rim fragments from Jerash, similar to our group 9–17, were discovered with Byzantine pottery dated to the fourth–fifth centuries (Dussart 1998: 56, Type BI.1211a and Pl. 3:4–6). Other rims from Amman and Jerash, with similar inclination, have a much wider date range from the second–third to the sixth–seventh centuries (Dussart 1998: 61, Type BI.1212 and Pl. 4:17–21). A few specimens of the smaller and deeper bowls from various sites in Jordan range in date from the Byzantine to Abbasid Periods (Dussart 1998: 66, Type BI.4213a21 and Pl. 6:17, 20, 21). A rim and side fragments from Jerash, similar to nos. 14 and 16, were dated to the Umayyad Period (Dussart 1998: 70, Type BI.5131 and Pl. 8:5). Bowl 18 is slightly different from the previous, having a carination from the rim to the straight in-sloping side. A bowl from Jerash with similar rim and profile was reconstructed as a shallow vessel with slightly concave base, dated fifth–sixth century, while other rims were dated to the fifth–seventh centuries (Dussart 1998: 64, Type BI.413 and Pl. 5:29, Type BI.4122 and Pl. 5:15, 17).

Rim 19 has a wide fold and straight tapering wall; it probably was a deep bowl. A similar fragment was found in locus 1007 (Area A), together with fragmentary material of Islamic nature. Bowls with broad folds are common in the Early Islamic Period until the late ninth century, a continuation of the Roman-Byzantine tradition.

1. 2049A/1, L 2300. Horizontally out-bent rim, d. 30.8 cm. Light bluish green glass, contains many small and minute, horizontally elongated bubbles.

2. 2060/1, L 2240. Horizontally out-bent rim, d. 37.6 cm. Light bluish green glass, contains small, horizontally elongated bubbles.

3. 2049/1, L 2202. Horizontally out-bent rim, d. 34.4 cm. Light bluish green glass, contains minute and medium horizontally elongated bubbles.

4. 2066/1, L 2240. Almost horizontally out-bent rim, d. 34.2 cm. Dull, light green glass, contains small, horizontally elongated bubbles.

5. 2055/2, L 2339. Diagonally out-bent rim, d. 23 cm. Bluish green glass, contains small, horizontally elongated bubbles on the fold.

6. 2020/1+2046/4, L 2304. Diagonally out-bent rim, d. 23 cm. The wall curves out below the rim, possibly forming a deep bowl. Green glass, contains few minute bubbles.

7. 2077/1, L 2222. Diagonally out-bent rim, d. 19.8 cm. Thin wall bent out below the rim to form a deep bowl. Light green glass, contains minute and small bubbles. Silvery weathering inside the fold.

8. 1099/1, L 1032. Almost vertical rim, d. 15.8 cm. Wall below rim vertical with a slight concavity. Light greenish blue glass, shiny whitish weathering.

9. 1014/1, L 1207. Out-bent rim with narrow fold, d. 15 cm. Side sloping inward. Light bluish green glass.

10. 2032/2, L 2112. Vertical rim, d. 17.8 cm. Body wall sloping inward. Brownish olive green glass, contains minute bubbles.

11. 1014/1, L 1207. Out-bent rim, d. 8.8 cm. Thick wall sloping in. Olive green glass, contains minute bubbles.

12. 2020/2, L 2304. Slightly out-bent rim, d. 13 cm. Side wall curving inward, indicating a shallow bowl. Light bluish green glass, contains many small, horizontally elongated bubbles in the fold.

13. 1080/1, L 1137. Almost vertical rim, d. 11.6 cm. Side wall sloping inward. Light green glass.

14. 1034/1, L 1010. Similar to previous, d. 10 cm. Light green glass, contains small and minute bubbles, some small ones are horizontally elongated.

15. 2065/1, L 2340. Rim fragment. Vertical rim, d. 14.8 cm. Vertical, slightly convex body. Green, bubbly glass, some horizontally elongated bubbles.

16. 1079/6, L 1137. Vertical rim, d. 13 cm. Wall curves slightly in. Green glass, contains small and minute bubbles, some are horizontally elongated. Iridescence on surface.

17. 1032/1, L 1100. Vertical rim, d. 11 cm. Straight wall slightly sloping in. Light green glass contains few small bubbles and few dark impurities.

18. 2018/1, L 2202. Vertical rim, d. 18.4 cm. Straight side wall curving in. Green glass, weathered surface, iridescence.

19. 1115/1, L 1040. Broad fold, vertical rim, d. 12 cm. Straight wall slightly sloping in. Light bluish green glass, shiny, flaking off weathering.

Bowls with double folded and collar rims (fig. 128:20–24)

Rims 20–21 are double folded. This type is uncommon at Shuni and Jalame. It is certain that bowls with double folded rim were not among the factory products at Jalame. A deep bowl, similar to nos. 20–21, from the wine press at Jalame was dated to 350–400 C.E. (Weinberg and Goldstein 1988: 49 and fig. 4–8:79).

Fragments 22–24 can be classified as a subgroup. The distinguishing characteristic is the broad folding of the rim, forming a collar. Most of these bowls are shallow, with a large diameter, mainly green in color. The depth of the bowl is the height of the collar, convex in most cases. None of these rims were preserved to their entire height, but the form is reconstructible. The broad fold creates an air space at the rim's upper section, while its lower edge is rolled out. Below it, the wall turns in horizontally toward the base, probably a tubular base ring. This type was classified by Isings (1957: 148) as Form 118, characteristic mainly in the eastern Roman Empire, dating to the fourth century. At Jalame, about 100 fragments of this type were identified, most certainly produced in the factory in the second half of the fourth century. Weinberg discussed their production and parallels (Weinberg and Goldstein 1988: 47 and fig. 4-7:71–73). Several fragments were discovered at Horvat Sugar and Kisra, dated to the fourth century (Aviam and Stern 1997: 96–97 and fig. 5:1; Stern 1997: 106–7 and fig. 1:6). The rims from Jerash were revealed from loci dated to the late fourth–fifth century (Meyer 1988: 190–91 and fig.6:L, M). Specimens from Jordan confirm the fourth-century date, but a few have a

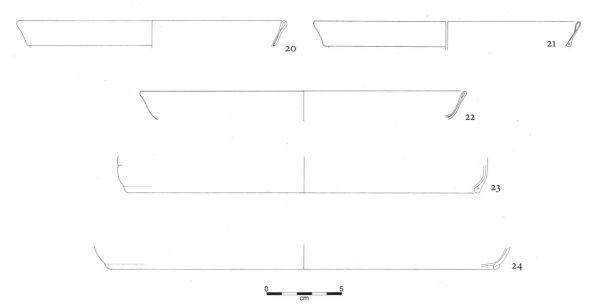

Fig. 128. Bowls with double folded and collar rims.

later date, suggesting the continuation of the type into the eighth century (Dussart 1998: 75, Type BII.311 and Pl. 11:2, 3, 7).

20. 2054/1, L 2300. Slightly out-bent rim, d. 18 cm. Wide fold with double tube. Greenish glass, contains few small bubbles.

21. 1073/5, L 1133. Wide fold, edge curved in. Light bluish green glass.

22. 1071/1, L 1127. Broad collar fold, curving in below the wall that curves in as well, d. 22 cm. Edge of fold broken. Green glass contains few small bubbles.

23. 0098/1, L 2041. Broken rim fragment. Lower part of wide collar fold, bent inward, d. 15.6 cm. Probably a shallow bowl. Light green glass, contains some horizontally elongated bubbles in the edge of the fold.

24. 2086/1, L 2252. Broken rim fragment. Lower part of wide, convex collar fold, maximum d. 27.8 cm. Horizontal side wall indicates shallow bowl.

Bowls with rounded and triangle shaped rims and bowls with a ridge below the rim (fig. 129: 25–37)

Number 25 belongs to a conical bowl, the earliest glass vessel on the site. It is part of a large homog-enous group of "cast grooved bowls," probably serving as drinking cups, with convex bases and horizontal grooves on the interior, below the rim; classified as Group A, from mid-second to mid-first century B.C.E. (Grose 1979: 55). These bowls were most probably produced in the Syro-Palestinian region. At Hellenistic Tel Anafa, large quantities of such bowls were uncovered (Weinberg 1970: 17–22 and Profiles 1–3; 1973: 35–42 and fig. 3:1–4). Cast grooved bowls have a wide distribution area in the Eastern and the Western Mediterranean, such as Sicily and Sidi Khrebish, Benghazi (Grose 1982: 20–29 and fig. 3; Price 1985: 287–91 and fig. 24.1:10,11).

The bowls with simple rounded and triangular rims are very diversified, encompassing flaring rims, S-shaped sides, upright rims, and inverted rims. Some of the rims (34–36) are similar to pot-tery vessels. The identification of some rims as bowls is not unequivocal. Fragment 26 is a flaring rim of a bowl of unknown size, showing similar-ity to a deep bowl from a burial cave at Kafr Yasif, dated to the third to first half of the fourth century (Gorin-Rosen 1997: 73 and fig. 3:3).

Rim and convex side of number 27 are similar to several fragments from Jordan, from Jerash and other sites, which are dated to the fifth–seventh centuries (Dussart 1998: 62, Type BI.31, Pl. 5:1–5). Several rim fragments with incurved are known

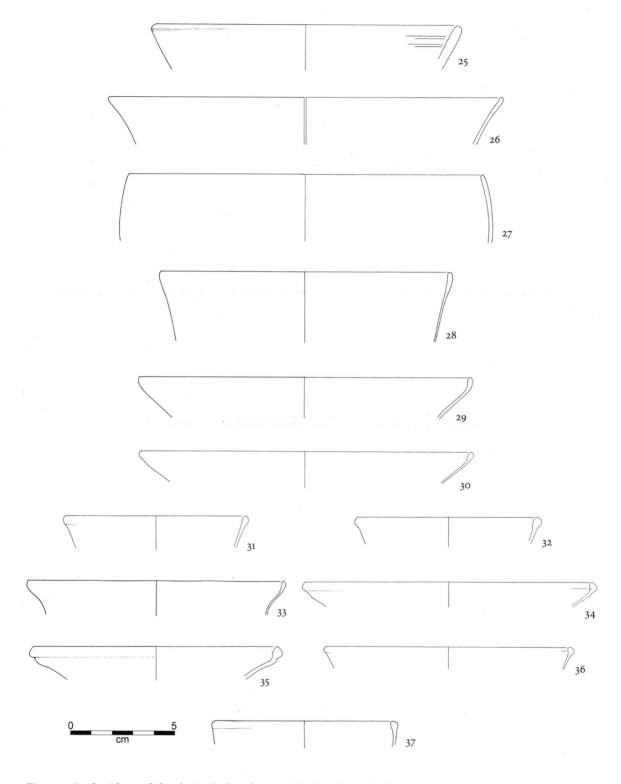

Fig. 129. *Bowls with rounded and triangle shaped rims and bowls with a ridge below the rim.*

from the burials at Lohamei Hagetaot, dated to the first half of the third century, although this group was dated to the third–fourth centuries (Peleg 1991: 135 and fig. 8:1–3). The shape of 28 is similar to the goblet cups, or lamps, but larger in diameter; it may be the bowl of a stemmed lamp or a deep bowl.

A similar bowl to 29, from Hamat Gader, was related to a type called "segmental bowl" from Hanita, dated to the third quarter of the third century. It is considered to be rather rare (Cohen 1997: 397–98 and Pl. I:4–5; Barag 1978: 18–19 and fig.9:29–30). Resemblance was found between nos. 30 and 33 and two bowls from Umayyad Beth Shean (Hadad 1998: 65 and fig. 1:14,15). Bowls 30, 33 and 35 have closely dated parallels at Beth Shean, from the shops built in 738 and destroyed by the earthquake of 749 (Hadad 1998: 65 and Pl. 20:340, 343).

Bowls 34–36 have triangular rims and in-sloping walls that might indicate shallow bowls. Numbers 31–33 and 37 seem to be deeper and smaller bowls. While at Tel Tanninim there is a variety of the type, it seems to be rare elsewhere. Two fragments similar to the small and deeper bowls are known from Amman, one of them dated to the Byzantine Period (Dussart 1998: 73, Type BI.631, Pl. 9:10–11). Another bowl similar to 32 was discovered at Jerash, and bears a late date of mid-eighth century, while a bowl fragment from Ain ez-Zara was dated to late first–second centuries (Dussart 1998: 69, Type BI. 512; Pl. 8:2, 3). A bowl from Horvat Aqav, similar to 33 was given a wide date-range of Late Roman to Byzantine Period (Cohen 2000: 167–68, 173 and Pl. I:13). The few available parallels for this group show the rarity of the type and the difficulties in dating it. Parallels to bowl 35 were found at Umayyad Beth Shearim and in the strata dating from the second half of the eighth to the eleventh centuries (Hadad 1998: 76–77 and Pl. 27:464, 497).

25. 1031/1, L 1117. Rounded rim, d. 14.4 cm, thick slanting wall. Two horizontal circular grooves inside, below rim. Cast bowl. Brownish green or olive green glass; remains of shiny whitish weathering.

26. 1069/3, L 1133. Rounded rim, wall sloping in, slightly concave. Light bluish green.

27. 1026/3, L 1112. Simple rounded rim, slightly bent in, d. 17 cm. Vertical convex wall. Colorless glass with pale greenish tinge (in section).

28. 1034/1, L 1115. Thickened rim, d. 14 cm. Thin, slightly concave wall. Light bluish green glass contains minute bubbles; thin iridescent weathering.

29. 1079/4, L 1137. Thickened upright rim, d. 16 cm. Angular below rim, straight wall sloping in. Green glass contains minute bubbles.

30. 2003/1, L 2201. Thickened rounded rim, d. 16 cm. Bent-in slanting wall, probably a shallow bowl. Light bluish green glass, contains bubbles. Weathered rough surface, some iridescence.

31. 2030/2, L 2112. Thickened rounded rim, d. 9 cm. Sidewall sloping in steeply. Green glass, contains horizontally elongated bubbles.

32. 2032/1, L 2112. Thickened, slightly angular rim, d. 8.8 cm. Sloping side wall. Green glass contains a few horizontally elongated bubbles.

33. 2049/2a, L 2300. Triangular rim, d. 12.2 cm. Side wall curves in before turning downward. Light green glass, rough surface.

34. 2037/2, L 2102. Thickened, defined triangular rim, d. 14 cm. Side wall bent in sharply with an angle. Light green glass, contains some horizontally elongated small bubbles. Translucent, filmy weathering partly covers the surface.

35. 1087/1, L 1026. Thickened, triangular rim, d. 11.8 cm. Angular side below rim; slightly concave wall sloping in. Deep emerald green glass; whitish iridescent weathering.

36. 2030/4, L 2112. Triangular rim, d. 10.8 cm. Side wall slightly bent-in. Light bluish green, bubbly glass.

37. 1071/2, L 1127. Rounded, thickened rim slightly bent in, d. 9 cm. Convex wall. Green glass, contains few minute bubbles.

Bowls with a horizontal ridge below the rim (fig. 130:38–39)

The characteristic feature of this class is the horizontal ridge below the rim on the exterior of the vessel. The bowls come in different forms, big and shallow such as 38, smaller and deeper as 39. The latter is less frequent. Barag (1970: 137 and Pl. 31) classifies this as Type 2.15, dated third to first half of fourth century, based on finds from Nahariya and Hanita. These bowls have low tubular base rings. Many fragments associated with this type were found at Jalame, most probably produced in the local factory, in the second half of the fourth century (Weinberg and Goldstein 1988: 45–47 and figs. 4–6). Other specimens are known from burial caves near Kabri, Horvat Sugar, and the winepress at Akhziv (Stern and Gorin-Rosen 1997: 19 and fig. 10:7; Aviam and Stern 1997: 96–97 and fig. 5:2–3; Syon 1998: 94 and fig. 14:2). Two fragments from Jordan were given different dates: one from Jerash was found with Roman pottery from the first to second centuries and another from Ain ez-Zara was dated to the period between the second half of the fourth and the first quarter of the sixth century. It seem that in Jordan this type is long-lived (Dussart 1998: 63, Type BI.4111b and Pl. 5:8, 9).

38. 1047/1, L 1123. Shallow bowl with upright simple rim, d. 18.4 cm. Slightly convex wall, circular horizontal ridge on the exterior of wall, 0.8 cm below rim. Light bluish green glass, contains minute elongated horizontal bubbles; shiny weathering.

39. 4152/1, Balk. Thickened, slightly out-turned rim, d. 12.4 cm. Straight wall almost vertical, bearing a horizontal rib on the outside, 1 cm below rim.

Bowls with rolled-in rims (fig. 130:40–42)

These are relatively scarce. The rim fragments found at Tel Tanninim indicate that bowls with infolded rims had assorted shapes, such as a shallow bowl with out-splaying rim (40), and a deep bowl with almost vertical rim (42). At Caesarea, two bowls with infolded rims were unearthed in a sealed locus, dated 650–750. This type of bowl did not appear in earlier or later layers. At Caesarea Stratum VIII it was considered to be a type characteristic only to the Umayyad Period (Pollak, 2002: fig. 1:1–2, in press), but we have to consider that the bowls from Tel Tanninim are slightly different. Rim 40 is similar to Dussart's Type BI.4222b2, which is based on finds from Jerash Stratum XII, dated to

the end of the seventh to eighth century. One rim was given a date of late sixth to seventh century; thus, the final date of this type is late sixth–eighth centuries (Dussart 1998: 69 and Pl. 7:20, 22, 23). The deep bowl 42 resembles Dussart's Type BI.4213b2. Specimens from Jordan give various dates: a rim from Jerash Stratum XI, sixth–seventh century; Ain ez-Zara fragment, from mid-fourth to first quarter of the sixth century (Dussart 1998: 67 and Pl. 6:26–28). Unfortunately, the closest parallel, from Umm Qeis, was not datable. Fragment 42 most resembles the bowls from Caesarea.

40. 2063/4, L 2340. Horizontal rim, folded up and in, d. 12 cm. Slanted wall. Light bluish green glass.

41. 2022/1, L 2112. Flaring rim, infolded, d. 11.8 cm. The rim continues the direction of the diagonal wall. Green glass, contains some small bubbles in the fold.

42. 2060/9, L 2240. Unevenly infolded vertical rim, slightly out-turned, d. 12 cm. Sidewall tapers down, slightly concave, probably forming a deep bowl. Green glass, contains small and minute bubbles.

Spittoon or bowl with wide horizontal rim (fig. 130:43)

This rim fragment can be interpreted in different ways. One of the options is that the vessel is a spittoon, although the known glass vessels are larger, the brims are not horizontal, and the vessels are ususaly decorated with enamel painting. They are dated to the fourteenth century, and also occur in other materials (Carboni and Whitehouse 2001: 272, Cat. 135). The rim might also be a small bowl, similar to a type of ceramic saucer with wide horizontal brim and hemispherical body, found at Caesarea Stratum II, and dating to the Crusader period (personal communication from Y. Arnon). Alternatively, it might be a type of bowl such as discovered from the shipwreck at Serçe Limani, with wide horizontal rim, cylindrical body, slightly convex wall, mold blown, and dating to the first half of the eleventh century (Bass 1984: 69 and fig. 51, Lledo 1997: 46 and fig. 1d).

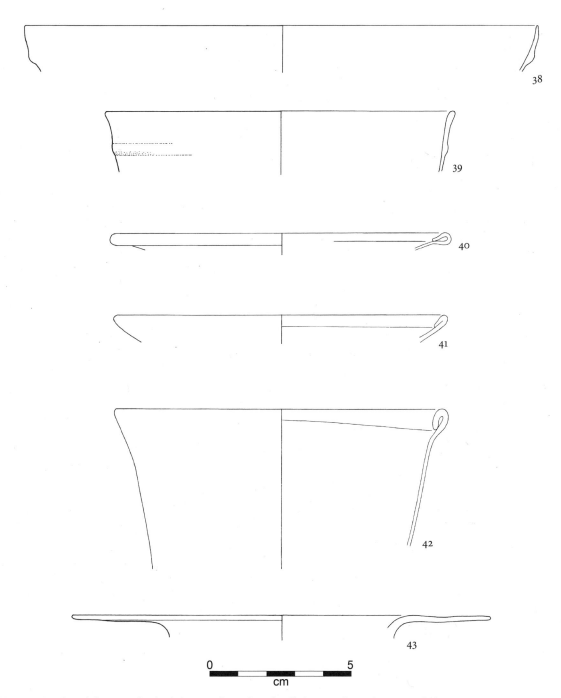

Fig. 130. *Bowls with horizontal ridge below rim (38–39); with rolled-in rim (40–42); spittoon (43).*

43. 1017/1, L 1110. Rim fragment. Horizontally out-splayed wide brim, max. d. 15 cm., mouth 7.6 cm. Brown glass, severe erosion forming reduced patches, iridescent weathering.

Bowls decorated with threads (fig. 131:44–51)

Threads wound around the upper part of the bowl near the rim are the main method of decoration. There are two main bowl types: with out-and-down folded rims and with simple rounded rims. Most of the decorated bowls have out-turning, simple rounded rims and concave sloping walls. Only one specimen (49) has an in-turning, thickened, rounded rim. The threads vary in color; on some bowls the threads are of the same color as the vessel, on others they are of contrasting colors, such as dark blue, turquoise or even opaque red. On part of the bowls, the applied threads are marvered in (44, 49). Bowls with flaring rims, decorated with applied threads similar to 44 and 46–48 were found at few sites. At Mezad Tamar, they were dated like the bowls with same shape, but without decoration, to the fourth–fifth centuries; at Ain ez-Zara Stratum II, dated 350/375–525; at Shuni (L 197) they were not dateable (Erdmann 1977: 107 and Taf. 5:515; Dussart 1998: 63, Type BI.4112 and Pl. 5:10; Pollak 2002, in press).

Bowls with flaring rims decorated with a single thread of contrasting color are also known from the Abbasid Period (ninth–tenth centuries) from Ramla (Gorin-Rosen 1999: 12, 14 and fig. 2:1) and Caesarea (Pollak 2002a: forthcoming). Fragment 47 can be seen as Islamic, based on the quality of the glass and the weathering type, in addition to the characteristics of other fragments from the locus (above L 1018), which contained material of Early Islamic date (75, 165). A similar bowl from Beth Shean was dated late eighth–eleventh century (Hadad 1998: 75 and Pl. 27:463).

Bowls similarly shaped to 45 were found at Jalame and Shuni (Weinberg and Goldstein 1988: 55 and fig. 4-17:129; Pollak 2002a: fig. 5:27, forthcoming). Bowls similar to 49, with in-turning, rounded rims decorated with applied threads, but not from the lip's edge, are known from Jalame (fourth century). The decoration continues into the fifth century (Weinberg and Goldstein 1988: 55, fig. 4-17:126, 128).

The bowls with out-and-down folded rims (50–51) are decorated with one or more threads, applied to the wall before the edge was folded down. Three similar bowls were found at Shuni, but not in datable context (Pollak 2002a: fig. 2:11–13, forthcoming). Several bowls with out-and-down folded rims with thread decoration within the fold were found in Beirut, dated to the Byzantine Period and classified as lamps (Foy

1997–98). A single bowl of this type was found at Jalame (Weinberg and Goldstein 1988: 42 and fig. 4-3:27).

44. 2088/1, L 2219. Flaring, thickened rim, d.16 cm. Decorated with threads from the edge of the lip downward on exterior of the side, fused to the vessel. The glass is bluish green and the threads are dark blue.

45. 1027/2, L 1041. Thickened, rounded out-bent rim, d. 8.2 cm. Wall probably sloping. Decorated with a single turquoise thread, fused to rim. Colorless glass with pale green tinge in section.

46. 1043/1, L 1112. Rounded rim, turning out, d. 17 cm. Straight wall sloping in. Two greenish turquoise threads decorate the wall. Colorless glass with pale greenish tinge in section, contains minute bubbles, horizontally elongated.

47. 1019/1, L 1007. Rounded edge of out-turning rim, d. 21.8 cm. Slightly concave sloping wall, decorated with single thread of same color as vessel. Colorless glass with greenish tinge; severely eroded surface, reduced thickness, patches and pitting. Thick, hard, enamel-like weathering.

48. 1072/1, L 1029. Simple, rounded, vertical rim, d.19 cm. Slightly concave wall sloping in, decorated with three thin threads of same color as body. Colorless glass, iridescent weathering.

49. 0060/1, L 2033. Thickened, rounded, inturned rim, d. 14.8 cm. Decorated with threads, fused to rim and side; sloping wall. Green glass, brown-red opaque threads.

50. 2042/1, L 2102. Out-and-down folded rim fragment, broad fold, d. 13.8 cm. Between the wall and the folded edge five threads were applied before folding. Greenish blue glass contains minute bubbles, dark blue threads.

51. 1124/1, L 1032. Small fragment of rim, distorted. A single thread was applied between wall and fold. Light bluish green glass, dark blue thread.

Bowls decorated with handles (fig. 131:52–53)

Fragments 52–53 are handles. Bowl 52 probably had a small basket handle attached to the top of the out-and-down folded rim, although such handles are

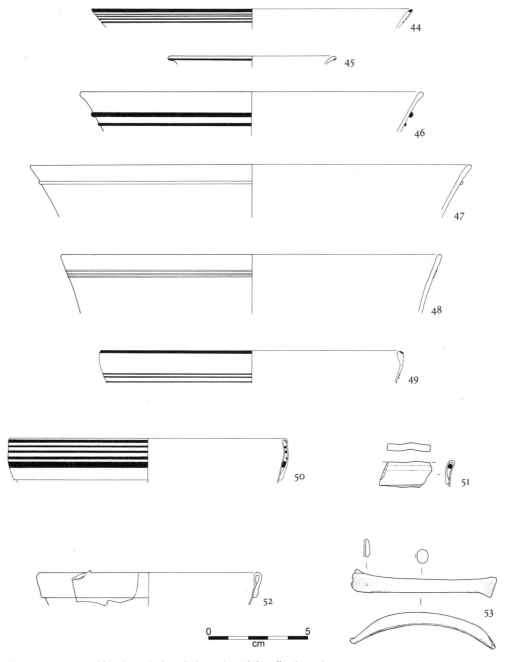

Fig. 131. *Decorated bowls: with threads (44–51); with handles (52–53).*

not typical. The vessel could have served as a lamp. Fragment 53 is a decorative coil handle attached to the body of a vessel of unknown form.

52. 1013/1, L 1207. Out-and-down folded rim, d. 11.2 cm. Sloping in wall; two small scars on the edge of the lip indicate some kind of handle attached to it, maybe a small basket handle. Pale bluish green glass, contains small bubbles.

53. 069/1, L. 1133. Decorative handle formed by a coil, flattened on both edges and applied to body. Green glass with darker stripe inside and dark impurities.

Pushed-in tubular bases (fig. 132: 54–64)

Only 13 fragments of pushed-in, tubular base ring fragments were uncovered, most of them associated with bowls. They come in different sizes and heights. The bigger bases probably belong to shallow large bowls, the smaller ones to deeper bowls. The small and low base rings may belong to jugs. The bases' colors are similar to those of the rims, mainly green of various tinges, bluish green and a single base of olive green glass.

Bases 54–59 are similar to bowls from Hanita, dated to the third and the first half of the fourth century (Barag 1978: 14, 20 and figs. 7:1; 10:34). Base 64 may show similarity to a shallow bowl with simple rim from Hanita, same date, and resembles several bases from Jalame (Barag 1978: 14 and fig.15; Weinberg and Goldstein 1988: 44 and fig. 4–4). Bases similar to 57 were found at Khirbat al-Karak, late fifth and early sixth century (Delougaz and Haines 1960: 49, 57 and Pl. 59:18). A base ring from Jerash, Early Byzantine (Meyer 1988: 192 and fig. 7:H), resembles our fragment 54.

54. 2082/1, L 2240. Fragment of out-splayed base ring, d. 11 cm. Faded, light green.

55. 2077/2, L 2222. Fragment of out-splayed base ring, d. 8 cm. Faded, light green.

56. 2018/1, L 2304. Fragment of tall, out-splayed base ring, d. 10 cm. Wall bent out horizontally. Bluish green glass, contains few small bubbles.

57. 0101/1, L 2041. High, slightly out-splayed base ring, d. 8.6 cm. Bluish green glass, covered by filmy translucent weathering.

58. 1063/2, L 1100. High, out-splayed base ring, d. 9 cm. Center probably flat or convex. Light bluish green; dulled surface, partly covered by shiny whitish weathering.

59. 2112, L 2249. Center of base ring. Thick, convex, with big pontil scar. Deep bluish green glass, contains minute bubbles.

60. 1020/1, L 1306. Thick base ring, d. 6.4 cm. Light green glass, contains bubbles; rough, weathered surface.

61. 1073/4, L 1133. High base ring, d. 5.8 cm. Slightly out-splayed. Green glass.

62. 1026/1, L 1112. Low base ring, out-splayed, d. 6.6 cm. Center probably concave. Deep olive green glass, translucent, filmy weathering.

63. 1032/2, L 1100. Low, slightly out-splayed base ring, d. 6.8 cm. Light green glass, contains small bubbles.

64. 2030/1, L 2300. Low base ring, d. 11.8 cm. Green glass.

OIL LAMPS

Five groups of oil lamps, used from Late Roman to Islamic times, are represented here.

Solid and hollow stemmed lamps (fig. 133:65–69)

These have a bowl- or goblet-shaped upper part and the lower part is a long cylindrical stem. Stemmed lamps were placed in bronze polycandela, mainly, but not exclusively, used in churches and synagogues, and are divided to two main subtypes: (A) lamps with solid stems and (B) lamps with hollowed stems. Fragments 65–68 are cylindrical solid stems. They vary from short and thick (65) to long and slender (67); some are more conical (66) and others are tooled (68). Most of these stems are made of green glass of various shades, some are deep bluish green, while olive green is rare.

Crowfoot and Harden dated the solid stems to the seventh century and claimed that they had been used only for a short time, in Late Byzantine and Early Islamic times, based on finds from Jerash and Beth Shean. These stems were mostly beaded and tooled (Crowfoot and Harden 1931: 203 and Pl. XXIX:21–23). New evidence shows that solid stems with modifications continue in use even up to the Mamluk Period (Hadad 1998: 66–69 and fig. 2–3, Type 2). The cylindrical type originated in the Late Byzantine Period (Hadad 1998: 69 and fig. 3, Type 3). The solid stems published by Barag (1970: 182 and Pl. 40:13.3–1, 4) are considered to be seventh century. A stem similar to 67 was found at Ramat Hanadiv, dated fifth–seventh centuries (Cohen 2000: 169 and Pl. II:24). Dozens of solid cylindrical stems were discovered at Shuni, some from sealed loci dating to the Byzantine Period (Pollak 2002a, forthcoming). They are similar to fragments 65–67.

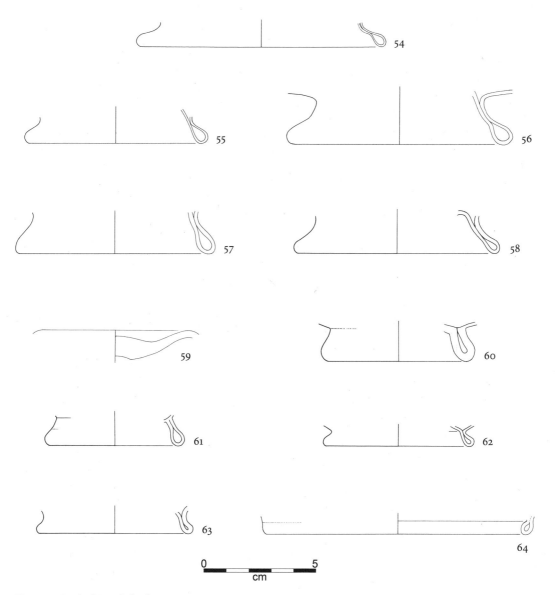

Fig. 132. *Pushed-in tubular bases.*

Similar stems from Jordan are dated to the seventh century and the Umayyad Period (Dussart 1998: 88, Type BVI.212; Pl. 16:9–10).

Only one fragment (69) represents the cylindrical hollow stem category. This subtype is contemporary with the previous, and is very common at Byzantine sites such as Mount Nebo, Samaria, Shavei Zion, Mezad Tamar, Rehovot-in-the-Negev and Caesarea (Saller 1941: 316 and Pl. 140:16–27; Barag 1967: fig.16:25, dated fifth–sixth century; Crowfoot 1957: 414 and fig. 96:6, below a fifth–sixth century floor; Erdmann 1971: Taf. 3:151;

Patrich 1988: 136, Type B, dated fifth–seventh centuries; Peleg and Reich 1992: 155 and fig. 20:1–9). Several examples from Jordan were dated to the Byzantine and Umayyad Periods (Dussart 1998: 86, Type BVI. 211; Pl. 16:1–8). Hollow stems found at Sardis, Type 3, were dated to the fourth–seventh centuries, although the largest quantity is concentrated between the fifth–sixth centuries (Saldern 1980: 50 and Pl. 23:274, 280).

65. 1079/1, L 1137. Cylindrical, short, solid stem, d. 1.4 cm, bottom of the cup curving up. Deep emerald green glass, contains few big bubbles and some

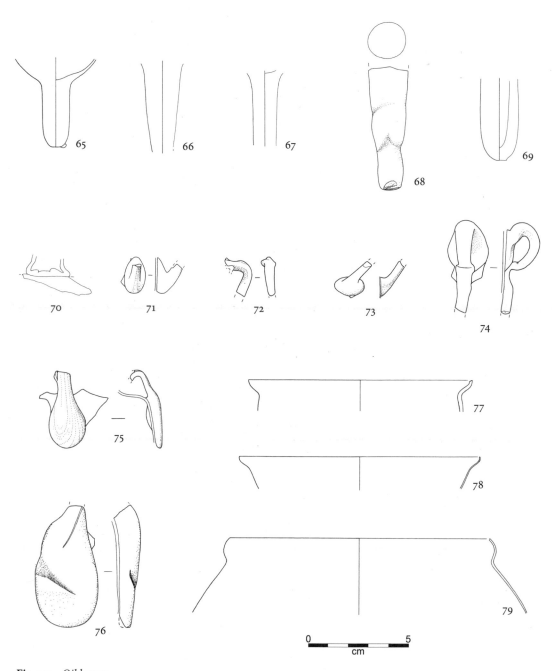

Fig. 133. *Oil lamps.*

small ones. Remains of filmy, shiny to iridescent weathering.

66. 2100/2, L 2249. Section of cylindrical to conical solid stem; broken on both ends. Green glass, contains big and small bubbles. Roughly weathered surface.

67. 2063/2, L 2340. Solid cylindrical stem, d. 1.2 cm. Broken at its lower end; at upper break bottom of cup is visible. Deep bluish green glass.

68. 0101/2, L 2041. Solid cylindrical stem, spirally twisted. Olive green glass.

69. 2037/1, L 2304. Hollow cylindrical stem, d.1.9 cm. Deep bluish green glass, bubbly.

Cup / bowl lamp with wick tube (fig. 133:70)

Tubes were applied to bowls or cups that served as lamps to hold the wick. Lamps with wick tubes first appeared in the Byzantine Period. Several lamps found in tombs or churches dated to Late Byzantine or Early Islamic times, others may be from the fifth–sixth centuries (Barag 1970: 184 and Pl. 40.13:13–16). Bowl fragments with wick tube were found at Nessana (Harden 1962: 84 and Pl. XX:47). Lamp fragments with wick tubes from Rehovot-in-the-Negev, Type A, were dated fifth–seventh century (Patrich 1988: 134 and Pl. XII:8–13). This type of lamp might be the same as that represented by handle fragments 71–73. Wick tubes continue to exist during the Islamic Period, in cylindrical bowl shaped lamps, such as those from Samarra (Crowfoot and Harden 1931: 205, Group 5; Pl. XXX:51–53), and later, in closed shapes like globular vessels with flared neck and several applied hanging handles, from the Fatimid era (Carboni and Whitehouse 2001: 77 and fig. 6; Carboni 2001: 165, Cat. 38a–c; Foy 1999: 186, 189 and figs. 4; 5:1; Pollak 2000: 240 and fig. 6:8).

70. 0101/3, L 2041. Fragment of concave base, lower section of wick tube fused to it. Body made of bluish green glass, tube of green glass.

Miscellaneous lamp handles (fig. 133:71–76)

Handle fragments 71–73 belong to bowl-shaped lamps. These bowls have out-and-down folded rims, in-sloping walls and concave bases (but other base forms occur as well). Three small handles are attached to rim and body. Barag's Types 13.12–14 are dated to Late Byzantine and the beginning of Early Islamic times, but Type 13.13 was also found in a context dated to the fifth century (Barag 1970: 184). Isings (1957: 162) presented examples from Italy, dating from the fourth and early fifth centuries, for her bowl lamp Form 134. No lamps found in the Eastern Mediterranean were dated earlier than the fifth century. Most of the finds dated Late Byzantine and later, as confirmed by examples from Rehovot-in-the-Negev (Patrich 1988: 134 and Pl. XII:1–7); Beth Shean (Hadad 1998: 49, 115 and Pls. 17:293–295; 51:872–876); and various sites in Jordan (Dussart 1998: 82, Type BVI.1221; Pl. 14:18–27).

Handle fragments 74–76 are related to lamps with closed shapes. 74 is a loop handle for suspension. It has a tail that may continue down to the base, tooled with pattern. The wall is straight and differs in color from the handle. This fragment is similar to a hanging lamp with vase shape, cylindrical neck, short shoulder and slightly conical body. It has six handles applied to the rim with tooled tails going down to the base, and in the interval six suspension rings with tooled tails from below the shoulder to the base. In this case, the body and the handles are of the same color. This lamp was dated eighth–ninth century (Carboni 2001: 165, Cat. 38a). The type of handle with tail occurred also in globular shaped or mosque lamps from the Fatimid Period (Foy 1999: 188 and fig. 5:1, 5, 7). Handle fragments 75 and 76 belong to mosque lamps with large flaring neck and globular body. Several handles were attached from shoulder to body. The lower part of the handle is drop-shaped, flattened when pressed to body. These lamps come in various sizes. Some are very small, such as the dark blue one from Caesarea, and another, colorless example from the Kuwait National Museum, both dated to the Fatimid era (eleventh century), as well as a handle fragment of turquoise glass and colorless body from Beth Shean (Pollak 2000: 240 and fig. 6:8; Carboni 2001: 166, Cat. 38b; Hadad 1998: 116 and Pl. 52: 891). Other lamps are large with similar handles. They are known from Beth Shean, where a handle fragment was discovered in the Abbasid–Fatimid layer, from Nishapur in Iran (tenth–eleventh century), Fustat in Egypt (eleventh–twelfth century) and the Serçe Limani shipwreck, ca. 1025 C.E. (Hadad 1998: 116 and Pl. 52:890; 1998: 72 and fig. 6:66–69; Kröger 1995: 182, No. 235; Foy 1999: 187ff. and figs. 5:3, 6:6, 7, 8; Jenkins 1986: 7).

71. 1069/2, L 1133. Lower part of small hanging loop handle. Body and handle of green glass.

72. 1032/1, L 1011. Upper part of small hanging handle, with the attachment point to rim. Light green glass.

73. 1038/1, L 1011. Lower part of small handle attached to body. Light green glass.

74. 1079/11, L 1137. Small loop handle attached to body. Extension of handle downward, broken.

Body of light green glass, handle dark blue, transparent to green glass, bubbly.

75. 1051/1, L 1018. Hanging handle, lower end attached to body and flattened. The vessel has an almost horizontal shoulder, curves up to neck, the body opens slightly downward. Body of colorless glass, eroded, reduced thickness, iridescent patches; flaking off weathering. Handle B of emerald green glass, eroded, rough surface, pearly weathering.

76. 048/1, L 1311. Lower end of mosque lamp handle, in shape of big drop, flattened and tooled. Body and handle of same yellowish, smoky glass, small and elongated bubbles.

Bowls and beakers with cracked-off or ground rims (fig. 133:77–79)

This group includes two hemispherical bowls and a deep bowl with squat globular body. The base was rounded or concave. Colors are varied tinges of green. They could have been used as lamps. These undecorated fragments may be considered variations of Isings' Form 96a, dated 250–450 based on European finds (Isings 1957: 113). Similar finds at Carthage were dated to the fourth century (Tatton-Brown 1984:197 and fig. 65:16). East Mediterranean hemispherical bowls with cracked-off rims, such as Barag's Types 2.5 and 13.10, and finds from the Jalame glass factory, were dated 350–400 (Barag 1970: 135, 183 and Pls. 30:5; 40:10; Weinberg and Goldstein 1988: 95 and fig. 4-49:481). Crowfoot and Harden's Group 2 (1931: 202 and Pl. XXX:17, 19) refers to bowl lamps of Late Roman date. At Caesarea, such bowls are dated fourth–fifth centuries (Pollak 1999: 324, 332 and fig. 1:17). The same date was given to a hemispherical bowl from Jerash, while two others were dated to the Late Byzantine period (Meyer 1987: 189, 197 and figs. 6:E; 7:GG-II). At Mezad Tamar and sites in Jordan the date range was fourth–seventh centuries (Erdmann 1977: 106 and Pl. 5:431–37, 439; Dussart 1998: 61, 224, Type BI.221; Pl. 4:22–25; 81, 253, Types BVI.1112b1–3; Pl. 13:15–20).

77. 1027/1, L 1041. Rim fragment, out-and-up curving, d. 11 cm. Polished edge; slightly convex wall, could form globular body. Dark olive green glass, contains many small and minute bubbles.

78. 1019/2, L 1041. Rim out-and-up curving, d. 12.9 cm. Thin, slightly convex wall sloping in. Probably hemispherical bowl. Yellowish green glass, translucent weathering.

79. 1080/8, L 1137. Rim and wall fragment of large bowl. Rim curving up and in, d. 13 cm. Convex wall sloping out, probably forming globular body. Green glass with minute bubbles.

CUPS

These three fragments (fig. 134) are possibly parts of cups. Cups with infolded rims occur at Ramla in the Umayyad layer (seventh–mid-eighth century); at Caesarea they are much more frequent in the following Abbasid era (Gorin-Rosen 1999: 11,13 and fig.1:1–3; Pollak 2002: fig. 2:21a–b, forthcoming). While 80 and 81 have straight slanting walls, the cups from Ramla and Caesarea have convex walls. Thus, these rims might be upper parts of goblets (Isings' Form 111), or a rim from Shuni (Isings 1957: 139; Pollak 2002a: fig.11:69, forthcoming).

The pinched handle forming a flat semicircular projection on the lower part of the handle is similar to features on handles from cylindrical cups of the Early Islamic Period. Occasionally the handle is decorated with more than a single pinch, such as a cup from Victoria and Albert Museum (Carboni and Whitehouse 2001: 72, Cat.1; eighth–tenth century) and two more at the Museum für Islamische Kunst, where the bodies of the vessels are decorated with tong pinching (Kröger 1984: 125, Cat. 108–109; ninth–tenth century). Fragment 82 has a carination on the side, a fact that might be problematic regarding cylindrical cups. Although in the examples brought here the handles are attached to the lower part of the vessels the side curving in toward the base.

80. 2037/1, L 2102. Rounded infolded rim, d. 9.4 cm, straight, slightly sloping-in side. Glass changes color from rim bluish green, bubbly, downward to green wall with few small bubbles and dark small impurities.

81. 2060/4, L 2240. Small rim fragment, infolded rounded, d. 9.8 cm. Wall slightly sloping in. Green glass, contains minute bubbles.

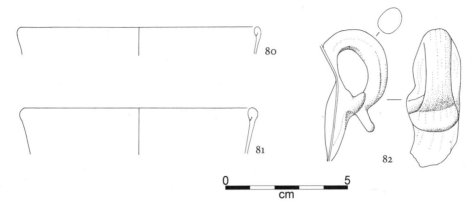

Fig. 134. Cups.

82. 2069/1, L 2240. Round handle of cup with pinched thumb rest; handle was attached to the lower part of an angular vessel. Green glass contains dark impurities, eroded by pitting, iridescence.

STEMMED GOBLETS (WINE GLASSES)

Bases and stems (fig. 135:83–94)

Stemmed goblets are a Mediterranean type first appearing in the Late Roman era (fourth century) and continuing until today (Isings 1957:139, Form 111). All the bases with stems discovered at Tel Tanninim are of the blown type, with pushed-in, concave bases and hollow stems. The glass colors are mainly light and deep greens and light and deep bluish greens. Stemmed goblets are very common among finds from churches; something that may point to either religious use or as lamps (Crowfoot and Harden 1931: 206, Group 4 and Pl. XXX:50). Goblets probably supersede the beakers with folded base rings (Weinberg and Goldstein 1988: 62). Barag (1970: 146 and Pl. 33:5.2–10) dated all the types to the Late Byzantine era. Goblets, dated fifth–sixth centuries, were found at the churches of Shavei Zion, Mount Nebo, and Khirbat al-Karak (Barag 1967: 67 and fig. 16:15–17; Saller 1941: 318 and Pl. 140:30–39; Delougaz and Haines 1960: Pl. 60:14, 21–22). Similar vessels from the painted tomb at Migdal Ashqelon were dated to the fifth–seventh centuries, and a base fragment from Caesarea is from the Late Byzantine Period (Katsnelson 1999: 70, 80 and fig. 2:9–14; Pollak 1999: 326, 329 and fig. 2:24).

Bases of this type from Jerash were dated to the Late Byzantine and Umayyad periods (Meyer 1988: 196, 199 and fig.8:Y,bb). Fragments from various sites in Jordan were dated mainly to the Byzantine period, but many fragments were from the Umayyad period and later (Dussart 1998: 115, Type BIX.1 and Pls. 27–28). Some goblets from the Basilica in Kourion were dated to the seventh century and considered to be of local production (Young 1993: 39).

83. 2063/1, L 2340. Foot and stem fragment. Pushed-in concave tubular base or foot, d. 6 cm max. Thick, cylindrical hollow stem ending in a small dome, projecting into the bottom of the cup; pontil scar on lower side of stem. Deep greenish blue glass, contains few tiny bubbles.

84. 0101/4, L 2041. Similar to previous, max. d. 4.6 cm. Concave wall of lower part of cup sloping out. Green glass, silvery weathering.

85. 0101/6, L 2041. Foot and stem. Pushed-in concave tubular foot, d. 6.2 cm. Hollow stem ending in a small dome at the bottom of the cup, pontil scar at lower end. Stem has a bead shape, formed by a slight constriction on both ends. Deep green glass, contains some bubbles.

86. 0101/7, L 2041. Foot, stem and lower section of cup. Pushed-in, tubular, thick foot, d. 5.6 cm. Concave; hollow, broad stem with rough bead shape, with pontil scar at its lower end, and small dome at upper end. The wall of the cup splays out horizontally. Light bluish green glass.

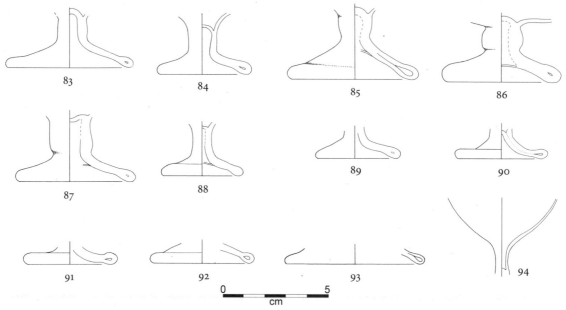

Fig. 135. *Stemmed goblets: bases and stems.*

87. 0101/8, L 2041. Foot and stem. Foot pushed in, concave with small pontil scar on the inside, d. 5.8 cm. Broad, hollow cylindrical stem, ending with a concavity. Constriction between foot and stem. Deep green glass, contains small bubbles.

88. 0101/5, L 2041. Foot and stem fragment. Concave, pushed-in base, d. 4 cm. Slim, hollow stem, pontil scar on its lower end. Bottle green glass.

89. 2018/2, L 2304. Foot fragment. Pushed-in, slightly concave base, d. 4 cm. Pontil scar. Greenish blue glass with olive green streak, contains some small bubbles.

90. 0101/9, L 2041. Foot fragment. Pushed-in, tubular base, d. 4.4 cm. Almost flat, concave at center. Deep bluish green glass.

91. 0092/2, L 2038. Small foot fragment. Folded, pushed–in, almost flat, d. 4.4 cm. Shallow concavity at center toward stem. Deep bluish green glass.

92. 2057/1, L 2202. Foot fragment. Pushed-in, tubular, concave base, d. 4.9 cm. Light bluish green glass; rough, weathered surface.

93. 1065/3, L 1132. Foot fragment. Pushed-in, concave base, d. 6.6 cm. Green glass, weathered surface.

94. 2023/1, L 2102. Stem and lower body of cup. Thin, delicate stem, hollow toward the cup. Convex wall of cup sloping out and up. Bluish green glass, contains bubbles at junction between body and stem.

Rims of goblets / stemmed lamps (fig. 136:95–106)

Several types of rims may belong to stemmed goblets or stemmed lamps. Most of the rims belong to the flaring type (95–103). Barag's Type 5.8 is a stemmed goblet with such a rim, dated to the early seventh century. The same date was given to stemmed lamps that have cups with similar flaring rims (Barag 1970:147, 182 and Pls. 33:5.8; Pl. 40:13.3–1). Numerous similar rims, from various sites in Jordan, are dated from the second half of the fourth to the eighth centuries. The largest number, however, appears during the Byzantine period (Dussart 1998:1 24–127, Type BIX.31; Pls. 30–31).

Fragment 98 resembles a rim from Jerash, dated from the end of seventh to the eighth century (Dussart 1998:124 and Pl. 30:36). Fragment 104 belongs to another sub-type of cups with a thickened, rounded rim and straight, vertical wall. Three stemmed goblets from Jerash have similar rims; they also have solid tooled bases. This type of base does not appear in the corpus of Tel Tanninim

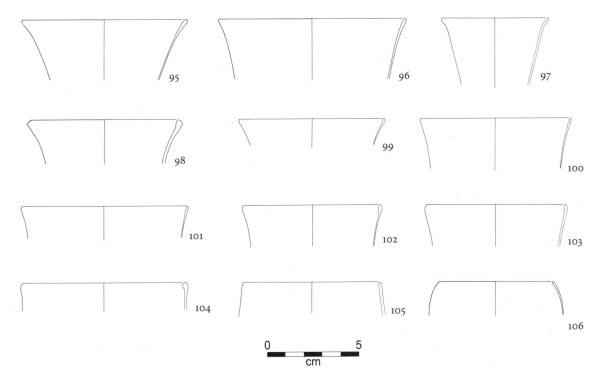

Fig. 136. *Stemmed goblets: rims.*

and is dated to Umayyad period (Meyer 1987:204 and fig. 10:X, Y, Z). Two hollow stemmed lamps have cups with similar flaring rims, dating to the Byzantine period (fifth–sixth centuries; Harden 1962:84–85, Pl. XX:51,52). Fragments 105 and 106 have thin, rounded rims. 105 has a vertical rim with an out-sloping wall that probably forms a sack-shaped cup. 106 has an in-curving rim and a convex body, similar to a rim from Khirbat al-Karak from the Byzantine period (Delougaz and Haines Pl. 59:14).

95. 1054, L 1125. Thickened, flaring rim, d. 8.9 cm. Thin wall sloping in. Light bluish green glass, contains small and minute bubbles and blowing spirals; thin, iridescent, flaking off weathering.

96. 1046/1, L 1114. Thickened, flaring rim, d. 9.8 cm. Thin wall slightly concave, sloping down and in. Bluish green glass contains minute and small bubbles close to rim, some are horizontally elongated. Thin, iridescent weathering.

97. 2099/1, L 2252. Out-bent, simple rim, d. 6 cm. Straight wall sloping in. Bluish green glass, more green at rim, contains few small bubbles.

98. 1090/1, L 1010. Thickened, flaring rim with in-curved edge, d. 8 cm. Light bluish green glass.

99. 2060/2, L 2240. Thickened, flaring rim, d. 8 cm. Thin, concave wall sloping in. Colorless glass with light bluish green tinge.

100. 0104/1, L 2041. Thickened, slightly out-turned rim, d. 8.2 cm. Thin, slightly concave wall. Pale bluish green glass, contains minute bubbles.

101. 0105/1, L 2041. Flaring rim, d. 8.9 cm. Slightly concave wall, sloping down. Green bubbly glass, contains small and few horizontally elongated bubbles.

102. 2023/2, L 2102. Thickened rim, d. 7.4 cm. Thin, concave wall sloping down. Bluish green glass contains minute bubbles and blowing spirals.

103. 0094/1, L 2038. Rounded, slightly in-turned rim, d. 7.6 cm. Slightly concave wall. Olive green glass.

104. 2026/1, L 2304. Thickened, rounded, slightly in-turned rim, d. 8.6 cm. Light bluish green glass.

105. 2031/1, L 2304. Simple rim, sloping in, d. 7.4 cm. Light bluish green glass contains minute bubbles in the direction of blowing spirals.

106. 1073/1, L 1133. Incurved rim, d. 6 cm. Convex wall. Bluish green glass, shiny, whitish weathering.

Decorated goblets (fig. 137:107–9)

Several cups bear decorations. Some of them have incurved rims and convex walls (109), others have thickened vertical rims (107, 108). These belong to goblets or wine glasses decorated with applied, fused-in threads. The threads are of dark blue color and in all cases are wound several times around the upper part of the cup from the rim downward. Similar rims of goblets were discovered in the painted tomb at Ashqelon (fifth–seventh century), and two more are known from Ras Abu Ma'aruf (Katsnelson 1999: 70, 80 and fig. 2:9–11, with bibliography; Gorin-Rosen 1999: 211 and fig. 2:23,24).

107. 2012/1, L 2300. Thickened rim, d. 7 cm. Vessel made of light bluish green glass and decorated with dark blue, translucent threads, fused to wall and rim.

108. 0133/1, L 2053. Small rim fragment. Thickened rim and thin wall of brownish olive green glass, several threads of dark blue glass, thin and thicker, are fused into wall.

109. 1048/1, L 1125. Small fragment of rim. Rounded rim, d. 9 cm. Convex wall of colorless glass with greenish tinge. Decorated with dark blue threads, fused-in.

JUGS AND JUGLETS

These vessels (fig. 138) were known in the Roman Empire in the first to second centuries, although in our region those early types are rare. They become more common in the Late Roman period. The majority of juglets discovered were from tombs. They are less prevalent in the Byzantine period. Vessels with one handle are not frequent at Tel Tanninim, only ten fragments were assigned to this group.

Handle fragment 110 resembles a Syro-Palestinian type from the fourth century, with an elongated pear-shaped body currently in the Newark Museum, similar to Isings' Form 120b (Auth 1976: 106, Cat. 121; Isings 1957: 150). Several ribbed strap handles were found scattered at the site at Jalame, not in the factory dump; thus, they were not con-

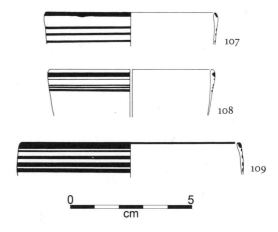

Fig. 137. *Decorated goblets.*

nected to the glass manufacture of the second half of the fourth century (Weinberg and Goldstein 1988: 66, 69 and fig. 4-30:250).

Fragment 111 is the upper end of a thick rod handle, attached to the neck of the jug. Only one example from the 23 types of jugs presented by Barag has a handle attached to the neck on its upper end. This was recovered from a Byzantine pit at Beth Shean (Barag 1970: 165 and Pl. 36: 8.23). Juglet 113 is a variation of the of Syro-Palestinian types, dated to the fourth century. Several similar examples are known from Hamat Gader and Kisra (Cohen 1997: 413, Type 3; Pl. 5:6–7; Stern 1997: 113 and fig. 3:28, with more references). Several juglets from the Dubkin Collection at the Israel Museum have some resemblance to 113, and are also dated to the fourth century (Israeli 2001: 183, Cat. 235–36).

Most jug fragments from Jalame have a funnel mouth and are decorated with a spiral thread or a single thick trail. Some have a single thread around the neck. They were found mostly in the factory dump (Weinberg and Goldstein 1988: 64–67 and figs. 4-27:208; 4-28:224). A juglet from Tomb 107 at Wadi Faynan, Jordan, dated to the Byzantine era (O'Hea 1998: 76, 78 and fig. 7, top) is similar in its funnel mouth and the handle attachment to the infolded rim of 113, but lacks the thread wound around the neck.

110. 0101/10, L 2041. Straight ribbon handle with 7–8 ribs, the two exteriors are more prominent than the interiors. Lower end of handle attached

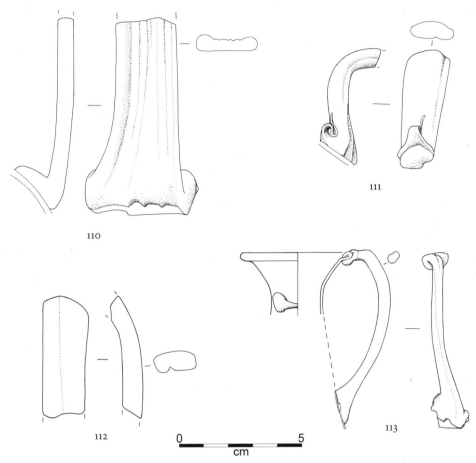

Fig. 138. *Jugs and juglets.*

to convex part of vessel, probably to shoulder. At attachment, part of the ribs were drawn out into short prongs. Both body and handle made of same bluish green glass. Silvery, filmy weathering.

111. 0101/11, L 2041. Upper part of flattened rod handle, with angular curving downward; attached to neck, with up and incurving upper end. Yellowish glass contains small elongated bubbles; iridescent surface underneath silvery weathering.

112. 1021/2, L 1112. Convex fragment of handle, flattened rod with fold on inside of handle. Pale green glass, rough surface, iridescent weathering, dark coating.

113. 2057/1, L 2340. Juglet: upper part, brim, neck, and handle, d. 4.8 cm. Infolded rim, funnel mouth, length of neck unknown. Thick thread handle, attached to lower end of neck or shoulder (the curving of wall attached to handle is of small diam-

eter) and to rim, then flattened. Remains of thread decoration on neck. Vessel, handle and thread are of same color: light bluish green. Handle contains several bubbles.

BOTTLES

The largest category among the vessels is that of the bottles (figs. 139–42). A total of 153 indicative fragments were identified as bottles. The identified fragments consist mainly of rims and a smaller number of bases and necks. Since this report deals with fragments, some doubt can arise concerning the shape of some of the vessels. Further division forms subtypes according to the characteristic features. Plain and decorated bottles will be presented separately. The main decoration method is applied threads. Few vessels were mold blown.

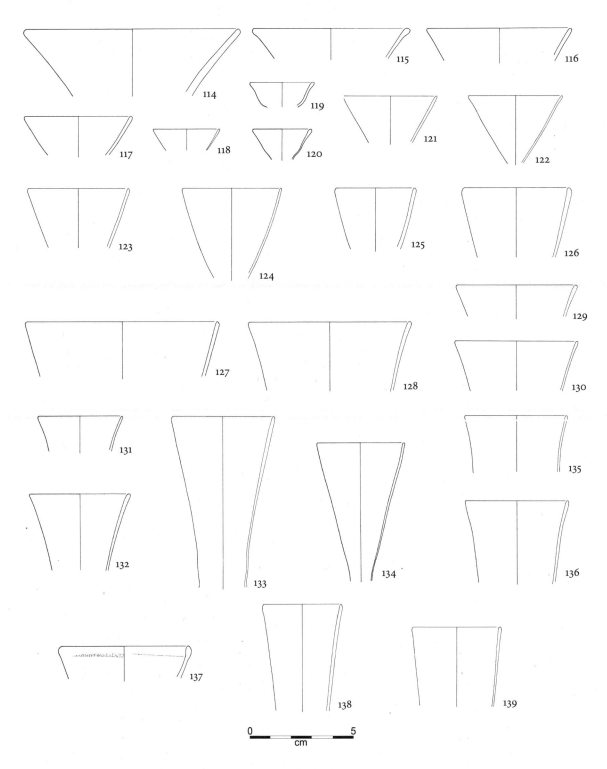

Fig. 139.   *Bottles with simple rim, funnel mouth or conical neck.*

Bottles with simple rims, funnel mouth
or conical necks (fig. 139:114–39)

Many of the bottles have flaring mouths. Only few are preserved enough to differentiate conical neck from funnel mouth that turns into cylindrical neck. Some funnel mouths are recognizable by the wide angle of the funnel. Conical necks are characteristic of the Byzantine period, although they are found in earlier contexts as well. The most common body shape for bottles with conical necks is the globular body with slightly concave base, such as Isings' Form 104b, from Western Mediterranean contexts (third–fourth century). Examples from Karanis and Jerash are dated later (fourth–fifth century; Isings 1957: 123–25). Barag discussed several bottles with globular bodies and conical necks (Type 15.12, dated fourth century), bottles with cylindrical necks and funnel mouths (Type 15.15; dated fourth and first half of the fifth century), or bottles with conical mouth and cylindrical neck (Types 5.24; 15.28) that may be fifth century (Barag 1970: 191 and Pls. 42–43). A bottle with globular body and cylindrical neck, slightly opening upward, probably developed from Types 15.12–13, is dated from the second half of the fifth to the sixth century (Barag 1970: 195 and Pl. 43:15.25).

Globular bottles are known from the painted tomb at Migdal Ashqelon (fifth century); a bottle with wide funnel mouth and cylindrical neck from Galilee (fourth century, probably from a tomb) and from the Akeldama Tombs in Jerusalem, three bottles with funnel mouth were found in Caves 1 and 2, together with Byzantine pottery (Katsnelson 1999: 72 and fig. 3:9–10, 12; Harden 1949: 153 and fig. 2:2; Winter 1998: 98 and fig. 5.6:2). Some bottles from Beit Ras are globular with conical neck (Harden 1964: 51 and fig.10, dated fourth–fifth century). Others include a rim from Shavei Zion (fifth–sixth century); several bottles with wide funnel mouth and simple rims from Hamat Gader (250–350); two bottles from a burial cave in Rafidiya (Shechem); and a large quantity of conical and funnel mouth from Shuni (Barag 1967: 65 and fig. 16:3; Cohen 1997: 419 and Pl. VI: 1–3; Hizmi 1997:126 and fig. 6:20–21; Pollak 2002: figs. 16:116–17; 17:118–23); Cyprus, third–fourth century (Vessberg 1952:

131 and Pl. 7:13–14); an intact bottle from a tomb at Umm Qeis, fourth to sixth/seventh century (Dussart 1998: 164, Type BXIII1121a1 and Pl. 51:8). Bottles with globular body and conical and funnel mouth were mostly used in the fourth century, with continuation into the fifth century, such as a bottle from Jerash with conical mouth, long cylindrical neck and globular body with slightly concave base (Dussart 1998: 142, Type BX.3111 and Pl. 39:1).

So far, only one option of the various vessels with conical neck was presented. There are other types of bottles with similar rims and necks. The cylindrical bottle with funnel mouth (Isings 1957: 160, Form 132) is a fourth-century variation of the previous bottle type with globular body. Bottles with pear-shaped body (Barag's Type 16.12) appear side by side with the globular bottles in some of the tombs, such as at Nahariya and Hanita, and are dated from the mid-third to the fourth century (Barag 1970: 202 and Pl. 44). This type was also found in burials at Lohamei Hagetaot, Kafr Yasif and Kabri (Peleg 1991: 139 and fig. 9:6, 8; Gorin-Rosen 1997: 74 and fig. 4:10; Stern and Gorin-Rosen 1997: 14 and fig. 16–17).

Barag's Type 16.13 is a development of the previous type, with longer neck. It appears in Byzantine burials (Barag 1970: 202 and Pl. 44:16.13-1). This later version is known from Samaria and Beit Ras (fourth–fifth century; Crowfoot 1957: 411 and fig. 95:7; Harden 1964: 51 and fig. 10, top, second from right). Rim and neck fragments 133–34 and 138–39 can be associated with this type.

Other bottles with funnel mouth have an angular body, like Barag's Type 17.5, such as the bottle from Samaria (fifth century) and Type 17.8 dated from the mid-fifth to sixth century (Barag 1970: 205 and Pl. 45; Crowfoot 1957: 411 and fig. 95:4).

Fragments 124–25 and 128–29 are similar to large bottles found at Jalame, dated ca. 350 C.E. (Weinberg and Goldstein 1988: 73 and fig. 4-35:298, 300). A rim fragment from Jerash resembling 125 was dated to the Late Byzantine/Umayyad periods (Meyer 1987: 205 and fig. 10:F).

Most of the datable rim fragments of conical necks are classified as Type BX.1113a1 (350/375–525). A few were given a later date (700–750), such as Types BX.1125a1 and BX.1132a1 (Dussart 1998: 128ff.

and Pls. 32:8–31; 33:1–18; 34:4–37; 35:1–13; 36:5–11). Another category within Dussart's classification contains a wide range of big funnel mouth fragments, Type BX.3241a, similar to our 114–18 and 121–23. Their date ranges from 350 to the Umayyad period, with some exceptions (Dussart 1998:144 and Pls. 40:10–25; 41:1–15). Funnel mouth and conical neck fragments were also recovered at Beth Shean, in the Umayyad and later strata, containing material from the mid-eighth to eleventh century (Hadad 1998: 35, 91 and Pls. 5:81–84, 91; 40:648–49).

Most of the rims are made of various tinges and shades of green glass, some are bluish green and yellowish green, while colorless pieces are rare. The rim diameter ranges between 3 and 10.5 cm. Most of the vessels are medium and big in size. Fragments 119 and 120 have a parallel from Tomb B at Lohamei Hagetaot (300–350), which has a long cylindrical neck and globular body; Hamat Gader (Peleg 1991:136 and fig. 9:1; Cohen 1997: 420 and Pl. VI:3), and Ras Abu Ma'aruf (fourth or early fifth century; Gorin-Rosen 1999: 206 and fig. 1:14).

114. 1026/2, L 1112. Rounded rim, d. 10.6 cm. Funnel mouth with slightly concave, thick wall. Yellowish glass, contains small and medium bubbles; erosion in form of patches reduces in section, thin iridescent flaking off weathering, dark thin coating.

115. 1019/1, L 1041. Rounded rim, d. 7.6 cm. Green glass, contains small and minute bubbles.

116. 1046/1, L 1010. Rounded rim, d. 7 cm. Emerald green glass.

117. 1079/8, L 1137. Rounded rim, d. 5.2 cm. Funnel mouth with slightly convex wall. Green glass, changes to olive green below rim, contains medium and small bubbles. Translucent, iridescent weathering.

118. 1079/7, L 1137. Funnel mouth with thin, convex wall, rim d. 3.2 cm. Greenish glass contains minute bubbles. Translucent, thin, filmy iridescent weathering.

119. 1072/1, L 1134. Rounded out-turned rim, d. 3.2 cm. Convex wall, cup shaped mouth. Pale bluish green glass, bubbles, some large, horizontally elongated; whitish, shiny weathering.

120. 1071/3, L 1127. Rounded, thickened rim, d. 2.9 cm. Funnel mouth with angular wall, curving downward to cylindrical neck. Light bluish green glass contains few medium size bubbles near rim. Remains of shiny weathering.

121. 2030/5, L 2112. Funnel mouth with straight wall, rim d. 4.6 cm. Deep green glass, contains minute bubbles.

122. 2103/1, L 2270. Funnel mouth with thin, straight wall, rim d. 4.6 cm. Light bluish green glass, contains minute bubbles and blowing spirals.

123. 2046/1, L 2304. Funnel mouth with straight wall, rim d. 5 cm. Green glass, contains many small dark impurities, bubbles and streak of a different shade of green.

124. 2102/2, L 2249. Funnel mouth with slightly convex wall, rim d. 4.9 cm. Light yellowish green glass.

125. 2099/2, L 2252. Funnel mouth with slightly convex wall, rim d. 3.8 cm. Bluish green glass contains elongated and minute bubbles and blowing spirals.

126. 2063/3, L 2340. Rim d. 5.2 cm. Thick wall sloping in. Green glass, contains tiny and small bubbles; part of surface dulled, rest iridescent. Interior surface rough.

127. 1080/4, L 1137. Rounded rim, d. 9.4 cm. Straight wall sloping in. Emerald green glass, contains small bubbles, some horizontally elongated. Shiny, whitish weathering, iridescence.

128. 2060/5, L 2240. Rounded rim, d. 7.8 cm. Slightly concave wall sloping in. Dulled green glass, contains minute bubbles.

129. 2049/2, L 2202. Rim d. 5.8 cm. Wall sloping in. Green glass contains minute bubbles.

130. 2086/2, L 2252. Thin wall sloping in, rim d. 6 cm. Light bluish green glass.

131. 1073/2, L 1133. Slightly concave wall sloping in, rim d. 4.1 cm. Greenish blue glass.

132. 1024/1, L 1004. Rounded rim, d. 5 cm. Slightly concave wall sloping in. Green glass, contains small bubbles.

133. 2060/7, L 2240. Rim d. 5 cm. Straight wall sloping in to form conical mouth that continues gently without angle into short cylindrical neck. Lower edge of neck curves out. Deep green glass.

134. 1079/2, L 1137. Rim d. 4.2 cm. Long conical mouth, continues with slender cylindrical neck. Green glass, contains small and minute bubbles. Whitish, thick weathering on outside, pearly weathering inside.

135. 2060/6, L 2240. Rounded rim, d. 4.9 cm. Rim lightly opens up with upper part of wall, below it cylindrical neck almost wide as rim. Bluish green glass, contains big bubbles.

136. 2030/1, L 2112. Conical mouth and neck, rim d. 5 cm. Green glass, contains small and minute bubbles in blowing spirals and some large ones.

137. 1036/1, L 1315. Unevenly thickened rim, d. 6.4 cm. Probably conical neck. Pale greenish glass, contains small bubbles; iridescent, translucent weathering, rough surface.

138. 0069/1, L 2031. Rounded rim, unevenly worked, d. 3.8 cm. Conical neck. Bluish green glass, contains minute to large bubbles, vertically elongated.

139. 0094/2, L 2038. Rounded rim, d. 4.2 cm. Conical neck. Light olive green glass, contains minute bubbles.

Bottles with cylindrical necks (fig. 140:140–48)

This category consists of various types of bottles, all having cylindrical necks. Numbers 140–46 are upright, simple, fire-rounded rims of big and smaller bottles. The colors of the glass are green, light green, bluish green, and a few specimens are olive green and sky blue.

Rims 140–46 resemble Dussart Type BX.5311, dated from 350 to the Umayyad period, although most of the examples are from the Byzantine period (Dussart 1998: 152 and Pl. 44). A few similar rim fragments were recovered at Ras Abu Ma'aruf (Pisgat Zeev East A). The date, based on parallels, ranges from Late Roman times to mid-sixth century (Gorin-Rosen 1999: 206 and fig. 1:9–10). Barag's Type 15.27 is a globular bottle with long and wide cylindrical neck and simple rim, dated to the fifth–sixth century. It differs from Barag's Types 15.6–8, 15.10 by the diameter and length of the neck, and by the constriction at the base of the neck. It represent types until the Late Byzantine

period (Barag 1970: 189ff. and Pls. 41, 43). More rims resembling 140–45 were found at Hamat Gader (second half of the fifth century to Late Byzantine), and in the painted tomb at Ashqelon (Cohen 1997: 422 and Pl. VII:6–10; Katsnelson 1999: 72 and fig. 3:9–12).

Fragment 146 is a small bottle with thick wall and globular body. It might be classified as Barag's Types 15.6–8, although it differs in the fire-rounded rim and lacks the constriction at the base of the neck. Resembling bottle necks of thick glass, with a slight constriction at the base of the neck, were found in the Umayyad strata at Caesarea. From Umayyad Beth Shean comes a bottle with similar neck and globular body, but it differs in the curving of the neck out toward the body (Pollak 2002: fig.1:3, in press; Hadad 1998: 35 and Pl. 5:87). Also similar to 146 is a rim and neck fragment from Beth She'arim Catacomb 20, dating to the Byzantine period (Barag 1972: 200 and fig. 97:16). Most resembling to 146 is a bottle from Susa Level II–III, dated 660–900 (Kervarn 1984: 224 and fig. 7:10).

The long cylindrical neck with the out-turned, tooled rim in our 147 might belong to a bottle with globular or bulbous body and high concave kicked-in base, a type known from ninth–tenth-century Islamic sites, like Beth Shean, in the stratum that contains material ranging from mid eighth–eleventh century and Caesarea (Hadad 1998: 109 and Pl. 47:797–800; Pollak 2002: fig.4:41–42, in press).

Rim and neck fragment 148 differs from the other bottles in color quality of glass and shape. It is known from Early Islamic sites as a bottle with wide and short cylindrical neck, upright rim and cylindrical or mold blown (hexagonal) body. Such bottles were found at Fustat (late eighth–ninth century) and at Caesarea (Shindo 1992: 599 and Pl. 6-14:33–36; Pollak 2002: fig. 2:23–24, in press).

140. 2071/1, L 2222. Rounded rim, d. 5 cm. Straight vertical wall. Green glass, contains small, minute and few big bubbles. Dulled interior.

141. 0111/2, L 2053. Rounded rim, d. 4.8 cm. Straight vertical wall. Light green glass, contains small and medium size bubbles in direction of blowing spirals.

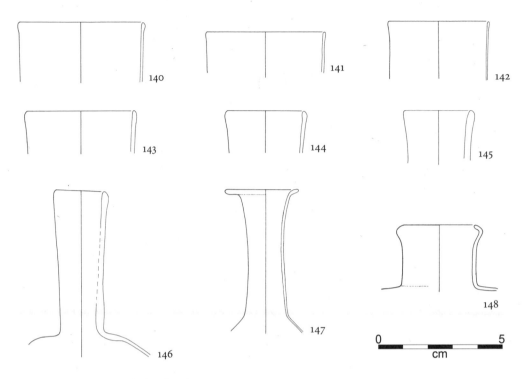

FIG. 140. *Bottles with cylindrical necks.*

142. 2065/2, L 2340. Rim d. 4 cm. Thin, vertical wall. Light olive green glass, contains few bubbles.

143. 2055/3, L 2229. Rounded rim, d. 4.5 cm. Green glass, contains small and medium-size bubbles and blowing spirals.

144. 2055/2, L 2229. Rounded rim, d. 3 cm. Slim cylindrical neck. Greenish blue glass contains minute and small bubbles.

145. 0103/1, L 2041. Rounded rim, d. 2.8 cm. Green glass with minute and some larger, elongated bubbles and blowing spirals.

146. TT98, B2, 2100/1, L 2249. Rounded rim, d. 2 cm. Long slender neck and convex, widely opening shoulder; emphasized, angular transition from neck to shoulder. Thick light green glass contains elongated bubbles in direction of blowing spirals.

147. TT99, B, 0101/12, L 2041. Rim, neck and shoulder fragment. Tooled rim, almost horizontally bent out, d. 3 cm. Long, cylindrical neck with slightly concave wall, diagonal shoulder from angular junction with neck. Dulled, light bluish green glass contains

mainly small, vertically elongated bubbles, and several big ones. Bluish, silvery, filmy weathering.

148. 1064/1, L 1100. Incurved rim, d. 3 cm. Short cylindrical neck, bent out at angle to horizontal shoulder. Sky blue glass, bubbly with blowing spirals; iridescent, thin weathering.

Bottles with infolded rims (fig. 141:149–58)

Bottles with infolded rim, funnel mouths or cylindrical mouths and necks, such as 150–55, have prototypes in the Late Roman period with various types developed from them in the Byzantine Period. Such rims and necks were found in the Early Islamic period as well.

Globular bottles with cylindrical necks and infolded rims were classified by Barag as Type 15.11 and 15.11-1 (third century to 350), based on the finds from Tomb XV at Hanita (Barag 1970: 191 and Pl. 41; Barag 1978: fig.13:51–53). Another bottle type with funnel mouth and tubular base ring, from the same tomb, was classified as Type 15.18 (Barag 1970: 193 and Pl. 42). A very similar bottle to the previous, but with flat and slightly concave base (Type 15.15) has a date range from the third to the beginning of the fifth century, based on examples from Nahariya (the earliest) and Gezer (Barag 1970: 192 and Pl. 42). Comparable rims were found at Mezad Tamar and Catacomb 20 (Late Roman–Byzantine) at Beth She'arim (Erdmann 1977: Taf. 4:277, 279–80, 283, 361, 364; Barag 1972: 200 and fig. 97:17, 19–20). Several large bottles found at Jalame have cylindrical and funnel mouths with infolded rims. They were considered to be factory produced, dated ca. 350 (Weinberg and Goldstein 1988: 72ff. and figs. 4-33; 4-34:296, 299). Hundreds of similar rim fragments were unearthed at Beirut, dated by parallels to the sixth century, but more abundant in the Umayyad period (Foy 1997–98). Conical mouths with rolled-in rims and cylindrical necks were found in large quantities at Caesarea Stratum VIII (640–750), where they are considered to be continuing types from the Byzantine period (unpublished).

A rim similar to the cylindrical mouth 154 from a painted tomb at Ashqelon is dated to the mid-fifth to seventh century (Katsnelson 1999: 72–74 and fig.3:8). Several examples of cylindrical mouths from Jordan are dated 350–525, a few rims were Umayyad and even Fatimid (Dussart 1998: 153, Type BX.5321 and Pl. 44:21–31). Bottles with infolded rims and funnel mouths were abundant in Jordan. Dussart divided them into three categories, differing in the slanting angle of the funnel. The majority are dated to the Late Byzantine period, with extension into the Umayyad era, few were dated earlier (350–525) or later to the Abbasid and Fatimid Periods (Dussart 1998: 135ff., Type BX.1125bb11 and Pl. 35:26–43, Type BX.1132 and Pls. 36:14–22; 37:1–6; 41:48–57; 42:1–12).

Bottles with conical and funnel mouth were found in the Umayyad layer at Beth Shean and were abundant at Caesarea Stratum VIII, (Hadad 1998: 35 and Pls. 6:102–8; 8:126; Caesarea is unpublished). Parallels to 155 from Caesarea were dated to the Umayyad period.

Rim fragments 156–58 belong to bottles of types known from the Early Islamic period. Rim 156 resembles a rim from Amman, dated to the Late Umayyad period, and a fragment from Tel Abu Sarifa, found in the earliest of the Islamic levels (IV; Dussart 1998: 132 and Pl. 33:34, Type BX.1113c; Adams 1970: 114 and Pl. 7: fig. 15:G-4).

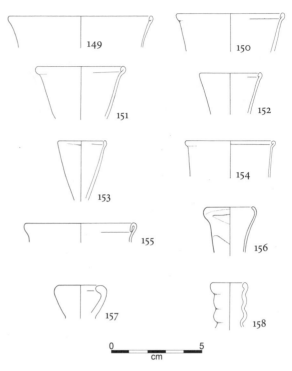

Fig. 141. *Bottles with infolded rims.*

The bulged mouth with in-curved rim fragment 157 has a parallel at Hama of similar purple glass. That bottle has a short neck and probably a wide body (Riis 1959: 46 and fig. 107). Various types of bottles from Fustat have bulging mouths and incurving rims, some of the bottles are decorated (Shindo 1992: Pls. 6-15:28, 34–35; 6-3:9). Several rims from Beth Shean are similar, dated second half of the eighth–eleventh century (Hadad 1998: 91 and Pl. 41:675–676, 678).

Diversely shaped bottles with beaded necks, like 158, are abundant in sites from the Early Islamic period: Fustat, second half of eighth–ninth century (Shindo 1992: 599 and Pl. 6-14:26–31; Scanlon and Plinder-Wilson 2001: 46 and fig. 20e–f); Beth Shean, second half of the eighth–eleventh century; Caesarea Stratum VII and VI, 750–950 (Hadad 1998: 95 and Pl. 42:709–20; Pollak 2002: fig. 2:25–28, in press). They are rare in the Umayyad layer at Beth Shean, and at Caesarea only one example was found in the Umayyad layer, where it is considered to be a forerunner of the type (Hadad 1998: 37 and Pl. 8:131; Pollak 2002: fig. 1:16, in press).

149. 2035/1, L 2304. Incurved, thickened rim, d. 7.8 cm. Sloping-in wall. Light greenish blue glass, contains horizontally elongated bubbles.

150. 0052/1, L 2031. Rounded rim, d. 5.8 cm. Sloping-in wall. Light bluish green, bubbly glass.

151. 0092/1, L 2038. Rounded rim, d. 4.8 cm. Slightly convex wall, sloping-in to form cup shape funnel mouth. Bluish green glass with some bubbles close to rim.

152. 2060/3, L 2240. Incurved rim, d. 3.2 cm. Straight wall sloping in. Dark blue, translucent glass.

153. 2055/3, L 2339. Infolded rim, d. 2.6 cm. Funnel mouth with slender neck. Light green glass contains bubbles, impurities and blowing spirals.

154. 2063/5, L 2340. Infolded, rounded rim, d. 4.8 cm. Straight vertical wall, cylindrical neck. Pale bluish green glass.

155. 1076/1, L 1127. In and down folded rim, rounded, d. 5.9 cm. Probably cylindrical neck. Green, bubbly glass.

156. 1065/1, L 1132. Slightly incurved rim, d. 2.6 cm. Cylindrical neck. Sky blue glass contains small and minute bubbles and blowing spirals. Iridescent surface.

157. 1105/1, L 1026. Horizontally incurved rim, d. 2.2 cm. Thick wall sloping in to form cup shape mouth, continues probably as cylindrical neck. Purple glass, rough surface, iridescent dark weathering.

158. 0101/13, L 2041. Rim and neck fragment. Rounded, incurved rim, d. 1.8 cm. Beaded neck. Deep bluish green glass, contains small and minute bubbles, whitish pearly weathering.

Bottles — Necks, Bodies and Bases (fig.142:159–74)

The following category contains necks, body fragments and bases of bottles. As was the case with the rims, it is difficult to define the complete shape to which the fragments belong, as various types possess similar parts. Though, it is of importance to present the diversity of types that can be, in some cases, connected to various rims displayed previously.

The neck and shoulder fragment 159 belongs to a large bottle that could have a funnel mouth, while the straight slanting shoulder indicates that the body was angular. It could be similar to Barag Type 17.5, which has a rounded concave base and is dated to the fourth to fifth centuries. Neck fragment 160 belongs to a smaller bottle than the former; the upper end of the neck opens up, probably to a funnel mouth. The slightly convex shoulder can be the upper part of globular body. It resembles Barag Types 15.15 or 15.18, which were discussed with the funnel mouth and infolded rims, above. Fragment 161 is of a bottle with short cylindrical neck and longer conical mouth and globular body. It is similar to Barag Type 15.28, dated to the fifth century (Barag 1970: 196. Pl. 43).

Fragments 162–64 belong to bottles with conical neck and globular body; they are mainly dated to the Byzantine period although this type is less common than the bottles that have a cylindrical transition between the conical part and the shoulder. Similar bottle necks and rims decorated with trails, of factory quality, were found at Jalame (350–380). Some were found in the wine press, which was filled in the late fourth to early fifth century (Weinberg and Goldstein 1988: 70 and fig. 4-32:272–75). Several similar bottles were found in various parts of a tomb at Khirbet Sabiya, in use from about 300–500 (Ayalon 1994: 32 and figs. 4:1–2; 5:2–4; 6). A neck with globular body from Jerash is dated by parallels (Kehrberg 1986: 368 and fig. 9:15). Two bottles from the museum at Bosra in Syria were dated to the fourth century, and a mold-decorated bottle from the museum at Kerak has a Byzantine form, although the decoration is more of Islamic nature (Dussart 1998: 132, Types BX.1121a–b and Pl. 33:35–37). A single bottle from the museum at Nazareth resembles our fragments, although it lacks the distinct transition from neck to shoulder (Bagatti 1967: 229 and fig. 4:88). Such bottles appear in the Islamic period as well, such as a plain one from Iran, dated to the tenth century (Lamm 1935: Pl. 16:K).

Fragment 167 belongs to a bottle from the Islamic period. The infolded horizontal interior rib, formed by tooling, characteristic to Iranian vessels from the twelfth century, but found in other regions

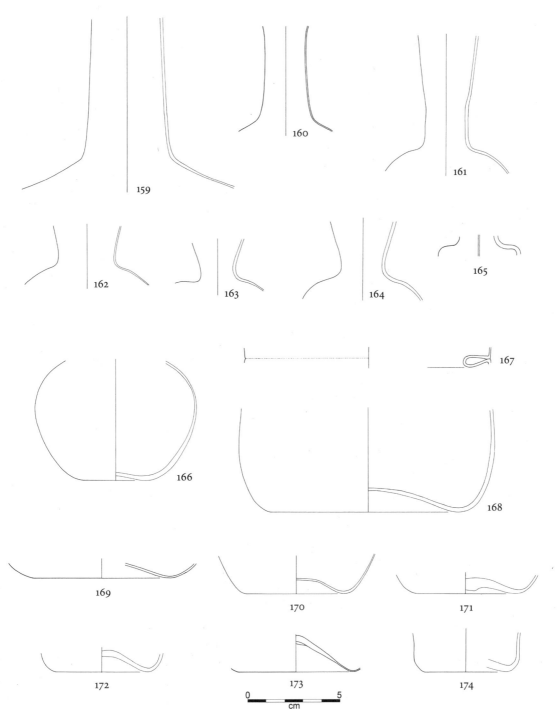

Fig. 142. *Bottles: necks, bodies and bases.*

as well and in earlier dates too. (Carboni 2001:182, cat. 46a–c, 3.28).

A wide range of concave bases (166, 168–74) display the variety of shapes that also include different forms of the bodies. 166 is globular, as could be 169–70, while 168 and 172 are probably ovoid shaped bottles. 174 seems to be a vessel with cylindrical body. Parts of the bases have pontil scars, which can be indication of further work on the vessel after the blowing process was completed, when further shaping of the rim or decoration is taking place.

159. 0081/2, L 2038. Neck and shoulder fragment. Long cylindrical neck, d. 4 cm. Neck opens at lower end to wide diagonal shoulder. Bluish green bubbly glass.

160. 1079/5, L 1137. Neck and shoulder fragment. Long cylindrical neck, slightly turned out at upper end, probably to conical or funnel mouth. At lower end, opens to wide diagonal shoulder. Green glass, pitted and patchy surface, shiny, whitish weathering.

161. 0101/14, L 2041. Neck and shoulder fragment. Neck upper edge missing, conical upper section and short cylindrical lower section of neck. Opens up to convex shoulder. Green glass contains small bubbles.

162. 2102/1, L 2249. Neck and shoulder fragment. Lower end of conical neck, opens to diagonal shoulder with slightly convex wall. Dulled, light green glass.

163. 2102/2, L 2249. Neck and shoulder fragment. Lower part of conical or funnel neck, opens to convex wall of unevenly formed shoulder. Light emerald green glass contains small, elongated bubbles.

164. 2031/2, L 2304. Neck and shoulder fragment. Lower part of conical neck, opens to convex shoulder. Thick bluish green glass contains small bubbles; faded surface.

165. 1051/2, L 1018. Shoulder fragment. Small vessel, approximate max. shoulder d. 4 cm. Narrow horizontal shoulder curves down to body. Neck d. approx. 1.8 cm. at lower end. Purple glass, iridescent bottle.

166. 2112/1, L 2249. Body and base fragment. Globular body, max. d. 8.8 cm. Slightly concave base, no pontil mark. Light green, bubbly glass.

167. 1024/1, L 1318. Fragment of interior, horizontal fold on body, d. 13.8 cm. Purple glass, contains few bubbles, rough surface.

168. 0052/2, L 2031. Thin, slightly concave base of big bottle, d. 10.6 cm. No pontil mark; curving up to convex wall of body, might be of sack form, max. d. 14 cm. Deep bluish green glass, contains minute and small bubbles.

169. 1080/7, L 1137. Thin, concave base fragment, d. 7.5 cm. Wall curves up and out from base, probably to form globular body. Light green glass, pitting and patches on surface, iridescent weathering.

170. 2102/4, L 2249. Thin, concave base, d. 5.4 cm. No pontil mark; wall curves up and out to form globular body. Bluish green glass, contains minute and small bubbles.

171. 2065/4, L 2340. Thickened, concave base, with big pontil scar, d. 5.6 cm. Wall curves up and out. Deep greenish blue, bubbly glass.

172. 2065/3, L 2340. Thin, concave, dome-like base, d. 5 cm. Pontil mark; wall curves up. Light bluish green, bubbly glass with brown streaks in base.

173. 1021/1, L 1112. High kicked concave base, thickened center with pontil mark, d. 6.4 cm. Thin wall curves up. Pale green glass, pitting and patches on surface, silvery iridescent weathering, dark coating.

174. 2037/2, L 2304. Thickened concave base fragment, d. 4.6 cm. Straight wall curves up vertically to form probably cylindrical body. Greenish blue glass.

THREAD-DECORATED BOTTLES AND JUGS

Thread-wound decoration is characteristic to the Byzantine period. It was widely used in the beginning of the Early Islamic period as a direct continuation of Byzantine traditions. The bottles in this category (fig. 143) have a funnel mouth and few are cylindrical. The rims are in most cases simple; several bear fused threads on the edge, and only one is rolled-in (a cylindrical). The threads are either the same color as the vessel or of a contrasting color.

Fragment 175 is decorated from the edge of the rim with a thick coil fused to it, as are two more rims (185–86) with cylindrical necks. Funnel mouth 177 was part of a big bottle. Decoration with thin threads and thick rings is characteristic of the Late Byzantine period (Barag 1970:194). The rim with the neck opening at its lower end (182) might have had a pear-shaped body.

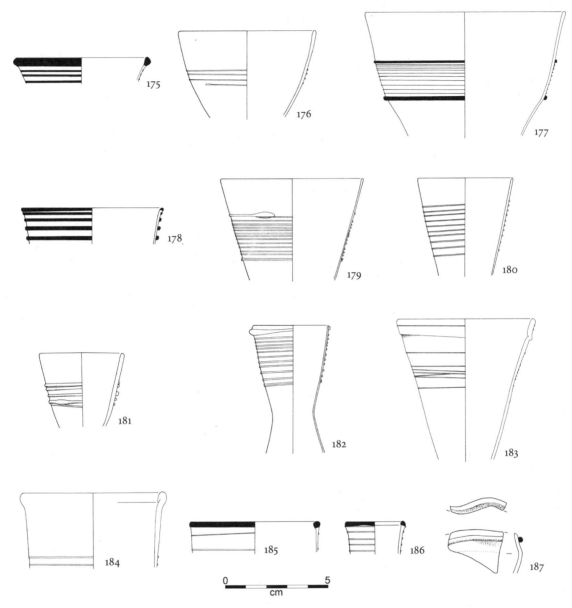

Fig. 143. *Thread-decorated bottles and jugs.*

Barag's Type 15.20 is similar to the mouth of 176 (fifth century to Late Byzantine). Such a mouth, decorated with threads of different color than the body, was found in the painted tomb at Migdal Ashqelon, where most vessels from the assemblage are dated fifth–early seventh century (Katsnelson 1999: 75 and fig. 4:5). Various bottles with thread decoration were found in the excavations at Ramat Hanadiv, including a cup shaped mouth. The date of the assemblage is fifth–sixth century, based on parallels (Cohen 2000: 170 and Pl. III:25–26,

29–36). Cup-shape funnel mouths similar to 176 were found at Beth Shean, Jerash and Caesarea, dated to the Umayyad period (Hadad 1998: 39 and Pl. 9:150; Kehrberg 1986: 368 and fig. 9:50; Caesarea is unpublished).

Bottles with thread-decorated mouth or neck are common at Byzantine dated sites and tombs. A tomb at el-Jish was generally dated to the fourth–fifth century, but Harden realized that new types appear. This means a "new milieu" and the tombs probably served longer, at least until the sixth century, such as the tomb at Kharjih, that contains similar bottles with thread decoration (Harden 1964:50 and figs. 9, 11). In a burial cave at Kefar 'Ara, three different intact bottles with globular bodies and several more rim fragments were found. They were dated to the late phase of use of the tomb: the intact vessels fifth–sixth century, the fragments fourth–sixth century (Sussman 1976: 96 and fig. 4:6, 7, 9 and Pl. XXVIII: 12–14). Thread-decorated bottles are known from various Byzantine sites, such as Shavei Zion, Kursi, Bet Shean, Khirbet al-Karak, Hamat Gader and others (Barag 1967: 5 and fig. 4–5; Barag 1983: 37 and fig. 9:2–3; Peleg 1994: 145 and fig. 15:9; Delougaz and Haines 1960: Pl. 59:1–3, 6; Cohen 1997: 420ff. and Pls. VI:12–13; VII:4–5, 8–14). Conical mouth 183 has a small fold below the rim, that could be unintentional, but which occurs often in vessels from the Umayyad period. This bottle resembles a rim from Beth Shean, although without decoration, from the Umayyad level (Hadad 1998: Pl. 5:86).

Fragment 187 may belong to a jug with pinched trefoil rim, decorated with a colored thread. It could be a jug from the late third–fourth century with globular body, such as Isings' Form 124a (1957: 154). A similar intact jug was found at Horvat Castra, dated fourth–early fifth century (Gorin-Rosen and Katsnelson 1999: fig. 51; Pl. III:6).

175. 2044/1, L 2202. Flaring rim, d. 6.4 cm. Sloping wall forms funnel neck. Rim thickened by fused coil, more threads wound below rim. Vessel made of light green glass, the decorating threads are of greenish turquoise; contains small bubbles and impurities.

176. 1080/2, L 1137. Rounded, vertical rim, d. 6.6 cm. Convex wall, forms cup-shaped mouth. Several thin threads of same color as vessel are wound 2 cm below rim. Green, bubbly glass; small and minute bubbles.

177. 2031/3, L 2304. Rounded rim, d. 9.8 cm. Convex wall forms cup-shaped funnel mouth. Wall decorated with wound thread, two thick threads delimit a group of thin ones on both edges. Vessel made of light green glass and threads of same color. The thick threads contain dark impurities. Vessel surface is dulled.

178. 1080/6, L 1137. Rim fragment, d. 6.8 cm. Wall slopes slightly in; threads are wound around from lip downward. Body made of light green glass, threads of dark blue glass.

179. 1066/1, L 1323. Funnel mouth of bottle, d. 6.9 cm. Decorated threads of same color as vessel. Green glass, exterior surface stained and pitted, interior iridescent.

180. 1080/3, L 1137. Conical neck of bottle, rim d. 4.6 cm. Straight wall sloping in, decorated with thin threads wound 10 times around neck. Body and threads of same green, bubbly glass. Stains and iridescence on surface; thin, whitish, shiny weathering.

181. 1067/1, L 1134. Rounded rim, d. 4 cm. Thick wall sloping in to form funnel mouth. Decorated with 5 applied threads, of same color as vessel. Light emerald green, bubbly glass, contains big dark impurities in threads; milky, whitish weathering.

182. 1079/3, L 1137. Conical neck with slightly convex wall, rim d. 3.6 cm. Neck opens at lower end. Upper part decorated from rim with applied threads of dark blue glass, wound 13 times around rim. Vessel made of green very bubbly glass; pitted surface.

183. 0081/1, L 2038. Conical or funnel shaped neck. Rounded rim, d. 6.6 cm. Uneven fold below rim, probably not intentionally done. Very thin threads of same color as vessel, wound on upper part. Light bluish green, bubbly glass.

184. 2066/2, L 2240. Rim and neck fragment. Incurved rounded rim, d. 6.8 cm. Cylindrical neck, decorated with applied thin threads of same color as vessel. Emerald green glass, contains minute bubbles.

185. 2074/1, L 2240. Rounded, thickened rim by coil fused to lip, d. 2.1 cm. Cylindrical neck, decorated with thin threads. Vessel made of bluish green glass, threads and coil of dark blue glass; contains small impurities.

186. 1076, L 1127. Thickened rim formed by thread fused to lip, d. 2.8 cm. Cylindrical neck decorated with applied thin threads. Greenish glass, threads of dark blue glass.

187. 1065/2, L 1132. Rim fragment. Curved or pinched fragment can indicate jug with spout. Dark blue thread is applied to exterior wall close to rim. Vessel made of green glass, rough surface with pitting; pearly weathering, iridescence.

MISCELLANEOUS DECORATION METHODS

Mold-decorated Vessels (fig. 144:188–89)

Mold-blown vessels, especially those decorated with diagonal or vertical ribbing or fluting, were popular in the fourth and fifth centuries, both in the East and West. This type of decoration appeared on bottles and jugs. Usually, the decoration was only on the body of the vessel. Rims with exterior horizontal fold, such as 188, appeared on small jars from the fifth century, but they were not mold blown, and on vessels of the Early Islamic period. The vertical ribbing was used for decoration on cylindrical bottles in the Late Roman period and on various forms of vessels in the Early Islamic period. Several such rims with folds below them are known from Soba, where they were found in level I, dated to the ninth–twelfth century (Harden 1955: 62, figs. 36:12; 37:31). Parallels with the squashed protruding base as 189 were not found.

188. 2055/1, L 2339. Rim of bottle or jug. Rounded vertical rim, d. 7 cm. On exterior, a horizontal fold protrudes 1 cm below rim; under it wall decorated with diagonal fluting, sloping in. Green glass.

189. 2102/5, L 2249. Lower section of body and base fragment. Flattened base curves up, inward and up again forming a projecting edge around base below the vertical wall of bottle. The wall is decorated by vertical fluting. Max. d. 5.8 cm. Deep green, bubbly glass.

Enamel painting and gilding (fig. 144:190)

Enamel painting on glass first appeared in Syria in the late twelfth or early thirteenth century. It was favored in the Islamic world during the thirteenth to fourteenth centuries, and by then production centers spread to Mamluk Egypt. Numerous mosque lamps were decorated with enamel painting and gilding, as were many other vessels for secular use, and both types bear inscriptions in most cases and decorative patterns.

Enamel is colored, opaque glass crushed to a rough powder and applied to the glass surface, then the vessel has to be reheated, probably more than once, for every color is fused to the glass at a different temperature (Carboni 2001: 323ff., Cat. 93a–d). The fragment from Tel Tanninim belongs to a big, unidentified vessel that was produced either in Syria or Egypt in the thirteenth to fourteenth centuries.

190. 1064/1, L 1322. Small, concave body fragment, or neck to shoulder, of colorless glass. Decorated with enamel painting in blue, brown, reddish brown and gold. The decoration can be divided into two parts, upper and lower. A band contains three stripes: two of gold and a brown in between. The upper part contains background in blue enamel for script that is unpainted, although incision along the borders of the letters might suggest outlining. It might have been an inscription, but we have only parts of two letters. Below the separating band, undefined pattern on clear glass painted with brown, thin reddish outlining and gold.

WINDOWPANES

All the windowpanes found at Tel Tanninim (fig. 144:191–96) belong to one type. The molten glass was placed on a flat surface and rolled out with a cylindrical rolling pin made of stone or metal, or another material resistant to the heat, with a smooth surface. This production process is evident in fragment 192, which bears the stretching marks on the lower side and the platform surface impression, straight but nor smooth. On the upper side, the pane is smooth, but the thickness varies in a way that left traces of the cylindrical roller. These marks are not visible in all cases. The edges are straight and might indicate rectangular or square panes. They were made of green, greenish blue and bluish green glass of light and deep shades. They come in thin and thick sheets. No plaster mark was found that can indicate incorporation in wall, but they could be incorporated in wooden frame as well. Most of these panes date to the Byzantine

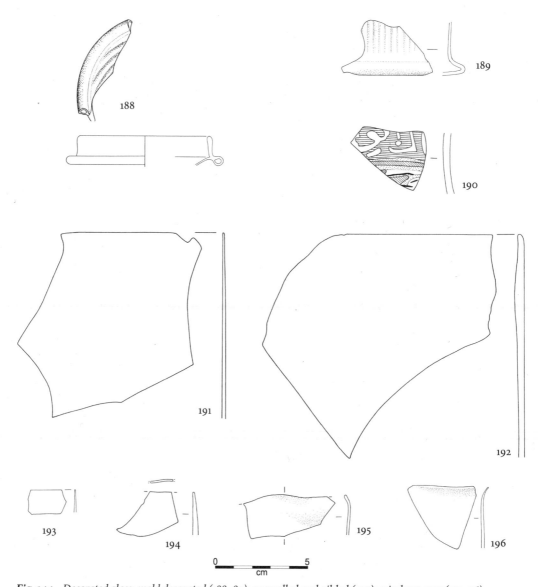

Fig. 144. *Decorated glass: mold decorated (188–89); enamelled and gilded (190); windowpanes (191–96).*

period, as several of the panes were recovered from sealed loci, such as fragments no. 192–93 and 195, dated to this period. Windowpanes are mentioned occasionally on some Byzantine sites, such as Shavei Zion, Caesarea, Jerash, and others (Barag 1967: 70; Peleg 1992: 160; Meyer 1987:194).

191. 2045/1, L 2304. Big fragment of pane with rounded, wavy edge. Greenish blue, bubbly glass, some iridescence.

192. 2100/1, L 2249. Big fragment of pane with rounded edge and uneven thickness. Deep bluish green glass, lower side bear starching lines, upper side smooth.

193. 2060/11, L 2240. Small fragment of pane with edge. Bluish green glass.

194. 1047/2, L 1123. Small fragment of pane with edge; thick green, bubbly glass.

195. 2103/2, L 2270. Pane fragment with thin curved edge. Light bluish green glass with dulled surface.

196. 1062/2, L 1011. Pane fragment with rounded, curving edge. Thin, light green glass, very bubbly, iridescent surface.

DATING SEALED LOCI

The dating of the loci is based on the dates given to each vessel in the typological category. Twenty-two sealed loci contained glass. Since no stratigraphic sequence was revealed of sealed loci that contained glass, the sealed loci will be presented in numerical order.

Only two sealed loci from Area A contained indicative glass fragments. Floor locus 1115 contained a single indicative bowl rim of a lamp (28), dated to the fifth–seventh century. The other locus from this area that contains glass was floor locus 1133, or rather the plaster foundation for a mosaic floor that was revealed under the surface locus 1100. The glass from this locus is composed of several bowl rims that are dated to the third–fourth century (26), and a distinctly dated bowl of the late fourth century. But two fragments are clearly of the Byzantine period: a rim of a stemmed goblet (106) and a fragment of a small hanging handle of a bowl lamp, a form dated to the Late Byzantine period, but continuing into the Early Islamic period as well. So this locus is dated to the Late Byzantine B and might be of the transition period. Several loci below 1133 form a sequence, down to locus 1137, that are not sealed loci, but all contained glass of the Byzantine period.

All the rest of the sealed loci are from Areas B and B2. Locus 2031 contains only few indicative glass fragments. The latest date is given to a rim of a bottle (150) that can be of Late Byzantine or Umayyad period date. This locus is below surface and relates to sealed locus 2038, which contains a larger amount of glass (fig. 145). The glass vessels were dated to the Late Byzantine (91, 151) and Umayyad periods (183). Another sealed locus related to the two previous, also below the surface locus, is 2041. This locus contained a large quantity of glass (fig. 146). Most of the glass is typical of Byzantine and Late Byzantine finds (fifth–seventh century), such as the stemmed goblets (84–88), the various oil lamps are types originating in the Byzantine period but they are more characteristic of the Umayyad (68) and the Abbasid periods, from the second half of the eighth to the mid-tenth century (70, 147, 158).

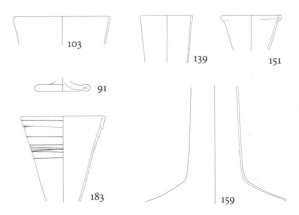

Fig. 145. *The glass assemblage from L 2038.*

The only fragment that represents locus 2033 is a thread-decorated bowl typical of the Byzantine period (45). From locus 2053 we have two vessel fragments: one is a bowl or cup of a goblet or lamp with thread decoration, dated to the Byzantine period, between the fifth and the seventh centuries (108), the other fragment is a rim of a cylindrical bottle (141), that has a wide range date from 350 C.E. until the Umayyad period. The locus is more likely of Late Byzantine period.

Locus 2102 (fig. 147) contains glass material dated from the Byzantine and Late Byzantine (50, 94, 102) to the Abbasid periods (fifth–ninth century). The cups with rolled in rims are typical of the Abbasid period (80) and the bowl with triangle rim (34) is Late Umayyad and Abbasid. Thus this locus is of Abbasid period.

Locus 2112 yielded glass material dating from the Byzantine to the mid-eighth century—the Umayyad period (fig. 148). A bowl with rolled-in rim (41) is a distinctive type that appears only in the Umayyad period. A few fragments of glass vessels came out of locus 2202. The earliest were dated to the second half of the fourth century (3, 129), and the latest, which date the locus, are from the Late Byzantine period (18, 92). From locus 2219 only a single indicative glass fragment (44), a thread-decorated bowl, indicates the Byzantine period, the fourth and fifth century. Three fragments represent locus 2222. A rim of a bowl and a base were dated to the second half of the third and the fourth century (7, 55) and a rim of a cylindrical bottle has a wide range date, from 350 C.E. to the Umayyad

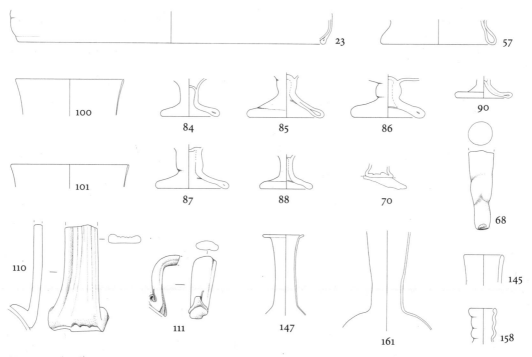

Fig. 146. *The glass assemblage from L 2041.*

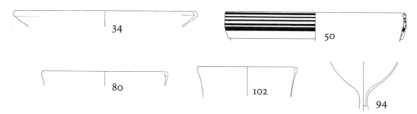

Fig. 147. *The glass assemblage from L 2102.*

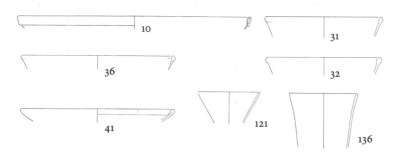

Fig. 148. *The glass assemblage from L 2112.*

period (140). The locus probably dates to the Early Byzantine period, based on the glass finds.

Locus 2240 was rich in glass finds (fig. 149). The earliest types of vessels were dated to the second half of the fourth and the fifth century (2, 4, 99) and the latest types were from the Umayyad and Abbasid periods (seventh to ninth century). Several bowls with rolled-in rim (42), which existed only in the Umayyad Period, were found in this locus. Cups that were common type in the

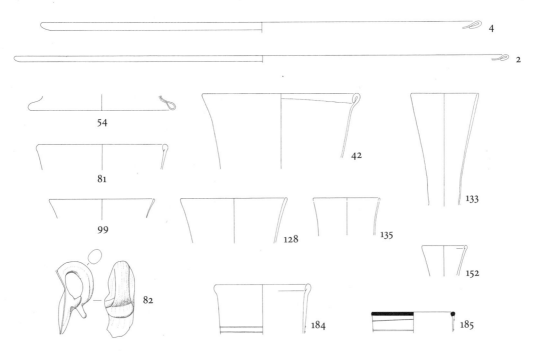

Fig. 149. *The glass assemblage from L 2240.*

Abbasid period, although scarcely appeared also in the Umayyad period (81). A handle of a cup or bowl (82) had an even later date: between the eighth and tenth centuries, but its identification is not accurate. Locus 2252 is below L 2240. It contained only few datable glass fragments. A distinct type of bowl with collar rim (24) is the earliest type, dated to the fourth–fifth century, although in one case its date continues to the eighth century. The other fragment is a rim of a bottle (125), dated to the Late Byzantine–Umayyad periods.

In locus 2249, plentiful of glass was revealed (fig. 150). Most of the vessel fragments belong to bottles of various forms. Large fragments of windowpanes were found as well (192). One of the stemmed lamps of the Late Byzantine period (66) comes from this locus. Most of the bottles were of Byzantine types, but one bottle is clearly of Islamic nature (146), with parallels from other Early Islamic sites dating to the seventh–ninth century.

The locus below the previous is 2258. It contained only one identified fragment of a bottle, with lopsided conical neck from the late fourth and early fifth century, not included in the typological catalog. Another locus that contained few indicative fragments, below 2249, is locus 2270. It

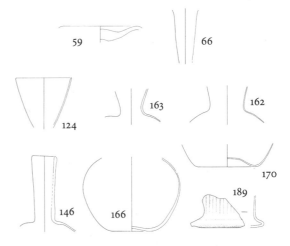

Fig. 150. *The glass assemblage from L 2249.*

contained the funnel-mouth rim of a bottle (122) and windowpanes (195) that were dated as Byzantine. Locus 2304 contained several glass fragments dating to the third and fourth century, but most of the glass is typical to the Late Byzantine period, such as the foot of the stemmed goblet (89), the hollow stem of a lamp (69) and some rims associated with these vessels (104, 105, 149), the funnel mouth of a big bottle decorated with threads (177), and windowpanes (191; fig. 151).

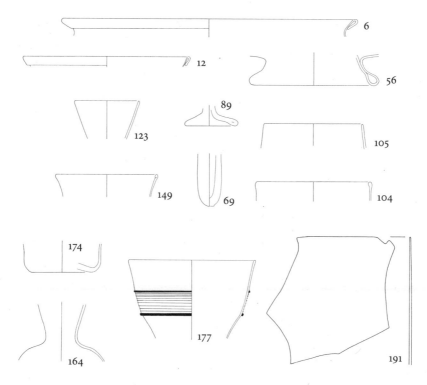

Fig. 151. *The glass assemblage from L 2304.*

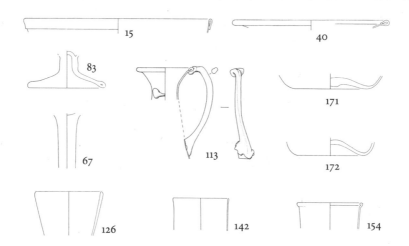

Fig. 152. *The glass assemblage from L 2340.*

The few glass fragments from locus 2339 can be dated to the Late Byzantine and Early Islamic periods (153, 188), but they were not accurately dated.

Locus 2340 yielded an assemblage (fig. 152) that consists of vessels characteristic of the Byzantine (12, 113), Late Byzantine and the beginning of the Early Islamic periods (67, 83, 142, 154, 126). The bowl with in-folded rim (40) is probably Umayyad, although the form of the bowl is not typical.

DISCUSSION

The glass from the excavations at Tel Tanninim consists of a large quantity of windowpanes that most probably were incorporated in buildings. Most of the windowpanes are associated with Byzantine or Early Islamic period loci. The glass vessels were found in fragmentary state; something that made the identification difficult and not accurate in some cases. The assemblage contains mainly common, domestic types of vessels, mainly of bluish-green color, probably of local production, that could have been produced in the vicinity. Although few chunks of unworked glass were found, it cannot give evidence to the existence of a glass factory on the site. The majority of the glass was dated from the Byzantine to the beginning of the Early Islamic periods, up until the Abbasid period. Many of the vessels were found in sealed loci.

The earliest vessel is a Hellenistic cast bowl, from L 1117; the only vessel from such an early period. There is a comparatively large group of vessels from the late third and fourth centuries, but as mentioned previously, the identification is not always accurate. Most of these are bowls and bottles.

Other than the periods presented previously, there is a small group of glass material dating from the tenth or eleventh to the thirteenth centuries, including an enamel-painted vessel and mosque lamp fragments. All the late material was found in loci in area A (loci 1110, 1018, 1311, 1322). Even though the glass material is poorly preserved, it provides a significant contribution to glass typology, mainly of simple, common vessel types for everyday use, especially in the period that is still difficult to define, the transition from the Byzantine period to the Early Islamic period.

2. The Lamps

by Ya'el D. Arnon

The TAP excavations yielded seventy-five diagnostic ceramic oil lamps and lamp fragments, dated from the Persian period to the Mamluk era (fifth century B.C.E. to the fourteenth century C.E.). In spite of the lack of historical evidence, the absence of the Early Islamic period material culture (late seventh–twelfth century) is still surprising. The lamps were analyzed according to their chronological typology. For example, the designation "Pa" represents Type "a" in the Persian period. In addition to their division into types by archaeological periods, the lamps within each period were counted to provide supplemental information on the volume of a specific era. The lamps were also located in a locus list, as a dating item for that locus. The 1990 edition of the Munsell Soil Color Charts were used for the clay hues description.

PERSIAN PERIOD

Type Pa (fig. 153:1)

This type is characterized by a saucer-shaped body, pinched at one edge in order to create a wick hole. Such oil lamps are well known in the Levant since the second millennium B.C.E. and extend up to the Hellenistic period, a life span of 1,700 years (Kennedy 1963: 70). The Persian-period oil lamp has a flattened base, while the earlier types (Bronze and Iron Ages) exhibit a concave one. Five fragments were retrieved in the excavations, namely, L038, L043, L044, L049 and L074. The Tel Tanninim specimens are made from a reddish-yellow clay 5YR 6/6, well levigated and containing very small white grits and grog inclusions. The outer surface is fired to a very pale brown hue 10YR 7/4. Such oil lamps were recorded at other sites such as Tel Mevorakh (Stern 1978: 39 and fig. 10:1–5; Pl. 26:7–9), Dor (Stern, Berg, Gilboa, Guz-Zilberstein, Raban, Rosenthal-Heginbottom, and Sharon 1995: 67, 214), Tel Keisan (Briend and Hambert 1980: 123 and Pl. 21:1–5), Tel Michal (Herzog, Rapp, and Negbi 1989: 143 and figs. 9;16:8) and Qadum (Stern and Magen 1984: fig. 9:2–4). At all the sites, except for Tel Michal, this type is dated to the Persian period.

HELLENISTIC PERIOD

Type Ha (fig. 153:2)

This type is characterized by a wheel-made round closed reservoir with a lug remnant at the shoulder, a small filling hole surrounded by two grooves, and a relatively long and flat nozzle, produced separately and attached to the body. Eleven specimens were unearthed in the excavations (see Table 1). The Tel Tanninim Type "Ha" is an Attic import product and was produced from a reddish yellow ware 5YR 7/6, finely levigated, well fired and potted. It has a black slipped exterior and reddish brown interior. Such a specimen corresponds to Howland's Type 25b found in the Athenian Agora (Howland 1958: 68; Perlzweig 1963: fig. 86), Scheibler's Type RSL 4 from the Keramikos (Scheibler 1976: 26), and Dor Type 7 (Rosenthal-Heginbottom 1995a: 234 and fig. 5:13), and is dated to the time span 400–250 B.C.E. The lug first appears around the middle of the fourth century B.C.E. (Rosenthal-Heginbottom 1995a: 235).

Type Hb (figs. 153:3–4; 156:1)

Type "Hb" was determined at Dor to be a local lamp (Rosenthal-Heginbottom 1995a: 235). It is characterized by a wheel-made, curved, closed body, flat or rounded rim, which is set off from the shoulders by a groove, but the main characteristic component is the long flat topped nozzle. The Tel Tanninim specimen consists of a pinkish clay 5YR 7/4, finely levigated, well fired and potted, and contains very small white grit and grog inclusions. Five fragments, numbered L003, L015, L028, L047 and L048, were excavated during the four seasons at Tel Tanninim. As mentioned above, this type

is well recorded at Dor, where it was classified as Type 6 and dated to the mid-fourth century B.C.E., extending up to the second century B.C.E. (Rosenthal-Heginbottom 1995a: 235 and fig. 5:14), and at Tel Mevorakh (Rosenthal 1978: 22–25 and fig. 2:22).

Type Hc (fig. 153:5)

A molded oil lamp consisting of a double convex body, convex on top with a central filling hole. Radial patterns often appear on the rim. This type is characterized mainly by its gray hue, probably as a result of a reduced firing process. Only three samples, L002, L005 and L032, were exposed, but this type is considered to be one of the most common types of the second century B.C.E. in the East. Type "Hc" is recorded and dated to the second and the beginning of the first century B.C.E. in sites such as: Yoqne'am (Avissar 1996:189 and fig. 15:3, No. 7), Dor Type 12 (Rosenthal-Heginbottom 1995: 238 and fig. 5:16), Tel Mevorakh (Rosenthal 1978: fig. 2:21), Tel Anafa (Weinberg 1971: 104–5 and Pl. 18), Delos (Bruneau 1965: 81–88 and Pl. 20) and Athens (Scheibler 1976: 70–71).

ROMAN PERIOD

Type Ra (fig. 153:6)

Its main characteristics are: a round mold-made body, flat base, a discus rim containing a central filling hole, absence of a handle, and a relief double-axe decoration on the shoulders. The lamp is very often red or reddish brown slipped on a light hue clay. The excavations unearthed seven specimens of this type (L009, L010, L016, L017, L037, L055, L068). This type of lamp is well distributed all over the Eastern Mediterranean, although Hayes designated it as a "Northern Palestinian" or "Southern Syrian" type (Hayes 1980: 86–88). Sussman in her study of the Caesarea lamps suggests that it is a local specimen and argues that the double-axe pattern is absent in the West of the Mediterranean (Sussman 1999: figs. 18, 20).

In Israel, rounded lamps decorated with a double-axe are recorded from Hanita in the north

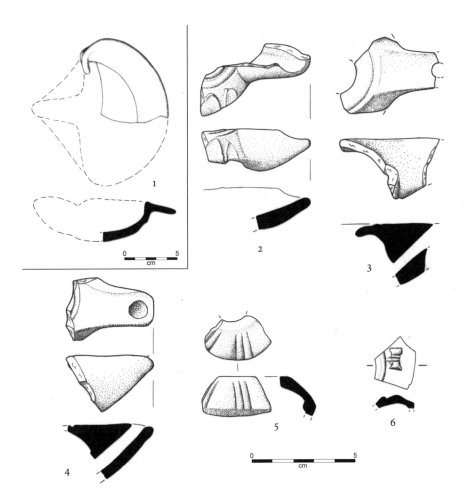

No.	Reg. No.	Locus	Type	Description
1	L049	1233	Pa	Reddish/yellow ware 5YR 6/6; pale brown surface 10YR 7/4.
2	L001	1007	Ha	Reddish/yellow ware 5YR 7/6; black slipped exterior, reddish slipped interior.
3	L047	1241	Hb	Pinkish ware 5YR 7/4.
4	L003	1018	Hb	Pinkish ware 5YR 7/4.
5	L032	1220	Hc	Gray ware 5YR 5/1.
6	L010	1125	Ra	Light brown ware 7.5YR 6/4; reddish brown slipped on exterior.

Fig. 153. *Persian, Hellenistic and Roman lamps.*

through Dor, Ramat Hanadiv, Caesarea and Rosh Ha'ayin in the central plain, to Maresha and Oboda in the south (Barag 1978: 36; Rosenthal-Heginbottom 1995: fig. 5:22, Type 26; Calderon 2000: 93–94 and Pl. 5; Sussman 1999: figs. 18, 20; Eitan 1969: fig. 14; Oren and Rappaport 1984: 123, and Negev 1986: 132–33). The double-axe sample appears in the study of Kennedy (1963: 75, Nos. 502–3), as well as that of Rosenthal and Sivan (1978: 85). The suggested date at the sites mentioned above is from the end of the first to the early third century C.E.,

but the peak according to all scholars is the second century C.E.

BYZANTINE PERIOD

Type Ba (fig. 154:7–12)

The most prominent type in the collection—twenty-eight lamps were found—is represented by Type "Ba." It is characterized by a coarse-ware, mold-made rounded reservoir with a decorated discus, a

Table 1. Lamp distribution by type and locus. Columns list the different types, while individual entries give information about registry number (bolded) and locus.

Pa (n=5)	Ha (n=11)	Hb (n=5)	Hc (n=3)	Ra (n=8)	Ba (n=28)	Bb (n=11)	Bc (n=1)	Bd (n=1)	Ma (n=3)
038 – 1233	001 – 1007	003 – 1018	002 – 2000	009 – 1114	006 – 1114	034 – 1204	064 – 2340	004 – 6000	053 – 1312
043 – 1234	013 – 1129	015 – 1130	005 – 1031	010 – 1125	007 – 1114	052 – 2304			054 – 1311
044 – 1234	014 – 1129	028 – 1200	032 – 1220	016 – 1127	008 – 1114	056 – 2304			062 – 1303
049 – 1233	030 – 1112	047 – 1241		017 – 1127	011 – 1125	057 – 2304			
074 – 1335	035 – 1204	048 – 1241		037 – 1201	012 – 1125	058 – 2304			
	036 – 1204			055 – 2339	017 – 1127	059 – 2327			
	046 – 1241			068 – 1331	018 – 1100	060 – 2304			
	063 – 1323				019 – 1100	066 – 2304			
	067 – 1331				020 – 1137	069 – 2342			
	070 – 1331				021 – 1127	073 – 2339			
	072 – 1331				022 – 1127	075 – 2355			
					023 – 1127				
					024 – 1127				
					025 – 1127				
					026 – 1127				
					027 – 1127				
					029 – 1127				
					030 – 1112				
					031 – 1112				
					033 – 1220				
					039 – 1229				
					040 – 1229				
					041 – 1205				
					042 – 1229				
					045 – 1241				
					051 – 1303				
					076 – 1125				
					077 – 1137				

small pyramidal knob handle, a bow shaped nozzle and a flat base. The similarity to the Beth Natif lamps was already noticed by Rosenthal and Sivan (1978: 125, Type 514) in their study of the Schloessinger collection, but the Christian ornaments suggest a later date. The molds from Caesarea are solid evidence of a local production (Sussman 1980: 76–79 and 1996: 354), moreover, one of the molds consists of a rosette ornament such as the Tel Tanninim specimen (fig. 154:8). Another unpublished mold with a palm tree pattern (fig. 154:12) exists in the Israel Antiquities Authority storage, under the registration No. 81–923 (Calderon 2000: 156). Such oil lamps, dated from the Late Byzantine era, late sixth to early seventh century C.E., were found at Ephesos (Bailey 1988: Nos. 3118–23), Beth She'arim (Avigad 1976: fig. 2), Jalame (Macdonnell 1988: No. 86), Ramat Hanadiv (Calderon 2000: 94–96 and Pl. 12), Caesarea (*ibid.*), and Ein Gedi (Barag and Porath 1970: 100).

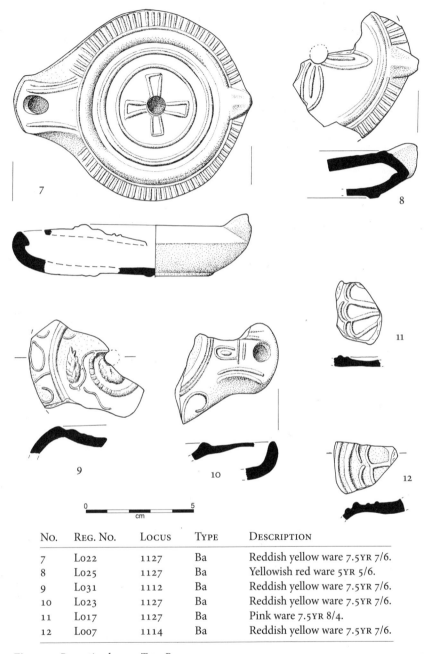

No.	Reg. No.	Locus	Type	Description
7	L022	1127	Ba	Reddish yellow ware 7.5YR 7/6.
8	L025	1127	Ba	Yellowish red ware 5YR 5/6.
9	L031	1112	Ba	Reddish yellow ware 7.5YR 7/6.
10	L023	1127	Ba	Reddish yellow ware 7.5YR 7/6.
11	L017	1127	Ba	Pink ware 7.5YR 8/4.
12	L007	1114	Ba	Reddish yellow ware 7.5YR 7/6.

Fig. 154. *Byzantine lamps, Type Ba.*

Type Bb (figs. 155:1–2; 156:2)

Type "Bb" is a well potted and fired lamp. The ware is usually orange pink 5YR 7/6, finely levigated. Eleven specimens were found in the excavations (see Table 1). A pointed, ovoid, mold-made oil lamp, characterized by a flat, ovoid, pointed ring base, a small sunken discus surrounded by a raised ridge, which extends onto the nozzle and circumscribes a definite trapezoidal channel; and a pyramidal knob handle opposite the wick hole. A relatively small filling hole is placed in the center of the discus, which is often decorated with relief ornaments comprising floral, geometric, zoomorphic and cultic symbols, such as a cross and even a depiction of Byzantine coins.

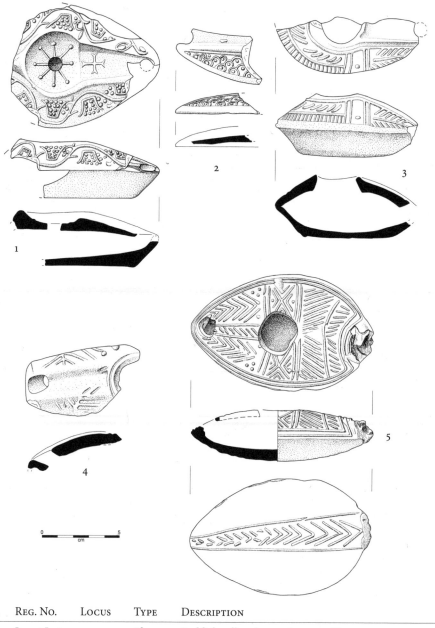

No.	Reg. No.	Locus	Type	Description
1	L057+L060	2304	Bb	Reddish yellow (orange) 7.5YR 7/6
2	L058	2304	Bb	Very pale brown ware 10YR 7/4.
3	L064	2304	Bc	Pink ware 5YR 7/4; fired to a pinkish gray hue 7.5YR 6/2.
4	L004	6000	Bd	Very pale brown 10YR 7/4; blackened by use.
5	L062	1303	Ma	Light red ware 10R 6/6; buff coated 2.5Y 8/3.

Fig. 155. *Byzantine and Mamluk lamps.*

In Caesarea, "Bb" is the most prominent (Arnon, in Press) and dated to the Byzantine–Islamic transition period—the second half of the seventh century C.E. The same phenomenon and date also appear in the study of Adan-Bayewitz (1986: 115).

Type "Bb" was also studied by Rosenthal and Sivan (1978: Types 510–11) and is well recorded in sites from the north of Israel, such as Beth Sheʿarim, Jalame, Shavei Zion, Nazareth, Capernaum and Hamat Gader (Avigad 1976: 3, Pl. 31, Type 3; Mac-

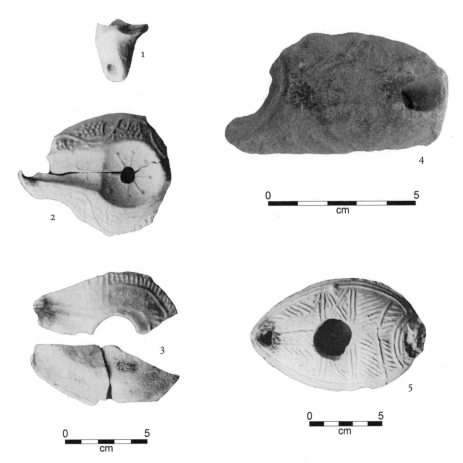

Fig. 156. *Photos of lamps: 003 (1); 057 (2); 064 (3); 004 (4); 062 (5).*

donnell 1988: figs. 4–6; 54; Prausnitz, Avi-Yonah, and Barag 1967: figs. 14–17; Bagatti 1969: fig. 236:2; Loffreda 1974: Photo 25 and fig. 18, Type L9; Peleg 1989; Coen Uzzielli 1997: fig. 11, Pl. 7:1–3; and Adan-Bayewitz 1986: figs. 123–25, Type 1).

Although at sites like Jalame (Macdonnell 1988: 116–35), Shavei Zion (Prausnitz, Avi-Yonah, and Barag 1967: 45–46) and Beth She'arim (Avigad 1976: 190–92) this type is dated to the fourth–sixth centuries, in Caesarea it is considered as a Transition Period lamp, for it was uncovered in Byzantine levels, as well as in post-Islamic conquest ones (Arnon, in press). Moreover, a specimen bearing a coin depiction was dated by Kindler (1958: 109) to 610–650 C.E. The data from Caesarea may allow us to suggest a relatively long time span for this type, beginning in the fourth century and extending until the seventh century C.E.

Type Bc (figs. 155:3; 156:3)

An ovoid, pointed, mold-made oil lamp. The ware is usually light red 2.5YR 6/6, or light brown 7.5YR 6/4, containing large quantities of small white grits. The surface is always fired to a light brown 7.5YR 5/2, or weak red 2.5YR 5/2 hue, probably as a result of a reduced firing. Only one specimen (number L064) was recovered, in Area B2. The lamp's characteristics are a relatively raised rim, a large central filling hole, often of an extended horseshoe-shape, a wide shallow channel, a flat base that follows the lamp's outline, and a small, relatively horizontal tongue handle. Projecting dots, herring bone patterns and net depictions are the most common decorations on the rim.

Type "Bc" is well recorded at sites such as Khirbet Karak (Delougaz and Haines 1960: Pl. 44:13), Capernaum (Peleg 1989: fig. 10:2), Nazareth (Bagatti 1969: fig. 234:27), Pella (Walmsley 1988:

Ill. 9:5), Kefar ʿAra (Sussman 1976: Pl. 26, Groups C, D), Hammat Gader (Coen Uzzielli 1997: fig. 12 and Pl. 6:1–2), Caesarea (Adan-Bayewitz 1986: Type 2, Ills. 126, 128b) and Beth Shean (Hadad 1997: figs. 31–34). All the sites mentioned above, except for Kefar ʿAra, which is a burial cave, were well established and prospered during the Byzantine era and continued to be occupied after the Islamic conquest as well.

In her study on the Samaritan lamps from Apollonia-Arsuf, Sussman considered "Bc" a Samaritan type and classified it as Samaritan Type IV. She has suggested a sixth–seventh century date for the type, but emphasizes that it continued in vogue into the Early Islamic period as well (Sussman 1983: 85). The finds from Beth Shean extend this date into the mid-eighth century (Hadad 1997: 168). In Caesarea, "Bc" lamps are absent in loci above the earthquake debris, therefore a seventh century or even beginning of the eighth century date will be an appropriate *terminus ad quem* (Arnon, in press).

Type Bd (*figs. 155:4; 156:4*)

An ovoid, pointed, mold-made oil lamp. The ware is usually reddish/brown 5YR 6/6, porous and often buff slipped 5Y 8/3. Only one specimen (**L004**) was recovered, in the surface layer of the test square in Area F. The type is characterized by a small sunken discus, often broken by use, surrounded by one ridge or more. The outer part extends onto the nozzle and forms a definite channel, sometimes slightly trapezoidal; a relatively horizontal knob handle and a sunken ring base, often containing a projecting pellet in the center. The rim decorations are composed of radial lines, diagonal streaks and projecting dots. Types "Bc" and "Bd" were uncovered in Caesarea in Area TPS on the Umayyad floor, below it, and in the earthquake debris, as well as in Late Byzantine levels (Arnon, in press). Type "Bd" corresponds more or less to Sussman's Type III, and it was dated at Apollonia-Arsuf to the fifth–seventh centuries. Yet it is important to indicate that in her study Sussman (1983: fig. 9:2 and Pl. 12:89) emphasizes that this type continues well into the Early Islamic period.

MAMLUK PERIOD

Type Ma (*figs. 155:5; 156:5*)

This type is characterized by a flattened, ovoid, pointed body, a concave base often decorated, and a pulled-up folded handle also known as a "duck tail handle." It seems that the mold was complete except for the wick hole, when the clay was pressed against it. The filling hole was cut with a pointed instrument when the clay was leather-hard. The ware is coarse and porous, containing large quantities of medium and small-size white grits and grog inclusions. The color is pink 2.5YR 6/6. The surface is always buff 5Y 8/3 coated. Three specimens were unearthed (**L053, L054, L062**), all within the "Crusader Tower" in Area A2.

Although absent at Crusader sites such as Caesarea (Arnon, in press), Athlit (Johns 1933, 1934, 1935, 1937) and Tell ʿArqa (Thalmann 1978; Hakimian and Salamé-Sarkis 1988), this type is well known at Medieval sites dated to the thirteenth–fourteenth centuries all over the region and even in Egypt (Kawatoko 1987: fig. 5:4, Type I:4). A hoard containing 66 coins dated to 1260–1277, which was found hidden in such an oil lamp, could be a solid proof for the date (Thompson 1973: 77, Pl. 14:A).

The Tel Tanninim specimen (**L062**) is decorated with geometric ornaments composed of herringbone patterns, projecting dots and diagonal streaks divided by metopes. A herringbone pattern, delimited by two parallel ridges, decorates the concave base. As noted above, similar samples were found at such sites as Hama (Riis and Poulsen 1957: 280), Beth Shean (Hadad 1997: figs. 4:16–18; 9:32–35), La Feve (Kedar and Pringle 1985: fig. 4:3), Yoqneʿam (Avissar 1996: 194–95, Type 3), Mount Carmel (Pringle 1984: fig. 5:9), Ramat Hanadiv (Boas 2000: Pl. 5:8–10), Burj al-Ahmar (Pringle 1986: 145, fig. 47), Abu Gosh (de Vaux and Steve 1950: fig. 33:1–2) and Jerusalem (Tushingham 1985: 151, fig. 45:1–3; Avissar 1992: 187, fig. 13:4).

DISCUSSION

The great majority of the oil lamps were retrieved from Areas A and A2, located on the top and slopes of Tel Tanninim. Only a few were intact and the rest were fragments or badly preserved specimens. The distribution of periods represents rather well the site's history from the middle of the first millennium B.C.E. to the fourteenth century C.E. As mentioned above, the absence of nearly 500 years representing the Early Islamic and Crusader periods is surprising, and the answer must be sought somewhere else, perhaps in other parts of the site. The lamp count by period demonstrates the intensity of settlement in each era. Although we are aware of the small amount of the samples used in this compilation—only 75 specimens—it seems that there are two occupational peaks: the first in the Hellenistic period and the second in the Byzantine era. Another interesting detail is the relatively high proportion of imported oil lamps in the Hellenistic period (Type "Ha"), while during the Byzantine era all the oil lamps were from local production. It should be emphasized that the oil lamp data do not stand by themselves, and that they must be looked at together with all other components of the excavations, in order to obtain a complete picture.

3. Miscellaneous Artifacts

by Robert R. Stieglitz

A. INSCRIBED OBJECTS

Two Sea Shells (figs. 157:1–2; 158:1–2)

Of the many dozens of common sea shells (*Glycimeris glycimeris Linnaeus*, 1758) unearthed in the various excavation areas, two were remarkable, as they were inscribed on their interior surface. Both shells were discovered in Area A (Square A1), locus 1127, a dark brown clayish soil north of W 1138. Their ceramic context included Gaza amphorae sherds datable to the Late Byzantine period, as well as an inscribed body sherd from another amphora (see below), and no less than nine oil lamps. Four of these lamps are illustrated above (Chapter IV.2, fig. 154:7–8, 10–11). The lamps are from the early sixth to early seventh century. In the same locus were also found twenty-one bronze coins. Of the latter, those that could be dated are of the fifth–sixth centuries. The inscribed shells can thus be attributed to a date in the sixth century.

On both shells, the writing is in faded black ink, executed in two lines in the center of the inner surface. On the first shell (I002), the four Greek letters on the top line are: Ο Μ Ο Φ. Below, executed in larger signs, are two more Greek letters: Ι Π. The signs on the second shell (I005) are severely faded and difficult to read. On the top line, the Greek letters appear to be Τ Ρ Ι Π Τ Ι. The signs in the second line below are not readily identifiable, due to their poor state of preservation. It is likely that the writings on both shells are abbreviations, and that the shells were used as tokens. They may have been utilized in the church, in Area A, where they were found, or perhaps in the bath-house, in Area D, which is situated directly below their find spot.

Byzantine Amphora Sherd (figs. 157:3; 158:3)

The sherd I003 was found with one of the inscribed shells (I002) in locus 1127. The cursive sign is the letter Μ, written on the exterior of the vessel in red ink. The bottom of sign is broken on both sides of the sherd, and it is possible there were other nearby signs, on either side of the sherd's edge, but this

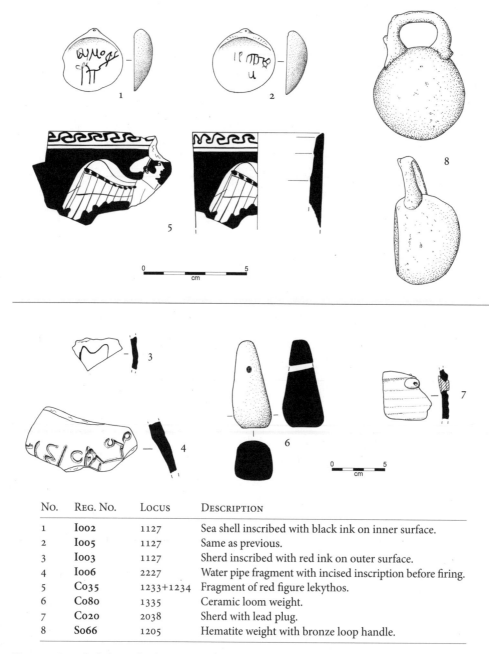

No.	Reg. No.	Locus	Description
1	I002	1127	Sea shell inscribed with black ink on inner surface.
2	I005	1127	Same as previous.
3	I003	1127	Sherd inscribed with red ink on outer surface.
4	I006	2227	Water pipe fragment with incised inscription before firing.
5	C035	1233+1234	Fragment of red figure lekythos.
6	C080	1335	Ceramic loom weight.
7	C020	2038	Sherd with lead plug.
8	S066	1205	Hematite weight with bronze loop handle.

Fig. 157. *Inscribed objects (1–4); ceramics (5–7); hematite weight (8).*

is rather unlikely. Single letters, in ink, appear on the upper parts of Byzantine amphorae usually to indicate capacity.

Water Pipe Fragment (figs. 157:4; 158:4)

This piece was unearthed with other ceramic pipe fragments in locus 2227 (Area B2; Square Q11),

in a location where a pipeline from the reservoir was found running westward. The ware is orange, with the upper edge curved inward, and remains of plaster on the exterior. The Greek letters had been incised into the wet clay of the pipe section (I006), using a thick stylus. The reading may be restored as a personal name, in the genitive case: ΗΣΙΟΔ[ΟΥ] 'Of Hesiod'. On the right, the letters

Fig. 158. *Photographs of inscribed objects (1–4) and ceramics (5–6).*

are followed by the upper part of a ligature, which may be a sign or an animal figure. The name on the pipe is either that of the pipe fabricant or that of an official in charge of the waterworks. Private names in the genitive are known from Roman lead pipes (*fistulae*), where they indicate the name of the waterworks official, the *curator aquarum* (see, for example, Corpus Inscriptionum Latinarum XV.7437, 7474, 7500).

B. CERAMIC FINDS

Painted Lekythos Fragment (figs. 157:5; 158:5)

Three sherds of an Attic red figure lekythos, later joined together (**C035**), were found in loci 1233 and 1234, Area A, Square B1. The fragment extends from the shoulder of the vessel to mid-wall. The ware is reddish orange, with exterior black glaze, and is 5.93 mm thick. The sherds were associated with diverse material culture, including many murex shells, bones, and brick fragments. The ceramic

assemblage was predominantly of the Persian period, and included basket amphora handles, body sherds, a juglet and two Persian era lamp fragments (**L043** in L 1234 and **L049** in L 1233). The preserved painted scene on the fragment depicts the head of a goddess flying to right with outstretched wings. She wears a snood (*sakkos*) over her hair, and earrings. Above the design panel is a band of meanders. The deity may be identified as rosy fingered Dawn (Eos), a popular figure on painted vessels of the fifth century B.C.E., perhaps bearing her son Memnon, who was slain at Troy according to tradition. The known corpus of imported Greek ceramics into Palestine during the Persian period is fairly extensive, having been found in over one hundred sites (Wenning 1990, with bibliography). These imports are found at both coastal and inland sites, and we can now add Tel Tanninim to the list of the coastal localities.

Loom Weight (figs. 157:6; 158:6)

The well preserved ceramic loom weight (C080) was found in locus 1335 (Area A), below a sand layer and the mortared foundations of the Byzantine church apse, and is datable to the Hellenistic period. Its shape is that of a slender pyramid with a rounded top. The sides are tapering and the square base is slightly concave with rounded corners. A hole for the yarn, with a diameter of 5.6 mm, had been punched through the weight along its centerline, near the top. The coarse sandy ware is strong brown 7.5YR 5/8 with tiny white grits. Parallels: Hellenistic Dōr (Stern 1981: 109) and a group of 150 such weights, from Late Hellenistic Yodfat in the Galilee (Aviam 1999: 97–98).

Byzantine Sherd with Lead Plug (figs. 157:7; 159:1)

Small holes in the shoulders of Byzantine bag-shaped amphorae are not uncommon finds. The hole vented the carbon dioxide gas formed in the fermentation process of new wine. One example was discussed previously (see above, Chapter III.2, No. 70), and another (fig. 159:2) was also unearthed in a Byzantine context. Less common are examples of holes that have subsequently been plugged. One such find at Tel Tanninim was the body sherd of a Late Byzantine to Early Umayyad period bag-shaped amphora (C020). The sherd was unearthed in locus 2038, situated inside the southern fishpond (L 2023) in Area B, within a compact multi-colored clay-like soil layer containing a massive concentration of broken pottery. The plug consisted of an elliptical lead ball fitted through the whole body of the vessel. A thin section of the lead plug was left protruding into the interior of the vessel. The exterior of the plug has a round hole near its right side.

Umayyad Flask (fig. 159:3–3A)

The nearly complete flask (R002) was found smashed, a few centimeters below the surface sand in Area B (L 2000), just south of the reservoir's western wall. A total of 41 sherds of the vessel, which had a creamy yellow fabric, were recovered and restored, but the restored vessel has unfortunately been lost. The flask had two handles and its profile featured a distinctive asymmetrical body, bulging out on one side only. A very similar flask from Pella is dated to ca. 720 C.E. (McNicoll, Smith, and Hennessy 1982: 169, No.1), a date which is consistent with the latest ceramics found in Area B, and is also appropriate as a *terminus post quem* for the abandonment of Area B at Tel Tanninim.

Ottoman Tobacco Pipes (figs.160–61)

Bowls and fragments of Ottoman tobacco pipes, known in the Eastern Mediterranean as *chibouk*, were uncovered in a 2 × 2 m test square (B-4), which was opened within the northwest corner of the water reservoir in Area B. Sometime after the Medieval period, when the reservoir had been out of use, this well-built *castellum* was converted into a dwelling. Two doorways were cut into its walls, one door (L 2042) was near the southeast corner, the other (L 2057) near the northwest corner. The ceramics and other finds from probe B-4 inside the structure indicated an intermittent use of the dwelling until the mid-twentieth century. The latest find was a cache of severely rusted 80-mm mortar shells, found buried in the northwest corner of the chamber, a probable remnant from the Israel War of Independence (1948–49). Local fishermen stated that the structure was occupied by a family about 50 years ago.

Another tobacco pipe bowl, of the disk-base type (C022, see below), was found in locus 1106 in Area A, indicating some Ottoman presence in the ruined structures in that region of Tel Tanninim. Some of the pipe bowls were complete, including the shank and termination-ring. The rest were body fragments of the bowls. The most common shapes of these tobacco pipes may be grouped into three general categories, which Robinson (1985) termed rounded, disc-shaped and lily-shaped. The Tel Tanninim tobacco pipes yielded all three types: two lily-shaped, one disk-based, and six rounded. Three additional bowl fragments were found: O002/2 (fig. 161:10) and two pieces of a seventh rounded bowl (C003; fig. 161:11–12).

Lily-shaped bowls

C012 (figs. 160:1; 161:1) is a petaled bowl with traces of burning inside, missing the shank. The ware is gray with a dark red gloss. On the shoulder, a wide lattice band, and below the petal flutes a row of carved concentric circles between thin lines of horizontal scoring. On the base V-shaped scored bands pointing forward. Inside diameter at rim 4.1 cm, outside height at base center 4.73 cm.

The second lily-shaped pipe bowl **C002** (figs. 160:2; 161:2) is represented only by a brown body fragment. The preserved design has a row of carved concentric circles between horizontal lines above the base and a scored band on the shoulder.

Disk-based bowl

C022 (figs. 160:3; 161:3) is a complete bowl with a long tapered shank and no wreath at the termination. The form of the bowl is nearly cylindrical and thus quite different from the two other groups. It is decorated with horizontal lines and punched rows of dots on the shoulder, and vertical scoring above base. The shank and disk base have pairs of scored parallel lines. A row of small incisions decorated the termination. The inside diameter at the rim is 2.11 cm. The outside height at the disk center is 3.78 cm, while the inside diameter of the termination is 1.24 cm. Probably dating to the nineteenth century.

Rounded bowls

C083 (figs. 160:4; 161:4) nearly complete with reddish brown clay. A wide band with lattice design decorates the shoulder. The wreath is stamped near its inner edge with a crescent seal depicting a row of dots near its periphery. The base has V-shaped scored bands pointing forward. Inside diameter at rim 3.16 cm, outside height base center 4.36 cm, inside diameter at termination 1.08 cm. This type has parallels inside and outside of Palestine: a shipwreck off Sharm ash-Sheikh, dated 1725–1750 (Raban 1974); Saraçhane in Istanbul (Hayes 1992: 391–95), where it is dated to the eighteenth century, and at Acre (Edelstein and Avissar 1997: 133, fig. 3b).

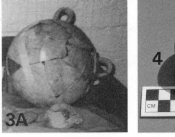

Fig. 159. *Photographs of ceramic objects (1–3A) and hematite weight (4).*

The pipes at Acre (Akko) have the same crescent seal stamp on the shank.

C013 (figs. 160:5; 161:5) is nearly complete, missing the rim, and has a dark red ware. The bowl is decorated with horizontal rouletted bands of lattice patterns and a pair of thin parallel lines. The shank is stamped near the wreath with a crescent seal depicting distorted dots near the periphery. The base has V-shaped scored bands pointing forward and a small stepped-ring near the apex. Inside diameter at rim (estimated) 3.10 cm, estimated height at base center 4.4 cm, inside diameter at termination 1.12 cm. Same parallels as for pipe **C083**, above.

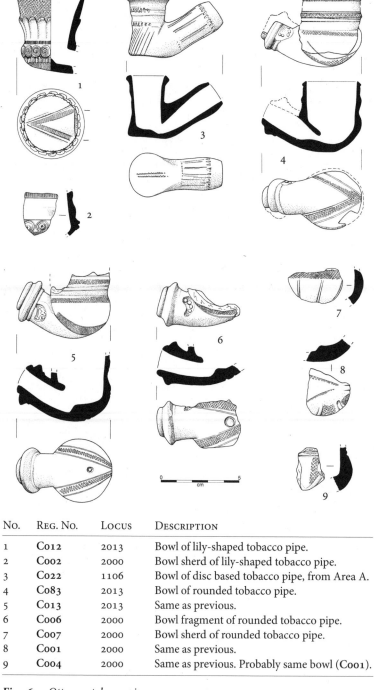

No.	Reg. No.	Locus	Description
1	C012	2013	Bowl of lily-shaped tobacco pipe.
2	C002	2000	Bowl sherd of lily-shaped tobacco pipe.
3	C022	1106	Bowl of disc based tobacco pipe, from Area A.
4	C083	2013	Bowl of rounded tobacco pipe.
5	C013	2013	Same as previous.
6	C006	2000	Bowl fragment of rounded tobacco pipe.
7	C007	2000	Bowl sherd of rounded tobacco pipe.
8	C001	2000	Same as previous.
9	C004	2000	Same as previous. Probably same bowl (C001).

Fig. 160. *Ottoman tobacco pipes.*

C006 (figs. 160:6; 161:6) has only its shank and about half the base preserved. The ware is pale pink to brown. A crescent seal is stamped in the center of the shank, depicting a row of dots near the periphery. The base has the V-shaped scored bands pointing forward with a stepped-ring near the apex. Inside diameter at termination 1.24 cm. Parallels as for pipes **C083** and **C013**.

C007 (figs. 160:7; 161:7) is a body fragment of a rounded pipe bowl, consisting of a brown ware. The preserved part has a lattice band below the rim and converging pairs of thin lines running to the base.

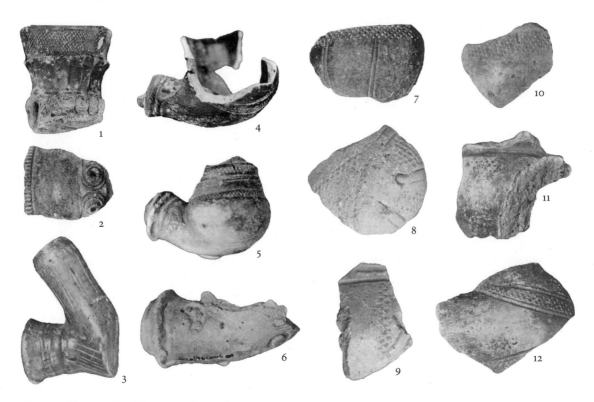

Fig. 161. *Photographs of Ottoman tobacco pipes.*

The two body fragments **C001** and **C004** (figs. 160:8–9; 161:8–9) are almost certainly parts of the same pipe bowl. The ware is very pale brown. The preserved decorations show a design of vertical bands of lattice and converging lines and thin lattice bands running towards the base.

The Ottoman pipes from Tel Tanninim, dated to the eighteenth–nineteenth century, have their closest parallels at Akko (Edelstein and Avissar 1997: fig. 2). The pipes were evidently of local manufacture, as they are quite distinct from the various types found at Greek sites (Robinson 1983; 1985). Tobacco pipe workshops in Palestine are known from Nazareth and Jerusalem (Ziadeh 1995: 211) and the Tel Tanninim pipes were likely manufactured in one of them.

C. HEMATITE WEIGHT

The well-preserved dome-shaped hematite weight (figs. 157:8; 159:4) is provided with an attached bronze ring, known as a loop-clamp. It was found in Area A, locus 1205, in a mixed fill of dark brown compact soil with Persian, Hellenistic and Byzantine pottery, as well as bone and glass fragments. Weights with metal loop-clamps are well attested since the Late Bronze Age at various sites in Syria-Palestine and Egypt (Eran 1982).

The heavy stone (specific gravity 5.2) is rounded and beveled, polished smooth, and has a flattened base. The loop-clamp is set at a slight angle, so that when the weight rests on its base the loop touches the surface. The hematite weight (**S066**) had a mass of 187.50 gr before cleaning, and after removing the bronze patina from the loop its weight was 186.60 gr. The weight mass fits into several regional weight standards. A parallel to our weight is a Hellenistic 2-*deben* unit (180.6 gr) found in Ashdod Stratum IV (Eran 1982: 95, note 28). A weight of this mass is suitable for weighing fresh fish.

D. MARBLE RELIQUARY FRAGMENT

Some 25 cm below the surface sand north of square A2 in Area A (L 1000), a smashed piece of a decorated marble chest was found, measuring 96 × 65 × 34 cm (figs. 162–63). The fragment (**A028**) was evidently from a reliquary casket, originally situ-

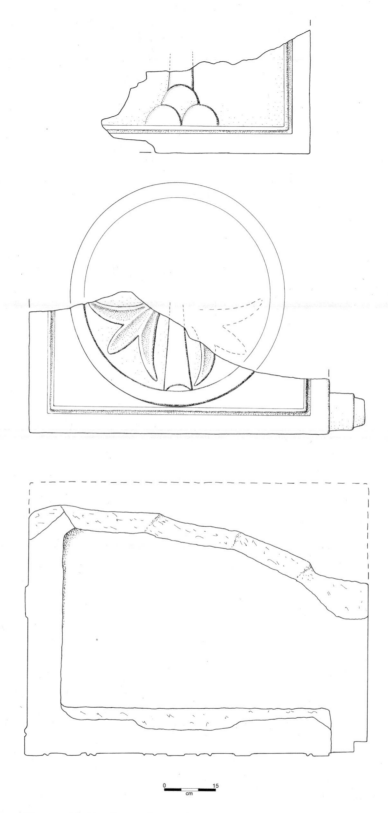

Fig. 162.   *Marble reliquary fragment.*

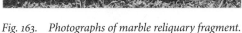

Fig. 163.   Photographs of marble reliquary fragment.

ated inside the large church that had been erected in Area A, on the summit of Tel Tanninim. The reliquary was probably broken into smaller pieces in order to burn the fragments for lime. Indeed, on the east slope of Tel Tanninim, just below the surface in Squares A3 and A4 of Area A, were found remains of a rounded stone installation, which may be those of an lime kiln (L 1006). There were signs of fire on the stones, and several sizeable marble fragments remained inside the structure. No ceramics were found in or near the structure, but its likely date is from the Ottoman period.

The interior was plain, except for a marble ridge left along the bottom of its long side wall. The casket exterior was decorated with reliefs. On the long side, a fleur-de-lis design was set in a circular frame, with a Byzantine cross carved over the circle's center. The panel on the short side depicted the partially preserved lower portion of a cross, set over three stylized rounded hills, a well-known rep-

Fig. 164.   Marble grating fragments.

resentation of the scene of the three crosses at the site of the crucifixion of Jesus and the two bandits at Golgotha in Jerusalem (Matthew 27:33).

E. MARBLE GRATING FRAGMENTS

Several fragments of marble grating were unearthed near the large fishpond in Area B2. They were carved out from white marble slabs, which were 1.4–1.9 cm thick. The plates were then drilled with rows of holes, spaced about 2–2.5 cm apart (fig. 164). The traces of mortar on their reverse indicate they had been cemented into place. The fishpond complex in Area B2 had been in use for a long period and underwent several building phases, as well as relying on two different water sources (the aqueduct or *castellum* water, or well water). The strainers were most likely used in connection with the open channels feeding water into the fishponds.

F. REPTILIAN BONE OBJECT

A fragment of a worked reptilian bone object (Z013) was unearthed in L 1204 (basket 1054), which contained 48 sherds, mostly Persian and some Hellenistic, and five murex shells. The context was a foundation fill of Stratum VI, whose material culture indicated it was derived from the Persian-Hellenistic strata below the fill (see above Chapter II.2). The bone had been cut and shaped into an irregular polygon, measuring 4.96 × 4.13 × 1.07 cm (fig. 165). On the top of the object was a pattern of concentric arcs, flanked on both sides by rows of hexagonal scales. The underside exhibits lengthwise striation and the cross-section shows what appears to be a bone structure. Upon discovery the piece was immediately called a "fossilized crocodile hide".

G. COINS

A total of 93 bronze coins was unearthed at Tel Tanninim. Most of them were of a very small denomination (the so-called *minimus*), extremely worn and thus illegible. The identifications for those legible examples were kindly provided by Mr. Peter Lampinen, the numismatist for The Combined Caesarea Expeditions.

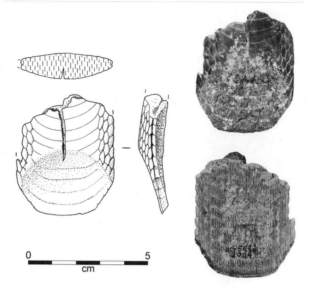

Fig. 165. *Reptilian bone object.*

A great majority of the undated coins are most likely of the Late Byzantine period and most of these were of the *minimus* denomination. The coins are listed by area and date of their excavation in the Appendix. The dates for the legible coins are based on either their legible surfaces or on their diameter typology. The earliest coin found at Tel Tanninim was Hellenistic, dated to the second century B.C.E. while the latest types, of pre-Ottoman date, were evidently from the Mamluk period.

Chapter V

The Fish Bone Remains

by Arlene Fradkin and Omri Lernau

This chapter examines the fish remains recovered during the 1996 through 1999 field seasons of the Tanninim Archaeological Project (TAP). The archaeological contexts from which the fish remains were recovered are discussed, followed by a description of the kinds of fish identified and estimates of their size. Finally, the fish assemblage at Tel Tanninim is compared to that of nearby Caesarea Maritima. We would like to thank Prof. Robert R. Stieglitz, director of the Tanninim Archaeological Project, for the opportunity to study the fish remains recovered at Tel Tanninim. We especially would like to express our appreciation to A. Asa Eger for providing detailed information on the cultural contexts of the fish samples we examined. Our thanks also go to Dr. Dani Golani for information on fishing techniques.

MATERIALS AND METHODS

The fish remains examined were recovered from two excavation areas. The bulk of the fish remains came from Area A2, in contexts dating to the Mamluk period, when the site inhabitants reused a Crusader tower for residential purposes. The rest came from Area A, the location, successively, of Persian and Hellenistic houses, a Byzantine church, and a nearby Crusader vault converted into residential quarters during the Mamluk occupation (see Chapter II, above).

Identification and analysis of the fish remains recovered at Tel Tanninim followed standard zooarchaeological procedures (Reitz and Wing 1999: 142–38). Specimens were identified by direct comparison with Lernau's private comparative reference collection. Identifications were carried out to the lowest taxon possible following standard zoological classification and nomenclature. For each specimen identified, a record was made of the element, its symmetry (right or left), and any evidence of modification (burnt, cut, and/or worked). Measurements of specimens were taken (Morales and Rosenlund 1979) and estimates of fish size (body length in cm) were determined using allometric formulas obtained from the literature (Desse and Desse-Berset 1996; Desse, Desse-Berset, and Rocheteau 1987; Van Neer 1989) and some generated from Lernau's reference collection. In this paper, estimated sizes of fish should be regarded as rough estimations only, yet sufficiently accurate for the present objectives.

Quantification of the animal remains included a count of the total number of identified specimens for each taxon (NISP) and calculated estimates of the minimum number of individual animals represented (MNI). The MNI figures were determined separately for each cultural context (e.g., all loci in a "living surface," which dated to the same cultural time period) and were based on the concept of paired elements and individual size.

RESULTS

In our study, we examined approximately 750 fish remains. However, we had to eliminate a small percentage of these in our analysis because they came from loci whose contexts were mixed and/or modern or for which sufficient contextual information was not available.

For those contexts used in our analysis, a total of 716 fish bone remains was recovered, of which 466 specimens were identified to the taxonomic level of family, and to the genus or species level where possible. Of the fish specimens identified, a total of 23 taxa, comprising 10 families, and an estimated minimum of 57 individual fish were represented. All taxa identified are listed in Table 2. Tables 3 and 4 present the cultural contexts of the fish remains in Areas A and A2, respectively. Quantification of the fish remains by family groupings of taxa and cultural period for the entire assemblage (i.e., Areas A and A2 combined) is provided in Table 5. Summary totals by cultural period are given in Table 6.

Area A

The assemblage of fish bone remains from Area A was quite small (see Table 3). From the Persian and Hellenistic houses, a total of 31 bones were identified, representing 8 families and 13 individuals. The several fish remains from the Byzantine period (NISP= 8) were from floor foundations associated with the construction of the church. Fish remains from the Mamluk period came from the reoccupied Crusader vault-turned-residence where 26 bones were identified, representing 4 families and 7 individuals.

Area A2

The fish bone remains from Area A2 constituted the larger of the two samples (see Table 4). This entire assemblage came from the Mamluk occupation of the Crusader tower as living quarters. A total of 401 bones were identified, representing 9 families and 33 individuals.

DESCRIPTIONS OF FISH

All the fish identified in Areas A and A2 naturally occur in local waters in the Tel Tanninim area. Table 7 shows the relative abundance of the fish remains identified for each cultural period according to their source. Table 8 gives summary tabulations by source for the entire assemblage. Local marine fish predominated, constituting 82 percent of the identified specimens (NISP) and 79 percent of the MNI. Local freshwater fish made up 18 percent of the identified specimens (NISP) and 21 percent of the MNI. No imported fish were represented in the fish samples.

In presenting the fish identified, we will first describe the various kinds of local marine fish represented in decreasing order of their relative abundance in the total archaeological fish bone assemblage and then similarly describe the local freshwater fish represented.

Local Marine Fish

The most common local marine fish identified at Tel Tanninim were grey mullets (*Mugilidae*). These are medium-sized fish, ranging from approximately 15 to 50 cm (6 to 20 inches) in length, and are very common in warm shallow inshore waters, lagoons, and estuaries along Israel's Mediterranean coast (Ben-Tuvia 1953: 1; 1971; 1986: 1197–203; Golani 1996: 30; Golani and Darom 1997: 196).

Two species of grey mullet were present: the flathead grey mullet (*Mugil cephalus*) and the thinlip grey mullet (*Liza* spp.). Although marine, these species typically enter brackish and even fresh waters. These mullets, particularly the young, often concentrate near freshwater outflows, or estuaries, and regularly ascend coastal rivers, but they return to the sea as adults for breeding. Feeding primarily on plant material, grey mullets typically move in dense schools, thus rendering them easy to capture in nets (Abraham, Blanc, and Yashouv 1966; Ben-Tuvia 1986: 1197–203; Lythgoe and Lythgoe 1992: 208). The grey mullets at Tanninim varied in size, ranging from 17 to 44 cm (7 to 17 inches) in length.

Mullets were well known to ancient Egyptians, who observed and described their migrations up the Nile River, which signaled the approach of the flood season. As in the past, mullets are regarded as an excellent food fish today and are an important commercial fish in Israel where they are typically raised in fish ponds (Abraham, Blanc, and Yashouv 1966: 156; Ben-Tuvia 1971: 18; Lernau and Lernau 1992: 133–34).

Other fish found in significant numbers included several members of the sea bream family (*Sparidae*). A very common fish group along Israel's Mediterranean coast, these medium-sized fish occur primarily in warm inshore waters and sometimes in brackish bays and estuaries. The young congregate in shallow waters, whereas adults are found in deeper waters (Bauchot and Hureau 1986: 883; Ben-Tuvia 1953: 23–24; 1971).

Several species of sea bream were identified. The gilt-head sea bream (*Sparus aurata*), the most common sea bream at Tanninim, is a shallow-water species and often enters brackish waters. Those at Tanninim were between 23 and 32 cm (9 to 13 inches) in length. Sea bream (*Diplodus* spp.) is a smaller sparid, 18 to 26 cm (7 to 10 inches) long at Tanninim, and is common along rocky coasts. Striped sea bream (*Lithognathus mormyrus*), also a small sparid, with an average size of 16 cm (6 inches) at Tanninim, is a gregarious species, sometimes swimming in large schools. Sea bream (*Pagrus* spp.) is a fairly large sparid and occurs in inshore waters over hard or sandy bottoms. This last sea bream averaged 25 to 26 cm (10 inches) in length at Tanninim. All four kinds of sea breams are carnivorous, feeding mostly on mollusks and crustaceans, and have powerful incisor- and molar-like teeth to crush and grind shells. A highly esteemed food today, these fish may be taken in nets (Bauchot and Hureau 1986: 883–906; Lythgoe and Lythgoe 1992: 113–15).

Groupers (*Serranidae*), another important fish family represented, are large marine fish that occur in the warm waters of the eastern Mediterranean and are also common along the coast of Israel (Golani 1996: 37–38). They are bottom-dwelling fish and voracious predators, feeding on other fishes as well as invertebrates. Many are valued as game fishes and are commercially important (Tortonese 1986: 780, 783).

Two species of grouper were identified at Tanninim. Dusky grouper (*Epinephelus marginatus*) is a fairly robust fish and is typically found on rocky bottoms where there are holes and caves. It is a solitary species, and larger individuals can be caught with hook and line (Ben-Tuvia 1953: 22; Lythgoe and Lythgoe 1992: 87; Tortonese 1986: 785–86). The dusky grouper at Tanninim was a rather small specimen with an estimated length of 36 cm (14 inches). Golden grouper (*Epinephelus costea*), a more slender-bodied fish, inhabits rocky, muddy bottoms, and the young often swim in small groups (Lythgoe and Lythgoe 1992: 86; Tortonese 1986: 784). The golden groupers at Tanninim averaged 29 cm (11 inches) in length.

Drums (*Sciaenidae*) are medium to large fish that inhabit shallow inshore waters and also occur along Israel's Mediterranean coast. Also carnivorous, they feed on small fishes, crustaceans, and mollusks (Ben-Tuvia 1971; Chao 1986: 865; Golani 1996: 40). Two species of drum were identified. Meagre (*Argyrosomus regius*), a large drum, is found in shallow coastal waters. Juveniles and subadults frequently enter estuaries and coastal lagoons. The meagres at Tanninim ranged from 21 to 47 cm (8 to 19 inches) in length. Brown meagre (*Sciaena umbra*), a smaller fish, is usually found on rocky and sandy bottoms. This fish had an estimated length of 35 cm (14 inches). Both species can be caught with nets or with hook and line (Chao 1986: 867, 871; Lythgoe and Lythgoe 1992: 106).

Several other local marine fish families were represented, though by only one or a few bones of a single species. Greater amberjack (*Seriola dumerili*) is a very large fast-swimming predaceous fish that can attain a maximum size of 2 m (6.6 feet). This fish is found worldwide, including the Mediterranean, as well as the West Atlantic, Gulf of Mexico, and Caribbean. A migratory fish, it moves in small groups and typically occurs in moderate to deep water. It can be taken with hook and line or with nets (Golani and Darom 1997: 166; Lythgoe and Lythgoe 1992: 103; Smith-Vaniz 1986: 837–38). The amberjack at Tanninim was 70 cm (28 inches) long. Seabass (*Dicentrarchus* spp.)

is a smaller marine predatory fish and migrates inshore during the summer where it frequently enters estuaries and ascends rivers (Lythgoe and Lythgoe 1992: 89–92).

Parrotfish (*Sparisoma cretense*) is a medium-sized fish that frequents rugged rocky areas along the Mediterranean coast and feeds on algae and small invertebrates. It is so-named for its gaudy colors and parrot-like beak, which it uses to scrape algae from encrusted rocks (Lythgoe and Lythgoe 1992: 140; Quignard and Pras 1986: 943–44). The parrotfish at Tanninim were between 19 and 21 cm (7 to 8 inches) in length.

In addition to bony fish, cartilaginous fish, represented by several shark or ray vertebrae (i.e., calcified *centra*), were in the Tanninim fish assemblage, but could not be identified.

Local Freshwater Fish

The most common local freshwater fish identified among the Tanninim fish remains was tilapia (*Tilapiini*). These are small- to medium-sized freshwater fish, up to 25 cm (10 inches) in length (Golani and Darom 1997: 244, 246), and are very common in many of Israel's rivers, lakes, ponds, and streams, particularly among stones and abundant vegetation. Several genera and species of tilapia naturally occur in the Lake of Galilee, the Jordan River, and/or Israel's coastal rivers (Goren 1974: 104; Trewavas 1942). The species found in the Tanninim area is the common St. Peter's fish (*Tilapia zillii*; Goren 1974: fig. 33). Like many other tilapias, this species may adapt to shallow marine waters and has been caught in the Mediterranean close to the shore. It feeds on aquatic plants and algae and is typically caught in nets (Trewavas 1982). The tilapias at Tanninim ranged from 16 to 31 cm (6 to 12 inches) in length. A popular table fish today, tilapias have been introduced into various parts of the world where they are raised on fish farms and are important in commercial and subsistence fisheries (Pullin and Lowe-McConnell 1982; Skelton 1993: 319).

The other freshwater fish at Tanninim was the Nile catfish (*Clarias gariepinus*). This is the largest freshwater fish in Israel and is the only catfish species in Israel today. This fish can attain a maximum length of 150 cm (59 inches; Golani and Darom 1997: 240) and a maximum weight of 20 kg (44 pounds). An inhabitant of lakes, large sluggish rivers, and slow water streams, the Nile catfish naturally occurs in Israel, in coastal rivers and in the Lake of Galilee and other waters of the Jordan River system, and throughout the Levant as well as in the Nile River in Egypt (hence the name Nile catfish) and in most areas of Africa. Like other members of the family *Clariidae*, this species has evolved an accessory air-breathing organ above the gills, which allows it to survive in such harsh conditions as poor oxygenation or desiccation. An omnivorous fish, the Nile catfish feeds on any available organic food source, including fish, frogs, reptiles, birds, small mammals, snails, crustaceans, and plant seeds and fruit, and may be caught by rod and hook or by nets (Goren 1974; Skelton 1993: 229–30). Estimated sizes of the Nile catfish at Tanninim ranged from 30 to 71 cm (12 to 28 inches) in length. This fish is considered edible and is an important food fish species in certain parts of the world today (Skelton 1993: 230).

COMPARISONS WITH CAESAREA MARITIMA

The fish bone assemblage at Tel Tanninim can be compared to that of nearby Caesarea Maritima (Fradkin and Lernau, in press). The two sites are located along the Mediterranean coast in close proximity to one another, and therefore their inhabitants would have had access to the same local fish resources.

Nevertheless, the two sites greatly differ in size and complexity. Caesarea Maritima was an important seaport city and a major commercial, industrial, administrative, and residential center in ancient and medieval times. Tel Tanninim was established before Caesarea (originally Straton's Tower), during the Persian period, and essentially remained a town throughout its various occupations. During the Byzantine period, Tanninim was a suburb of Caesarea, tapping into the water from Caesarea's High-level aqueduct and supplying Caesarea's markets with fish, presumably raised in its several *piscinae*, or artificial fishponds (Stieglitz 1998; 1998a). In Crusader times, Tanninim was a coastal estate that had been sold by the Lord of Caesarea to one of the military orders of knights. Both Tanninim and Caesarea were destroyed in 1265 C.E. Later, in the fourteenth century, the Mamluks occupied the few Crusader structures at Tanninim but did not build a permanent settlement there. Tanninim was abandoned by about 1400 C.E. (Stieglitz, this volume, Chapter VI).

The fish bones identified at the two sites came from various cultural contexts and time periods. At Tanninim, fish remains were recovered from Persian and Hellenistic houses, a Byzantine Christian church, and Crusader structures converted into residential quarters during the Mamluk occupation. That no fish bones were found in the *piscinae*, which were in use during the Byzantine and Early Islamic periods (Eger 1998), may have been because the fish raised in these installations were removed while still alive, after having attained a certain designated size, and then were distributed to markets in the local area. At Caesarea, fish remains were identified from a Roman temple, Byzantine warehouse, Byzantine church, Islamic and Crusader houses, and Late Islamic and Crusader monumental public buildings (Fradkin and Lernau, in press).

The two fish assemblages are compared in terms of the kinds of fish identified, their relative abundance based upon MNI figures, estimates of their size, and skeletal elements represented. At Tel Tanninim, a total of 716 fish bones was recovered, of which 466 were identified, representing an estimated 57 individuals. At Caesarea, 941 fish bones were recovered, of which 389 specimens were identified and 157 individuals represented (Table 9). The smaller percentage of bones identified at Caesarea was due to the poorer condition of some of the remains. The higher MNI, on the other hand, resulted from the much greater number of loci from which fish remains were recovered. At Tanninim, there were far fewer loci and some of these were combined for analysis purposes.

In general, similar resources were used at both sites, though Caesarea exhibited greater fish diversity. At Caesarea, 32 taxa comprising 17 families were represented, whereas 23 taxa comprising 10 families were recorded for Tanninim (see Table 9). Of the local marine fish, several differences included the presence of sand tiger, thicklip grey mullet, common sea bream, herring, horse-mackerel, grey triggerfish, bluefish, and snapper exclusively at Caesarea, and the occurrence of *Diplodus* sea bream, golden grouper, greater amberjack, and parrotfish only at Tanninim. Local freshwater fish, tilapia and Nile catfish, were represented at both sites, but Tristram's St. Peter's fish and barbel were identified only at Caesarea (Table 10).

One significant difference between the site assemblages was the presence of two nonlocal species—Nile perch and bagrid catfish—at Caesarea and their complete absence at Tanninim. Both are freshwater fish that naturally occur in the Nile River in Egypt, as well as in other rivers and lakes in Africa and therefore were imported to Caesarea. Nilotic fish remains, particularly Nile perch, have been recovered in fairly large quantities from many archaeological sites throughout Israel in contexts spanning various time periods (for example, Lernau 1986/87; Lernau and Lernau 1992; Lernau 2000). Most likely, these fish were an important trade item in ancient and medieval times. A major seaport city, Caesarea surely had access to resources from other regions through its various trade networks. Tanninim, on the other hand, was a small coastal settlement and probably was not involved in long-distance trade, thereby relying solely on locally available resources.

In terms of the relative representation of different kinds of fish, the two assemblages appear very similar, the various families occurring in an almost identical order of abundance at each site. At both Tanninim and Caesarea, local marine fish predominated. Grey mullets were most common, followed by sea breams, groupers, and drums. All other marine fish were represented by only one to a few bones each. Local freshwater fish, however, differed proportionally at the two sites. At Tanninim, tilapias/cichlids were far more common than Nile catfish (see Table 2), whereas at Caesarea, Nile catfish was more abundant (see Fradkin and Lernau, in press).

Size estimates for each kind of fish represented at Tanninim were comparable to those calculated for the same fish at Caesarea. Furthermore, for all major fish taxa identified, both cranial and vertebrae (i.e., meat-bearing bones) were represented in both site assemblages.

DISCUSSION

The recovery of the fish remains primarily from within domestic structures indicates that the fish identified were used for local consumption. Living on the Mediterranean coast, the residents of Tanninim had ready access to a rich source of fish in the immediate vicinity and appear to have eaten a variety of fish.

The majority of the fish bones came from the Mamluk occupation, when several Crusader structures were converted into temporary living quarters. As the Mamluks never established a permanent settlement at Tanninim, no markets existed there during this period. Consequently, the Mamluk inhabitants captured and processed themselves any fish they consumed (Stieglitz, pers. comm.). The marine fish were obtained from the Mediterranean Sea and local estuaries, whereas the freshwater fish were probably initially collected from Nahal Tanninim (Crocodiles River) and/or the nearby Kabbara marsh (Stieglitz 1998: 65).

Based upon several lines of archaeological evidence, the site of Tel Tanninim had a series of occupations throughout its history. During certain periods, it was economically linked to the nearby city of Caesarea, and, at other times, it functioned independently. The presence of several piscinae from the Byzantine period indicates that Tanninim maintained a fishing industry at that time, most likely provisioning the markets at Caesarea and perhaps others in the local region. The recovery of fish bone remains in domestic contexts from Persian, Hellenistic, and Mamluk occupations is evidence that this resource was solely for consumption by the residents of Tel Tanninim during those periods.

Table 2. Taxon list for Areas A and A2 in decreasing order of relative abundance (× indicates presence).

Scientific Name	Common Name	NISP	MNI	Area A	Area A2
LOCAL MARINE FISH					
Chondrichthyes	**Cartilaginous Fishes**				
Elasmobranchii	sharks/skates/rays	3	1		×
Osteichthyes	**Bony Fishes**				
Mugilidae	grey mullets	157	6	×	×
Liza spp.	grey mullet	5	3		×
Mugil cephalus	flathead grey mullet	3	2	×	×
Sparidae	sea breams	82	4	×	×
Diplodus spp.	sea bream	6	3	×	×
Lithognathus mormyrus	striped sea bream	3	1		×
Pagrus spp.	sea bream	3	1		×
Sparus aurata	gilt-head sea bream	16	5	×	×
Serranidae	groupers	67	5	×	×
Epinephelus spp.	grouper	9	1		×
Epinephelus costea	golden grouper	2	1		×
Epinephelus marginatus	dusky grouper	1	1		×
Sciaenidae	drums	13	4	×	×
Argyrosomus regius	meagre	2	2	×	×
Sciaenia umbra	brown meagre	1	1	×	
Carangidae	jacks	2	1		×
Seriola dumerili	greater amberjack	1	1	×	
Moronidae	seabasses				
Dicentrarchus spp.	seabass	2	1		×
Scaridae	parrotfishes				
Sparisoma cretense	parrotfish	2	1	×	
LOCAL FRESHWATER FISH					
Osteichthyes	**Bony Fishes**				
Cichlidae	cichlids	67	5	×	×
Tilapiini	tilapia	11	5	×	×
Clariidae	catfishes				
Clarias gariepinus	Nile catfish	8	2	×	×

Table 3.   Area A — Cultural contexts of fish bone remains.

Period	Structure	Context	Locus	# Fish Bones	NISP	MNI
PERSIAN	Domestic habitation	"living surface"	1234	3	1	1
		sandy mix	1233	43	22	7
PERSIAN/ HELLENISTIC	Domestic habitation	foundation fill for Byzantine church	1204	22	8	5
BYZANTINE	Church	earliest floor foundation for church	1114	7	5	2
		Byzantine horde under a later Byzantine floor	1127 1137	5	3	2
MAMLUK	Mamluk reuse of Crusader vault	"temporary living surface" covered by destruction or collapse of wooden ceiling	1107	14	10	4
		upper fill	1105	25	16	3
TOTALS				119	65	24

Table 4.   Area A2 — Cultural contexts of fish bone remains.

Period	Structure	Context	Locus	# Fish Bones	NISP	MNI
MAMLUK	Mamluk reuse of Crusader tower	"temporary living surfaces"	1307 1319 1322	78	56	9
		fill over Crusader stairs/floor in stairwell and over floor in large room	1303 1305	510	341	23
		fill	1309	2	0	0
		fill associated with sealing of tower entrance	1315	7	4	1
TOTALS				597	401	33

Table 5. Quantification by family and cultural period for entire fish bone assemblage.

Family	Persian		Persian/Hellenistic		Byzantine	Mamluk	
	NISP	MNI	NISP	MNI	NISP	NISP	MNI
LOCAL MARINE FISH							
Chondrichthyes							
Elasmobranchii						3	
Osteichthyes							
Mugilidae	6	1	1	1	2	156	
Sparidae	3	2	2	1		105	11
Serranidae	2	1	1	1		76	
Sciaenidae	2	1			5	9	
Carangidae	1	1				2	
Moronidae						2	
Scaridae			2	1			
LOCAL FRESHWATER FISH							
Osteichthyes							
Cichlidae	8	1	2	1	1	67	
Clariidae	1	1				7	
TOTAL	23	8	8	5	8	427	40

Table 6. Totals by cultural period for entire fish bone assemblage.

Period	# Fish Bones Recovered	% Fish Bones Recovered	NISP	NISP %	MNI	MNI %	# Families Represented
PERSIAN	46	6.42	23	4.94	8	14.04	7
PERSIAN/ HELLENISTIC	22	3.07	8	1.72	5	8.77	5
BYZANTINE	12	1.68	8	1.72	4	7.02	3
MAMLUK	636	88.83	427	91.63	40	70.18	9
TOTAL	716	100.00	466	100.00	57	100.00	

Table 7.   Local marine and local freshwater fish by cultural period for entire fish bone assemblage.

Period	Local Marine		Local Fresh	
	NISP	MNI	NISP	MNI
PERSIAN	14	6	9	2
PERSIAN/HELLENISTIC	6	4	2	1
BYZANTINE	7	3	1	1
MAMLUK	353	32	74	8
TOTAL	380	45	86	12

Table 8.   Totals for local marine and local freshwater fish for entire fish bone assemblage.

Source	NISP	NISP %	MNI	MNI %
LOCAL MARINE	380	82	45	79
LOCAL FRESHWATER	86	18	12	21
TOTAL	466	100	57	100

Table 9.   Comparison between Tel Tanninim and Caesarea Maritima fish bone assemblages.

	Tel Tanninim	Caesarea Maritima
# FISH BONES RECOVERED	716	941
NISP	466	389
MNI	57	157
# FAMILIES REPRESENTED	10	17

Table 10. Comparison of fish taxa at Tel Tanninim and Caesarea Maritima in decreasing order of relative abundance (× indicates presence).

Scientific Name	Common Name	Tel Tanninim	Caesarea Maritima
LOCAL MARINE FISH			
Chondrichthyes	**Cartilaginous Fishes**		
Elasmobranchii	sharks/skates/rays	×	×
Odontaspididae	sand tigers		×
Odontaspis taurus	sand tiger		×
Osteichthyes	**Bony Fishes**		
Mugilidae	grey mullets	×	×
Chelon labrosus	thicklip grey mullet		×
Liza spp.	grey mullet	×	×
Mugil cephalus	flathead grey mullet	×	×
Sparidae	sea breams	×	×
Diplodus spp.	sea bream	×	
Lithognathus mormyrus	striped sea bream	×	×
Pagrus spp.	sea bream	×	×
Pagrus pagrus	common sea bream		×
Sparus aurata	gilt-head sea bream	×	×
Serranidae	groupers	×	×
Epinephelus spp.	grouper	×	×
Epinephelus costea	golden grouper	×	
Epinephelus marginatus	dusky grouper	×	×
Sciaenidae	drums	×	×
Argyrosomus regius	meagre	×	×
Sciaenia umbra	brown meagre	×	×
Carangidae	jacks	×	×
Seriola dumerili	greater amberjack	×	
Trachurus sp.	horse-mackerel		×
Clupeidae	herrings		×
Balistidae	triggerfishes		×
Balistes carolinensis	grey triggerfish		×
Moronidae	seabasses		
Dicentrarchus spp.	seabass	×	×

Table 10. continued.

Scientific Name	Common Name	Tel Tanninim	Caesarea Maritima
LOCAL MARINE FISH			
Scaridae	parrotfishes		
Sparisoma cretense	parrotfish	×	
Pomatomidae	bluefishes		×
Pomatomus saltator	bluefish		×
Lutjanidae	snappers		×
Lutjanus sp.	snapper		×
LOCAL FRESHWATER FISH			
Osteichthyes	**Bony Fishes**		
Cichlidae	cichlids	×	×
Tristramella sp.	Tristram's St. Peter's		×
Tilapiini	tilapia	×	×
Clariidae	catfishes		
Clarias gariepinus	Nile catfish	×	×
Cyprinidae	carps/minnows		×
Barbus spp.	barbel		×
IMPORTED FRESHWATER FISH			
Osteichthyes	**Bony Fishes**		
Centropomidae	snooks		
Lates niloticus	Nile perch		×
Bagridae	bagrid catfishes		
Bagrus sp.	bagrid catfish		×

Chapter VI

Summary and Conclusions

by Robert R. Stieglitz

The TAP excavations during 1996–1999 unearthed a sequence of settlements at the coastal site of Tel Tanninim, from initial activity during Iron Age IIC (700–586 B.C.E.) to the abandonment of the settlement after ca.1350 C.E., followed by intermittent Ottoman activity until the twentieth century. The lowest stratified level of the settlement was reached in a very limited area, one of only a few square meters (Stratum VIII) directly above the bedrock in Area A. In that location, the pottery and material culture indicated that occupation was not earlier than fifth century B.C.E. Pottery analysis from the entire sequence of strata in Area A revealed the presence of ceramics from Iron Age IIC, indicating that the earliest settlement was established several generations before the beginning of the Persian period (586–332). The discrepancy between the earliest stratified evidence and that of the earliest ceramic finds is doubtlessly due to the small area exposed at the lowest level of the excavations. The finds from our Stratum VIII did not provide a representative sample of the earliest settlement, which had been established on the low coastal mound, situated at the mouth of the Crocodile River.

The new settlement founded at Tel Tanninim during the Iron IIC period was likely connected with the renewed urban activities at the large urban cite of Dor, situated about 9 km to the north. The latter city had evidently been incorporated into the Assyrian province of Samaria, following the regional reorganization in 712 B.C.E. undertaken by the Assyrian King Sargon II (722–706). The extent and nature of the first settlement at Tel Tanninim, which we shall term Stratum IX, is now unknown, since it is attested only by a limited ceramic assemblage. Perhaps it was a fishing village, linked economically to Dor. The nearby settlement at Tel Mevorakh, situated to the east, on the south bank of the Crocodile River (fig. 3), was unoccupied during this phase of the Iron Age. The location for the earliest settlement at Tel Tanninim was no doubt due to its advantageous situation at the river mouth (fig. 166), a site that offered good anchorage for fishing boats, as well as easy access the adjacent Kabbara marsh with its ample fowl wildlife.

Early in the fifth century B.C.E., another geo-political event again changed the status of the central Levantine coastal strip. The Persian emperor Darius I (521–486) ceded nearly the entire Plain of Sharon—from the major port of Dor in the north to the harbor of Jaffa in the south—to his loyal vassal King Eshmunʿazor II of Sidon (501–487; on the dates, see Kelly 1987: 52). Soon afterwards, several new sites were founded in the ceded coastal strip. The enterprising Sidonians, together with the local population of Samaria, were joined by the active participation of the Tyrians, who were then allies of Sidon. The coastal plain of the Sharon possessed three excellent harbor sites at Athlit, Dor and Tel

Fig. 166. *Aerial view of Tel Tanninim in 1994 (courtesy of M. Laner).*

Mikhmoret, but was also noted for its fertile grain producing hinterland. Thus there were ample opportunities for a network of coastal trading posts, linked to the hinterland, which was the hallmark of Phoenician maritime activities.

Among the settlements of the fifth century B.C.E. was one at the earlier Iron Age IIC site on the mouth the Crocodile River. The surface finds on a smaller mound, about 120 m southeast of Tel Tanninim, suggest that the Persian period settlement included that mound as well, thus indicating a significant expansion of the older settlement during the Persian period. The evidence of the storage jar assemblage from the Persian period, and the relatively large quantity of Greek imported ceramics, both recovered from a very limited area of the Persian settlement, strongly suggests that Tel Tanninim functioned primarily as a fishery.

This Persian period site, whose name remains unknown, was likely of Sidonian foundation, like its neighbor at Tel Mevorakh (Stratum VI). Tel Tanninim (Stratum VIII) constituted one in a string of Phoenician towns and trading posts established along the Levant coast, stretching from the Lebanon to the Egyptian frontier in Sinai. These coastal settlements were designed to extend the commercial and colonial horizons of the Sidonian kingdom and, by mutual agreement, those of her neighboring kingdom of Tyre. We know from historical records that even citizens of other Canaanite city states, such as Byblos, occasionally participated in the Phoenician colonization enterprises during the Persian period.

After the entire Levant was transformed by the swift military conquests of Alexander the Great (332–323), Tel Tanninim continued to be occupied in the following Hellenistic era (Stratum VII). The stratigraphy and ceramics, albeit still from a small area of the early settlements at Tel Tanninim, do not indicate a clear distinction or break between these settlements. The excavated evidence suggests a continuity of occupation with no destruction, a situation also known from contemporary sites in Palestine and from the historical sources. It is likely, however, that during the early Hellenistic period Tel Tanninim was sparely settled, or even abandoned briefly, as Early Hellenistic ceramics are rare. At nearby Tel Mevorakh there is also a gap between the final Phoenician phase (Stratum IV) and the Hellenistic settlement (Stratum IIIB).

By the third century B.C.E., Tel Tanninim was evidently refounded, perhaps by Macedonian and Greek settlers. The new rulers may have been accompanied by Phoenician settlers and Samaritans, as was the case at other sites in the Sharon Plain. Sometimes during the third to second centuries B.C.E. the settlement acquired its Greek name Krokodeilon polis, being named after the river flowing into the sea along its northern edge, a river then called the *Crocodilon* (Pliny, *NH* 5.17.75). This newly founded Hellenistic settlement at Tel Tanninim was probably established by Ptolemy II Philadelphus (283–246), who was very active in developing the maritime horizons of his kingdom, both in the Mediterranean and the Red Sea. One of his principal policies was settling Macedonian veterans in various outposts of his realm (Stieglitz 1993: 649). At the same time, Ptolemy II evidently founded (or re-founded) the settlement at Straton's Tower (Στρατωνος πυργος), the site later rebuilt and renamed Caesarea by King Herod of Judaea. Since Straton's Tower was a much larger site than Krokodeilon polis, had better anchorage facilities, and was situated only about 5 km south of the Crocodile River, the Hellenistic settlement of Krokodeilon polis was not established to serve as regional port. It was, rather, founded to serve as a suburban fishery for Straton's Tower.

The settlement at Krokodeilon polis was abandoned in the early part of the first century B.C.E., due to the political activities of the Hasmonaean King Alexander Jannaeus (103–76) along this sector of the Mediterranean coast. Jannaeus had

actually managed to purchase the coastal strip, stretching from Dor to Straton's Tower, which was previously controlled by a local Hellenistic ruler named Zoilos. In June of 103/02 B.C.E., Jannaeus annexed this valuable coastal sector to his growing kingdom (Josephus *Antiquities of the Jews* 13.324; Stieglitz 1997: 302). Straton's Tower, which by now had acquired fortification walls, and still possessed good port facilities, continued to be utilized by Jannaeus, and was now given the Hebrew name Migdal Śar 'Commander's Tower' (Stieglitz 1996: 598). The small coastal settlement at Tel Tanninim, which was not particularly useful to Jannaeus, was abandoned during his reign or shortly afterwards, as was the settlement at Tel Mevorakh (Stratum IIIA). By the second half of the first century B.C.E., the site of Krokodeilon polis was only an historical memory, as noted by Strabo (16.2.27).

After the Hellenistic period, there was a major gap in occupation at the mound of Tel Tanninim. The surface surveys and the material culture from the excavated areas produced virtually no Roman finds. However, Roman period activity at Tel Tanninim is indicated by the finds of a few Roman sherds, seven Roman oil lamps, and fragments of a bronze coin that can be dated to the first–second century C.E. (No66). The finds suggest an intermittent Early Roman presence at Tel Tanninim, most likely in connection with the major construction project of the High-level aqueduct to Caesarea Maritima. The aqueduct required maintenance of its water pipes, as well as its structural elements, activities that were undertaken during the Early Roman era (first–second centuries C.E.). The repairs are attested by inscription plaques embedded in the aqueduct arches.

At a high spot on the *kurkar* ridge, situated about 1 km southeast of Tel Tanninim, numerous sherds of the Early Roman period were found on the surface. These suggest some extensive Roman activity at this location as well, although no surface structural remains were seen there. We can surmise that between the first century B.C.E. and the fourth century C.E. the mound of Tel Tanninim was not occupied except for intermittent activity, connected primarily with the waterworks of Caesarea. The Roman coastal road between Caesarea and Dor passed by the ruined structures at the mouth of the river and travelers, as well as military units, no doubt paused at the site on various occasions.

A significant settlement at Tel Tanninim was renewed with a burst of building activity in the Early Byzantine era, when the foundations were also laid for the large church structure in Area A on the summit of the mound (Stratum VI). The first phase of the church revealed a massive apse and eastern wall indicating a basilica plan (an apse with a radius of 5.50 m to its exterior side, nave and side aisles). The dimensions of the excavated wall sections indicate they were exterior and that the apse was external. The deep foundations dug for the planned church came to rest on the earlier settlement layers of the Persian-Hellenistic site, just above bedrock. Parallels to this church plan have been excavated at Shavei Zion (on the coast north of Akko), Nessana in the northwest Negev, Kursi on the Sea of Galilee, and other sites in the region. There is little doubt that this newly founded Christian suburb, now known in Aramaic as *Migdal Malhaʾ* 'Saltworks Tower', and almost certainly called *Turris Salinarum* in Latin, was directly linked to the urban expansion of Caesarea Maritima.

The new name of the site referred to a prominent structure on the site, whose foundations were also laid in the Early Byzantine period. It was a tower, strategically placed directly below and east of the church foundations in Area A2. The Byzantine tower, which was completed before the church, overlooked the road and the bridge spanning the Crocodile River. It no doubt served as a checkpoint for the newly expanded northern territorial boundary of Caesarea. The new city limits were now marked by the settlement at Tel Tanninim, and the prominent tower gave its name to the new site.

It is likely that this particular spot overlooking the river mouth was also of wider regional significance. The Bordeaux Pilgrim (333 C.E.) notes that the frontiers (*fines*) of Syria and Phoenicia were situated just north of Caesarea, which I interpret to mean at the Crocodile River. This geographical tradition is actually already attested by Pliny (5.14.69) who says that [Caesarea] Prima Flavia is the frontier of Palestine, after which [northward]

comes Phoenicia (on the coast) and Samaria (inland). In another passage, Pliny (5.17.75) again places the beginning of Phoenicia at the *Crocodilon* River. A control tower at this location also makes good sense as a frontier toll post on the Roman road to and from Dor.

The archaeological evidence from all of the excavated areas on Tel Tanninim, both architectural and ceramic, revealed that the heyday of the settlement (Stratum V) was clearly achieved in the Late Byzantine centuries (ca. 450–640). During that period, the site boasted a complex of fish farms, primarily destined for the markets at Caesarea, at least two bath-houses, and was supplied with running water by the High-level aqueduct of Caesarea. The settlement of Late Byzantine times was dominated by a large basilica church, built atop the mound (fig. 167).

The primary economic base for the settlement was fish farming, most likely including a small scale production of sea purple dye, made from the abundant supply of the purple shellfish found along the coast during that era. The presence of fishponds (sea and freshwater) at Tel Tanninim also brings to mind the advice of Columella (*De Re Rustica* 8.16.6), written ca. 60 C.E., concerning the establishment of fish farming: "The first step in this direction is to examine the nature of the ground where you have decided to construct your fishponds (*piscinae*), for every kind of fish cannot be kept on every coast." Tel Tanninim was evidently chosen because it afforded the possibility to keep fish nourished by seawater, as well as freshwater species. Water for the freshwater fishponds was initially supplied by the High-level Caesarea aqueduct. When that source failed, or was disrupted, the fishponds relied on two coastal wells (Area B2). The excavated evidence clearly shows that at least one of these wells supplied a continuous water flow via a water-wheel. The latter is called in contemporary Talmudic sources (Ruth R. II, 19; Lev. R. 34) an *ʾantilayyaʾ*-wheel (also *ʾantelayyaʾ*), after the *ʾantal*-jars, which were lashed to its rim or suspended from a chain attached to the rim of the wheel.

During the sixth century, the region of Caesarea was devastated by both natural disasters and

Fig. 167. *Reconstruction of Tel Tanninim in the Byzantine period (drawing by J. Macsai).*

political turmoil. Several major earthquakes are attested (Russell 1985), notably in 525 (estimated intensity 6.7), and especially the massive tremor in July 551 (7.8). These events, coupled with the two major Samaritan revolts (529, 555–56), caused severe economic disruptions in the entire region (Mayerson 1988). Both the settlements and aqueducts were adversely affected, but the community at Tel Tanninim survived these upheavals. The major repairs undertaken on the water reservoir (*castellum*) in Area B are evidently connected with one or more of these disruptions.

In the seventh century, the settlement (Stratum IV) began to experience a rapid decline as a result of more dramatic political events. In 614, the Persian invasion of Palestine under the Sassanian King Chosroes II (591–628) resulted in the capture of Caesarea without a battle. For the next thirteen years, the Persians occupied that city, and, no doubt, the flourishing suburban settlement at Tel Tanninim. A generation later, the Arab conquest of Caesarea in 640/41 finally terminated the long

Byzantine era. The Arabs initiated a process which witnessed the gradual cultural transformation of the region into Muslim lands. In the period immediately following the Muslim conquest, the Christian settlement at Tel Tanninim, with its church and fishing industry, continued to exist, although on a reduced scale.

By the end of the seventh and the beginning of the eighth century, the large basilica church built in Area A had fallen into disuse. The fish farms at Tel Tanninim in Areas B and B2 were certainly abandoned. The numerous robbing trenches and destruction of the many mosaic floors, both within the church, as well as in the nearby structures atop the mound, indicate that in the Early Islamic II period, the site (Stratum III) was no longer occupied. Throughout the Abbasid–Fatimid centuries (750–1099), the sporadic ceramic finds and the continuing robbing trenches indicate that the previously flourishing settlement was being systematically quarried for building materials, presumably for use in nearby Islamic Caesarea.

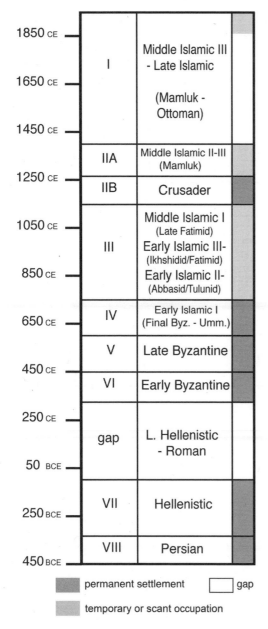

1850 CE	I	Middle Islamic III - Late Islamic (Mamluk - Ottoman)
1650 CE		
1450 CE		
1250 CE	IIA	Middle Islamic II-III (Mamluk)
	IIB	Crusader
1050 CE	III	Middle Islamic I (Late Fatimid) Early Islamic III- (Ikhshidid/Fatimid) Early Islamic II- (Abbasid/Tulunid)
850 CE		
650 CE	IV	Early Islamic I (Final Byz. - Umm.)
	V	Late Byzantine
450 CE	VI	Early Byzantine
250 CE	gap	L. Hellenistic - Roman
50 BCE		
250 BCE	VII	Hellenistic
450 BCE	VIII	Persian

■ permanent settlement   □ gap

■ temporary or scant occupation

Fig. 168. Stratigraphic sequence at Tel Tanninim, as revealed by the TAP excavations, 1996–99.

After the establishment of the Crusader Kingdom of Jerusalem (1099), Caesarea was fortified anew by the Crusaders and a small town rebuilt within its walls. The ruined ancient port was activated and used as a small naval base by the Crusader knights. Their primary harbors were situated at Athlit (*Castellum Peregrinorum* 'Pilgrims' Castle') and at Akko (St. Jean d'Acre). A coastal estate, named Turris Salinarum in Cru-

sader sources, was established at Tel Tanninim (Stratum IIB). Settlement was confined to Areas A and A2. The Crusaders made use of the ruined Late Byzantine structures, in Areas A and A2, and built directly over them. They thus built over the ruined church and incorporated an earlier barrel vault into one of their buildings. Nearby, in Area A2, a rather large rectangular tower was now built. Aerial photographs indicate a structure of about 17 × 10 m, but the probes along the edges did not reveal all its exterior walls. It is likely that these were robbed, particularly for use in the Ottoman bridge, as their lower courses were constructed of fine large ashlars. The northwest corner of the Crusader tower, with its spiral staircase, was found still well preserved at its lower courses. Floors were either of beaten earth or plastered.

Under the Crusaders, Turris Salinarum was within the jurisdiction of Caesarea, and in 1166 the estate was transferred to the Hospitallers. The location of the site, at the outflow of the Crocodile River, continued to benefit the coastal estate. The site was now a strategic location on the coastal road connecting Crusader Caesarea to their fortress at Merle (Dor). As noted in Chapter I above, sometimes after 1191 the Order of the Hospitaller Knights of St. Lazarus was granted two estates situated near Caesarea. One was named the Tower of Saint Lazarus, the other was the Church of Saint Lawrence. It is possible that the former of these may be the same as Turris Salinarum, having been renamed by the Order of St. Lazarus. The Order also acquired a small fleet in 1253 and thus had an increased interest in coastal estates.

The final occupation horizon of Tel Tanninim took place immediately after the destruction of the site in 1265. Following the conquest of Caesarea in that year by the forces of the Sultan Baybars, the Mamluk presence at the site utilized the Crusader buildings, particularly the tower (Stratum IIA). After the expulsion of the Crusaders from the Holy Land in 1291, the Mamluk rulers systematically destroyed all Crusader harbor installations (Ayalon 1965). The only military facilities on the coast they retained were designed to serve as lookouts for hostile naval activity. Tel Tanninim did not possess port facilities, nor was its tower sufficiently important, and thus it was abandoned, probably after the middle of the fourteenth century.

In the following centuries (1350–1700), the site was not settled. During the eighteenth–nineteenth centuries there is evidence for intermittent Ottoman presence (Stratum I). At the end of the nineteenth century, most activities at the site consisted of continued quarrying of stones from the ruined buildings, which were still visible on the mound. In 1898, a fine new stone bridge was built over the Crocodile River by the Ottoman authorities, in order to accommodate the impending coastal journey planned for the visit of the German Kaiser Wilhelm II. The stones for the bridge were taken from the building remains on the site. The lime kiln, constructed on the eastern slope of Tel Tanninim, most likely belongs to this phase, rather than the earlier Mamluk occupation. The kiln produced lime from broken marble pieces for the great volume of the mortar mix required in the bridge construction.

The stratigraphic sequence in Figure 168 summarizes the occupation history of the site as revealed by the TAP excavations of Tel Tanninim (1996–99). The evidence derived from the analysis of the stratigraphy and architecture in Areas A and A2 (Chapter II.2), the ceramics (Chapter III), as well as the small finds (Chapter IV), indicates discontinuous occupations of the site, beginning in the Iron IIC period and extending to the Ottoman era.

Appendix

Excavated Coins by Area and Date

Year	Area	Date	Basket	N	Locus	Date
96	A	7/01	1013	001	1000	
96	A	7/07	1028	006	1007	
96	A	7/17	1067	010	1011	
96	A	7/21	1084	011	1029	
96	A	7/22	1096	012	1034	
96	A	7/23	1099	013	1032	
96	A	7/23	1099	014	1032	
96	A	7/23	1099	016	1032	
96	A	7/23	1099	017	1032	
97	A	7/08	1069	046	1133	5th century C.E.
97	A	7/08	1071	047 (n=8)	1127	5th–6th century C.E.
97	A	7/09	1073	48 (6)	1127	5th–6th century C.E.
97	A	7/10	1076	049 (6)	1127	5th–6th century C.E.
97	A	7/14	1080	051 (13)	1137	5th–6th century C.E.
97	A	7/14	1081	052	1127	5th–6th century C.E.
97	A	7/14	1082	053	1139	383–395 C.E.
98	A	6/09	1032	055	1204	1st B.C.E.–1st C.E.
98	A	6/09	1034	056	1221	
98	A	6/16	1051	062	1200	Abbasid
98	A	6/18	1053	066	1220	1st–2nd century C.E.
98	A	6/18	1053	067	1220	
98	A	6/23	1072	059	1220	
98	A	6/23	1074	060	1239	
98	A	6/24	1076	058	1241	
99	A	8/11	1067	082	1323	Late 4th century C.E.
99	A	8/17	1084	089	1332	4th century C.E.
99	A	8/17	1084	090	1332	2nd century B.C.E.
99	A	8/17	1084	091	1332	
99	A	8/17	1084	092	1332	
99	A2	7/28	1016	083	1301	
99	A2	7/29	1020	075	1306	
99	A2	7/29	1023	076	1311	Mamluk?
99	A2	7/29	1023	077	1311	Mamluk?
99	A2	7/29	1023	078	1311	Mamluk?
99	A2	8/04	1041	079	1315	
99	A2	8/04	1041	080	1315	6th century C.E.

Year	Area	Date	Basket	N	Locus	Date
96	B	7/04	0021	002	2013	5th century C.E.
96	B	7/04	0024	003	2013	Mamluk?
96	B	7/07	0025	004	2013	19th century Ottoman
96	B	7/07	0029	005A	2000	565–578 C.E.
96	B	7/07	0029	005B	2000	518–527 C.E.
96	B	7/14	0059	007	2031	
96	B	7/14	0061	009	2031	351–361 C.E.
98	B2	5/27	2002	054	2201	5th century C.E.
98	B2	6/16	2055	065	2229	
98	B2	6/18	2058	068	2240	577/578 C.E.
98	B2	6/19	2060	057	2240	5th century C.E.
98	B2	6/19	2061	063	2229	5th century C.E.
98	B2	6/22	2066	064	2240	5th century C.E.
98	B2	6/22	2069	069	2249	5th century C.E.
98	B2	6/22	2069	070	2240	5th century C.E.
98	B2	6/22	2069	071	2240	6th century C.E.
98	B2	6/23	2075	061	2222	
98	B2	6/26	2093	072	2240	
99	B2	7/23	2006	084	2300	
99	B2	7/29	2025	073	2304	
99	B2	7/29	2027	074	2314	
99	B2	8/05	2046	081	2304	
99	B2	8/11	2057	085	2340	
99	B2	8/12	2063	086	2340	
99	B2	8/17	2072	087	2355	5th–6th century C.E.
99	B2	8/17	2072	088	2355	
97	D	6/10	4000	surface (5 coins)	4000	
97	D	6/12	4000	surface (2)	4000	570/571 C.E.
97	D	6/13	4000	surface	4000	
97	D	6/13	4001	surface	4010	
97	D	6/17	4004	surface	4000	
97	D	7/10	4152	050	Square D8 balk	

Note on Locus Numbers
and Object Categories

TAP locus numbers are coded by years and excavation areas, as follows:

Year	Areas A & A2	Area B	Area B2	Area D
1996	1000–1044	2000–2069	—	—
1997	1100–1141	2100–2124	—	4000–4021; 4050–4068
1998	1200–1244	2201-2274	2201-2274	—
1999	1300–1337	—	2300–2358	—

Object registration numbers are coded by a letter category, followed by three digits:

A = architectural object, or fragment
B = bone, ivory or horn object, or fragment
C = ceramic (pottery) object, or sherd
F = fabric, cloth or leather
G = geological or soil sample
H = human skeleton, or skeletal fragment
I = inscribed object
J = jewelry
L = lamp, whole or fragment

M = metal object or fragment
N = numismatic (coin)
P = plant, or botanical sample
R = restored ceramic object
S = stone object, or fragment
V = vitreous (glass) object, or fragment
W = wood object, fragment, or sample
Z = zoological (animal bone, or shell)

Volunteers of the
Tanninim Archaeological Project 1996–1999

Margaret L. Allen, Washington, DC
Frederic E. Andersen, Washington, DC
Kathleen P. Bailie, Toronto, Ontario
Joyce L. Bashew, Metuchen, NJ
Richard J. Bautch, Notre Dame, IN
Ari D. Bergen, West Orange, NJ
James S. Bucko, Alexandria, VA
L. Ann J. Cameron, Vancouver, British Columbia
John W. Carveth, Lakewood, CO
Per Skov Christensen, Kvaerndrup, Denmark
Gerda Cole, Scarborough, Ontario
Ruth A. Corson, New York, NY
Nancy L. Cusick, Chicago, IL

Abigail Daly, Glasgow, Scotland, UK
William M. Damon, Lithonia, GA
Kathleen Derzipilski, New York, NY
A. Asa Eger, Morristown, NJ
Karen & Jordan A. Egertson, Thousand Oaks, CA
Anne Fleming Eggleston, Baltimore, MD
Janet E. Gans Epner, Libertyville, IL
Gail L. Epstein, Newtown Square, PA
Jacqui Roitman-Estrin, Vancouver, British Colombia
Tina Faller, Bühl-Neusatz, Germany
Ingrid Fiallo, Little Falls, NJ
Marleny Franco, Little Falls, NJ
Stephan Frühling, Barsbüttel, Germany

Katherine C. Gay, Baltimore, MD

Benjamin D. Gordon, Sponsylvania, VA

Jacqueline S. Gregoor, Leiden, The Netherlands

Mary & Daniel Guillochon, Charleston, WV

Shankar Gupta, Roanoke, VA

Jennifer F. Harland, York, UK

Bruce Hartel, Littleton, CO

Gregory S. Hobson, Bedford, VA

Helene A. Holzman, Jersey City, NJ

Jessica M. Houser, Bristol, TN

Arnout Hyde, Jr., Charleston, WV

Sara F. Jacoby, Ridgewood, NJ

Isabelle A. Julian, Falmouth, Cornwall, UK

Dania M. Kafka, Livingston, NJ

Hadas Karkowski, Kibbutz Ma'agan Mikhael, Israel

Joyce S. Kline, Cambridge, MA

Brian L. Kolber, Manasquan, NJ

Benjamin T. Leech, Portland, OR

Gary Liebesman, Morristown, NJ

Kathrin Lingl, Bühl, Germany

Jane Y. Lucas, Woodmere, NY

Geraldine Macsai, Evanston, IL

Annette Malka, Kfar Yona, Israel

Joseph D. Manese, West New York, NJ

Maurice M. Margulies, Rockville, MD

Peter J. McHugh, Elizabeth, NJ

Bonnie & Garry F. Mohr, Monrovia, CA

Craig R. Morrison, Toronto, Ontario

Alexandra Moss, New York, NY

Marjoleine Motz, Amsterdam, The Netherlands

Sarah H. Parcak, New Haven, CT

Simon D. Penn, Ilford, Essex, UK

Lisa A. Piascik, Falls Church, VA

Christopher J. Pitera, Morristown, NJ

Naomi Pomerantz, Kfar Monash, Israel

Robert W. Rausch, Tiburon, CA

Jay P. Regosin, Jerusalem, Israel

Joan L. Reid, Mississauga, Ontario

Fiona A. Robertson, Sutherland, Scotland, UK

Shyrell K. Salminen, La Puente, Ca

Thomas M. Salminen, La Puente, CA

Cynthia Sanchez, Paterson, NJ

Henry D. Schilb, Bloomington, IN

Lisa F. Schneider, Brooklyn, NY

George H. Schwartz, Kew Gardens, NY

Harva L. Sheeler, Vienna, VA

Wendy Siegel, Vernon Hill, IL

Guy Singer, Bedford, NY

Susan L. Sjoblom, Hopkins, MN

Ruth Slater, New Rochelle, NY

David W. Spivey, Fayetteville, NC

Jennifer A. Stabler, Abell, MD

Suzanne S. Stichman, Washington, DC

Daniel E. Stieglitz, Forest Hills, NY

Lydia S. Szafranski, Williamsville, NY

Kenneth D. Taylor, Sierra Madre, CA

Bibliography

Abel, F.-M.

1914   Le littoral palestinien et ses ports. *RB* 11: 556–90.

Abraham, M.; Blanc, N.; and Yashouv, A.

1966   Oogenesis in Five Species of Grey Mullets (*Teleostei, Mugilidae*) from Natural and Landlocked Habitats. *Israel Journal of Zoology* 15: 155–72.

'Ad, U.

2000   Nahal Tanninim. *HA* 111: 39–41 (Hebrew).

Adams, R. Mc.

1970   Tell Abu-Sharifa: A Sassanian-Islamic Ceramic Sequence. *Ars Orientalis* 8: 87–119.

Adan-Bayewitz, D.

1986   The Pottery from the Late Byzantine Building (Stratum 4) and Its Implications. Pp. 90–129 in *Excavations at Caesarea Maritime, 1975, 1976, 1979, Final Report*, eds. L. I. Levine and E. Netzer. Qedem 21. Jerusalem: IA-HU.

Aharoni, Y.

1964   *Excavations at Ramat Rahel II: Seasons 1961 and 1962*. Rome: Centro di Studi Semitici.

Amiran, R.

1969   *Ancient Pottery of the Holy Land*. Ramat Gan: Masada.

Armstrong, P.

1991   A Group of Byzantine Bowls from Skopelos. *Oxford Journal of Archaeology* 10: 335–47.

Arnon, Y. D.

1999   The Islamic and Crusader Pottery of Area I, 1993–1994, A Stratigraphical/Typological Study. Pp. 225–52 in *Caesarea Papers 2*, eds. K. G. Holum, A. Raban and J. Patrich. *JRA* Supplementary Series 35. Providence, RI: JRA.

1999a   The Fatimid Hoard from Caesarea: A Preliminary Report. Pp. 232–48 in *L'Egypte fatimide: son art et son histoire*, ed. M. Barrucand. Paris: L'Université de Paris.

in press The Ceramic Oil Lamps of the Transitional and Medieval Period from Caesarea Maritima (640–1300): A Chronological and Typological Study. *BASOR*.

Artzy, M.

1980   The Utilitarian 'Persian' Storejar Handles. *BASOR* 238: 69–73.

Artzy, M., and Lyon, J.

2003   The Ceramics. Pp. 183–202 in E. Linder and Y. Kahanov, *The Ma'agan Mikhael Shipwreck* I, ed. E. Black. Jerusalem: IES and University of Haifa.

Atil, E.

1973   *Ceramics from the World of Islam*. Washington, DC: Smithsonian Institution.

Auth, S.

1976   *Ancient Glass at the Newark Museum*. Newark, NJ: Newark Museum.

Avi-Yonah, M.

1949   *Historical Geography of Palestine*. Jerusalem: Mossad Bialik (4th ed., 1984; Hebrew).

1959   Latin Inscriptions from Ma'agan Michael. *BIES* 24: 36–41 (Hebrew).

Avi-Yonah, M.; Cohen, R.; and Ovadiah, A.

1993   Early Churches. Pp. 305–14 in *The New Encyclopedia of Archaeological Excavations in the Holy Land, Vol. 1*, ed. E. Stern. Jerusalem: IES – Carta.

Aviam, M.

1999   Yodfat—Uncovering a Jewish City in the Galilee from the Second Temple Period and the Time of the Great Revolt. *Qadmoniot* 32: 92–101 (Hebrew).

2001   Shavei Ziyyon. *HA* 113: 9.

Aviam, M., and Getzov, N.

1998   A Byzantine Smithy at Horvat 'Ovesh, Upper Galilee. *'Atiqot* 34: 63–83 (Hebrew).

Aviam, M., and Stern, E. J.

1997   Burial Caves near Horvat Sugar. *'Atiqot* 33: 89–102 (Hebrew).

Avigad, N.

1976   *Beth She'arim III: Report on the Excavations during 1953–1958*. Jerusalem: IES.

Avissar, M.

1992   Medieval Pottery from Area A1 and G. Pp. 187–90 in *Excavations in the City of David 1978–1985, Vol. III*. Qedem 33. Jerusalem: IA-HU.

1996   The Medieval Pottery. Pp. 75–172 in *Yoqne'am I: The Late Periods*, eds. A. Ben-Tor, M. Avissar and Y. Portugali. Qedem Reports 3. Jerusalem: IA-HU.

Avizur, Sh.

1990   Ancient Water Power Structure in the Ma'agan Michael Nature Preserve. Pp. 327–33 in *HaSharon: Between Yarkon and Karmel*, eds. D. Grossman, A. Degani, and A. Shmueli. Tel Aviv: Eretz – Ministry of Defence (Hebrew).

Avshalom-Gorni, D.

1997   *Storage Jars from the Hellenistic, Roman and Byzantine Periods in Western Galilee—Chronological, Typological and Regional Aspects*. Ph.D. Dissertation, Bar-Ilan University, Ramat Gan (Hebrew).

Ayalon, D.

1965   The Mamluks and Sea Power. Pp. 116–28 in *Western Galilee and the Coast of Galilee*, The 19th Archaeological Convention, October 1963. Jerusalem: IES (Hebrew).

Ayalon, E.

1979   The Jar Installation of Khirbet Sabiya. *IEJ* 29: 175–81.

1994   A Roman-Byzantine Mausoleum at Khirbet Sabiya, Kefar Saba. *'Atiqot* 25: 27–39 (Hebrew).

1998   Ancient Kefar Saba in the Light of Recent Discoveries. *'Atiqot* 34: 8–9.

1999   Yavne-Yam: 'Persian-Wheel' (*Saqiya*) Well. *HA* 109: 72–73.

2000   Typology and Chronology of the Water-Wheel (*Saqiya*) Pottery Pots from Israel. *IEJ* 50: 216–26.

Bagatti, B.P.

1967   I vetri del museo francescano di Nazaret. *Liber Annuus* 17: 222–40.

1969   *Excavations in Nazareth I: From the Beginning till the XII Century*. Studium Biblicum Franciscanum 17. Jerusalem: Franciscan (Italian).

Bailey, D. M.

1988   *A Catalogue of Lamps in the British Museum III: Roman Imperial Lamps*. London: British Museum.

Bar-Nathan, R., and Adato, M.

1986   The Promontory Palace Pottery. Pp. 75–160 in *Excavations at Caesarea Maritima 1975, 1976, 1979: Final Report*, eds. L. I. Levine and E. Netzer. Qedem 21. Jerusalem: IA-HU.

Barag, D.

1967   Glass. Pp. 65–70 in M. W. Prausnitz, M. Avi-Yonah and D. Barag, *Excavations at Shavei-Zion: the Early Church*. Roma: Herder.

1970   *Glass Vessels of the Roman and Byzantine Periods in Palestine*. Ph.D. Dissertation, The Hebrew University, Jerusalem (Hebrew).

1972   Glass Vessels. Pp. 198–213 in *Beit She'arim, Report on the Excavations during 1953–1958, Vol. III: Catacombs 12–13*. Jerusalem: IES and IA-HU.

1974   A Tomb of the Byzantine Period near Netiv Ha-Lamed He. *'Atiqot* 7: 81–87.

1978   Glass Vessels. Pp. 10–33 in *Hanita, Tomb XV: A Tomb of the Third and Early Fourth Century C.E. 'Atiqot* 13.

1983   Glass Vessels. Pp. 37–38 in *The Excavations of Kursi-Gergesa*, ed. V. Tzaferis. *'Atiqot* 16.

Barag, D., and Porath, Y.

1970   The Synagogue at En-Gedi. *Qadmoniot* 3: 97–100 (Hebrew).

Baramki, D. C.

1944   The Pottery from Khirbet el Mefjer. *QDAP* 10: 65–107.

Barnett, R. D.

1940   Mersin, The Greek Pottery. *Liverpool Annals of Archaeology and Anthropology* 26: 110–32.

Bass, G. F.

1982   The Pottery. Pp. 155–88 in *Yassi Ada I: A Seventh Century Byzantine Shipwreck*, eds. G. F. Bass and F. H. van Doornick. College Station, TX: Texas A & M University.

1984   The Nature of the Serçe Limani Glass. *JGS* 26: 64–69.

Bauchot, M.-L., and Hureau, J.-C.

1986   Sparidae. Pp. 883–907 in *Fishes of the North-eastern Atlantic and the Mediterranean, Vol. 2*, eds. P. J. P. Whitehead, M.-L. Bauchot, J.-C. Hureau, J. Nielsen, and E. Tortonese. United Kingdom: UNESCO.

Baumgarten, Y. Y.

2000 Evidence of a Pottery Workshop of the Byzantine Period at the Foot of Tel Ashdod ('Ad Halom' Site). '*Atiqot* 39: 69–74 (Hebrew).

Ben-Arieh, R.

1997 The Roman, Byzantine and Umayyad Pottery. Pp. 347–81 in *The Roman Baths of Hammat Gader: Final Report*, ed. Y. Hirschfeld. Jerusalem: IES.

Ben-Tor, A.; Portugali, Y.; and Avissar, M.

1978 Excavations at Tel Yokne'am. *IEJ* 28: 74–76.

Ben-Tuvia, A.

1953 Mediterranean Fishes of Israel. *Bulletin of the Sea Fisheries Research Station, Haifa*, No. 8: 1–40.

1971 Revised list of the Mediterranean fishes of Israel. *Israel Journal of Zoology* 20: 1–39.

1986 Sciaenidae; Mugilidae. Pp. 865–74; 1197–204 in *Fishes of the North-eastern Atlantic and the Mediterranean, Vol.* 2, eds. P. J. P. Whitehead, M.-L. Bauchot, J.-C. Hureau, J. Nielsen and E. Tortonese. United Kingdom: UNESCO.

Bennett, W. J., Jr., and Blakely, J. A.

1989 *Tell el-Hesi Stratum V: The Persian Period.* Winona Lake, IN: Eisenbrauns.

Berlin, A. M.

1988 *The Hellenistic and Early Roman Common-Ware Pottery from Tel Anafa.* Ann Arbor, MI: University Microfilms.

1992 Hellenistic and Roman Pottery: Preliminary Report, 1990. Pp. 112–28 in *Caesarea Papers: Straton's Tower, Herod's Harbour, and Roman and Byzantine Caesarea*, ed. R. L.Vann. *JRA* Supplementary Series 5. Ann Arbor, MI: University of Michigan.

1997 The Plain Wares. Pp. 1–211 in *Tel Anafa II, i, The Hellenistic and Roman Pottery*, ed. S. C. Herbert. *JRA* Supplementary Series 10.2. Ann Arbor, MI: *JRA*.

Beyer, G.

1936 Das Gebiet der Kreuzfahrerherrschaft in Palästina. *ZDPV* 59: 1–91.

Bjelajak, L.

1989 Byzantine Amphorae in the Serbian Danubian Area in the 11th–12th Centuries. Pp. 110–18 in *Recherches sur la ceramique byzantine*, eds. V. Deroche et J. M. Spieser. *BCH* Supplement 18. Athens/Paris: Ecole française d'Athènes.

Blakely, J. A.

1993 Area CV (Vault Project). Pp. 61–68 (*Part I*); 93–101 (*Part II*) in *The Combined Caesarea Expeditions: Field Report of the 1992 Season*, eds. A. Raban, K. G. Holum, and J. A. Blakely, Haifa: University of Haifa and The Recanati Center for Maritime Studies.

Boas, A. J.

1994 The Import of Western Ceramics to the Latin Kingdom of Jerusalem. *IEJ* 44: 102–22.

1997 Late Ceramic Typology. Pp. 382–95 in *The Roman Baths of Hammat Gader: Final Report*, ed. Y. Hirschfeld. Jerusalem: IES..

2000 Medieval and Post Medieval Finds. Pp. 211–26 in *Ramat Hanadiv Excavations*, ed. Y. Hirschfeld. Jerusalem: IES.

Bonifay, M., and Piéri, D.

1994 Amphores du Ve au VIIe s. à Marseille: nouvelles données sur la typologie et le contenu. *JRA* 8: 94–120.

Briend, J., and Humbert, J.-B.

1980 *Tell Keisan (1971–1976): une cité phénicienne en Galilée.* Orbis Biblicus et Orientalis, Series Archaeologica I. Fribourg, Switzerland: Éditions universitaires.

Bruneau, Ph.

1965 Les lampes. Pp. 81–88 in *Exploration archeologique de Delos* (Fasc. XXVI). Paris: Editions Boscard.

Bruun, Chr.

1991 *The Water Supply of Ancient Rome, A Study of Roman Imperial Administration.* Helsinki: Finnish Society of Sciences and Letters.

Calderon, R.

1999 The Pottery. Pp. 135–48 in *The Early Byzantine Monastery at Khirbet ed-Deir in the Judean Desert: The Excavations in 1981–1987*, ed. Y. Hirschfeld. Qedem 38. Jerusalem: IA-HU.

2000 Roman and Byzantine Pottery. Pp. 91–162 in *Ramat Hanadiv Excavations: Final Report of the 1984–1998 Seasons*, ed. Y. Hirschfeld. Jerusalem: IES.

Carboni, S.

2001 *Glass from Islamic Lands: The al-Sabah Collection, Kuwait National Museum.* New York: Thames and Hudson.

Carboni, S., and Whitehouse, D.
2001 *Glass of the Sultans*. New York: Metropolitan Museum of Art.

Catling. H. W.
1972 An Early Byzantine Pottery Factory at Dhiorios in Cyprus. *Levant* 4: 1–82.

Chao, L. N.
1986 A synopsis on zoogeography of the Sciaenidae. Pp. 570–89 in *Indo-Pacific fish biology: Proceedings of the Second International Conference of Indo-Pacific Fishes,* eds. T. Uyeno, R. Arai, T. Taniuchi, and K. Matsuura. Tokyo: Ichthyological Society of Japan.

Christou, D.
1996 *Kourion: Its Monuments and Local Museum.* Nicosia: Filokipros.

Coen Uzzielli, T.
1997 The Oil Lamps. Pp. 319–46 in *The Roman Baths of Hamat Gader: Final Report*, ed. Y. Hirschfeld. Jerusalem: IES.

Cohen, E.
1997 Roman, Byzantine and Umayyad Glass. Pp. 396–431 in *The Roman Baths of Hamat Gader: Final Report*, ed. Y. Hirschfeld. Jerusalem: IES.
2000 Roman and Byzantine Glass. Pp. 166–76 in *Ramat Hanadiv Excavations: Final Report of the 1984–1998 Seasons*, ed. Y. Hirschfeld. Jerusalem: IES.

Colt, H. D.
1962 *Excavations at Nessana, 1*. London: British School of Archaeology in Jerusalem.

Conder, C. R., and Kitchener, H. H.
1882 *The Survey of Western Palestine*, Vol. II: *Samaria*. London: PEF.

Cook, Th.
1900 *Cook's Tourist Handbook for Palestine and Syria*. London: Thomas Cook & Son.

Crowfoot, G. M.
1957 Glass. Pp. 403–38 in J. W. Crowfoot, G. M. Crowfoot, K. M. Kenyon, *Samaria-Sebaste III: The Objects from Samaria*. London: PEF.

Crowfoot, G. M., and Harden, D. B.
1931 Early Byzantine and Later Glass Lamps. *JEA* 17: 196–208.

Crowfoot, J. W.
1941 *Early Churches in Palestine*. London: Oxford University.

Crowfoot, J. W.; Crowfoot, G. M.; and Kenyon, K. M.
1957 *Samaria-Sebaste III: The Objects from Samaria*. London: PEF.

D'Angelo, F.
1995 La Protomaiolica di Sicilia e la ricerca delle sue origini. *Archeologia Medievale* 22: 455–60.

Dayagi-Mendels, M.
2002 The Akhziv Cemeteries: The Ben-Dor Excavations 1941–1944. *IAA Reports* 15. Jerusalem: IAA.

de Vaux, R., and Steve, R. M.
1950 *Fouilles à Qaryat el Enab, Abu Gosh, Palestine*. Paris: Gabalda.

Delougaz, P.
1960 The Objects. Pp. 30–52 in P. Delougaz and R. H. Haines, *A Byzantine Church at Khirbat al-Karak*. The University of Chicago Oriental Institute Publication 85. Chicago: University of Chicago.

Delougaz, P., and Haines, R. C.
1960 *A Byzantine Church at Khirbet al-Karak*. The University of Chicago Oriental Institute Publication 85. Chicago: University of Chicago.

de Sandoli, S.
1980 Sabino de Sandoli, *Itinera Hierosolymitana Crucesignatorum (saec. XII–XIII), Vol. II.* Jerusalem: Franciscan Printing Press.

Desse, J., and Desse-Berset, N.
1996 Osteometrie et Archeozoologie de la Daurade Royale (*Sparus aurata* Linne, 1758). *Fiches d'Osteologie Animale pour l'Archeologie*. Juan-les-Pins, France: Centre de Recherches Archeologiques du CNRS, APDCA.

Desse, J.; Desse-Berset, N.; and Rocheteau, M.
1987 Contribution a l'Osteometrie du Mulet, *Liza (Liza) ramada* Risso, 1826 (= *Mugil capito* Cuvier, 1829). *Fiches d'Osteologie Animale pour l'Archeologie*. Juan-les-Pins, France: Centre de Recherches Archeologiques du CNRS, APDCA.

Donceel-Voûte, P.
1988 *Les pavements des églises byzantines de Syrie et du Liban: décor, archéologie, et liturgie*. Louvain-la-Neuve: College Erasme.

Dothan, M.

1971 *Ashdod II–III: The Second and Third Seasons of Excavations 1963, 1965, Soundings in 1967.* 'Atiqot 9–10.

1976 Akko: Interim Excavation Report, First Season, 1973–74. *BASOR* 224: 1–48.

Dussart, O.

1998 *Le Verre en Jordanie et en Syrie de Sud.* Bibliothèque archéologique et historique 152. Beyrouth: Institut français d'archéologie du Proche-Orient.

Duval, N., and Caillet, J. P.

1982 Khan Khaldé (ou Khaldé III). Les fouilles de Roger Saidah dans les églises, mises en œuvre d'après les documents de l'auteur. Pp. 320–46 in *Archéologie au Levant, recueil à la mémoire de Roger Saidah.* Lyon: Maison de l'Orient.

Edelstein, G., and Avissar, M.

1997 A Sounding in Old Acre. *'Atiqot* 31: 129–36.

Eisenberg, E., and Ovadiah, A.

1998 A Byzantine Monastery at Mevo-Modi'in. *'Atiqot* 36: 1–19 (Hebrew).

Eger, A. A.

1998 *The Piscinae at Tel Tanninim: A Comparative Study of Ancient and Modern Aquaculture in Israel.* Undergraduate Honors Thesis, Rutgers University, New Brunswick, NJ.

Egloff, M.

1977 *Kellia: la poterie copte. Quatre siècles d'artisanat et d'échanges en Basse-Egypte,* 2 Vols. Geneva: Georg.

Eitan, A.

1969 Excavations at the Foot of Tel Rosh Ha'ayin. *'Atiqot* 5: 49–68 (Hebrew).

Elgavish, J.

1968 *Archaeological Excavations at Shikmona, Field Report No. 1: The Levels of the Persian Period, Seasons 1963–1965.* Haifa: City Museum of Ancient Art (Hebrew).

1974 *Archaeological Excavations at Shikmona, Report No. 2: The Level of the Hellenistic Period—Stratum H, Seasons 1963–1970.* Haifa: City Museum of Ancient Art (Hebrew).

Empereur, J.-Y., and Picon, M.

1989 Les régions de production d'amphores impériales en méditerranée orientale. Pp. 223–48 in *Amphores romaines et histoire économique: dix ans de recherche.* Paris and Rome: École française de Rome.

Eran, A.

1982 The Weights. Pp. 91–100 in *Ashdod IV: Excavations of Area M,* eds. M. Dothan and Y. Porath. *'Atiqot* 15.

Erdmann, V. E.

1977 Die Glasfunde von Mezad Tamar (Kasr Gehainije) in Israel. *Saalburg-Jahrbuch* 34: 98–146.

Everman, D.

1992 Survey of the Coastal Area North of Caesarea and of the Aqueducts: Preliminary Report. Pp. 181–93 in *Caesarea Papers: Straton's Tower, Herod's Harbour, and Roman and Byzantine Caesarea,* ed. R. L. Vann. *JRA* Supplementary Series 5. Ann Arbor, MI: University of Michigan.

1997 *The Water Supply System of Caesarea Maritima: A Historical Study.* Ph.D. Dissertation, University of Maryland, College Park, MD.

Fehervari, G.

1973 *The Islamic Pottery - Barlow Collection.* London: Faber & Faber.

Feigl, E.

n.d. *Momento - Der militärische und hospitalische Orden des heiligen Lazarus von Jerusalem.* Vienna: Druck.

Fischer, M.

1989 Hellenistic Pottery (Strata V–III). Pp. 177–87 in *Excavations at Tel Michal, Israel,* eds. Z. Herzog, G. Rapp, and O. Negbi. Publication of the Tel Aviv University Institute of Archaeology No. 8. Minneapolis: University of Minnesota and Tel Aviv University.

Foy, D.

1997–98 Les verres du contexte 24 du chantier 002 à Beyrouth. *Bulletin de l'Association française pour l'archéologie du verre* 1997–98: 8–11.

1999 Lampes de verre fatimides à Fostat; le mobilier des fouilles d'Istabl'Antar. Pp. 179–96 in *L'Egypte fatimide: son art et son histoire,* ed. M. Barrucand. Paris: L'Université de Paris – Sorbonne.

Fradkin, A., and Lernau, O.

In press The Fishing Economy at Caesarea Maritima, Israel. In *Caesarea Papers 3,* eds. K. G. Holum and A. Raban. *JRA* Supplementary Series.

Frankel, P. L.
1986   *Water Lifting Devices*. Rome: FAO.

Frierman, J. D.
1975   *Medieval Ceramics: VI–XIII Centuries*. Los Angeles: University of California.

Galili, E., and Sharvit, Y.
1999   Jisr Az-Zarqa, Underwater Survey. *HA* 109: 57–58.

Galling, K.
1938   Die syrisch-palästinische Küste nach der Beschreibung bei Pseudo-Scylax. *ZDPV* 61: 66–96.

Gichon, M.
1993   Die Keramik des Kastells. Pp. 129–256 in *En Boqeq: Ausgrabungen in einer Oase am Toten Meer, Band I*, ed. M. Gichon. Mainz: von Zabern.

Gilboa, A.
1995   The Typology and Chronology of Iron Age Assemblages. Pp. 1–16 in *Excavations at Dor, Final Report, Volume IB, Areas A and C: The Finds*, eds. E. Stern, J. Berg, A. Gilboa, B. Guz-Zilberstein, A. Raban, R. Rosenthal-Heginbottom, and I. Sharon. Qedem Reports 2. Jerusalem: IA-HU.
2001   *Southern Phoenicia during Iron Age I–IIA in the Light of the Tel Dor Excavations: The Evidence of the Pottery*. Ph.D. Dissertation, The Hebrew University, Jerusalem.

Gjerstad, E.
1960   Pottery Types: Cypro-Geometric to Cypro-Classical. *Opuscula Atheniensia* 3: 105–22.

Golani, D.
1996   The Marine Ichthyofauna of the Eastern Levant: History, Inventory and Characterization. *Israel Journal of Zoology* 42: 15–55.

Golani, D., and Darom, D.
1997   *Handbook of the Fishes of Israel*. Jerusalem: Keter.

Goren, M.
1974   The Freshwater Fishes of Israel. *Israel Journal of Zoology* 23: 67–118.

Gorin-Rosen, Y.
1997   A Burial Cave at Kafr Yasif. *ʿAtiqot* 33: 71–77 (Hebrew).
1999   Glass Vessels from Recent Excavations in Ramla: A Preliminary Representation. Pp. 10–15 in *Ramla: The Development of a Town from the Early*

Islamic to Ottoman Periods, ed. Sh. Bison and F. Vitto. Jerusalem: IAA.

Gorin-Rosen, Y., and Katsnelson, N.
1999   The Glass Vessels. P. 38 in *Horvat Castra: 1993–1997*, eds. Z. Yeivin and G. Finkelstein. *HA* 109.

Gorzalczani, A.
2000   Hellenistic Period Remains at Ramat Aviv. *ʿAtiqot* 38: 25–32 (Hebrew).

Greenhut, Z.
1998   Horvat Hermeshit (1988–1990). *ʿAtiqot* 34: 121–72 (Hebrew).

Grose, D. F.
1979   The Syro-Palestinian Glass Industry in the Later Hellenistic Period. *Muse* 13: 54–67.
1982   Early Blown Glass: The Western Evidence. *JGS* 21: 9–29.

Guerin, V.
1875   *Description géographique, historique et archéologique de la Palestine. Seconde Partie - Samarie* (Tome II). Paris: L'Imprimerie Nationale.

Guz-Zilberstein, B.
1995   The Typology of the Hellenistic Coarse Ware and Selected Loci of the Hellenistic and Roman Periods. Pp. 289–433 in *Excavations at Dor, Final Report, Volume IB, Areas A and C: The Finds*, eds. E. Stern, J. Berg, A. Gilboa, B. Guz-Zilberstein, A. Raban, R. Rosenthal-Heginbottom, and I. Sharon. Qedem Reports 2. Jerusalem: IA-HU.

Hadad, S.
1997   Oil Lamps from the 3rd–8th centuries CE at Beth Shean (Skythopolis). *Dumbarton Oaks Papers* 51: 147–88.
1998   *Glass Vessels from the Umayyad through Mamluk Periods at Bet Shean (7th–14th Centuries C.E.).* Ph.D. Dissertation, The Hebrew University, Jerusalem (Hebrew).
1998a   Glass Lamps from the Byzantine through Mamluk Periods at Bet Sheʾan, Israel. *JGS* 40: 63-76.

Hakimian, S., and Salamé-Sarkis, H.
1988   Céramique mediévale trouvée dans une citerne à Tell ʿArqa. *Syria* 65: 1–61.

Harden, D. B.
1936   *Roman Glass from Karanis: found by the University of Michigan Archaeological Expedition in*

Egypt, 1924–1929. Ann Arbor, MI: University of Michigan.

1949 Tomb Groups of Glass of Roman Date from Syria and Palestine. *Iraq* 11: 151–59.

1955 Glass. Pp. 65–70 in *Excavations at Soba.* Occasional Papers No. 3. Khartoum: Sudan Antiquities Service.

1962 Glass. Pp. 76–91 in *Excavations at Nessana, Vol. I,* ed. H. D. Colt. London: British School of Archaeology in Jerusalem.

1964 Some Tomb Groups of Late Roman Date in the Amman Museum. *Annales du Congrès* 3: 48–55.

Hayes, J. W.

1972 *Late Roman Pottery.* London: The British School at Rome.

1980 *Ancient Lamps in the Royal Ontario Museum I: Greek and Roman Clay Lamps.* Toronto: Royal Ontario Museum.

1980a *A Supplement to Late Roman Pottery.* London: The British School at Rome.

1985 Hellenistic to Byzantine Fine Wares and Derivatives in the Jerusalem Corpus. Pp. 181–94 in *Excavations in Jerusalem 1961–1967, Vol. I,* ed. A. D. Tushingham. Toronto: Royal Ontario Museum.

1992 *Excavations at Saraçhane in Istanbul, II: The Pottery.* Princeton: Princeton University.

Hennessy, J. B.

1970 Excavations at Samaria-Sebaste, 1968. *Levant* 2: 1–21.

Herzog, Z.; Rapp, G.; and Negbi, O.; eds.

1989 *Excavations at Tel Michal, Israel.* Publication of the Tel Aviv University Institute of Archaeology No. 8. Minneapolis: University of Minnesota and Tel Aviv University.

Higginbotham, J.

1997 *Piscinae: Artificial Fishponds in Roman Italy.* Chapel Hill, NC: University of North Carolina.

Hill, D.

1997 *A History of Engineering in Classical and Medieval Times.* London: Routledge.

Hirschfeld, Y.

1990 List of the Byzantine Monasteries in the Judean Desert. Pp. 1–89 in *Christian Archaeology in the Holy Land: New Discoveries.* Essays in Honor of V. C. Corbo, OFM. Jerusalem: Franciscan.

Hizmi, H.

1997 Two Burial Caves in Rafidiya (Shechem). *'Atiqot* 32: 125–30 (Hebrew).

Holum, K. G.

1998 Combined Caesarea Expeditions: 1998 Summer Season. http://digcaesarea.org/Documents/WWWrept.98.html

Horowitz, S.

1994 Archaeological Survey of Jisr az-Zarqa Marina: Preliminary Report. Presented to the Israel Lands Administration (unpublished; Hebrew).

Horton, F. L., Jr.

1996 A Sixth-Century Bath in Caesarea's Suburbs and the Transformation of Bathing Culture in Late Antiquity. Pp. 171–89 in *Caesarea Maritima: A Retrospective after Two Millennia,* eds. A. Raban and K. G. Holum. Leiden: Brill.

Howland, R. H.

1958 *Greek Lamps and their Survivals: The Athenian Agora,* Vol. IV. Princeton: Princeton University.

Isings, C.

1957 *Roman Glass from Dated Finds.* Groningen: Wolters.

Israeli, Y.

2000 *Ancient Glass at the Israel Museum: the Dubkin Collection and Others Presents.* Jerusalem: Israel Museum.

Jenkins, M.

1986 *Islamic Glass: A Brief History.* New York: Bulletin of the Metropolitan Museum of Art 44.2: 1, 10–56.

Johns, C. N.

1932 Excavations at 'Athlit (1930–31): The South-Eastern Cemetery. *QDAP* 2: 41–104.

1933 Medieval Slip-Ware from Pilgrims' Castle, 'Athlit (1930–31). *QDAP* 3: 137–44; Excavations at 'Athlit (1930–31). *QDAP* 3: 145–64.

1934 Excavations at Pilgrims' Castle, 'Athlit (1931–32). *QDAP* 4: 122–37.

1935 Excavations at Pilgrims' Castle, 'Athlit (1932–33). *QDAP* 5: 31–60.

1937 Excavations at Pilgrims' Castle, 'Athlit (1933). *QDAP* 6: 121–52.

Johnson, B. L.
1988　The Pottery. Pp. 137–226 in *Excavations at Jalame: Site of a Glass Factory in Late Roman Palestine*, ed. G. D. Weinberg. Columbia, MO: University of Missouri.

Johnson, B. L., and Stager, L. E.
1995　Ashkelon: Wine Emporium of the Holy Land. Pp. 95–109 in *Recent Excavations in Israel*, ed. S. Gitin. Boston: American Institute of Archaeology.

Kahanov, Y.
1998　*The 'Sewing System' in the Hull Construction of the Ma'agan Mikhael Shipwreck: A Comparative Study with Mediterranean Parallels.* Ph. D. dissertation, University of Haifa (Hebrew).

Katsnelson, N.
1999　Glass Vessels from the Painted Tomb at Midgal Ashqelon. *Atiqot* 37: 67–82.

Kawatoko, M.
1987　Oil Lamps from al-Fustat. *Orient* 23: 25–53.

Keay, S.
1984　*Late Roman Amphorae in the Western Mediterranean: A Typology and Economic Study, The Catalan Evidence, Vol. 2.* BAR International Series 196. Oxford: BAR.

Kedar, B. Z.
1991　*Looking Twice at the Land of Israel.* Aerial Photographs of 1917–18 and 1987–91. Tel Aviv: Ministry of Defence – Yad Izhak Ben-Zvi (Hebrew).

Kedar, B. Z., and Pringle, D.
1985　La Feve: A Crusader Castle in the Jezreel Valley. *IEJ* 35: 164–79.

Kehrberg, I.
1986　Summary Report on Glass. Pp. 375–84 in *Jerash Archaeological Project 1981–1983, I*, ed. F. Zayadine. Amman: Department of Antiquities of Jordan.

Kelly, Th.
1987　Herodotus and the Chronology of the Kings of Sidon. *BASOR* 268: 39–56.

Kennedy, C. A.
1963　The Development of the Lamp in Palestine. *Berytus* 14: 67–115.

Kennedy, H.
1994　*Crusader Castles.* Cambridge: Cambridge University.

Kervarn, M.
1984　Les niveaux islamiques du secteur oriental du tépé de l'Apadana, III: les objects en verre, en pierre et en métal. Pp. 211–35 in *Cahiers de la délégation archéologique française en Iran* 14. Paris: Guethner.

Kindler, A.
1958　A Seventh Century Lamp with Coin Decoration. *IEJ* 8: 106–09.

Kingsley, S. A.
1994–1995 Bag-Shaped Amphorae and Byzantine Trade: Expanding Horizons. *Bulletin of the Anglo-Israel Archaeological Society* 14: 39–56.
1999　The Sumaqa Pottery Assemblage: Classification and Quantification. Pp. 263–329 in *A Roman and Byzantine Jewish Village on Mount Carmel, Israel*, ed. S. Dar. BAR International Series 815. Oxford: BAR.

Klein, Sh.
1923　The Sea-Coast Road. Pp. 1–13 in *Scripta Universitatis I*. Jerusalem: Hebrew University (Hebrew).

Kletter, R., and Rapuano, Y.
1998　A Roman Well at Khirbet Ibreiktas. *Atiqot* 35: 43–57.

Kogan-Zehavi, E.
1999　A Painted Tomb of the Roman Period at Migdal Ashqelon. *Atiqot* 37: 189–209 (Hebrew).

Kröger, J.
1984　*Glas: Islamische Kunst. Loseblattkatalog unpublizierter Werke aus deutschen Museen,I.* Mainz: von Zabern.
1995　*Nishapur: Glass of the Early Islamic Period.* New York: Metropolitan Museum of Art.

Kuhnen, H.-P.
1987　*Nordwest-Palästina in hellenistisch-römischer Zeit: Bauten und Gräber im Karmelgebiet.* Weinheim: VCH.

Lamm, C. J.
1935　*Glass from Iran in the National Museum, Stockholm.* Stockholm: Fritze.

Lamon, R. S., and Shipton, G. M.
1939　*Megiddo I, Seasons of 1925–1934, Strata I–V.* Chicago: The Oriental Institute.

Landels, J. G.

1980   *Engineering in the Ancient World*. Berkeley: University of California.

Landgraf, J.

1980   Keisan's Byzantine Pottery. Pp. 51–100 in *Tell Keisan (1971–1976): une cité phénicienne en Galilée*, eds. J. Briend and J.-B. Humbert. Orbis Biblicus et Orientalis, Series Archaeologica I. Fribourg, Switzerland: Éditions universitaires.

Lane, A.

1937   Medieval Finds at Al Mina in North Syria. *Archaeologia* 87: 19–78.

Lehman, G.

2002   The Iron Age Pottery. Pp. 178–222 in A. Kempinski, *Tel Kabri: The 1986–1993 Excavations*, eds. N. Scheftelowitz and R. Oren. Tel Aviv: Tel Aviv University Institute of Archaeology.

Lenzen, C. J.

1983   *The Byzantine/Islamic Occupation at Caesarea Maritime as Evidenced through the Pottery*, 2 Parts. Ph.D. Dissertation, Drew University, Madison, NJ.

Lernau, H.

1986-87 Subfossil Remains of Nile Perch (*Lates* cf. *niloticus*): First Evidence from Ancient Israel. *Israel Journal of Zoology* 34: 225–36.

Lernau, H., and Lernau, O.

1992   Fish Remains. Pp. 131–48 in *Excavations at the City of David 1978–1985, Final Report, Vol. 3*, eds. A. De Groot and D. T. Ariel. Qedem 33. Jerusalem: IA-HU.

Lernau, O.

2000   Fish Bones. Pp. 463–77 in *Megiddo III: The 1992–1996 Seasons*, eds. I. Finkelstein, D. Ussishkin, and B. Halpern. Tel Aviv: Tel Aviv University Institute of Archaeology.

Linder, E.

1991   The Ma'agan Mikhael Shipwreck Excavations. *Qadmoniot* 24: 39–46 (Hebrew).

Linder, E., and Rosloff, J.

1995   The Ma'agan Michael Shipwreck. Pp. 275–281 in *Tropis* III: 3rd International Symposium on Ship Construction in Antiquity, Athens, 1989, ed. H. Tzalas. Athens: Hellenic Institute for the Preservation of Nautical Tradition.

Lledo, B.

1997   Mold Siblings in the 11th Century Cullet from Serçe Limani. *JGS* 39: 43–56.

Lofferda, S.

1974   *Cafarnao II: La Ceramica*. Studium Biblicum Franciscanum 19. Jerusalem: Franciscan.

Loud, G.

1948   *Megiddo II, Seasons of 1935–1939*. Chicago: The Oriental Institute.

Lyons, U.; Lyons, M. C.; and Riley-Smith, J. S. C.

1971   *Ayyubids, Mamlukes and Crusaders*, Vol. 2. Cambridge: Heffer.

Lythgoe, J., and Lythgoe, G.

1992   *Fishes of the Sea: The North Atlantic and Mediterranean*. Cambridge, MA: MIT.

Macdonnell, A. M.

1988   The Terracotta Lamps. Pp. 116–36 in *Excavations at Jalame, Site of a Glass Factory in Late Roman Palestine*, ed. G. D. Weinberg. Columbia, MO: University of Michigan.

Magness, J.

1992   Late Roman and Byzantine Pottery: Preliminary Report, 1992. Pp. 129–53 in *Caesarea Papers: Straton's Tower, Herod's Harbour and Roman and Byzantine Caesarea*, ed. R. L. Vann. *JRA* Supplementary Series 5. Ann Arbor, MI: University of Michigan.

1992a   Various Reports: The Late Roman and Byzantine Pottery from Areas H and K. Pp. 149–68 in *Excavations at the City of David 1978–1985 Directed by Y. Shiloh, Vol. III*, ed. A. De Groot and D. T. Ariel. Qedem 33. Jerusalem: IA-HU.

1993   *Jerusalem Ceramic Chronology Circa 200–800 CE*. Sheffield: Sheffield Academic.

1995   The Pottery from Area V/4 at Caesarea. *Annual of ASOR* 52: 133–45.

Majcherek, G.

1993   Roman Amphorae from Marina el-Alamein. *Mitteilungen des Deutschen Archäologischen Instituts Abteilung Kairo* 49: 213–20.

1995   Gazan Amphorae: Typology Reconsidered. Pp. 163–78 in *Hellenistic and Roman Pottery in the Eastern Mediterranean: Advances in Scientific Studies, Acts of the II Nieborow Pottery Workshop*. Warsaw: von Falck.

Marchese, R.

1989   Aegean and Cypriot Imports in the Persian Period. Pp. 145–80 in *Excavations at Tel Michal, Israel,* eds. Z. Herzog and G. Rapp. Tel Aviv: Tel Aviv University Institute of Archaeology.

1995   Athenian Imports in the Persian Period. Pp. 127–81 in *Excavations at Dor, Final Report, Volume IB, Areas A and C: The Finds*, eds. E. Stern, J. Berg, A. Gilboa, B. Guz-Zilberstein, A. Raban, R. Rosenthal-Heginbottom, I. Sharon. Qedem Reports 2. Jerusalem: IA-HU.

Mayerson, Ph.

1986   Choricius of Gaza on the Water Supply System of Caesarea. *IEJ* 36: 269–72.

1988   Justinian's Novel 103 and the Reorganization of Palestine. *BASOR* 269: 65–71.

Mazar, A.

1985   *Excavations at Tell Qasile, Part Two: The Philistine Sanctuary.* Qedem 20. Jerusalem: IES.

McNicoll, A. W.; Smith, R. H.; and Hennessy, J. B.

1982   *Pella in Jordan 1: An Interim Report on the Joint University of Sydney and College of Wooster Excavations at Pella, 1979–1981.* Canberra: Australian National University.

Megaw, A. H. S.

1972   Supplementary Excavations on Castle Site at Paphos, Cyprus 1970–71. *Dumbarton Oaks Papers* 26: 323–46.

Melkawi, A.; ʿAmr, K.; and Whitcomb, D. S.

1994   The Excavations of Two Seventh Century Pottery Kilns at ʿAqaba. *Annual of the Department of Antiquities of Jordan* 38: 447–68.

Meyer, C.

1988   Glass from the North Theatre Byzantine Church, and Soundings at Jerash, Jordan, 1982–1983. Pp. 175–222 in *Preliminary Reports of ASOR-Sponsored Excavations, 1982–1985*, ed. W. E. Rast. *BASOR* Supplement 25. Baltimore: Johns Hopkins University.

Meyers, E. M.; Kraabel, A. T.; and Strange, J. F.

1976   *Ancient Synagogue Excavations at Khirbet Shema, Upper Galilee, Israel.* Annual of *ASOR* 42. Chapel Hill, NC: Duke University.

Mook, M. S., and Coulson, W. D. E.

1995   East Greek and Other Imported Pottery. Pp. 93–125 in *Excavations at Dor, Final Report, Volume IB, Areas A and C: The Finds*, eds. E. Stern, J. Berg, A. Gilboa, B. Guz-Zilberstein, A. Raban, R. Rosenthal-Heginbottom, I. Sharon. Qedem Reports 2. Jerusalem: IA-HU.

Morales, A., and Rosenlund, K.

1979   *Fish Bone Measurements. An Attempt to Standardize the Measuring of Fish Bones from Archaeological Sites.* Copenhagen: Steenstrupia.

Morgan, P., and Leatherby, J.

1987   Excavated Ceramics from Sirjan. Pp. 23–172 in *Syria and Iran: Three Studies in Medieval Ceramics*, eds. J. Allen and C. Roberts. Oxford: Oxford University.

Mülinen, E. Graf von

1907–08 Beiträge zur Kenntnis des Karmels (2 Teile). *ZDPV* 30: 117–207; 31: 1–258.

Müller, C., ed.

1855   *Geographi Graeci Minores, I.* Paris (reprinted: Hildesheim: G. Olms, 1965).

Nahshoni, P.

1999   A Byzantine Site in the Migdal Neighborhood, Ashqelon. *ʿAtiqot* 39: 99–111 (Hebrew).

Negev, A.

1986   *The Late Hellenistic and Early Roman Pottery of Nabataean Oboda: Final Report.* Qedem 22. Jerusalem: IA-HU.

Northedge, A.

1992   *Studies on Roman and Islamic Amman, Vol. I: History, Site and Architecture.* Oxford: Oxford University.

O'Hea, M.

1998   Glass Vessels and Plaster Disks, in *The Wadi Faynan Project: The South Cemetery Excavation, Jordan 1996, a Preliminary Report*, by G. Findlater, M. El-Najjar, A.-H. Al-Shiyab, M. O'Hea and E. Easthaugh. *Levant* 30: 69–83.

Olami, Y., and Peleg, Y.

1977   The Water Supply System of Caesarea Maritima. *IEJ* 27: 127–37.

Oleson, J. P.

1984   *Greek and Roman Water-Lifting Devices: The History of a Technology.* Toronto: University of Toronto.

1985   A Roman Water Mill on the Crocodilion River near Caesarea. *ZDPV* 100: 137–52.

Oleson, J. P.; Fitzgerald, M. A.; Sherwood, A. N.; and Sidebotham, S. E.

1994　*The Harbours of Caesarea Maritima, Vol. II: The Finds and the Ship*. BAR International Series 594. Oxford: BAR.

Onn, A.

1999　Tombs of the Persian Period near Tell er-Ras. *'Atiqot* 37: 1–78 (Hebrew).

Oren, E. D.

1993　A Christian Settlement at Ostrakine in North Sinai. Pp. 305–14 in *Ancient Churches Revealed*, ed. Y. Tsafrir. Jerusalem: IES.

Oren, D. E., and Rappaport, U.

1984　The Necropolis of Maresha-Beth Govrin. *IEJ* 34: 114–53.

Ovadiah, A.

1970　Corpus of the Byzantine Churches in the Holy Land. *Theophaneia* 22.

Papanikola-Bakirtzis, D.

1989　Medieval Pottery from Enkomi: Famagusta. Pp. 233–46 in *Recherches sur la céramique byzantine*, eds. V. Deroche et J. M. Spieser. *BCH* Supplement 18. Athens/Paris: Ecole française d'Athènes.

1999　*Byzantine Glazed Ceramics: the Art of Sgraffito*. Athens: Archaeological Receipts Fund.

Patrich, J.

1988　The Glass Vessels. Pp. 134–41 in *Excavations at Rehovot-in-the-Negev, Vol. I: The Northern Church*, ed. Y. Tsafrir. Qedem 25. Jerusalem: IA-HU.

Patrich, J., and Tsafrir, Y.

1993　A Byzantine Church Complex at Horvat Beit Loya. Pp. 265–72 in *Ancient Churches Revealed*, ed. Y. Tsafrir. Jerusalem: IES.

Peacock, D. P. S.

1984　Petrology and Origins. Pp. 6–28; in *Excavations at Carthage: The British Mission, Vols. 1–2*, eds. M. G. Fulford and D. P. S. Peacock. Sheffield: Sheffield Academic.

1984a　The Amphorae: Typology and Chronology. Pp. 116–40 in *Excavations at Carthage: The British Mission, Vols. 1–2*, eds. M. G. Fulford and D. P. S. Peacock. Sheffield: Sheffield Academic.

Peleg, M.

1989　Domestic Pottery. Pp. 31–113 in *Excavations at Capernaum 1972–1982, Vol. I*, ed. V. Tzaferis. Winona Lake, IN: Eisenbrauns.

1991　Persian, Hellenistic and Roman Burials at Lohamei Hagetaot. *'Atiqot* 20: 134–52.

1994　Beit She'an: A Paved Street and Adjacent remains. *'Atiqot* 25: 139–55.

Peleg, M., and Reich, R.

1992　Excavations of a Segment of the Byzantine City Wall of Caesarea Maritima. *'Atiqot* 21: 137–60.

Peleg, Y.

2000　The Characteristics of Water Distribution in Roman Towns. Pp. 241–46 in *Cura Aquarum in Sicilia: Proceedings of the Tenth International Congress on the History of Water Management and Hydraulic Engineering in the Mediterranean Region, Syracuse, May 16–22, 1998*, ed. G. C. M. Jansen. Bulletin Antieke Beschaving Supplement 6. Leiden: Bulletin Antieke Beschaving.

Perlzweig, J.

1963　*Lamps from the Athenian Agora*. Princeton: American School of Classical Studies in Athens.

Picirillo, M.

1993　*The Mosaics of Jordan*. Amman: American Center of Oriental Research.

Pococke, R.

1745　*A Description of the Orient and Some Other Countries, Vol. II, Part 1*. London.

Pollak, R.

1999　Glass from the Sediments of the Inner Harbour (Area I14). Pp. 323–32 in *Caesarea Papers 2*, eds. K. G. Holum, A. Raban and J. Patrich. *JRA* Supplementary Series 35. Providence, RI: *JRA*.

2000　Glass Vessels of a Fatimid Hoard from Caesarea Maritima. *Annales du Congrès* 14: 238–42.

2002　Early Islamic Glass from Caesarea: A Chronological and Typological Study. *Annales du Congrès* (in press).

2002a　The Glass Vessels and Objects from Shuni (forthcoming).

Porath, Y.

1984　Lime Plaster in Aqueducts: A New Chronological Indicator. Papers at the Symposium on Historical Water Development Projects in the Eastern Mediterranean, Jerusalem, 21–22 March 1983. *Leichtweiss-Institut für Wasserbau der Technischen Universität Braunschweig, Mitteilungen* 82: 1–16.

1988　Tel Tanninim—Aqueduct. *HA* 92: 22 [= *ESI* 7–8 (1990) 175].

1989   Plaster in Aqueducts as Chronological Indicator. Pp. 69–78 in *The Ancient Aqueducts of Eretz Israel*, eds. D. Amit, Y. Hirschfeld, and J. Patrich. Jerusalem: Yad Ben-Zvi (Hebrew).

1993   Level Aqueduct to Caesarea (Jisr az-Zarqa). *HA* 99: 25–26 [= *ESI* 12 (1994) 28–29].

1996   The Tunnel of Caesarea Maritima's High Level Aqueduct at the Kurkar Ridge (Jisr ez-Zarqa). *'Atiqot* 30: 126–27.

Porath, Y.; Paley, S. M.; and Stieglitz, R. R.

1993   Tel Mikhmoret. Pp. 1043–46 in *The New Encyclopedia of Archaeological Excavations in the Holy Land, Vol. 3*, ed. E. Stern. Jerusalem: IES – Carta.

Porath, Y.; Yannai, E.; and Kasher, A.

1999   Archaeological Reports (Chapters 1–4; 7–8). *'Atiqot* 37: 1–78 (Hebrew).

Prausnitz, M. W.; Avi-Yonah, M.; and Barag, D.

1967   *Excavations at Shavei Zion: The Early Christian Church*. Rome: Herder.

Price, J.

1985   Late Hellenistic and Early Imperial Vessel Glass at Berenice: A Survey of Imperial Tableware found during Excavations at Sidi Khrebish, Benghazi. Pp. 287–96 in *Cyrenaica in Antiquity*, eds. G. Barker, J. Lloyd and J. Reynolds. BAR International Series 236. Oxford: BAR.

Pringle, D.

1982   Some More Proto-Maiolica from 'Athlit (Pilgrims' Castle) and a Discussion of its Distribution in the Levant. *Levant* 14: 104–20.

1984   Thirteenth Century Pottery from the Monastery of St. Mary of Carmel. *Levant* 16: 91–111.

1985   Medieval Pottery from Caesarea: The Crusader Period. *Levant* 17: 171–202.

1986   *The Red Tower (al-Burj al-Ahmar): Settlement in the Plain of Sharon at the Time of the Crusaders and Mamluks, A.D. 1099–1516*. London: British School of Archaeology in Jerusalem.

1997   *Secular Buildings in the Crusader Kingdom of Jerusalem*. Cambridge: Cambridge University.

1998   *The Churches of the Crusader Kingdom of Jerusalem, Vol. II*. New York: Cambridge University.

Pullin, R. S. V., and Lowe-McConnell, R. H., eds.

1982   *The Biology and Culture of Tilapias*. Proceedings of the International Conference on the Biology and Culture of Tilapias, no. 7. Manila, Philippines: International Center for Living Aquatic Resources Management.

Quignard, J.-P., and Pras, A.

1986   Scaridae. Pp. 943–44 in *Fishes of the North-eastern Atlantic and the Mediterranean, Vol. 2*, eds. P. J. P. Whitehead, M.-L. Bauchot, J.-C. Hureau, J. Nielsen, and E. Tortonese. United Kingdom: UNESCO.

Raban, A.

1974   The Shipwreck off Sharm-el-Sheikh. *Archaeology* 24: 146–55.

1976   The Phoenician Jars from the Wrecked Ship off Philadelphia Village. *Sefunim* 5: 48–58.

Rapuano, Y.

1999   The Hellenistic Through Early Islamic Pottery from Ras Abu Ma'aruf (Pisgat Ze'ev East A). *'Atiqot* 38: 171–203.

Reitz, E. J., and Wing, E. S.

1999   *Zooarchaeology*. Cambridge, UK: Cambridge University.

Riis, P. J., and Poulsen, V.

1957   *Hama: Fouilles et Recherches 1931–1938, IV/2*. Copenhague: Fondation Carlsberg.

Riley, J. A.

1975   The Pottery from the First Season of Excavation in the Caesarea Hippodrome. *BASOR* 218: 25–63.

1979   The Coarse Pottery from Berenice. Pp. 91–467 in *Excavations at Sidi Khrebish, Benghazi (Berenice), II*. Supplements to *Libya Antiqua V*. Tripoli: Secretariat of Education, Department of Antiquities.

1981   Pottery from Cisterns 1977.1, 1977.2 and 1977.3. Pp. 85–124 in *Excavations at Carthage 1977, Vol. VI: Conducted by the University of Michigan*, ed. J. A. Humphrey. Ann Arbor, MI: University of Michigan.

Robinson, H. S.

1959   *The Athenian Agora, Vol. V: Pottery of the Roman Period*. Princeton: Princeton University.

Robinson, R. C. W.

1983   Clay Tobacco Pipes from the Kerameikos. *Mitteilungen des Deutschen Archäologischen Instituts Abteilung Athen* 98: 265–85.

1985 Tobacco Pipes of Corinth and of the Athenian Agora. *Hesperia* 54: 149–203.

Rochman-Halperin, A.
1999 Excavations at Givʿat Yasaf (Tell er-Ras), 1984–1985. *ʿAtiqot* 37: 83–124 (Hebrew).

Röhricht, R., ed.
1893–1904 *Regesta Regni Hierosolymitani (1097–1291)*. Innsbruck: Oeniponti.

Roller, D. W.
1982 The Northern Plain of Sharon in the Hellenistic Period. *BASOR* 247: 43–52.

Rosen-Ayalon, M.
1971 Islamic Pottery from Susa. *Archaeologia* 24: 204–8.
1974 La poterie islamique (Ville royale de Susa 4). *Mémoires de la délégation archéologique en Iran* 50. Paris: Guethner.

Rosenthal, R.
1978 The Roman and Byzantine Pottery; The Pottery [Hellenistic]. Pp. 14–19; 23–25 in *Excavations at Tel Mevorakh (1973–1976), Part One: From the Iron Age to the Roman Period*, ed. E. Stern. Qedem 9. Jerusalem: IA-HU.

Rosenthal, R., and Sivan, R.
1978 *Ancient Lamps in the Schloessinger Collection*. Qedem 8. Jerusalem: IA-HU.

Rosenthal-Heginbottom, R.
1988 The Pottery. Pp. 78–96 in *Excavations at Rehovot-in-the-Negev, Vol. I: The Northern Church*, ed. Y. Tsafrir. Qedem 25. Jerusalem: IA-HU.
1995 Imported Hellenistic and Roman Pottery. Pp. 183–288 in *Excavations at Dor, Final Report, Volume IB, Areas A and C: The Finds*, eds. E. Stern, J. Berg, A. Gilboa, B. Guz-Zilberstein, A. Raban, R. Rosenthal-Heginbottom, I. Sharon. Qedem Reports 2. Jerusalem: IA-HU.
1995a Lamps. Pp. 234–51 in *Excavations at Dor, Final Report, Volume IB, Areas A and C: The Finds*, eds. E. Stern, J. Berg, A. Gilboa, B. Guz-Zilberstein, A. Raban, R. Rosenthal-Heginbottom, I. Sharon. Qedem Reports 2. Jerusalem: IA-HU.

Rotroff, S.
1997 *The Athenian Agora XXIX: Hellenistic Pottery, Athenian and Imported Wheelmade Table Ware and Related Material*. Princeton: Princeton University.

Russell, K. W.
1985 The Earthquake Chronology of Palestine and Northwest Arabia from the 2nd through the Mid-8th Century A.D. *BASOR* 260: 37–59.

Sagona, A. G.
1982 Levantine Storage Jars of the 13th–4th Century B.C. *Opuscula Atheniensia* 14: 73–110.

Saʿid, ʿA.
2002 Nahal Tanninim Dam. *HA* 114: 34–41 (Hebrew).

Saldern, A. von
1980 *Ancient and Byzantine Glass from Sardis*. Cambridge, MA: Harvard University.

Saller, S. J.
1941 *The Memorial of Moses on Mount Nebo, Part I: The Text*. Jerusalem: Franciscan.

Sanders, G.
1989 Three Peloponnesian Churches and their Importance for the Chronology of the Late 13th and Early 14th Century Pottery in the Eastern Mediterranean. Pp. 189–99 in *Recherches sur la ceramique byzantine*, eds. V. Deroche and J. M. Spieser. *BCH* Supplement 18. Athens/Paris: Ecole françasie d'Athènes.

Sarre, F.
1925 *Die Ausgrabungen von Samarra II: Die Keramik von Samarra*. Berlin: Propyläen.

Scanlon, G. T.
1974 Fustat Expedition: Preliminary Report 1968, Part I. *JARCE* 11: 81–91.
1984 Molded Early Lead Glazed Wares from Fustat: Imported or Indigenous. Pp. 65–96 in *In Quest of Islamic Humanism, Arabic and Islamic Studies in Memory of Mohamed al-Nowaihi*, ed. A. H. Green. Cairo: American University in Cairo.

Scanlon, G. T., and Pinder-Wilson, R.
2001 *Fustat Glass of the Early Islamic Period*. London: Altajir World of Islam Trust.

Scheibler, I.
1976 *Griechische Lampen. Kerameikos, Vol. XI*. Berlin: De Gruyter.

Schioler, Th.
1973 *Roman and Islamic Water-Lifting Wheels*. Odense: Odense University.
1989 The Watermills at the Crocodile River: a Turbine Mill Dated to AD 345–380. *PEQ* 121: 133–43.

Schlesinger, D.
1984   More on Slingstones. *Qadmoniot* 17: 89 (Hebrew).

Schumacher, F.
1887   Researches in the Plain North of Caesarea. *PEFQSt* 1887: 78–85.

Shindo, Y.
1992   Glass. Pp. 304–35 in *Egypt Islamic City: al-Fustat, Excavation Report 1978–1985*, eds. K. Sakurai and M. Kawatoko. Tokyo: University of Tokyo.

Siegelmann, A.
1973   Aqueducts in the Caesarea Region. *HA* 46: 6–8.
1989   Upper Nahal Tanninim—Aqueducts. *HA* 93: 52.
1993   Aqueducts in the Upper Nahal Tanninim Region. *HA* 99: 26–27 [= *ESI* 12 (1994) 29–30].
1996   Horvat Castra, 1988. *'Atiqot* 29: 77–92 (Hebrew).

Siegelmann, A., and Yankelevitch, Sh.
1981   Tel Tanninim. *HA* 77: 13–14.

Siegelmann, A., and Rawak, Y.
1995   Aqueducts in the Upper Nahal Tanninim Region. *HA* 103: 45–46 [= *ESI* 15 (1996) 51–52].

Singer-Avitz, L.
1989   Local Pottery of the Persian Period (Strata XI–VI). Pp. 115–44 in *Excavations at Tel Michal, Israel*, eds. Z. Herzog, G. Rapp, and O. Negbi. Publication of the Tel Aviv University Institute of Archaeology No. 8. Minneapolis: University of Minnesota and Tel Aviv University.

Skelton, P. H.
1993   *A Complete Guide to the Freshwater Fishes of Southern Africa*. Halfway House, South Africa: Southern Book Publishers.

Smith, R. H.
1973   *Pella of the Decapolis, I: The 1967 Season of the College of Wooster Expedition to Pella*. Wooster, OH: The College of Wooster.

Smith, R. H., and Day, L. P.
1989   *Pella of the Decapolis II*. Wooster, OH: The College of Wooster.

Smith, R. H.; McNicoll, A. W.; and Watson, P.
1992   The Byzantine Period. Pp. 145–82 in *Pella in Jordan 2*, eds. A. W. McNicoll, P. C. Edwards, J. Hanbury-Tenison, J. B. Hennessy, T. F. Potts, R. H. Smith, A. Walmsley and P. Watson. Sidney: Meditarch.

Smith-Vaniz, W. F.
1986   Carangidae. Pp. 815–44 in *Fishes of the North-eastern Atlantic and the Mediterranean, Vol. 2*, eds. P. J. P. Whitehead, M.-L. Bauchot, J.-C. Hureau, J. Nielsen, and E. Tortonese. United Kingdom: UNESCO.

Sparkes, B. A., and Talcott, L.
1970   *The Athenian Agora XII: Black and Plain Pottery*. Princeton: Princeton University.

Spier, V.
1993   *Methods of Growing and Holding Fish in Fish Ponds (Piscinas) and Other Facilities along the Coasts of Israel and Italy in the Roman Period*. M.A. thesis, University of Haifa.

Stacey, D. A.
1995   *The Archaeology of Early Islamic Tiberias*. A thesis submitted externally, for the degree of Doctor of Philosophy at the University of London (unpublished).

Stager, L. E.
1991   *Ashkelon Discovered*. Washington, DC: Biblical Archaeology Society.

Stern, E.
1973   *The Material Culture of the Land of the Bible in the Persian Period 538–332 B.C.E.* Jerusalem: Bialik Institute and IES.
1978   *Excavations at Tel Mevorakh (1973–1976), Part One: From the Iron Age to the Roman Period*. Qedem 9. Jerusalem: IA-HU (Hebrew).
1981   Hellenistic Dor. *Qadmoniot* 14: 103-11 (Hebrew).
1982   *The Material Culture of the Land of the Bible in the Persian Period*. Warminster: Aris and Philips.
1995   Local Pottery of the Persian Period. Pp. 51–92 in *Excavations at Dor, Final Report, Volume IB, Areas A and C: The Finds*, eds. E. Stern, J. Berg, A. Gilboa, B. Guz-Zilberstein, A. Raban, R. Rosenthal-Heginbottom, I. Sharon. Qedem Reports 2. Jerusalem: IA-HU.

Stern, E., and Magen, Y.
1984   A Pottery Group of the Persian Period from Qadum in Samaria. *BASOR* 253: 9–28.

Stern, E.; Berg, J.; Gilboa, A.; Guz-Zilberstein; B., Raban, A.; Rosenthal-Heginbottom, R.; and Sharon, I., eds.
1995   *Excavations at Dor, Final Report, Volume IB, Areas A and C: The Finds*. Qedem Reports 2. Jerusalem: IA-HU.

Stern, E. J.

1977   Excavations of the Courthouse Site at 'Akko: The Pottery of the Crusader and Ottoman Periods. *'Atiqot* 31: 35–70.

1997   Burial Caves at Kisra. *'Atiqot* 33: 103–35 (Hebrew).

Stern, E.J., and Gorin-Rosen, Y.

1997   Burial Caves near Kabri. *'Atiqot* 33: 1–22 (Hebrew).

Stieglitz, R. R.

1993   Straton's Tower: The Name, the History, and the Archaeological Data. Pp. 646–51 in *Biblical Archaeology Today, 1990* (Proceedings of the Second International Congress on Biblical Archaeology, Jerusalem, June–July 1990). Jerusalem: IES – Israel Academy of Sciences & Humanities.

1996   Stratonos Pyrgos – Migdal Sar – Sebastos: History and Archaeology. Pp. 593-608 in *Caesarea Maritima: A Retrospective after Two Millennia*, eds. A. Raban and K. G. Holum. Leiden: Brill.

1997   Ptolemy IX Soter II Lathyrus on Cyprus and the Coast of the Levant. Pp. 301–6 in *Res Maritimae: Cyprus and the Eastern Mediterranean from Prehistory to Late Antiquity*, eds. S. Swiny, R. L. Hohlfelder, H. W. Swiny. Cyprus American Archaeological Research Institute Monograph Series, Vol. 1. Atlanta: Scholars.

1998   A Late Byzantine Reservoir and *Piscina* at Tel Tanninim. *IEJ* 48: 54–65.

1998a   Hydraulic and Fishing Installations at Tel Tanninim. *Near Eastern Archaeology* 61: 256.

1999   *Excavations Tel Tanninim, Preliminary Report* (unpublished).

Stillwell-Mackat, T.

1967   More Byzantine and Frankish Pottery from Corinth. *Hesperia* 36: 249–328.

Sullivan, M.

1984   *The Arts of China*, 3rd ed. Berkeley: University of California.

Sussman, V.

1976   A Burial Cave at Kefar 'Ara. *'Atiqot* 11: 92–101.

1980   Moulds for Lamps and Figurines from a Caesarea Workshop. *'Atiqot* 14: 76–79.

1983   The Samaritan Oil Lamps from Apollonia-Arsuf. *Tel Aviv* 10: 71–96.

1996   Caesarea Illuminated by its Lamps. Pp. 346–58 in *Caesarea Maritima: A Retrospective after Two Millennia*, eds. A. Raban and K. G. Holum. Leiden: Brill.

1999   Terracotta Oil Lamps. Pp. 115–36 in *The Sdot Yam Museum Book of the Antiquities of Caesarea Maritima*, ed. R. Gersht. Tel Aviv: Hakibbutz Hameuchad.

Syon, D.

1998   A Winepress at Akhziv. *'Atiqot* 34: 93–99 (Hebrew).

Tampoe, M.

1989   *Maritime Trade between China and the West, an Archaeological Study of the Ceramics from Siraf (Persian Gulf), 8th–15th Centuries A.D.* BAR International Series 555. Oxford: BAR.

Tatton-Brown, V. A.

1984   The Glass. Pp. 195–212 in *Excavations at Carthage: The British Mission, Vol. I.1*, eds. H. R. Hurst and S. P. Roskams. Sheffield: Sheffield Academic.

Thalmann, J. P.

1978   Tell 'Arqa (Liban Nord), campagnes I–III (1972–1974), chantier I: rapport préliminaire. *Syria* 55: 22–118.

Thompson, O. H.

1973   Area C. Pp. 72–88 in *Heshbon 1971: The Second Campaign at Tell Hesban*, eds. R. S. Boraas and S. H. Horn. Andrews University Seminary Studies 6. Berrien Springs, MI: Andrews University.

Thomson, W. M.

1880   *The Land and the Book: Southern Palestine and Jerusalem*. New York: Harper & Brothers.

Tibble, S.

1989   *Monarchy and Lordships in the Latin Kingdom of Jerusalem 1099–1291*. Oxford: Clarendon.

Tomber, R.

1999   Pottery from Area I14 Inner Harbour Sediments. Pp. 295–322 in *Caesarea Papers 2*, eds. K. G. Holum, A. Raban, and J. Patrich. *JRA* Supplementary Series 35. Providence, RI: *JRA*.

1993   Quantitative approaches to the investigation of long distance exchange. *JRA* 6: 142-66.

Tortonese, E.

1986   Serranidae. Pp. 780–92 in *Fishes of the Northeastern Atlantic and the Mediterranean, Vol. 2*, eds. P. J. P. Whitehead, M.-L. Bauchot, J.-C. Hureau, J. Nielsen, and E. Tortonese. United Kingdom: UNESCO.

Trewavas, E.

1942   The Cichlid Fishes of Syria and Palestine. *Annals and Magazine of Natural History* (series 11) 9: 526–36.

1982   Tilapias: Taxonomy and Speciation. Pp. 3–13 in *The Biology and Culture of Tilapias*, eds. R. S. V. Pullin and R. H. Lowe-McConnell. Proceedings of the International Conference on the Biology and Culture of Tilapias, No. 7. Manila, Philippines: International Center for Living Aquatic Resources Management.

Tubb, J. N.

1986   The Pottery from a Byzantine Well near Tell Fara. *PEQ* 118: 51–65.

Tushingham, A. D.

1985   *Excavations in Jerusalem 1961–67*. British Academy Monographs in Archaeology Vol. 1. Toronto: Royal Ontario Museum.

Tzaferis, V.

1983   The Excavations at Kursi-Gergesa. *'Atiqot* 16: 1–48.

Uscatescu, A.

1996   *La Ceramica del Macellum de Gerasa (Jarash, Jordania)*. Amman: Informes Arqueologicos.

Ustinova, Y., and Nahshoni, P.

1994   Salvage Excavations in Ramot Nof, Be'er Sheva. *'Atiqot* 25: 157–77.

Van Alfen, P. G.

1996   New Light on the 7th Century Yassi Ada Shipwreck: Capacities and Standard Sizes of LRA1 Amphoras. *JRA* 9: 189–213.

Van Neer, W.

1989   Contributions a l'Osteometrie du Nil *Lates niloticus* (Linnaeus, 1758). *Fiches d'Osteologie Animale pour l'Archeologie*. Juan-les-Pins, France: Centre de Recherches Archeologiques du CNRS, APDCA.

Venit, M. S.

1987   The Painted Tomb from Wardian and the Decoration of Alexandrian Tombs. *JARCE* 25: 71–91.

1988   The Painted Tomb from Wardian and the Antiquity of the Saqiya in Egypt. *JARCE* 26: 219–22.

Vessberg, O.

1952   Roman Glass in Cyprus. *Opuscula Archaeologica* (Lund, Sweden) 7: 109–165.

Vitto, F.

1996   Byzantine Mosaics at Bet-She'arim: New Evidence for the History of the Site. *'Atiqot* 28: 115–46.

Walmsley, A. G.

1988   Pella/Fihl after the Islamic Conquest (635–900 C.E.). *Mediterranean Archaeology* 1: 142–59.

Watson, P.

1992   Change in Foreign and Regional Economic Links with Pella in the Seventh Century A.D.: The Ceramic Evidence. Pp. 233–47 in *La Syrie de Byzance à l'Islam, VIIe–VIIIe siècles*, eds. P. Canivet et J.-P. Rey-Coquais. Damas: Institut Français de Damas.

Weinberg, G. D.

1970   Hellenistic Glass from Tel Anafa in Upper Galilee. *JGS* 12: 17–27.

1973   Notes on Glass from Upper Galilee. *JGS* 15: 35–51.

Weinberg, G. D., and Goldstein, S. M.

1988   The Glass Vessels. pp. 38–102 in *Excavations at Jalame: Site of a Glass Factory in Late Roman Palestine*, ed. G. D. Weinberg. Columbia, MO: University of Missouri.

Weinberg, S. S.

1971   Tel Anafa: The Hellenistic Town. *IEJ* 21: 104–5.

Wenning, R.

1990   Attische Keramik in Palästina: Ein Zwischenblick. Pp. 157–67 in *Transeuphratène 2* (Actes du colloque international *La Syrie-Palestine à l'époque perse*, Paris, 1989), eds. J. Elayi and J. Sapin. Paris: Gabalda.

Whitehouse, D. B.

1967   The Medieval Pottery of Lazio. *Papers of the British Academy at Rome* 35: 40–86.

Williams, C.

1989   *Anemurium: The Roman and Early Byzantine Pottery*. Subsidia Mediaevalia 16. Toronto: Crescent East.

Winter, T.

1998   The Glass Vessels from Horvat Hermeshit (1988–1990). *'Atiqot* 34: 173–77 (Hebrew).

Yadin, Y.; Aharoni, Y.; and Amiran, R.

1961   *Hazor III–IV*. Jerusalem: IES.

Yankelevitch, Sh.
1981   Tel Tanninim—Milestones. *HA 76*: 18.

Yeivin, Z.
1992   Excavations at Carmiel (Khirbet Bata). *'Atiqot 21*: 109–28.

Yeivin, Z., and Edelstein, G.
1970   Excavations at Tirat Yehuda. *'Atiqot 6*: 56–69 (Hebrew).

Young, S. H.
1993   A Preview of Seventh-Century Glass from the Kourion Basilica, Cyprus. *JGS 35*: 39–47.

Zemer, A.
1977   *Storage Jars in Ancient Trade*. Haifa: National Maritime Museum Foundation.

Ziadeh, G.
1995   Ottoman Ceramics from Ti'innik, Palestine. *Levant 27*: 209–45.

Index

PERSONS

PLACE NAMES